The History of the Nigerian Railway
Vol. 1

The History of the Nigerian Railway Vol. 1

Opening the Nation to sea, air and
road transportation

Francis Jaekel

Safari Books Ltd.
Ibadan

Published by
Safari Books Ltd.
Ile Ori Detu
1, Shell Close
Onireke
Ibadan.
Email: info@safaribooks.com.ng
Website: http://safaribooks.com.ng

© 1997, Francis Jaekel
First Published 1997
Reprinted, 2020

I am delighted that this series on **The History of the Nigerian Railway** written by my father 23years ago is still considered relevant today. The Publisher, Joop Berkhout, who originally published the first edition in 1997, defiled all odds to get across to me as the eldest son of the author to seek for my permission to transfer the rights to his new company, Safari Books, for reprinting. I obliged him, considering the value of the book to the history of Nigeria and the railway sector in particular.

Miles Jaekel

All rights reserved. This book is copyright and so no part of it may be reproduced, stored in a retrieval system, or transmitted, in any form or by any means, electrical, mechanical, electrostatic, magnetic tape, photocopying, recording or otherwise, without the prior written permission of the author.

ISBN: 978-978-57696-2-3

Contents

Dedication	vii
List of Illustrations	ix
Acknowledgements	xi
Foreword	xv
Preface	xvii

Chapter 1
Exploration, Trade and 20th Century History — 1

Chapter 2
Physical Geography, Game and Climate — 20

Chapter 3
Peoples, Languages, Demography, Cultures and Artifacts — 31

Chapter 4
Ocean Passage from Sail to Conference Lines — 46

Chapter 5
Inland Waterways — 61

Chapter 6
Road Networks — 79

Chapter 7
Ports, Harbours and Terminals — 97

Chapter 8
Aviation and Airports — 132

Chapter 9
Electricity Undertakings — 153

Chapter 10
Public Water Supplies — 176

Chapter 11
Opening up a Hinterland — 193

Index — 211

Dedication

To
the cherished memory of
Alhaji, the Hon. Sir Abubakar Tafawa Balewa, KBE
Federal Minister of Transport 1954–1957
Prime Minister of the Federation 1957–1966

List of Illustrations

1.	Mungo Park and Lander Memorial, Jebba	4
2.	Cemetery on Government Hill, Jebba	5
3.	Trading Station, Old Calabar	7
4.	Lugard Hall, Kaduna	11
5.	A Hill on the Jos Plateau	21
6.	The Gurara River Waterfall near Abuja	24
7.	Baobabs by the Niger	26
8.	Bushcow at Tungan Giwa, 1966	29
9.	Speaker's Chair, House of Assembly	36
10.	An Onitsha Lady	38
11.	A Developed Craft: The Gates of Anglican Cathedral, Onitsha	39
12.	Fulani Herd-boys	42
13.	Bornu Camelmen dressed for a Durbar	43
14.	Dye Pits in Kano	44
15.	MV 'Aureol' at Las Palmas in 1971	50
16.	The Torpedoing of the 'Falaba' on 28/3/1915	53
17.	The Niger Delta	65
18.	The Niger/Benue Confluence in Lokoja	66
19.	Borassus palm dugout canoe on River Sokoto	69
20.	Government River Steamer Circa 1912	72
21.	The Niger South Channel and Juju Rock at Jebba	75
22.	The Onitsha Bridge over the Niger on the Benin-Enugu road opened in 1965	85
23.	Opening of the Second Carter Bridge in 1931	86
24.	7:30 am on Carter Bridge in 1956	88
25.	The Road to Keffi near Abuja	91
26.	Iddo Wharf, 1906	110
27.	Iddo Wharf, 1917	111
28.	Mailboat & Boat Train at Apapa Quay in the 30s	113
29.	Port Harcourt Wharf, 1915	116
30.	Port Harcourt Harbour Works, 1921	117
31.	Early Bi-plane Landing in Nigeria	136
32.	Herald on the Approach of an Aircraft to Kano Airport	137
33.	BOAC 'York' Aircraft at Ikeja Airport	142
34.	Kurra Falls Power Station on the Plateau	154
35.	Shaki Dam in Progress, 1965	181
36.	Shaki Rising Main, 1965	183
37.	Intake for Yola Water Supply	189
38.	Rock Cutting towards Ibadan, 1900	200
39.	Gradient Profiles of Nigerian Railways showing locations of stations	201
40.	Rock cutting on the Kogun Kloof, 1926	204
41.	Canadian Class Locomotive No. 769 breasting the 4324ft summit on the Kafanchan-Jos branch in 1959	207
42.	Terrain between Zaria & Gusau, 1929	208

Acknowledgements

I am greatly indebted to the late Freddie Page of the Crown Agents Archives for visits lasting over two years and to Dorothy Codling, widow of Charles of the Nigerian Railway and Ruston and Hornsby, for the gift of his copious notes on the locomotives of the system. I was touched that Marjorie Simson took pains to see that all the railway effects of her late cousin, Tommy Welch, came to me; Tommy saw long service in Nigeria and was a devoted 'running man'.

It is a pleasure to record the assistance and hospitality rendered by four Nigerian Railway officers who had retired to other spheres of work in England: John Phillips, Managing Director of Gloucester Railway C&W Co. Ltd. for details of Nigerian rolling stock; Trevor Astley, Chairman & Managing Director; Bill Houghton, Director of Pandrol Ltd, for details of Nigerian track fastenings; and Roy Farmer, Marketing Manager of GEC Traction Ltd. for information concerning locomotives built for Nigeria by six British companies by then within the control of GEC.

Turning now to works executed for the Nigerian Railway: for the Borno Extension I remain grateful to the late John E.G. Palmer CBE, Consultant to Rendel Palmer & Tritton, for introductions and good cheer, to Mr. J.A. Platt, their Librarian, for the sorting of archives and the loan of album and project reports and to Mr. J.R. Sweetapple, Associate, who was their Resident Engineer for Gombe-Ashakpa works and for clarification of bridge designs. The second job concerned the MAS scheme for Kafanchan executed by Westinghouse Brake & Signal Co. Ltd. whose Resident Engineer was Christopher Napper. His appointment facilitated a transfer of 'know-how' to my decided advantage. When, later, Westinghouse Signals Ltd. came to install tokenless block on two lengthy stretches I became indebted to Mr. H.W.J. Everitt, Signal Engineer Export, for details and schematics.

I was greatly obliged to Hunslet (Holdings) Ltd. I had known grandfather, father and sons; I refer to the Alcocks, particularly the late John and Peter. It can be said that they engineered almost the whole stock of Nigerian Railway's steam shunters over fifty-five years and their records in which Geoffrey Horsman assisted proved invaluable.

My thanks are due to Freddie Beasant, Director, and Brian Law, of Brush Electrical Machines Ltd., for user statistics of the Nigerian Railway Corporation's diesel electric shunters built at Loughborough and to Messrs S. Oakes and C. Higgs of F.H. Lloyd & Co. Ltd., Wednesbury, for details of the 1911 and 1977 designs and trailing loads of the ABC coupler. I wish to acknowledge the assistance given by Messrs D. Wallace and R. Brewis of Vickers Elswick Works, Armament Division, in relation to Sir W.G. Armstrong Whitworth locomotives supplied to Nigeria and to Mr. M.A. Swallow, Director/Sales Manager of Hawthorn Leslie (Engineers) Ltd. who passed me on to Mr. J.F. Clarke of Newcastle-upon-Tyne Polytechnic Faculty of Education and Humanities for research into Hawthorn Leslie built engines for the Nigerian Railway.

I am grateful to Davis & Lloyd (1955) Ltd. of River Don Works for bogie detail, to Mr. J.E. Atkinson, Sales Director of D. Wickham and Company Ltd. for engineer's inspection car and trolley orders for Nigeria, and to Neville Cooley of Design Group for Industry, Kenilworth, for information relating to NRC intention as to maintenance and training.

Mr. D.H. Boot of Henry Boot Engineering Limited gave me details of turnouts supplied to the Nigerian Ports Authority; Mr. K.G Hibbitt, Export Sales, Horseley Bridge and Thomas Piggott, Clarke Chapman Ltd., spent time on pressed steel water storage tank installations. Harry While, F.H. Jeffery and Ian F. Dallison of the London Office, Messrs J.S. Roberts and R. Bright of the Workington and Barrow Works of the British Steel

Corporation (Exports) Ltd. went to pains for me over Nigerian Railway's track detail supplied.

I had many meetings down in Kent with Evelyn Bunning, widow of Arthur John. Allen Civil, author of a history of W.G. Bagnall Ltd., filled me in with details of his company's products on Nigerian Railway metals. Miss C. Whinton of the Church Missionary Society gave me slides of Nigerian rail scenes taken by David Pluckrose. Frank Dunn-Abbott MBE, who spent many years in Nigeria on water, assisted with plates depicting Oyo State installations. Mr. S.J. Hancock of Royal Engineers Corps Library searched records for the Royal Engineers' involvement in Nigerian Railway construction and came up with a good deal about Sir Percy Girouard.

A gentleman of considerable assistance was Mr. C.H. Minns of the Foreign and Commonwealth Office Library. Equally helpful was Donald Simpson of the Royal Commonwealth Society. Colonel Peter Castle-Smith gave me correspondence from his maternal grandfather about the Nigeria of 1866. The libraries of the 'Civils', 'Mechanicals' and the Chartered Institute of Transport (CIT) were of inestimable benefit.

I consulted these works: *Command 2325, 2782, 2787, 4523, Blue Books, Colonial Office Reports, Railway Engineer, Locomotive C&W Review, Railway Gazette, Railway Magazine, Modern Railways, West Africa, Lagos Weekly Record, Nigerian Magazine, Nigerian Field Society* and *West African Chartered Engineer*; I drew on the books by C.R. Niven, Nicholson (1913), Temple, Mrs Larymore *(A Resident's Wife in Nigeria)* Schram *(Nigerian Health Services),* Miller *(Lagos Steam Tramways),* Hastings *(Railroads),* Redman *(Railway Foundry),* Holt *(A Hunslet Hundred),* HMSO *(Reshaping of BR)* and Lloyd *(Search for the Niger).*

Invaluable research was afforded by Capt. C.W.J. Orr RA's *The Making of Northern Nigeria,* Capt. H.O. Mance DSO RE's lecture to the RUSI of 1913, and the IBRD Reports of the early 1950s. Most informative was the *Red Book of West Africa* by Allister Macmillan FRGS published by Frank Cass in 1920 and republished by Spectrum Books Ltd. Ibadan in 1994 — acclaimed the first ever of its kind published.

To the late C.T. Quinn-Young and to those officers after my retirements: K.C. Bansal and Jasbir Pal Singh of RITES, Dr Jakpa of the Ministry and Nigerian Railway Corporation's officers retired or in post: N.C.U. Okoro, A.F.A. Babatunde, T.O. Griffin, E.E. Henshaw, Alhaji Oduntan, M.U.A. Okakpu, Tom Duncan, J.K. Cole, Olu Holloway, J.N. Iloenyosi, the late M.A. Crane, W.A. Adegoroye, F.A.O. Phillips, the late M.O.D. Oshosanwo, G.H. Whiteside, J.O. Ogunlesi and A.O. Talabi.

The majority of the plates are reproductions and almost entirely the work of Derek Ransley of Berkhamsted Photographic. The line drawings are exclusively the work of F.A. Alabi of Interlink Consult, New Bodija, Ibadan.

The publication of this work would have been impossible without the financial commitment of Diamond Bank Limited. I therefore acknowledge with happiness my debt to Diamond Bank for sponsoring the publication of one thousand copies of this work as their contribution to the dissemination of knowledge and promotion of the history of Nigeria.

Spectrum Books Limited undertook the styling and publishing of the three-volume history. I acknowledge especially Tony Igboekwe and Layi Ajani for their editorial skills.

Picture Credits

Government of Nigeria: Mungo Park Memorial, Old Calabar Trading Station, Lugard Hall, Baobabs, Gurara Falls, Hill on Jos Plateau, Onitsha Cathedral, Speaker's Chair, Onitsha lady, Niger South channel, Niger/Benue confluence, Borassus palm canoe, Carter bridge in 1956, Road of Keffi, Onitsha bridge, Mailboat at Apapa, York aircraft, Herald at Kano Airport, Kogum Kloof 1926, Terrain Zaria-Gusau, Lagos Steam Tramway routes, "Nupe" on the BKR, Enugu "ETS" instruments, Profile of the BLR, Obwetti yard, D'Enghien Ateliers tank wagon, Naira conversion table, Cattle grazing, Kolanuts, Groundnuts, Tin dredge, River class at Kaduna North.

Nigerian Railway Corporation: Iddo wharf, Port Harcourt harbour, Kurra Falls, Profile of 3ft. 6in. system, The 4324ft. summit, Iddo terminus 1901, Engine 51 in 1902, 1st Ogun bridge, Barijuko engine, Tram crossing 1st Carter bridge, Minna station, Kano station, Train over the Gulma bridge, Lagos Volunteers, Iddo yard, Port Harcourt station, Ferry "Munshi", Gerti monument, Kafanchan Jc 1926, NRC logo, Matissa tamper, Leopard killed, Jebba bridges & Juju Rock, Structure gauge, Mokwa diagram, Ebute Metta workshops 1923, Enugu workshops, NR No. 502, 207 class diagram, Iva Colliery, 1st coal at Port Harcourt, Hopper wagons, Collier "Diana", 1101 class diagram, 1201 class diagram, 1401 class diagram, Ebute Metta Jc signalling, Chafe spillway, Saloon built 1919, Cattle wagon conversion, Lease/Lend conversions, Offa station, Zungeru station, Zaria station, Kaura Namoda terminus, Oshogbo & Ilorin buildings, Ebute Metta HQ 1935, Organisations in 1926 & 1934 & 1973, Pie chart earnings, Pie chart distribution, Accounts HQ building extensions, Bar chart imports, Bar chart exports, Earl of Plymouth visit, T.B. Welch retirement, Sir Ralf Emerson retirement, Speech by Capt. Mance, HQ conference with Dr Ikejiani and J.C. Egbuna, Junior Service estate, Hockey team, Stationmaster in uniform, Communication facilities, Microwave communications, Timetable of 1899, Aro stone, Jebba express, Down Limited 1934, Mileage chart, Limited train leaving Ibadan, Tickets, Japanese 3rd class interior, Fulani girls, Train climbing Kloof, Leyland Comet, Road service Gusau-Sokoto Mercedes-Benz trucks, Lalupon disaster, Site plan of disaster, Printing office, Gibson and trainees, "Freedom Day", Aids in Zaria workshops, Police dog trials, St John Brigade, London Office, Medical Centre.

Crown Agents for Oversea Governments and Administrations: Jebba cemetery, Opening of 2nd Carter bridge, Iddo wharf 1906, Port Harcourt wharf 1915, Cutting towards Ibadan 1900, Children's Special, Bogie low-sided open 1901, Bogie covered goods, Hunslet No. 11, Hawthorn Leslie No. 22, Jebba south slipway, "Fabius" leaving Jebba, Barijuko tramway map, Opening of Lagos Steam Tramway, Turner covered goods, Hudswell Clarke No. 1, Birmingham Railway explosives van, Kitson No. 57, Leeds Forge 3rd class, Birmingham Railway platform wagon, Turner covered goods of 1914, 1st loco for Nigerian Railway, Earthworks Imo swamp, Brickworks, Offa summit, Labour at Bokani, River at Opeki bridge, Ferrying loco No. 2 over River Ilo, Kaduna bridge construction at Zungeru, The Kaduna at Zungeru in flood, Benue bridge, Benue bridge caisson sinking rate, Iddo Island workshops, 1st engine erected in Colony, LGR No. 13, Iddo coal transporters, Ebute Metta shed 1900, Port Harcourt loco yard 1922, NER watering facilities, Water tank wagon, Metro-Cammell Twinberrow bogie, Inspection saloon on slipway 1911, Bristol Carriage 3rd class, Japanese 3rd class carriage, Midland Railway postal van, Canadian Car 20 ton low-sided bogie, Hurst Nelson stone wagon, Birmingham Railway high-sided bogie, Cravens covered cattle wagon, Hurst Nelson benzene tank wagon, Agege double-storey station building, Officer quarters 1898, Craven steam crane, Ransome & Rapier steam crane

C.N. Napper Esq: M.V. Aureol, Pump trolley, Tyer's KT instrument, Kafanchan NX panel, Kafanchan MAS commissioning, Coaling of River class engine at Kafanchan, NRC loco 1608 at Lagos, Kafanchan sheds in 1972, Brake van and tail board at Kafanchan, Cattle empties, Hunslet No. 89, Limited train near Kagoro, NRC Hitachi loco 1611, Bauchi Meat Products.

The late T B Welch: 1st train over Benue bridge, Loco 631 on the bridge over the River Ebba, Engine 686 ex Gold Coast, Engine 174 at Ebute Metta, Ibadan turntable, Ebute Metta Jc water bridge, Down limited at Jebba, Head of department residence, Drivers' rest house at Ibadan, loco 605 and cattle, Departure of 1st Eastern Limited, Loco 519 at Bukuru, Gerti disaster.

GEC Traction Limited: 1st diesel loco in Nigeria, The Queen and HRH leaving Iddo, NRC loco 1001 on River Kubani bridge, Loco 455 at Darlington, Cab of loco 455, Loco 101 at Newton-le-Willows, Loco 1007 at Preston,

Zaria diesel shed, Head Wrightson transporter, Royal Train awaiting departure, Loco 1401 leaving Ibadan.

International Railway Gazette: Carriage & Wagon group 1933, Carriage & Wagon organisation 1934, Cravens 1st class sleeper 1952, Chief Engineer's conference, District Superintendent's conference, Mobile Instruction Unit, Sectioned injector, Sectioned SKF bearing.

The Nigerian Field Society: Bushcow, Fulani herd-boys, Bornu camelmen, Dye pits, Government river steamer, Early biplane landing, Zaria leatherworker

Gloucester Railway Carriage & Wagon Co. Ltd.: Brake van at Gloucester, Horse-box, 6-door 1st class carriage, Interior of dining saloon 1913, 25 ton low-sided wagon 1923, 20 ton frameless covered goods

Rendel Palmer & Tritton: Kuru-Bauchi plains, Bridge between Kuru and Bauchi, Gongola bridge, Bauchi opening, Prime Minister at the Bauchi opening

The late Maurice Crane: Loco 807 at Newton-le-Willows, North Mail boat train 1930s, Freight train from Nguru

Nigerian Railway Clerical Staff Association: Eastern District party for Herbert Kille with 1st Nigerian lady stenographer featured, Retirement of Mr Adebiyi HQ 1957, African Loco Drivers Union presentation to author

G.H. Whiteside Esq.: Washout at mile 363, Trestle pier erection as site of waashout, Bridge deflection at site of washout.

Hunslet Holdings Limited LGR No. 31 at Leeds, Lagos Steam Tramway engine 104 at Leeds, NRC 51 class at Leeds

Mak Maschinenbau GMBH Bogie of NRC 1201 class, NRC No. 901 showing engine exposed

Water Corporation of Oyo State: Shaki dam, Shaki rising main

Institution of Mechanical Engineers: Sentinel-Cammell steam railcar, Diagram of train paths Zaria-Kano

Daily Mirror: Torpedoing of the "Falaba"

Weidenfeld & Nicolson: The Niger Delta

Institution of Civil Engineers: Yola intake

The late S. Marchant: Author in Cravens saloon on tour

Foreign & Commonwealth Office: Map of the Bauchi Light Railway

The late Mrs Sutherland: Opening of the Niger bridge at Jebba

Nigerian Daily Times: Prince of Wales entraining at Iddo in 1925

D. Wickham and Company Limited: Engineer's inspection car

H.H. Abbott Esq.: Zaria diesel workshop

F.A.O. Phillips Esq.: Organisation of mechanical department 1958

F.H. Lloyd & Co. Limited: ABC coupler

Anonymous: Tank cars and covered goods derailed, St John ambulance team at Zaria

Author: Last Bauchi train from Jos, Ebute Metta Jc semaphores, Diagram of running shed locations, Enugu shed in 1949, Diagram of steam watering points, Diagram of bogie designs employed, Diagram of NER wayside station layouts, Diagram of maximum permitted speeds, Pictorial representation of timetables 1916, 1924, 1932, 1949, 1956, 1962, 1966 and 1980, Station stops of express trains, Diagram of station earnings over 12 year period, Diagram of freight net ton miles yearly maxima, Gauge "O" model railway

Foreword

Nigeria is currently passing through a critical period of national reconstruction of her political, economic and social infrastructures. As part of this inevitable process of transformation, the Nigerian Railway is undergoing expansion and modernisation as the gauges are being expanded and new coaches acquired.

In times like these, the past becomes as important as the future, if not more so, as we seek to lay down beacons that will guide us and illuminate our path in our march to the 21st century.

For me, who at a very crucial and sensitive period of our national history had to carry the mantle of leadership in the search for national unity and the advancement of Nigeria's domestic and international interest, to be invited to read and contribute to a seventeen years' work on the history and analysis of railways in Nigeria, is both pleasant and challenging. Not for anything, but principally for the central role the railways played in opening up our contact with the outside world and its contribution to the development of a Federal service. The railways were arteries of our national life, and the railways can become once more the fine fibres of our national integration.

When Francis Jaekel discovered that "no printed word recorded the endeavours of Nigerians and expatriates" in developing the railways; when he became angry that "the influence of the extending railway, driven to open up the country at nil profit, on the Nigerian environment" is unacknowledged; when he set out to sacrifice himself for seventeen years to do something about it; and now that he, equipped with thirty-seven years spell of office in Nigeria has finished forty-nine chapters of network analysis of the history and impact of the railways on the Nigerian, I salute his tenacity of purpose.

To cater for the reader with no knowledge of the country, three chapters deal with history, geography, peoples and cultures. Such is the importance of Nigerian rivers that a separate chapter deals with inland waterways. Because of the Railway's influence on the economic environment, there follows six chapters detailing that influence. Nine chapters deal with the history of the nine tramway/railway systems and thirty chapters analyse every facet of working from land through training to medical provision. Over 300 plates accompany the text.

Upon reflection, I keep wondering what this nation would have been if not for the railways. It was the railways that made it possible for agricultural products to move smoothly from the hinterlands to the ports. It was the railways that made it possible for people to move at relatively no cost over long distances for trade and other occupational pursuits. It was the railways that gave support and strength to military operation and the movement of heavy duty equipment and materials needed for industrial works and development. The railways were then the life-line of the national economic development.

In presenting this history of Nigerian Railway, Francis Jaekel went beyond rail lines to deal with the purposes and human virtues that powered the railway projects. This text is therefore a celebration of the conquest of the human spirit and a great lesson in human industry. By drawing our attention to Nigeria's rivers and waterways, this text opens up reflections on the need for Nigeria to explore her rivers and waterways. In discussing the whole process of training and development of the human resources associated with the railways, the text focuses our attention as we reconstruct, on the need to develop our manpower base properly if we are to achieve sustainable development.

Against the background of my own experience in Government, I hope that this book would be read by all who are or may be in public life. It opens the future while placing under our steps the milestones of the past.

I commend Francis and recommend this text to all, students and practitioners alike.

General (Dr) Yakubu Gowon
Yakubu Gowon Centre
Abuja
11th April, 1997

Preface

No single enterprise or venture set the seed to the development of this vast country than did the railway which rapidly assumed a mantle of paternalism, and a historian in acknowlegement and tribute must be found.

I knew the country for forty-seven years. I commenced to write in 1971 at Berkhamsted in Hertfordshire and completed the manuscript seventeen years later in 1988 at Woodhall Spa in Lincolnshire. The text is of my making alone. Place name spelling adopted is that in use at each material time; units quoted are both metric and imperial and money is stated in LSD, £p or Naira/Kobo terms and no excuse is made for this lack of uniformity which arises from historical necessity. A Naira/Sterling conversion table is given.

Tafawa Balewa, a Vice-President of the Britain-Nigeria Association, to whose memory this work is dedicated, said of the British 'whom we have known first as masters, then as leaders, finally as partners, always as friends.' At the pre-independence talks in London he had said:' The building of our nation shall proceed at the wisest pace.' Lord Boyd of Merton gave riposte with the Hausa proverb 'At the same time as the wall itself is built the finger marks on it are made.' General Gowon on a State Visit to England in 1973 summed up to Ted Heath with the words 'We are not here to sign a special treaty. We are not here to negotiate a special agreement. We are here to illustrate the reality of contacts and relations that go on all the time, every day, on many fronts and in many spheres.'

I believe that pretensions to a sufficiency in education fall on no man until he has lived in another man's country. In Nigeria, I quickly became immersed in herpetology and then followed forestry, agriculture and the insect world. I grew to admire African beauty and carriage. It was a Nigerian who taught me the difference between a laugh and a smile — the first the mark of the uncivilised, the second a glimpse of culture. My wife, Madge, was in the country for some thirty-one years and is mentioned not only for the Nigerian adage 'behind every successful man lies a woman.' My three children, Sandra, Miles and Roderick, made countless sorties to the coast and met so many people that, grown up, they had become masters of conversation in cosmopolitan society. The pages of this book unfold many problems but throughout my span of attachment I remained stress-free and happy. I have found that the friends whose passing I lament are mostly those who recall to me my days under the sun.

I want this book to be read by Nigerians of post-independence generations. The British officers resident to 1960 were naturally a very different bunch to the British contractors visiting after 1960 and I am anxious that the Nigerian of today should judge my race by an understanding knowledge of the former, one of whose outstanding contributions lay in the creation of the Nigerian Field Society.

In the land of the mother of railways, domestic literature continues to pour forth from the presses. The Nigerian Railway was at one time the largest colonial system and its history must not escape library shelves, especially a treatise comprehensive in scope. Comparisons have been made but they are of a technical nature. In many ways 'Nigeria the country' cannot be divorced from 'Nigeria the railway' as the history will reveal.

I acknowledge with gratitude that in 1932 I received training from the London Midland and Scottish Railway in no less than three departments. In the course of time it was to be that I would serve the Nigerian Railway likewise.

The aim of the Indian systems in 1916 was to develop industries, foster trade, elevate the welfare of the peasant, increase revenue and decrease taxation. Nigerian railway systems were built to procure stone, export cotton, distribute indigenous coal, export groundnuts, ease cocoa production and open up the vast plains of Borno, all in that precise order.

In 1977, Nigeria was fourth in the OPEC league and sixth in proven resources. There is a future in natural gas once markets have been found. She had become Britain's largest importer of pharmaceuticals and she was the sole source of columbite. Much of her light industry had become 'heavy'. Cars on the roads were growing at 15.5% per annum. Telephone and electricity remained problem areas but much attention had been paid to water supplies. British investment in the country reached £1400 million in 1970. Nigeria's main pre-occupation after Independence was to turn from an export orientation to the need to explore local substitute materials and products to save foreign exchange but the need for this latter to fund plant maintenance and capital works was to dog her for years. Great strides had been made in sea and air ports. Nigeria is second only in the continent in production off the presses and the Nigerian is avid for news. Nigeria, by its association with bodies like UNESCO and ECOWAS, had from the first remained global in outlook, as well it must, for one out of every four Africans is a Nigerian.

I have been condemnatory of the railway only in one chapter and have borne in mind Dr. Jakpa's request that at all times I be truthful in fact and endeavour but for all arms of government I must be like-inclined with regard to statistical analysis and reporting. To throw away the need in the 70s for exploration to determine basic units of cost and work done, or to produce them years later so that their relevance was in question, is indeed serious and must be remedied.

On the railway in 1962/63, gross trailing ton miles per locomotive in use per annum reached 27.45 million. Peak rail passenger carriage reached 1,022,069/month. In 1973, the average length of haul per ton over the whole year was 874km; in Spain it was 307, in Sweden 265, in Switzerland 148; what wonderful potential therefore for Nigeria. I agree with Professor Obaro Ikhime, then President of the Historical Society of Nigeria, who has blamed ignorance of Nigerian history for failure to evolve meaningful strategies for the country's development. Otherwise there is much humour and reference in the narrative of the African scene from which prayer has not been omitted. I have been careful to record the 'real' Nigeria and not restrict myself to cosmopolitan Lagos. The work is written for the cadet as much as for the head of department, whether at home or abroad.

Like the USA, Nigeria's rail history is best thought of in terms of Links-In anniversaries; there were 3:

1st January 1912   LGR and BKR joined at Minna;
12th July 1926   Northern & Southern NER approaches joined near Gerti;
27th August 1958   Inauguration of the Works to join NRC and BER near Kuru.

Railroads are an imported technology but the transport of goods and passengers does not earn foreign exchange. The creation of a New Lines Department was a good thing but the Nigerian is as ever over-enthusiastic and too many simultaneous schemes killed the golden goose. Certainly, Sokoto requires a railhead and now Katsina with its rolling mills demands treatment. The railway must not close the Idogo branch but instead revitalise it. In the UK the good and bad of the late Dr Beeching, the 'good' for his approach to analysis, the 'bad' for his feeder line closures, has long been digested and rail cuts have long ceased to be the norm. For many years the Nigerian Railway was less than fairly treated by its Ministry. In the UK, that portfolio now embraces all modes except inland waterways. More must be expected of the All Nigeria Transport Authority.

The European Economic Community governments are thinking of plans to relieve systems of responsibility for maintaining their infrastructure. This is a matter for careful consideration by the Nigerian authorities.

Nigeria's plans to install 1435mm standard gauge for their 1067mm gauge earned universal condemnation in the 70s. The rail gauge is only important for speed — and on the 3ft. 6in. very high velocities have been reached — the important issue is the structure gauge and here, Nigeria is well endowed. The Nigerian scheme would have committed successive governments to an on-going task for twenty to twenty-five years and put paid, without transhipment, to future connections to adjoining territories.

The Nigerian Railway lost its expatriate personnel most skilled in their network after Independence and for a time, and a long time at that, unfortunately suffered from a high turn-over of its indigenous officers. Recovery where experience is involved must needs be a lengthy business. The most pressing need today is for new locomotives, not for new rolling stock since utilisation of existing assets has been depressed only because of inadequate motive power.

On my last day in Nigeria, 27th April 1985, Marubeni Corporation kindly dined me at the Bacchus Restaurant in Ikoyi and invited railway heads to join us there.

Francis Jaekel OBE
Pinetrees
Woodhall Spa
LN10 6UZ

Exploration, Trade and 20th Century History

The first explorers were the birds of northern Europe. Only one versed in knowledge of African exploration would understand the significance of the quotation: 'Nile a river without a source, the Niger a source without a river.' A history of slaving eclipsed by a history of traffic in palm oil along a littoral attractively described as Grain Coast, Ivory Coast, Gold Coast, Slave Coast and Oil Rivers, but the purist will be delighted to learn that it was proved in Zanzibar that paid labour was more productive than slave. There were many ditties about the danger of penetration to the 'White Man's Grave' and one version ran

> Beware and take care of the
> Bight of Benin
> For the few that come out
> There are many go in.

A number of words were introduced into the English language from the West Coast: popinjay, guinea, gorilla, eserene and palaver. The British laid out townships at Kaduna, Port Harcourt and Jos, the last derived from 'Gwosh' mispronounced for 'Jos'. Colonies were territories formally annexed by the British Crown, protectorates countries which accepted the protection afforded by British rule, mandates countries for which only administration was given. Further technical differences arose according to the manner in which the legislative council was given legal stance.

Years ago Allister Macmillan, author of *The Red Book of West Africa,* produced the classic from which these verses are taken, their impact being as applicable today as it was at the turn of the century.

> Also in the towns of commerce do not look for privacy;
> There are many weary fellows thinking of it longingly;
> And you'll find the bush is better for a season of content
> Than the unrelaxing pressure of the socially intent.
> In the splendour of its forests, in the riches of its ore,
> In the wonder of its exports that are ever growing more,
> In its rivers and its peoples, in its plenitude and death,
> There is not another region like West Africa on earth.'
> All West Africa is calling for more of the men it needs-
> Men of courage and discernment, strong in purpose, straight in deeds-
> And it offers splendid prospects, which for many ills atone;
> But if lacking in essentials, better to stay at home.

Ancient

Many people today have come to realise that the origin of man is more likely to be found in East Africa than along the banks of the Euphrates. In 1965 Professor Thurstan Shaw excavated in a forest zone fifteen miles from Akure, a skeleton charcoal radiocarboned to around 9250 BC, the most ancient find of Homo sapiens yet found in West Africa. Plant life goes back much further. Lycopodium cernum is one hundred million years younger than Psilotum found only in Nigeria and one other place in the world.

In 600 BC the Phoenicians navigated the entire African continent but 500 BC, the same epoch that saw the voyage to West Africa of the Carthaginian Hanno, marks the oldest trace of a living culture — the Nok people with their terra cotta figurines living around Katsina Ala. As in England after the Roman occupation there then came a blank in the country's history but it is known that circa AD 800 Arab flag bearers of Islam traversed the desert to found the long surviving dynasty of Kanem, that desert whose approximate southern limits only were known to the ancient world. Contemporary with Kanem were the empires of Ghana, Mali and Songhay.

The Yorubas who were to make their capital Old Oyo and their religious fount Ife came from the Middle East sometime between 1000 BC and AD 800. The influence of Benin extended down to Lagos. The Hausas (Hausa is a language and not a race) and the Fulanis emigrated from the north to meet a country peopled by long forgotten tribes and the former founded the original seven states, their southernmost emirate being at Ilorin in Yoruba country. They were in Kano by the 10th century when Sokoto was the seat of the Caliph and Bida the capital of Nupeland.

Early European Contact

A French map of 1351 showed the coastline with some fair accuracy, a Venetian reached the Gambia in 1456 whilst Europeans saw the coasts of Liberia and Cameroun in 1462 and 1469 respectively.

The Portuguese bought pepper and ivory in Benin in 1472 and their countrymen had the monopoly of slaving. Lagos was discovered in the same year and named by the caravel captain, Lancelot de Freitas, as Lagos de Curamo, finally Lagos, displacing the Yoruba name, Eko, years later resuscitated by the Holiday Inn Group. This was in the time of Prince Henry the Navigator, grandson of John O' Gaunt, Duke of Lancaster. Main trade routes continued across the desert until the coast became better known during the 15th century when contact was further established with Fernando Po and Sao Tome so that Nigeria became tapped on its northern and southern limits with no stranger gaining access to the interior.

Songhai overran Katsina, Zaria and Kano in 1513 and Hassan Ibn Mohammed El Wazzan El Zayyati, best known as Leo Africanus, published a record of West African empires in 1526. The first English sea captain to make land was Captain Windham in 1553 who took on board a cargo of Benin pepper. A year later the dynasty of Biu was founded. Palm oil from Benin was first taken aboard in 1588 by the Englishman Captain Welsh and by 1601 the Dutch were examining trade potential. Ethiopia had become the best known country to Europe, statehood was known to be most developed in Senegal and sixteen names were now on the map of what was to become Nigeria, one of which was Bonny.

Age of Exploration

Africa was the first continent to be visited by whites, but was the last to be explored; a survey was made the more difficult because of the multiplicity of names and identification difficulties. In 1749 the French map showed outline without interior. Exploration parties usually started off from Tripoli 'over the shining sand and under the burning sky,' or from the Gambia, dominated by the quest for the Niger or the spoils of the rich interior. Explorers were often pawns in the hands of the various tribes and many testified to the saving of their lives by the succour afforded by African womenfolk. In 1823 one of them wrote of buffalo, elephant and good looking girls. Many explorers were of low standing at home; most found it convenient to adopt temporarily the religion of Islam and to profess to have medical knowledge. All knew that to speak well of christians invited certain trouble.

The first Lamido of Adamawa reigned from 1808, the Kingdom of Oyo stretched west to Asante in the Gold Coast, the Delta, Calabar, Ibadan and Abeokuta had been pinpointed. Six years before, Othman dan Fodio preached the Holy War and as Sarkin Musulmi, made himself master of Sokoto. Portuguese influence dwindled in the 16th century as the Dutch/French/English made their many sorties on the coast having been stimulated by the demand for slaves for the plantations of America and the Spanish West Indian Colonies. Ships of all nations became familiar with the river mouths between Lagos and Calabar. European goods were found in the Kano markets by 1851.

One party from Tripoli was driven back by Arabs, another from the Gambia was murdered, while yet another from Sierra Leone was forced to retire, Two Germans from Cairo died in the attempt, Mungo's son went out and died, a Senegal party lost its leader, six other failures followed. To personalise the scene, there were Mungo Park (1795), Denham, Clapperton & Oudney (1823), Landers (1825), Rene Caillie (1828), Barth (1850), Baikie (1854) and Gerhard Rohlfs (1865).

A great fillip was given to exploration in 1788 with the founding in London by Sir Joseph Banks of the Association for Promoting the Discovery of the Interior Parts of Africa (merged in 1831 with the Geographical Society) which, though biassed in favour of East Africa, remained undeniably curious about the true course of the Niger. Mungo Park, Scottish surgeon, made two voyages, captivity and hardship notwithstanding, reaching the Niger at Segu, Bambara, on 20th July 1796. His character is best revealed by these quotations:

> "Looking forward I saw with infinite pleasure the great object of my mission, the long sought for, majestic Niger... flowing slowly to the *eastward*.... I hastened to the brink.... lifted up my fervent thanks in prayer, to the Great Ruler of all things for thus far having crowned my endevours with success", and, "although all the Europeans who are with me should die, and though I were myself half dead, I would still persevere; and if I could not succeed in the object of my journey, I should at least die on the Niger."

Small wonder that in England there was a sense of guilt for many years after his death.

On his second trip with rank of captain when 75% of his thirty-five soldiers died before even glimpsing the Niger, he reached Bussa in 1805, only to die in ambush, so they say, or to drown because of shouted warnings from the banks to his craft of impending rapids being misunderstood, so they say, or fired upon because they were thought to be raiding Fulanis. He shares a memorial by the Niger, just beyond Jebba railway station, with Richard Lander who later completed the Niger discovery, and the simple obelisk bears these charming words, "Both died in Africa for Africa." Every British schoolboy knows of Mungo Park because of the quaintness of his name. The obelisk inscription is sufficient testimonial.

The end of the Napoleonic wars with their drain on manpower gave added impetus to exploration. The ill-assorted trio, Oudney, Denham and Clapperton, set out via Tripoli to Chad to behold the great Lake on 4th February 1823. They split up, Denham to Borno, Oudney to Benue, Clapperton to Kano and Sokoto, the death of Oudney having been predicted by El Kanemi. Clapperton's mission was to negotiate a treaty between Sultan Bello and the British Government. He entered Kano on 20th January 1824 — unnoticed. He came out again via Badagry with his servant, Richard Lander, and marched over the Yewa to Shaki, Old Oyo, Bussa, Yelwa and Sokoto, losing three Europeans enroute, himself to die from dysentery, being buried five miles south east of Sokoto at Jungarie by his servant. A stone in Sokoto cemetery commemorates: "Commander Hugh Clapperton RN — Explorer — died 13th April 1827."

Mungo Park and Lander Memorial Jebba

Richard Lander, wont to play his bugle horn on his travels, carried on. Altogether he made three trips, on the last two accompanied by his younger brother, John. On his return from the first trip at the instigation of the Portuguese who disliked him for his anti-slavery feelings, the King of Badagry had him tried as a spy and to prove his innocence, he had to submit to trial by ordeal by drinking red water tree bark Erythrophleum guineense, alkaloid erythropleine; only one in a thousand survived; he was one of the thousand. The second trip at the bequest of Lord Bathurst was to continue from where Mungo Park left off and trace the Niger from Bussa to its mouth. On the 25th October they discovered the confluence of the Niger and Benue at Lokoja. The year was 1830. They arrived at the Delta one month after leaving Lokoja. Lander claimed that the waterway would become the highway to civilisation. On the voyage the casualty rate was 90%. On his third trip he was shot while passing Angiama in the Delta but he carried on to die in Fernando Po from gangrene in February 1834.

Cemetery on Government Hill Jebba October 1908

Rene Caillie of Poitou, a baker's son, was the first to reach Timbuktu and return, setting out in 1828 from Sierra Leone and returning across the Sahara to Tangier. Dr Heinrich Barth of Hamburg, a cartographer and contemporary of Livingstone, produced nine African dictionaries and wrote 3000 pages of text on his travels described as a classic of penetration into the emirates. He marched ten thousand miles sucking his own blood in lieu of water and was the first to enter Yola in 1851 and discover the upper waters of the Benue. He died in Germany "with the arrogant quality of the Arab" but not before receiving a tumultuous welcome in Prussia and stimulating the first rumblings of the European scramble for Africa.

Dr Baikie in 1861 founded the site of Lokoja carrying out the functions of Consul for six years. Gerhard Rohlfs was the first to travel from the Mediterranean to the Gulf of Guinea in 1865. He was one of the few to return and not be at loggerheads with learned societies — because his journey "had not the fascination of a Nile discovery."

British naval squadrons were in Nigerian waters from 1810 to police slave dealing suppression, first entering the river Bonny in 1826. An aquatint depicted HMS Primrose capturing the slaver Veloz Passajaero in 1830 hanging in the Maritime Museum. British influence extended steadily after the Congress of Vienna and in 1833, slavery was abolished in the British Empire, some three years after Denmark had taken a similar step. With the Portuguese about on Lagos roads, returned slaves were sent ashore via Dahomey for Abeokuta. However cessation of the traffic closed the boundaries of Benin to other trade for so long that decay set in with the territory robbed of outside influence. The Royal Navy rescued the slave who was to be the future Bishop Crowther. The principal unit of exchange in the traffic was the manilla, not the cowrie, and the copper and lead content of the "coin" was redeemed in 1948 at an eventual cost of £284,000.

Missions

The Turks had suzerainty over Algiers, Tunis, Tripoli and Egypt between 1830-1880. Ethiopia had become an empire in 1897 and Egypt was under British occupation in 1891. Condominium, Kingdom, Mandate, were to describe areas of Africa by 1924. Republics were to come later. Sierra Leone became the third African country to issue stamps, after Natal and Cape of Good Hope. Lagos (not Nigeria) followed in 1874. The Rev. Thomas Freeman, his father an African, his mother English, was the first Wesleyan missionary, arriving at Cape Coast Castle in 1838 and Badagry in Nigeria on 24th September 1842. Here he built a mission house on coconut palms with bamboo walls.

In all Africa forty Protestant and thirteen Roman Catholic Missions were set up, the first in Northern Nigeria at Lokoja in 1865. On 17th January 1845 there followed a CMS Mission with Mr Townsend and the Rev. Samuel Ajayi Crowther, freed from slavery and future bishop. In April of that year Mrs Gollmer, wife of a reverend in the party, died and earned for herself an immortality by becoming the first person in Nigeria to receive a christian burial. A two-storey church house was built and that too earned fame as 133 years later it was declared an antiquity. Wesleyans figured later at Abeokuta; Presbyterians at Calabar were made famous by Mary Slessor's work of thirty-eight years, and the Baptists came to Victoria in Cameroun. The Catholics concentrated in the east. The foundation stone of the first Lagos church, Christ Church, was laid in 1867 by the Administration.

Trade

Brazil established trade at Badagry from the 17th century and much later their architectural heritage was to be seen at Lagos. By 1831 the eastern coastline had been dubbed "Oil Rivers". The French who had occupied Forcados from 1786 vied for trade with the Dutch, British, Portuguese, and the Spanish. The latter had taken possession of Fernando Po. The news of the

Niger's true course fired MacGregor Laird, son of a principal Liverpool shipowner, with the urge to explore and trade. Very soon, with Consul Beecroft, he was urging His Majesty's Government to retain use of Fernando Po as it was the key to Central Africa and a good base for navigation. He set up a trading company in 1832 and with Dr Oldfield, Lt. Allen and Richard Lander explored the Niger as far as the Nupe Capital, Rabba, and part of the Benue then known as the Chadda. They used the vessels *Columbine*, 176 tons, *Quorra*, 83 tons, and *Alburkah*, 35 tons. The first depended on sail; the others were paddle steamers. The *Quorra* broke up off Fernando Po.

Trading Station Old Calabar

In 1841, the Admiralty sent out the three steam vessels, *Albert, Wilberforce* and *Soudan,* carrying a crop of English specialists, picking up Kroomen at Sierra Leone as deck hands, and, at the request of the Church Missionary Society, the two missionaries, J.F. Schon and Samuel Crowther. The object was to lay the seeds for a trading and agricultural station at Lokoja but the expedition was a failure, losing fifty-three men of a complement of 303.

MacGregor Laird then formed a Society of Merchants to settle trade disputes on the Niger, having by then established for himself an outstanding reputation for riverine business. From 1854 he had company — Dr Baikie trading at Lokoja. In 1852, merchants of different nationalities at the Port of Lagos were about equal but one decade later, the British outnumbered combined French, Italian, German and Brazilian sea captains by 45%. In 1857, the *Dayspring* set out, famous to all acquainted with Nigerian history. She was 77 tons, 30 HP, and she had on board Dr Baikie, Rev. Crowther, and a certain Lt. John Glover RN who was a hydrographer. The Dayspring reached Lokoja in thirty-one days from Liverpool where Crowther established a mission at nearby Igbobi. Baikie carried on but the vessel was wrecked on the Juju Rock at Jebba on the 7th October 1857 stranding the ship's company at Rabba for a year. Baikie's use of quinine saw him to the Niger, rather than the Sahara, the obvious route from which to open up the country. MacGregor Laird moored a hulk just below the confluence in that year and called it "Laird's Town". He died four years later.

On the 29th June 1864 at a Convocation at Canterbury Cathedral, Dr Samuel Ajayi Crowther, first ordained clergyman of the Church of England in West Africa, married to a grand-daughter of the Alafin of Oyo, captured by the Portuguese, rescued by the British, associated with two Niger expeditions, confidant of Laird and Baikie, entered into the Bishopric of the Niger Mission.

Another well-known name came to the fore in 1876: I.T. Palmer, a Sierra Leonean, who started up the palm oil trade for Miller Brothers on the Niger, became Diplomatic Agent for the Royal Niger Company, and became known everywhere as "Warrior" because of his hatred of slavery and twin murder. In 1928, he was Warri-Benin-Division nomination for the Legislative Council of (united) Nigeria.

In 1877, Sir George Taubman Goldie, realising the potential of the river trading stations, persuaded the firms that strength lay in combination and that a common purse could buy out the French — the impediment to the granting of a Royal Charter. Goldie, who virtually succeeded Laird, gave the combination the name "National Company of Africa" and on 10th July 1886, the Royal Charter was bestowed and with it the responsibility for the territory north of the Niger. A Constabulary was created and born along with the Oil Rivers Protectorate. The National Company of Africa had become UAC and finally Niger Company in 1879. Britain and France, the latter with most government support for the British were still sluggish in their thinking, raced to secure approval for Borgu, the former becoming the victor and Goldie following up with land acquisition from Ilorin northwards. Captain Lugard served in the RNC. 1886 saw the first returns of revenue and expenditure for Lagos Township, former returns having appeared over the Gold Coast mantle. Southern and Northern Nigeria were not in a position to follow suit until 1899.

Law and Order

The Colonial Office started up as a Committee of the Privy Council "for the Plantaccons" in 1660 and did not enjoy a minister of sole responsibility for the colonies until 1930. Fifteen per cent of the Royal Navy fleet patrolled West African waters but gave traders no protection inland. John Beecroft in 1835 ascended the Niger to Lokoja; five years later almost to Bussa; and in 1845 as far as Rabba, having in the interval explored the Benin and Old Calabar rivers. The first direct connection between Britain and Nigeria might be said to rank from his appointment as Consul for the Bights of Benin and Biafra from Santa Isabel in Fernando Po in 1849. But Santa Isabel was too far away and Consul Campbell was appointed at Lagos in 1861. Twenty years passed after Beccroft's voyage before the lower reaches of the Niger were surveyed by Glover.

Viscount Palmerston, future British Prime Minister, considered that notorious slave ports like Lagos should be annexed and a British naval force entered Lagos on the 26th December 1851, destroyed the slave market, deposed King Kosoko, put King Akintoye in his place, and made Badagry as a substitute port redundant. Things did not prosper in the required way and on the 6th August 1861 the new King Dosumu ceded Lagos to the British Crown.

In 1862 H.S. Freeman was made the first Governor and High Commissioner of the settlement of Lagos but a better remembered appointment came up in 1866 when Lt. John Glover was made Harbourmaster for Lagos. Later the Governor of the Colony of Lagos and C.A. Maloney assumed command, Lagos Colony being in 1875 enlarged by the addition of Badagry. Control moved nearer, in 1874, to the Gold Coast and C.C. Lees took up the first appointment with the rank of Lt. Governor. Maloney appeared back on the scene in 1883 with the rank of Deputy Governor of Lagos. Both Glover and Maloney are remembered by Glover Hall and Maloney Street.

France's aspirations to territory arose from the wish to compensate for the loss of Alsace and Lorraine. G.L. Gaiser of the German firm persuaded King Mahin of Okitipupa to cede nine miles of the coastline to his Emperor on behalf of Consul Nachtigal after whom a cape in Ambas Bay was named. In 1885 came the Berlin Conference when agreement on the award of territory in Africa was to be based "on effective occupation". Britain was able to claim that her interests in Nigeria so prevailed and the existence of a British Protectorate was recognised. Britain made treaties with Chiefs on the banks of the Niger Delta and called the parcel of land "Oil Rivers Protectorate" (ORP). Administration was by the Foreign Office but proved ineffective and it was left to the Royal Niger Company, Chartered and Limited, to take the lead in opening up the Niger further up-country.

In 1886 the separate Colony of Lagos was established by Letters Patent and viewed as the modern map of Nigeria, the country consisted of Lagos Colony, ORP, RNC, and the great remainder "area of British Influence". Everything was to change by 1900 but meantime ORP, enlarged, became the Niger Coast Protectorate in 1893 and a separate Yorubaland Protectorate was created in the same year to facilitate administration. The Governor of the Colony of Lagos in 1889 was Capt. G.C. Denton, remembered for Denton Causeway, and in 1893 Sir G.T. Carter, whose name was still commemorated a hundred years later in respect of the three generation bridge, the Iddo Island-Lagos Mainland bridge. The High Commissioner of the ORP in 1891 was Major C.M. Macdonald who carried on with the Niger Coast Protectorate with a knighthood followed by Sir Ralph Denham Rayment Moor who contributed much to railway argument. Nigeria's international boundaries were drawn up in 1893 with the Camerouns, 1898/1906 with Niger and 1906 with Dahomey.

A famous, or is it infamous, name then turned up. Roger Casement, with years of experience in the Congo, in the Survey Department of NCP, 1892-1895, associated with Elder Dempster and H.M. Stanley; from Calabar to Lourenco Marques, as Sir Roger, in World War I, executed in Ireland by the British for treason to the British 'Crown, having escaped an explorer's death in the Consular Service. In 1897 Lagos was under the Colonial Office, the interior under a private company, the coast under the Foreign Office. But under Chamberlain all became Colonial Office responsibility.

In the north Lugard, when not on skirmish, was preoccupied with his capitals. Lokoja, established by river penetration and trade in a territory where it must have been at its lowest ebb but for flotsam and jetsam, proved unhealthy despite Mount Patti and a good source of water. It started off well enough: 0720 hours 1st January 1900 and the

RNC flag lowered and the Union flag hoisted at a parade of arms with all civilians in uniform. The House of Commons had deliberated the position of the RNC in July 1899, a trading concern, "surely impossible position when disputes arose with foreign states" The Charter was revoked on the last day of 1899, the territory becoming Protectorate of Northern and Southern Nigeria, the latter absorbing the NCP. Sir Frederick Lugard became the first High Commissioner and Lokoja was to remain the capital until a substitute was found. The RNC became Niger Company Limited, was acquired by Lever Brothers in 1920, to become United African Company in the years that were to follow and that is why on 1st January 1900 there was much flag ceremony and the taking of oaths. Within months Lugard moved to Jebba, still on the same river, Lokoja losing out to Baro as the terminus on the Niger of the Baro-Kano Railway. Jebba had been a strategic camp for newly raised West African Frontiers Force during the French crisis of 1897 and was kept as a military base against Kontagora and Bida.

In May 1900 Lugard sent Col. Morland and recce parties up the Kaduna and the Gurara, away from the unhealthy spots, towards the Hausa States. On studying the surveys he much favoured the Bauchi Highlands but with his meagre resources was afraid to be too far away from the transportation offered by the waterways. A railway up the escarpment would have been prohibitively costly. The best choice was Kaduna that gave eighty miles free from rapids and he chose Dungeru but changed the name to Zungeru because the "Z" looked more native. Zungeru was just a few miles from the accessible port of Gwari-Juko, corrupted to Barijuko. They moved in September 1902. He had awaited a new Director of Public Works and found him in John Eaglesome who paved the way to attainment of the cantonment.

When the Yorubaland Protectorate had been formed, Egbaland within had been excluded in consideration of the right to build a railway through its territory. The exclusion of the Egba capital, Abeokuta, proved a thorn in the flesh of the Administration, peace being maintained by a force at Ibadan until the treaty of independence was terminated in 1914. Fear of French and Egba threats led to the appointment of a British Resident at Ibadan. The first High Commissioner for the Protectorate of Southern Nigeria was Sir Ralph Moor. The Governor of Lagos as his contemporary was Sir William MacGregor, remembered for railway and MacGregor Canal.

Indirect Rule was not Lugard's invention. The Romans applied it and some form of it was to be found in India and Fiji. In Nigeria Sir Claude MacDonald had advocated it in the Delta in 1891. It was practised in the Yoruba States and Goldie suggested it for the Northern States. It was least practised in Plateau State inhabited by the British in 1902 as part of a plan to forestall French occupation of Borno. Lugard married Flora Shaw, Colonial Correspondent of *The Times* and she was the one who suggested the name 'Nigeria' for the British Protec-torate.

The first white woman in many parts of Northern Nigeria was Mrs Constance Larymore in 1902; her husband was on Lugard's staff. The first British army officer on the scene at Biu was in 1904. Tribute was paid to the famous Dr Walter Miller by the imposition of 14-day examinations in Hausa for British civil servants. His church at Wusasa near Zaria was a beautiful mud built structure:

In 1905 there were 342 Europeans in the whole of Northern Nigeria including 120 soldiers. A year later another railway-interested Governor appeared for Lagos — Sir Walter Egerton, and the Protec-torate of Southern Nigeria became divided up into West, Central and East Provinces with capitals at Lagos, Warri and Calabar. The Parliament decreed around this time that the official language of the railway should be English, that Erse should not be encouraged in Ireland, and that Hungarian should apply on the railway in the Croation district. Lugard went to Hong Kong in 1907 and Sir Percy Girouard, his replacement, lost no time in seeking a better site for a capital than

Zungeru. He thought of Kano but listened to the Canadian, Australian and South African views that a new capital was better sited in virgin territory. In the end the view prevailed that a site on the projected line of the latest railway should be sought and the choice settled on Kaduna, 570 miles from Lagos. The Great War stopped occupation until 1917.

Lugard Hall Kaduna

In 1863, Lagos had a civil police force and a semi-military police force, 1861 having seen their birth. The RNC raised a constabulary foiling French and German intentions and the rank of detective in the country was created in 1879. Consul Annesley drew up a force in the Oil Rivers Protectorate (ORP) in 1880 and in the country generally, police and military police became separated in 1886. Five years later, there appeared Night Water Police but by 1894 more reliance was placed on the military forces than on the constabulary of the NCP. A Drum & Fife Bugle band was first heard in 1897, a year after the formation of "The Lagos Police". In 1906, there were then three forces, Colony of Lagos, Protectorate of Northern Nigeria and Protectorate of Southern Nigeria. Until World War 1 the type of firearm used was influenced by the practice of the Royal Irish Constabulary.

On thinking over the French menace Chamberlain, then Colonial Secretary, decided in 1897 that the various military forces should be amalgamated in West Africa and there be created the West African Frontier Force, WAFF (pronounced WOFF). Colours were presented in 1922 and in 1928 King George V bestowed the "Royal". The first commandant on 26th August 1897 was Captain and Brevet Major (local Colonel) Frederick Dealtry Lugard. Born in India in 1858 he had been commissioned in the East Norfolk Regiment. He set up HQ at Jebba. His selection arose from his appointment under Goldie of RNC in 1894 where he was required to negotiate a treaty with the King of Borgu for trading rights in the face of French competition. The Force was financed by the Imperial Government and officered by the British Army.

In 1898 an Engineering Unit of 20 Madrass Sappers was posted under Lt. Charles RE. Lt. Glover, on the Dayspring with Dr. Baikie, freed a number of slaves with which he formed "Glover's Hausas" for the Lagos Constabulary and these men formed the backbone of Lugard's army. A West Indian detachment formed the Garrison of Lagos. The NCP had a force raised by Ralph Moor who was a former Inspector of the Royal Irish Constabulary called the Oil Rivers Irregulars and nick-named the Forty Thieves. At HQ Calabar, they became the Niger Coast Constabulary and in 1898 became the nucleus of the 3rd Ballalion WAFF, Southern Nigerian Regiment. WAFF regimental marches became "Father O' Flynn", "La Paloma", and "Lancashire Poacher". Jebba HQ trained two battalions of infantry, two battalions of artillery, and a company of engineers.

The first Inspector General of WAFF was Brigadier G.V. Kendall, appointed 23rd July 1901 when both Lagos and Southern Nigeria forces each had a native officer. As a consequence of Lord Selbourne's Committee, the Royal Engineer's attachment was disbanded in April 1903. From this year, WAFF officers wore the Crown Bird crest on their helmets. In the mess was a medical officer, Dr. E.C. Adams, called Adamu, famous for his ballads "Lyrae Nigeriae" and part author of the play, "White Cargo", popular in London for many years.

The Sultan of Sokoto's Standard was presented to the 2nd Battalion Leicestershire Regiment in June 1904. It was returned to Nigeria on Independence in 1960. It was the original standard raised by Othman dan Fodio during the Jihad. In 1906 the Lagos Battalion amalgamated with the Southern Nigeria Regiment and in 1907 the strength of the Northern Nigerian Regiment was 2797 rank and file made up of 1738 Hausas, 361 Kanuris, 362 Yorubas, 215 Fulanis and 121 others, After the move to Kaduna, Zungeru remained a WAFF base.

There were skirmishes. King Shodeke wisely established a base at Abeokuta for defence against the Dahomeans in 1825 in good time for later defence of the famous Amazonians — women dressed as soldiers. Internally, Capt. Bower was sent to Ibadan to stop Ilorin raiding south for slaves in 1895 and his name is commemorated in Ibadan to this day. Lugard dealt with potential French hostility in Borgu in 1897 but the most important event of the year was the Benin massacre of all but two Europeans when Consul Phillips marched on Chief Overami with inadequate forces. Bida and Kontagora yielded up slavery only by forcible persuasion and until 1902 Yola, Bauchi and Borno were in the same boat.

In April 1900 Lugard had to send troops to the Gold Coast for the Ashanti Campaign, a field force led by Major Baden Powell, later to achieve Boy Scout immortality.

From 1st January 1900, any child born in Nigeria was born free. In 1901/02 the Long Juju Fetish at Arochuku and its sacrifices had to be subdued. In 1903 Resident Maloney was murdered by the Magaji of Keffi who was given asylum by the Emir of Kano. In the resulting expedition the Victoria Cross was awarded to Lt. Wallace Wright whilst a sapper on duty with the Anglo-French Boundary Commission. Major C.H. Fouljes captured Aliyu, the Emir. Kano was taken on 3rd February 1903. Sokoto, Katsina, Kano and Gwandu were the last to fall to British arms but there was still trouble further south Bende/Onitsha, slave trade and sacrifice, which had to be brought under control and the gentleman in charge was Brevet Major H.M. Trenchard. The year was 1905/06 and the Major was to see further service as Marshall of the Royal Air Force.

The last incident to cause loss of British lives in the country was the Satiru Rising in Sokoto in 1906 and it proved the first reverse suffered by the WAFF. A self-styled Mahdi preached Holy War against the infidel, three officers lost their lives, and a punitive expedition had to be launched.

One Nigeria

The first railway in West Africa was the 1881 Kayes-Koulikoro in present day Mali but the first time steam was seen on the actual coast was at the time of the first Ashanti Campaign when Sappers employed a steam traction engine in the bush.

The first proposals for a united Nigeria were along the lines of a Maritime and a Soudan state. Fortunately, with one of those rare instances of foresight seldom exhibited by any government, the man appointed to rule was sent out a year early so that he could make up his mind as to what should be done. This was Sir Frederick Lugard upon whom was bestowed the personal rank of Governor-General. The task was to amalgamate the Nigerias as the Colony and Protectorate of Nigeria as from 1st January 1914 with Abeokuta, the last remaining independent kingdom, joining in. The Colony meant "British Subject"; the Protectorate "British Protected Person". The Protectorate was made up of the Northern and Southern Provinces. The first Lt. Governor of the former was C.L. Temple CMG and of the latter A.G. Boyle CMG. Lugard decided that the federal departments should be railway, WAFF, colliery, audit, treasury, posts and telegraphs, judicial, survey and legal. The police forces were not however amalgamated. The WAFF consisted of four battalions infantry, one battalion mounted infantry and two batteries artillery.

On the appointed day 30,000 horsemen drawn from Sokoto to Chad gave the Salute of the Desert at the Kano Durbar. A new flag was introduced together with a new colonial badge of two interlaced green triangles on a pink circle within a green square presenting a crown in yellow at the centre line intersections. This was known as Solomon's Seal and lasted till independence from Britain in 1960.

On the 5th August 1914, RSM Alhaji Grunshi, Gold Coast Regiment, in the Togoland Campaign, fired the first shot in anger, the first by any soldier of the allies in the Great War. Grave danger threatened Nigeria from Cameroun and Nigerian forces were mobilised meeting with such heavy losses in the valleys of the Benue and Cross Rivers that on the 1st September following, larger forces were fitted out under Major General Sir Charles Dobell. Douala fell but not the rest of the country so a second force under Brigadier General Cunliffe entered from the north, reduced Garua, joined up with the first force and took the country by 18th February 1916. Thereafter the Camerouns were administered on the authority of a mandate, the British portion being under the wing of a Protectorate. The Victoria Cross went to Capt. J. Butler, Kings Royal Rifle Corps, London Gazette 23-8-1915.

In a despatch to the War Office Sir Charles said "give me the Hausa soldier — no day too long — no task too difficult." Then came the East African Campaign, General Smuts, Commander-in-Chief Eastern Section and the comment, "the green caps never retired," a reference to the green Kilmarnock cap that replaced the fez of 1903. Mahiwa was a principal battle, Nigerian troops holding the lines with great bravery Casualties were:

combatants   killed 475; died of disease 208
carriers   killed 38; died of disease 472

Lugard retired in 1919 and said "christian missions played a great part in education; Nigeria always stood on its own feet." He left the WAFF, strength marked by twenty-six barracks, to the never forgotten sound of the "Hausa Farewell", a long melody of bugle calls based on Hausa tunes and played at the last railway station or Port of Lagos.

Bishop Crowther had a grandson. He was Herbert Macaulay, a gifted civil engineer, a force behind the scenes at the Democratic Party of 1922, his picture on the one naira note reprint of 1979 as a national hero.

The first representative Legislative Council with jurisdiction over Lagos and the Southern Provinces sat in 1922. The man most responsible for recruitment at the Colonial Office and for the "Devonshire Courses" of the Administrative Service was Major Sir Ralph Furse. In 1929 came the tragic "Womens Riots" of Aba and N'bawsi upon whom Lt. Richard Hill and his force were forced to shoot when only paces away. The cause was the unfounded fear of female taxation. Taxation troubles were by no means isolated in the long history of Nigeria. The Nigerian Police Force came into being, at last, in April 1930.

Before 1920 there were twenty-two Provinces, among them the now forgotten Munshi, Muri, Nassarawa and Nupe. In 1926, Plateau was carved out of Muri, Nassarawa and Bauchi. In 1932, there were twenty-one Provinces among them Ijebu and Adamawa. In 1949 Katsina, Benin and Rivers were created. The RWAFF was reorganised in 1933. Northern and Southern elements, each under a Lt-Col and a European Reserve Force came into being, including an Engineer Cadre. A Lagos Defence Force was authorised just before the Munich crisis. On 1st April 1939, the Southern Provinces was split into the Western Province and the Eastern Province. The principle that colonies must be self-supporting was finally destroyed in 1940. In February of that year the British Government issued a White Paper on the subject of Colonial Development and Welfare. It announced legislation providing £5 million a year for ten years for colonial development schemes to be used for agriculture, education, health, housing, as well as economic development and research. The measures were to apply to Colonies, Protectorates and Mandated Territories alike.

In 1941, it was decided that the RWAFF should consist only of infantry units. Technical arms such as the engineers became the West African Engineers.

World War II

Almost immediately there was the fall of France and the entry of Italy and later the loss of Malaya on the abandonment of Indo-China. The father of the RWAFF was now Major-General G.J. Gifford, soon General Sir George Gifford and at the commencement, five battalions quickly grew to twenty-three. The headquarters was Achimota College in the Gold Coast. In addition, General Sir Hugh Stockwell was at the East African Front and Burma Campaign and there was Major-General C.R.A. Swynnerton who signed the Order of the Day which included my commission after an Officer Cadet Training Unit (OCTU) at Enugu.

The Nigerians fought in the Italian East African Campaign and in Burma as part of the 81st and 82nd Divisions. The Nigerian Police Force raised a battalion and went to Burma. There was a shortage of officers despite the presence of Imperials and two hundred Polish officers who were drafted in. An early problem was whether the Germans would goad the Vichy French into taking action against a British Colony in West Africa — fortunately the Trans-Saharan railway had remained a project and was not in the making.

On the 7th June 1941, the War Office signalled an alert because only Chad under Governor Felix Eboue failed to fall into line. So as second in command to Captain Freddie Maw, with a team of British and Nigerian Sappers, I set out to prepare all border bridges in the north for demolition. Eventually, Equatorial Africa and French Cameroun adopted the stance of Chad but the danger completely passed after the appearance of De Gaulle on the scene. There were eight African schoolmasters per battalion for service abroad and I never really forgot my basic Hausa. At Arakan, Nigerian units operated with General Wingate behind Japanese lines. A captured Japanese diary said of the RWAFF 'because of their belief they are not afraid to die even if their comrades have fallen; they keep advancing as if nothing had happened.'

There was a cruiser *HMS Nigeria*. The name was carried on after independence by *NNS Nigeria* and the former became the Indian cruiser *Mysore*. The casualty list in the 1944/45 campaigns was:

	killed	wounded	missing	total
Officers	32	103	3	138
British ORs	24	81	1	106
African ORs	494	1731	54	2279

The RWAFF won 66 Battle Honours: Nigeria Regiment 28, Gold Coast Regiment 24, Gambia 8 and Sierra Leone 6 and from 1948 Nigeria has celebrated as an annual day of remembrance the battle fought at Myohaung where the greatest number of men took part. Her Majesty Queen Elizabeth II visited Nigeria in 1956 and named the unit 'The Queen's Own Nigeria Regiment'. Headquarter's West African Command closed down in June 1956, Ghana severed its connection in March 1959 and the last Colonel Commandant, General Sir Lashmer Whistler, relinquished his appointment in August 1960, one day after the RWAFF ceased to be. There can be no more attractive name carried by a regiment than that of 'Frontier Force'.

Pre-Independence

It will have become apparent that this racing analysis has concerned itself with law and order and politics once exploration had paved the way. The missing material, that makes or breaks a country's position in the world league, will be found in sufficient depth in a companion volume.

In 1947, there came (Governor) Richards Constitution. He was later Lord Milverton. In 1951 came the constitution providing for a Central Council of Ministers, House of Representatives and Regional Houses of Assembly and Houses of Chiefs in Northern and Western Nigeria giving rise to the emergence of political parties. Then in 1952 came (Governor) Macpherson Constitution which was an improvement on the Richards Constitution which was going down in history disliked.

In 1954, the rank of Governor-General was resuscitated. A new Federal Constitution made its way in October 1954 in which Regional Legislatures were given increased autonomy. They called this the pre-independence constitution, the country having spent much time in deliberating a date for the attainment of complete independence during which the national press was at pains to make life more unpleasant for the expatriate — an issue glossed over as being natural in retrospect.

Independence came to Ghana in 1957 and in 1960 to Cameroun, Chad, Niger, Dahomey, Togo, Ivory Coast, and Upper Volta. Inside Nigeria self-rule was granted to Western and Eastern Regions on the 8th August 1957 and in that year the first Federal Prime Minister, Alhaji Abubakar Tafawa Balewa, was appointed and ex-officio British officials ceased to be members of the Nigerian Federal Council of Ministers.

In 1958, the year 1960 was set down as target date for the Federation and cutting of the British tie. On March 15th 1959, Northern Nigeria attained self-rule, a later celebration being attended by the Duke and Duchess of

Gloucester. On January 16th 1960, the Federal House unanimously passed a motion that "this House authorises the Government of the Federation of Nigeria to request Her Majesty's Government in the United Kingdom as soon as practicable to introduce legislation in the Parliament of the United Kingdom providing for the establishment of the Federation of Nigeria on October 1st 1960, as an independent Sovereign State, and to request at the appropriate time support with the other Member Governments of the Commonwealth, Nigeria's desire to become a member of the Commonwealth."

So, almost a century after the Dosumu Treaty, on 1st October 1960, there was formed the Federation of Nigeria consisting of Northern Nigeria, Western Nigeria, Eastern Nigeria and the Federal Territory of Lagos. It was not of course an act of returning a country to its nation because there was no such nation, by name or area, at the time it was taken. Nigeria was a British creation handed back to those people who lived upon its lands.

On Friday 30th September, 1960 the ceremony of flag raising and display of fireworks was held. The national press reported one case of drunkenness and disorderliness in the whole of metropolitan Lagos. On the Saturday, we witnessed the Independence Ceremony. A Guard of Honour was furnished by the 3rd Battalion, Queens Own Nigeria Regiment for the presence of the Prime Minister, His Excellency the Governor General and Lady Robertson, and HRH Princess Alexander of Kent who presented the Constitutional Instruments.

Back home, in the United Kingdom, all with knowledge looked forward to a prosperous and safe rule for the new nation.

Post Independence

There was a great parade of all the appointed ministers along the Marina. The Prime Minister of the Federation was Alhaji Sir Abubakar Tafawa Balewa whose party was the Northern Peoples Congress. The Premier of Northern Nigeria was Alhaji Sir Ahmadu Bello, the Sardauna of Sokoto, Leader of the Northern Peoples Congress. The Premier of Western Nigeria was Chief S.L. Akintola of the Action Group. The Premier of Eastern Nigeria was Dr. M.I. Okpara of the National Council of Nigeria and the Cameroons. The President of the Senate of the Federal Parliament was Dr Nnamdi Azikiwe while the Leader of the Opposition in the Federal Parliament was Chief Obafemi Awolowo. At the Federal level, Parliament consisted of the Senate of forty-four members and the House of Representatives of 312 members. Each Region was self-governing and had a bicameral legislature consisting a House of Chiefs and a House of Assembly. Membership at the Senate were North 76, West 52 and East 63 while the House of Representatives had, for the North 136, West 80 and East 84.

The Armorial Bearings depicted an eagle on a black shield supported by two white chargers and coctus spectabilis, a Nigerian colourful flower. The shield was bisected by two silver bands representing the Niger and the Benue. The arms depict strength and dignity. The motto is "Unity and Faith". The National Flag was green-white-green in equal parts representing agricultural wealth, unity and peace. The three verse National Anthem included the words

> Though tribe and tongue may differ,
> In brotherhood we stand,

but was only to last nineteen years because it was written by an English woman, strange in a sense, as all else British has persisted.

Nigerians held senior posts in the judicial, legal and medical departments because they had entered the professions at an early age but there were few appointments to the administrative service. At the Federal level, all heads were British including the Secretary to the Prime Minister but excluding the Secretary to the Council of Ministers. Sir James Robertson carried on as Governor-General for a month and in November 1960 was succeeded by Dr Nnamdi Azikiwe, the first Nigerian appointment to the highest office in the land. On the

9th August 1963, full circle once again established itself by the creation of the Mid-Western Region.

Republic and Military Coups

On 1st October 1963, Nigeria became a Republic with Dr. Azikiwe as President and Commander-in-Chief. The country also became a member of the Commonwealth and the United Nations. It mattered nothing to UK/Nigeria relations. In October 1965, there was a general election characterised with vote rigging by the Akintola faction and about 2000 people lost their lives in the resulting melee. The hallmarks of the 1966 assassinations were set, I fear, as it was rumoured that Chief Akintola and Sir Ahmadu Bello had negotiated a deal to conspire that federal troops should be brought to Ibadan to deal with the former's opposition. Young army officers, fed up with ministerial extravagance, needed no further fuel, and they struck, blindly in some directions, on January 15th 1966, led by Major Kaduna Nzeogwu (a Mid-Western Ibo) and four other Sandhurst-trained officers, killing the Prime Minister (Hausa), Sir Ahmadu Bello (Fulani), Chief Ladoke Akintola (Yoruba) and Chief Festus Okotie-Eboh (Itsekiri), long time Federal Minister of Finance. Lt. Colonel Arthur Unegbu was the only Ibo killed, he for gallantly refusing to hand over the keys to the armoury. Killed with him were nine senior army officers.

The coup had degenerated and the pattern of killings and decline in discipline left no doubt of this. The Prime Minister, who had been warned of the impending coup by a friendly power, went quietly to his end after prayer. Neither was the senior wife of the Sardauna spared. In disgust, Dahomey and Niger closed their borders.

Akintola had been a railway clerk; he had held portfolio as Minister for Communications & Aviation. The Sardauna was the most powerful political figure in the country, every inch an aristocrat and every inch of him dressed like one. In 1963 he had defined the unity of Nigeria as "the rivers of the Niger and Benue, the road, railway and communications systems, our openings to the outside world, the ports of Lagos and Apapa, and Kano airport. Each part of the country depends on the others for one service or another, and for one type of produce or another."

On January 16th 1966, Major-General Johnson Aguiyi-Ironsi took over. He was the last UN soldier to leave Congo soil in 1964, the first to succeed the British G.O.C. Nigerian Army, Major-General Welby-Everard. He was Aide-de-Camp (ADC) to the Governor back in the 50s and Extra Equerry to the Queen for the Nigerian visit of 1956.

The General was an Ibo. He suspended the Constitution and appointed Military Governors to run the four Regions. The important posting of these four lay in the assignment of Lt.-Col. Chukwuemeka Odumegwu-Ojukwu to the East. Unfortunately for Nigeria and the General, the latter adopted a wholly sectarian attitude in listening to advice.

On 24th May 1966, General Ironsi took unilateral action and abolished the federal system based on Regions thereby altering the fundamentals. Within five days violence had erupted. On 29th July, troops mutinied and the General was killed at Ibadan. With him went a gallant gentleman, Lt.-Col. Adekunle Fajuyi, Military Governor of the West, who as host, had refused to yield up his guest to the insurgents. Ten senior army officers lost their lives in the fighting in circumstances in which also Northern retaliation for the January coup figured. It had been a particularly sore point that on coming to power, no courts-martial had been ordered by the General. A year after his assumption of office the General's remains were given a state funeral upon being re-interred and buried at Umuahia but they had to find an Englishman to drive the train — G.O. Urion —retired Assistant General Manager (Operation). On August 1st 1966 Lt.-Col. Yakubu Gowon with the look of classical youth about him, took over as Supreme Commander.

Civil War

The Republic of Biafra was proclaimed by Lt.-Col. Ojukwu from 30th May 1967 and lasted until Major-General Phillip Effiong and Biafra surrendered on the 12th January 1970. Ojukwu's father had been a very wealthy Lagos businessman of Eastern origin.

The Federal Government at the Aburi Meeting in Ghana in January 1967 bent over backwards in making far-reaching concessions. Gowon did the one thing for which he will never be forgotten. On 27th May 1967 he laid the foundation stones for a Nigeria devoid almost of North or West or East connotation by the creation of twelve States to replace the Regions: North Western, North Central, Kano, North Eastern, Benue-Plateau, Kwara, Western, Lagos, Midwest, East Central, South Eastern and Rivers states.

On Friday June 30th Ojukwu announced to the world "total war" against Nigeria. They started in earnest with attempts to dynamite Lagos and from 6th July the action was intensified. A day later Gowon ordered mobilisation and a bloody civil war lasted for 2½ years and caused untold suffering and havoc. The war was well planned with a large stock of railway tank cars in Eastern hands but to anyone who knew Nigeria, there could only be one end — surrender. Sanctions of course had been applied and ships warned off eastern waters.

Militarily, Lagos had the initiative. Biafra was waging a war on four fronts: Onitsha-Enugu axis, Ogoja, Port Harcourt and Calabar. Genocide was mentioned many times and 1967 passed with neither side sufficiently weakened to sue for terms. For too long the British Government tried to remain neutral. A year later it was said that "It is not a military campaign waged to decimate the Ibos as a group. The Ibos are no enemies; they are Nigerians who, however, must learn to accept constituted authority." Biafra's survival will merely perpetuate internecine tribal wars and such a pocket of power will encourage and promote international conspiracy.

Biafra was swollen with refugees and both sides suffered heavy casualties. The Federal Military Government repeated quite often that it would stop action if the rebels renounced secession and accept the new structure of twelve States in Nigeria. But the disintegration of Nigeria was not negotiable. Asaba fell in 1968 but Awgu was captured. Portuguese arms came to the help of the Biafrans but Holland and Belgium, after much doubt, supported neither side.

Ojukwu's public relations was a better weapon than Gowon's in spite of the shortage of funds which the former had to contend with. Tanzania, Gabon, Ivory Coast and Zambia recognised Biafra. Port Harcourt, Afam and Aba fell as the war dragged on. The Nkalagu cement factory was destroyed, and the largest market in West Africa, Onitsha, shelled. The University of Nigeria, Nsukka was damaged. Soviet strike aircraft were sent to Gowon with Egyptian pilots who were not too happy in their assignment. Nigeria remained the key to the independence of African States and the stability of the African hemisphere. If Nigeria were to break up, other States would soon become the victims of the forces always ready in the wings.

Owerri fell next and Ojukwu's men were squeezed into an area centred on Umuahia only, a fraction the size of what had been the starting of the Ibo empire — some 4000 square miles. Upon the conclusion of the war, General Gowon behaved with great magnanimity to the defeated.

An Executive Presidency

The 1912 West African Currency Board was wound up and Nigeria introduced the Naira (₦) with 100 Kobo to the unit from January 1st 1973, one Naira being worth 10/- in British (old) currency on creation. By 1974 the High Commissioner to Nigeria had become one of the most important UK postings. On the 29th July 1975 General Gowon, whilst away at the OAU Summit Meeting at Kampala, was deposed in a bloodless coup. There was too much extravagance among State Governors and plans to return to civilian rule were awaited. His asylum in the United Kingdom created some ill-feelings in Nigeria. His place was taken by an undoubted strong man, Brigadier Murtala Mohammed. By a political masterstroke he cancelled the 1973 census, always a suspect figure, and brought the 12-States country up to 19 States, abolishing in their names this time any reference to the points of the compass. The new States were Oyo, Ogun, Lagos, Kwara, Niger, Bendel, Rivers, Imo, Cross River, Anambra, Benue, Plateau, Gongola, Bauchi, Borno, Kano, Kaduna, Sokoto and Ondo.

A Committee, the Aguda Committee, was set up to report on the desirability of establishing a new capital to replace overcrowded Lagos and recommended a 3000 square mile Federal Capital Territory around latitude 9 and 7 East longitude in the region of Abuja, a very attractive area. Most tragically, General Mohammed was assassinated whilst driving his car to Dodan Barracks in Lagos on the morning of Friday 13th February 1976. International relations were not helped by suggestions of foreign involvement and unease persisted for some time. The assassin was Lt.-Col. Dimka who duly met his deserved fate. A shocked nation then learnt that among those to follow him to the firing squad for complicity in the outrage was Major-General I.D. Bisalla, Defence Commissioner.

Lt.-General Olusegun Obasanjo, a Sapper, the first of the Yoruba nation to hold this office, took up the lead and prepared the country for a return to civilian rule. The Constitution of the Federal Republic of Nigeria 1979 was drawn up with the appointed day, 1st October 1979, making provision for the executive powers of the Federation to be vested in a President. On the 1st October 1979 Alhaji Shehu Shagari, Fulani, native of Sokoto, became first Executive President of the Second Republic.

Physical Geography, Game and Climate

Within the compass of small England, every variety of scenery is to be found and those unacquainted with Nigeria may believe all to fall within the pattern of a tropical uniformity. Words strung together in this exercise may easily fascinate and be thought to guild the lily but the treatment given is susceptible of proof to indigenes and visitors who care to wander. This "geography" is written mainly in the present tense.

Africa has the largest area of tropic of any of the continents and its coastline is remarkable for its minimum of indentation. Nigeria within Africa occupies 356,670 sq. miles (923,768) sq. km and lies as a simple quadrilateral massif off the west coast, lying between 3 and 14° East and 4 and 14° North bounded by Benin, Niger, Chad, Cameroun, and the Gulf of Guinea. It is larger than France and Italy combined. The southern-most tip of the former Gongola State in the east is but a few miles north of Lagos in the west, a fact realised by few of the inhabitants. So vast is the country. If one factor alone had dictated the ecology it is the inhibiting presence of the tsetse-fly.

The Nigerian shore, lacking natural harbours, is a low sandbar coastline with entrances continually silting up, free of coral reef except for occurrences in the Bight of Benin. In the west, Badagry is separated from the sea by a sand spit and fresh water creek, introducing the continuous lagoons that are such a significant means of communication and broken open naturally at Lagos alone from there to the Delta. But although it is possible to move by inland water as far as Opobo protected from the surf seventy miles east of Lagos, the shore line sand becomes the mud of a delta that over the centuries has pushed the sea back whilst accommodating the piggy back sand of the Niger. The shelf quickly descends to 100 fathoms off Lagos but the gradient has eased off by the coast of Cameroun. Palm Point separates the Bights of Benin and Bonny. The construction of the Lagos harbour moles has in a span of fifty-eight measured years brought about the advance of Lighthouse Beach by 400 metres and the retreat of Victoria Beach by 1250 metres.

The geology is varied. The coast features plains, ridges, mangrove, deltaic and sediment deposition. In the south west there are quartzite ridges, sandstone plains, granite hills, syenite and garnet, with scattered inselbergs less scattered around Iseyin where the domed monsters capture the imagination. Flood plains abound all over the country, detritus and alluvium never far away, a potent warning to bridge and road construction teams. Eastwards are the shale and clay, the Imo an example of a fault-guided valley, the famous Ameki formation of migmatite and undifferentiated igneous and metamorphic rocks, to the Oban Hills of Calabar on Pre-Cambrian basement.

No new term is required to describe Kwara but ironstone capping is met and the man-made Kainji Lake covers a stretch of the Niger crossing the Kontagora anticline in the series of rapids and gorges encountered by Mungo Park. Oolitic Ironstone is found as the centre of Nigeria is reached and in Benue where the limestone at Yandev is of the highest quality, the Rift features craters breeched by later eruptions of basaltic lava and extinct cinder cones. Hard shale as Enugu is left to the south with Plateau State described as a "Giant's Causeway" of six-sided basaltic columns between Vom and the Ganawari Hills and elsewhere described as a mixed bag of porphyritic biotite granite reaching the Kudaru Hills, fluvio volcanic deposit, siltstone, and lacustrine sediment. The 295m high Wase Rock is a volcanic neck.

A Hill on the Jos Plateau

In the far north-east, aeolian sand, clay, dune depression and degraded flood plains mark Borno with a lava plateau at Biu and require the Lake Chad fishermen to make use of oxen and horse bones to weigh their nets in the absence of any stone. In the far north-west, white clay and red sandstone cheek by jowl with iron-capped hills, gneiss and schist, flood plains along the Sokoto/Rima basins and good examples of pediment forming, in neighbouring Niger State, a pediplan. The Federal Capital Territory boasts the 600-feet Zuma Rock of granite. Between the east and the west, much of what has been said invites repetition but for the landlocked granary Kano where but for two ugly rocks in the city, hardly a stone is to be found.

Turning to the soil, one is faced with Africa's greatest problem — erosion. Orchard scrub in the west holds the ground together; in the Delta mangrove trees act as a cement until solid ground is reached. Fertility is assured in Imo by the glabrous shrub, Acioa barteri, not far away from soil erosion at its worst — the Enugu-Onitsha axis whilst the river Orashi ends up in innumerable gullies beaten for size by those of the Udi cuesta, best viewed from the aeroplane. Much soil is infertile because it lacks humus forcing a hard life upon the people who for example dwell in such territory. The Niger-Benue is alluvial, the Middle Belt lateritic, the northern zone chestnut steppe and the fine light-coloured wind blown dust called loess. Borno is distinctive for clay accumulation with organic matter, called 'firki' giving rise to black cotton soil and a ground in the dry season bedevilled with open cracks.

It is true that a line drawn from the west of Cape of Good Hope to the Ethiopian Highlands divided the continent, east, to a panorama of African beauty and wildlife, west, to the desert and low lying shores. It is also true that Nigeria is on the "wrong" side of this line, yet it does not lack the scene to captivate the eye. Before part of Cameroun became part of Nigeria, a table was published that few will have seen of the range of elevation above sea level according to the area in square miles at each chosen increment. This is reproduced as a percentage area of the whole country:

Under 400 feet	24.02%
400 and under 800 feet	22.91%
800 and under 1200 feet	21.39%
1200 and under 2000 feet	24.26%
2000 and under 3200 feet	6.75%
3200 and under 4400 feet	0.67%

The statistics deals with tableland and not with peak. The highest land, west of the Niger, is 2236 feet, north of the Niger/Benue 5841 feet, and east of the Niger, South of the Benue, 6700 feet. Away, off the border, above the swamps of the Rio Del Rey, lies Africa's second highest mountain, an active volcano, Mount Cameroun at 13,350 feet. The record climb, up and down, was accomplished in 7 hours 50 minutes by H.N. Milne of the Nigerian Administrative Service. He found the temperature to be 44°F at 1200 feet.

A range of highlands then separates Cameroun from Nigeria. The Adamawa Plateaus, among them, reach 8000 feet And on the Nigerian side of the border is found the beautiful landscape of the Sonkwala Ridge with a peak at 6200 feet, home of the gorilla and the blue green fern salaginellis. Few rivals for wealth of scenery can touch the Plateau, always the Jos Plateau and never the so often misnamed Bauchi Plateau. Approached from the south by the Kagoro Hills to arrive at the Shere Hills of altitude 5841 feet on the contour map, the impression is the proverbial pin cushion. Jos is the geographical centre of Nigeria and the ultra-violet radiation induces the growth of roses, carnations and delphiniums. Scarp surrounds except to the north east where the country drops to a greener landscape. To the north, there is formed the watershed between the Niger and Lake Chad systems.

Biu in Borno, an undisturbed backwater for the ornithologist, enjoying both Guinea and Sahel vegetation, has a plateau of 2000 sq. miles at 2500 feet. Ekiti in present-day Ekiti State, presents an area of unparalleled rock climbing potential and the Semorikas with their 'tie tie' ropes are said to be as skilled as the Sherpas of Nepal and Tibet.

Lying on an air corridor, the peaks of the too high Idanre Hills in Ondo State were determined at 3100 feet. Their sheer granite walls fire the mountaineer's imagination. The plains of Sokoto occupy 1/20th of the area of the Federation. Vast rock massifs in Kaduna State, land of sugar-cane, secret the hyena. The Udi Plateau, a cuesta, peaks at 1715 feet and the film "Daybreak at Udi" featured, under District Officer E.R. Chadwick OBE, the greatest community effort in development in the land. Where the cashews grow and along the road, his name will be remembered.

The scarplands from below Awgu to ninety miles north, form the watershed between the rivers draining through into the Niger and those flowing east into the Cross. The valley of the Cross is the most extensive of the southern plains. The country around the seat of the capital, Abuja, ranges from 800 to 2000 feet with nearby Niger State offering many an example of saddle or col. Ibadan dominates the plains of Oyo. West of the Niger/Benue confluence is the Patti Ridge at 1340 feet looking like an amputated starfish. Finally is the classic example of the gorge, Olokemeji, where railway takes advantage of the Ogun hillside cut.

From relief, attention turns to drainage. Rivers with a length of 125 miles or over in Nigeria include:

River	Length	Rises	Flows
Niger	730	Sierra Leone	Gulf of Guinea
Benue	495	Cameroun	Niger
Sokoto	390	Kaduna State	Niger
Kaduna	340	Plateau State	Niger
Cross	335	Cameroun	Gulf of Guinea
Gongola	330	Plateau State	Benue
Komadugu Yobe	290	Kano State	Swamps of Chad
Ka	235	Sokoto State	Sokoto
Yedseram	220	Mandara Mts	Swamps of Chad
Katsina Ala	215	Bamenda Highlands	Benue
Zamfara	210	Sokoto State	Sokoto
Hadejia	205	Kano State	Komadugu Yobe
Ogun	190	Oyo Plains	Lagos Lagoon
Mariga	185	Kaduna State	Kaduna
Donga	175	Mambilla Plateau	Benue
Osse	165	Kwara State	Delta
Imo	140	Imo State	Gulf of Guinea
Anambra	130	Benue State	Niger
Mada	125	Plateau Foothills	Benue

Rivers, wet and dry, abound everywhere. The Niger, at 2600 miles, is the third longest river in the continent, passing through almost every climatic zone of West Africa, and draining over 50% of the country. Its main tributaries are the left bank ones, Sokoto, Kaduna, Benue, the last and the parent forming a great letter "Y" superimposed over the country. Whilst the Gambia is most adapted for ocean-going navigation, the Niger is divided into four sections by rapids at Bussa in Nigeria, Niamey in Niger, and Bamako in Mali. Amazingly, by the pattern of distributaries in Mali, it forms an inland delta. The coastal delta of 25,000 square miles over a shore line of 200 miles with twenty-one distributaries, the largest in Africa, is arcuate and built up over the centuries by alluvium deposits — the whole never forgotten when one is airborne.

The creeks support the largest of the mangroves, Rhizophora racemosa, mudskippers and hermit crabs, all in an absence of "ozone". The channels of which the main are the Nun and Forcados were once thought of as the separate outlets of the "Oil Rivers". Enroute, the Niger passes through Leaba with dangerous rapids, "crocodiles and constant drowning", but is set off by flamboyants, frangi-pane and acacias in the Borgu territory of the solemn Fish Eagle and river oysters.

Jebba is a white cemetery signifying duty doggedly done with the famous Juju Rock and elephant and lion still abundant in 1938, through Mureji old time caravan station to the meetings of the waters to coin an Irish phrase at Lokoja, reminiscent of highland scenery, with the roar of the lion once heard on the banks of the tributary the Mimi, seen best from Mt. Patti. At Onitsha, the Niger is in rejuvenation terrain.

Unlike the Niger, the Benue is not hampered by rapids in its course through Nigeria, a characteristic owed to the fact that the valley is cut through sedimentary rocks below Yola, a place name meaning "rising ground". It is clearer than the Niger, traverses some lovely sceneries and has flat banks which a continually flooded in the rains when it discharges 10,000 cubic metres per second, draining 120,000 sq. miles of territory. The gradient is from 550 feet to 250 feet and its total length from confluence to source is 650 miles. The main tributaries are the Gongola and Mada on the right bank and the Katsina Ala and Donga on the left. The Katsina Ala drains the Obudu Plateau and the Sonkwala Mountains in an example of rectangular drainage.

The Gurara River Waterfall near Abuja

North East Nigeria drains into the only large lake in the country, Chad, with no outlet to the sea, but in strict terminology Cameroun provides the inflow via the Chari/Logone systems, the Nigerian rivers Komadugu Yobe, Komadugu Gana and Yedseram being lost in a trough before they reach the lake. Altogether the supply is on a radial pattern. Lake Chad, shrinking but once the size of the Caspian Sea is again enlarging after the drought of 1972-4 and may be any size from 6,400 to 16,000 sq. km at a maximum depth of 4.6m in the south. Twenty-five per cent of the surface lies in Nigeria.

The largest of the coastal rivers is the Cross, always spoken of as the Cross river, never the river Cross, with the best example in Nigeria of a broad tidal channel. All eastern rivers flow into the Bight of Bonny: western coastal including the Ogun, Oshun, Oni, flow into the Lagos and Lekki Lagoons. The Yewa flowing near Badagry is a good example of trellis drainage. The high plains of Bauchi to Sokoto offer negligible relief so that the Gulma, for example, has an average gradient of 0.3 metre per kilometre. The Sokoto and Rima dominate Sokoto State and prosper cultivation in the three-mile wide fadamas. The former was chosen in 1975 to accommodate the Bakalori Dam, one of the world's longest, designed to irrigate 70,000 acres. Mountain streams tumble down the Plateau. The finest waterfall lies near the Federal Capital Territory on the Gurara, an area sought by the seeker after gold. The Gurara gives rise to many tributaries to a dendritic pattern in the territory.

Only the Kaduna river remains to be mentioned, named from the Hausa plural for crocodile, studded in places with islands. The Jibwa, off the Kaduna, has twenty-seven tributaries, a not untypical feature of Nigerian river supply. Nigerian rivers are either too low to permit navigation in dry season or too much in flood in wet season to ensure full economic use. Containment of the floods is now engaging the attention of the country to lessen the menace and assist agriculture. Neglecting the dry season, the country may be said to be well watered but there are large areas in central Borno, northern Kano, and where the Benue and Gongola run parallel courses where there is no effective drainage. The river map of the country is long overdue for revision but the Inland Waterways Department Hydrological map does clearly portray the watershed — the Atlantic Divide.

The word "jungle" is not used in Nigeria where forestry covers 30% of the land area and food crop cultivation another 10%. In thousands of square miles, mangrove occupies 0.7, high forest 14.5, and savanna 104.2 according to the World Bank in 1953. There are said to be 900 species of trees any one of which can be identified by the noting of sixteen characteristics with the best commercial timbers, mahogany, iroko and obeche in the Mid-West and the West. As recently as 1979 it was said that 12% of the land was threatened by encroachment of the Sahara. In the riverine strips grow *Berlinia grandiflora,* Vogel's Napoleona, the corkwood tree, and the African Tulip tree while introduced exotics include cashew, pawpaw, gourd, mango, avocado pear, guava, cassia, the flamboyants, and the casuarina.

Technically speaking, from the east of Lagos to the east of Port Harcourt is mangrove, then across the country a belt of fresh water swamp, the two between them lying ten to sixty miles wide, then a zone of rain forest whose northern tip just penetrates Kwara State. A great area of Guinea Savanna then traverses the map with Sudan Savanna topping it but descending to the latitude of Yola in the east. Sahel Savanna is found in northern Borno and Montane in the east north of latitude 6° towards the Cameroun border. Very serious inroads have been made into the virgin forest by centuries of shifting cultivation and the bulk of vegetation consists of secondary growth.

The vegetation map illustrates the divisions now described. Where the breakers fall the casuarina may be found on sandy soil, so called after the cassowary bird whose feathers resemble the needle-like branchlets of the tree. Otherwise the mangrove from Senegal to Angola with the largest swamps in the delta features the screw pine, Raphia hookeri, and the three mangroves on aerial shoots in an impenetrable maze of ooze, termite free, reaching 70 feet dominated by the red rhizophora racemosa, provider of tannin. Inland, the fresh water swamp exhibits sudd and papyrus.

Baobabs by the Niger

The rain forest features the oil palm Elaeis guineenis, probably the most important tree in Nigeria, taller than Raphia hookeri, the wine palm, and in general the flora is the richest in West Africa with the semi-deciduous camwood, Bombax, Ceiba the silk cotton, iroko, Sapele mahogany, red ironwood, and terminalia superba, often intertwined with an undergrowth of lianas and other climbing plants. Around Ilesha every third bush is a custard apple and in the evergreens, colas, the beloved by ants common canthium, ebony, pink African cedar, tallow, and the rubber plantations. In Cross River State is Gmelina arborea, host to the bat, furnishing 300,000 tons of paper pulp per annum.

Guinea is a parklike savanna of grass and fire resisting trees beautiful to behold with the Biblical baobab, Adansonia digitate, as sentinel, its fruit as large as footballs and beloved by the Red Patas monkey. The zone includes broadleafed, riparian, transition, of mature and secondary growth, much to a mosaic pattern with farm cultivation as in Benue. Guinea runs out north of the Plateau with its bare highland grassland. Plantations include pine, eucalyptus, kenaf and sugar on the Bacita estate and the many trees to be found in the belt include the silk cottons bombax buonofozense, the red flowering, and ceiba pentandra, the white flowering, the former providing the material for thorn carvings and the kapok of lifebelts.

Other trees include the locust bean, shea, wild date, tamarind, and borassus aethiopium, the fan palm whose palm wine is allied to the arrack of India. Oil and wine palms are still found. The dreaded euphorbia balsamifera, a fleshly spurge used as an anti-marauding hedge, is found in many areas. In secondary forests, maidenhair albizia and umbrella tree musanga cecropioides are to be seen. Aloe grows on the inselberg and the main inventory closes by reference to rubber, berlinia grandiflora, parkia clappertoniana (in tribute to the explorer), afrormosia laxiflora, lophira lanceolata, teak, the acacias, vegetable ivory from the dum palm hyphaere thebaica, and watermelon.

The drier Sudan savanna, supporter of many crops, consists of scrubby vegetation interspersed with tall trees many of which have been named in Guinea savanna. Part of the zone embraces the so-called Middle Belt, a landstrip of imprecision to many but in fact lying between 8 and $10\frac{1}{2}°N$ separating the savanna from the rain forest. The Sudan savanna is also the cattle belt so that the area of the tsetse-fly has been defined. Sokoto in the west, about to have the benefit of the Bakalori Dam to ease water shortage, is largely agricultural with aquatic grasses along its rivers and thorny and non-thorny thickets in abundance. Some small lakes are to be seen and 'new' trees are the thirsty thorn, West African laburnum, African rosewood, nocturnal water lily, acacias of variety, and independent of moisture the neem, no less than a million growing in the east in Borno. The former Gongola State presents the greatest variety.

The Sahel savanna enjoying eight dry months in the year represents the last refuge before the desert and supports acacia seyal, thorn and gum arabic while the grass fails as a complete carpet, being tussoky and interspersed with sand dunes. The firki clay plains herald the reeds of Lake Chad.

Montane on the Cameroun-Gongola/Cross River border and around $6° 20'N$ is typically seen on the Mambilla Plateau with canopied forest rich in ferns, mosses, herbs, epiphytes, lichens and the only specimen of the tufted perennial eragrostis camerunensis. The outlook is indeed most easy on the eye.

Seven species of tree reach 200ft. in Nigeria; they are:

1. Triplochiton scleroxylon, known by the Bini name Obeche; its timber leads in export.
2. Ceiba pentandra, silk cotton tree.
3. Gossweilerodendron balsamiferum, an evergreen.
4. Daniellia oblonga.
5. Pachyelasma tessmannii, an evil smelling wood.
6. Cylicodiscus gabunensis Harms. The bole of this tree is up to 37ft. in girth.
7. Entandrophagma cylindricum, a first class mahogany known as Sapele Wood; one

tree may yield 12,000 cubic feet of timber.

All these trees are found in the rain forest except for the third, found in Guinea savanna.

Large areas of Nigeria remain relatively unopened up. They are Western Oyo, coastal Edo/Delta, the "epicentre" of Cross River, riverain strips in Plateau Edo/Delta/Kwara boundary, inland of Chad, and, most of all, large tracts of the former Gongola.

Nigeria has scrapped the 1973 population census figures and conducted another one in 1991. Of more interest is a census of wild game. It is commonly said that there is little left. The foregoing paragraphs have mentioned game incidence and the lesser known country will harbour animal life because game will thrive where man lives not. Of the one-time abundance of game in this country there can be no doubt from the following observations made at the turn of the century and later.

In 1918 "elephants crashed about in Borno at pleasure" and one shot yielded 61 lbs of ivory — Rowland Ward's biggest but one for Nigeria. The circumference of the forefoot before preservation was within one inch of a world record. The elephant is still found in Benue/Plateau, in the delta, and Ogoja. In July 1977 one hundred were sighted 130 kms from Maiduguri in Borno and four months later many farms were destroyed by the animals near Kaura Namoda in Sokoto. The Kaduna/Niger border still trembles to their tread. The record with which I started the elephant sage was eclipsed in 1941: an animal taken near Owo in Ondo State gave 63½ lbs for the tusks which measured 7ft. 3in. on the outside curve with a girth of 16½in.

Lions had been seen at Burra in Bauchi, in Ondo in 1901, by the Benue in 1925, near Wum in Cameroun quite often. A new record for the python was established quite close to where this was being written, established by a Geological Survey Party in 1934 at Lanlate, river Ogun, Oyo State, 34ft. head to tail. In all, 106 species of snake crawl the country. In 1925, fourteen rhinoceros were counted in Yola, Adamawa and they are still thought to inhabit the Kelenge river of that State, possibly their only location. Giraffes were never seen in old Muri Province close to present day Yankari Game Reserve, but were found in Borno and said to be in SW Niger. The buffalo is in the Delta, Benue/Plateau boundary, in Tiv country, in what was Ogoja Province, on the banks of the Niger, and I have myself seen seven on Enugu airport in the 50s. Manatee, relative of the dugong, still inhabits the Cross River. The hippopotamus are in the northern reaches of the Cross, in the Benue and the Niger, in the rivers feeding Chad, and were once too many to count in the Katsina Ala. I saw five in 1979 of the fifty counted in 1974 in the Oil river in the Borgu Game Reserve. In World War II, I counted seventy crocodiles in one evening where the Shemankar joins the Benue at Ibi.

Mary Kingsley was friendly with the gorillas in the east; they along with the chimp are still to be found in what was Ogoja Province. Leopards have been known in Ondo and Bauchi, and are still found elsewhere along with other members of the cat family. In 1942, I met a caracal in the eaves of the Gusau Club, water buck off Jebba, roan antelope off Kaiama and Katagum and hartebeest off Ibi with Kabba so rich in antelopes as to have a town, Okene, named from the vernacular "Garden of Antelopes". The best snipes were as far apart as Ilorin and Yola and in 1965, I lost count of the cranes on the Maiduguri-Fort Lamy road. The tsetse bush of Kaiama teemed with wildlife, Shaki in Oyo was the start of big game; Ondo, Benue and the Ningi bush saw animals in the hundreds in the dry season. The primates are well represented and are as close to Ibadan as seven miles away.

In the 60s, a report prepared for the IUCN and the American Committee for International Wildlife Protection by Professor Petrides declared as extinct in Nigeria the black rhinoceros, eland, dama and dorcas gazelles, pigmy hippo and white oryx, and announced as endangered the gorilla, chimpanzee, lion, cheetah, leopard, manatee, hippo, giraffe, klipspringer and ostrich. One takes heed but does not necessarily agree. The Government introduced the **Borgu** and

Yankari Game Reserves and are moving too slowly to further conservation. A lead has been taken by the Bauchi State Wildlife and Hotels Board.

Bushcow at Tungan Giwa, 1966

Textbooks usually commence with an introduction to climate. I prefer to conclude with the subject. In a nutshell, expatriates prefer the drier north but are healthier in the humid south and indigenes unaccustomed to travel to temperate climates fall sick on return. Those who perspire freely feel fittest. If Jos was the sought-after haven by the European then Akure in Ondo was said to rank second. Adamawa enjoys 'delicious' nights in February and Buea in Cameroun a 'European' climate. Neither Mauritanian coastal nor monsoonal climates fall within Nigeria where the four zones are described as:

Equatorial	Rain every month with two maxima;
Semi-seasonal Equatorial	Up to 4 months dry/low total rainfall with two maxima;
Monsoonal Equatorial	Rain every month and very high rain total;
Tropical	One rainfall maximum.

Off the coast, there are the Gulf and equatorial opposing currents and the SW Monsoon winds of June to September bring about the coastal rains. But the weakened December-March are in opposition with the harmattan from the north and rainfall is depressed. The harmattan is really Sahara dust, excellent for northern cultivation, lasts 5-7 months and reaches down to latitude 5°N. In the south, precipitation exceeds evapo-transpiration by 6-9 months, the far north by 1-3 months and tornadoes, more properly called line squalls, bring the heavy rain heralded by a mass of black cumulus cloud.

In the wet season, the country is zoned into ten bands of rainfall intensity, in the dry, five. Although Debundscha nets 383in. in the Cameroun, Nigeria's bottom zone starts off with 105in. around Port Harcourt and by the time NE Borno is reached, the intensity is down to 20in. The headwaters of the Katsina Ala receive 100in. but its parent at Yola receives 39in. Zungeru, one time Northern capital, in the 51in. belt received 2.64in. in one day in 1904. Sokoto where a mosquito net can be dispensed with for many months in the year, can get down to 27in. Rainfall in Lagos lies between 65 and 112in. and is noticeably less in Ibadan.

Night and day are almost equal and the norm for sunshine does not exceed nine hours. Lagos temperature figures reflect:

Grass minimum	63° F
Absolute shade minimum	71° F
Mean temperature	80° F
Absolute shade maximum	89° F
Mean solar maximum	142° F

Yola attains 110° F mean and Argungu 115° F mean. Humidity reaches 98% in Lagos maximum and falls to 12% minimum at Kano, 10% in the desert.

Chapter 3

Peoples, Languages, Demography, Cultures and Artifacts

Retired officers of the British Colonial Service will have a natural bias in favour of the indigenes of this diverse land, a sympathy and understanding markedly absent in the post-independence visits by the expatriates of many countries, resident for works to the benefit of the country, but resident also far too often for reasons of pecuniary gain alone. The distinction is one of considerable importance. A second generation Nigerian will grow up to assume that the lack of interest in his country by the expatriate was equally manifest in the lifetime of his parents when an alien country governed his territory.

The Soviet influence common in some other African regions is not to be felt in Nigeria. Neither will any foreign power be likely to secure a foothold in the land. Such is the independence of the Nigerian peoples. In religion the Muslims are in a majority right across Northern Africa except for Ethiopia, but in Nigeria it is estimated that they represent half the population. The language family is Niger-Congo+Kordofanian, sub groups Benue-Congo, and Adamawa Eastern, and, sub group Chad of Afro-Asiatic or Hamito-Semitic. The Camerounians claim that their country is the melting pot where Sudanic and Bantu meet English and French. The School of Oriental and African Studies states that there are 1500 languages in Africa apart from the European tongues spoken and that of these, about a thousand are heard in West Africa. The most widely spoken of the 1500 is Swahili — understood in Angola, Zaire, Central Africa, and of course East Africa. It is a member of the Bantu Group.

The international boundaries which were drawn up by the super powers were not to ethnographic lines: French West Africa/Nigeria divided the Hausa, Dahomey, born of French West Africa/Nigeria divided the Yoruba, Cameroun/Nigeria divided the Kanuri. Ghana, where a feature of the culture acknowledges matrilineal descent, has a male population in excess of female, the reverse of Nigeria which, in common with six other countries in the world, gives to men a higher life expectancy than women. South of the Sahara, Nigeria is richest in sculptural traditions with Cameroun retaining the best preserved folklore.

In nine African countries, the growth rate is 3%, in thirty, 2%+, in six the statistics is unreliable. Twenty-two European countries yield under 1% by contrast. On the other hand, life expectancy in Nigeria is below forty years and Liberia has an infantile mortality rate of 159.2 deaths per thousand live births. The determining factor in population explosion is the proportion under fifteen years of age. One of every five Africans is a Nigerian. Independence to the French territories meant little to the French. In 1960 one hundred thousand were still to be found closely integrated whilst less than half that number of the British remained to live in West Africa. The Lebanese tended to make their homes on the coast and did not retire to their mother country.

The factors at work in determining the concentration of the population were many and varied. They included tribal tradition, even to an extent with the Ibos, of continuing to live in a mediocre environment when better land was nearby, the effects of the slave trade, water, swamp, river blindness, sleeping sickness, civil wars of the last century and spread of roads and railways.

West Africa has 20% of the land area of Africa but contains 33% of her peoples, and within Africa, no country is as populated as Nigeria. The world's races are classified not by colour but by the ratio:

$$\frac{\text{Maximum width of skull}}{\text{Maximum length of skull}}$$

and this is known as the Cephalic Index. Accordingly, the true negro is not a native of Nigeria but the semi-negroid is found before Nigeria's south eastern border.

Population of West Africa

Of the fifteen countries comprising West Africa, Nigeria has the largest area and the greatest population, Gambia the smallest in both directions. In 1974 the total population was about 121 million of which 58.7% lived in Nigeria. As usual, the pattern of migration was everywhere inland to the sea coast. Density reached four figures per square kilometre in a few small areas but was as low as 3/sq.km. inland. Country averages were, in 1970, Nigeria: 60 and Mauritania: 1 only per sq. km. The demographic map shows very large tracts of 3-12 per sq. km. with Nigeria ranging from 3-5 to four figures. The term 'sparse population' would include Chad basin, Cross River district, western Ivory Coast, eastern Senegal and much of Mali.

Population of Nigeria

In 1911 the population of Lagos was 73,766 and in 1919 Lugard gave the country population and area as then surveyed as:

Province	Area Sq. Miles	Population in Thousands
Sokoto	35,400	1,262.3
Kano	28,600	3,398.3
Bornu	32,800	679.7
Bauchi	24,700	679.7
Zaria	9,850	390.3
Nupe	18,450	388.5
Kontagora	27,000	118.4
Ilorin	14,100	330.1
Nassarawa	17,900	582.6
Munshi	17,000	471.0
Muri	15,600	407.8
Yola	14,300	291.3
Total, Northern Provinces	255,700	9,000.0
Oyo	14,872	1,027.0
Owerri	7,613	1,272.0
Abeokuta	6,694	552.0
Calabar	6,248	871.0
Ogoja	8,211	1,066.0
Onitsha	7,519	1,342.0
Ondo	6,051	384.0

Benin	8,799		567.0
Warri	9,342		515.0
Lagos Colony	1,335		154.0
Total, Southern Provinces & Colony	76,684		7,750.0
Grand Total	332,384		16,750.0

In 1931 the population was 20 million, growing at the rate of 150,000 per annum. On the basis of twelve States to the Federation, recorded statistics were, area in square miles, population in millions, that for 1973 provisional, density in persons per square mile for the 1963 census:

State	Area	1953 Census	1963 Census	1973 Census	Density
Lagos	1,381	0.50	1.44	2.47	251
Western	29,100	4.36	9.49	8.92	289
Mid-Western	14,922	1.49	2.54	3.24	168
Rivers	7,008	0.75	1.54	2.23	223
East-Central	8,746	4.57	7.23	8.06	711
South-Eastern	13,730	1.90	3.62	3.46	263
Kwara	28,672	1.19	2.40	4.64	82
Benue-Plateau	39,204	2.30	4.01	5.17	95
North-Eastern	105,025	4.20	7.79	15.38	78
Kano	16,630	3.40	5.77	10.90	339
North-Central	27,108	2.35	4.10	6.79	158
North-Western	65,143	3.40	5.73	8.50	88

East-Central and South-Eastern had boundary adjustments and area figures do not necessarily agree at each count but the combined areas of the two remained unaffected.

On the basis of Regions the reported statistics were, in millions:

Region	1953 Census	1963 Census
North	16.840	29.759
East	7.218	12.394
West	6.087	10.266
Mid-West		2.536
Lagos	0.272	0.665

On the basis of the 19-State Federation created in February 1976, the statistics have been projected back into the census of 1953 and 1963. The figures in this table are presented in descending order of State population at the 1963 count, area in square miles, population in millions.

State	Area	1953 Census	1963 Census	% Increase 1953-63
Kano	16,630	3.40	5.77	69
Oyo	14,216	2.43	5.21	114
Sokoto	39,577	2.80	4.54	62
Kaduna	27,110	2.40	4.09	70
Cross River	13,730	1.76	3.60	105
Imo	4,847	2.32	3.47	50
Benue	18,565	1.69	3.04	80
Gongola	37,407	1.36	3.00	121
Borno	41,498	1.56	2.99	92
Anambra	6,701	2.24	2.94	31
Ondo	8,162	0.95	2.73	187
Bendel	14,920	1.49	2.47	66
Kwara	23,690	0.83	2.31	178
Bauchi	25,971	1.40	2.19	56
Plateau	20,833	0.85	2.03	139
Rivers	7,010	0.73	1.72	136
Ogun	6,722	0.98	1.55	58
Lagos	1,380	0.50	1.44	188
Niger	25,566	0.06	1.19	98

In the 1953 census 44.3% were under age 15 and 8.1% were over 50. Some 51.1% of the total population were female, a preponderance everywhere evident except in Lagos township. 47.7% were in employment, 54.3% of the males, 41.2% of the females. The number employed in agriculture has declined. The number employed by the Federal Government at 31/12/1977 had reached 124,503, 90.7% male, the largest group being judicial, justice, police and prisons but the overall shortage of managerial and professional staff had long been evident, a deciding factor in the continued employment of expatriates. The West has 50% of the largest townships including that "enigma", Ibadan, about whose size people are confused. What is to be understood is that it is third in size on the continent, ranking after Cairo and Johannesburg but first in size in tropical Africa.

By 1951 the population was greater than Canada, Australia and New Zealand put together and from 1931 to 1964 the rate of increase was seen to be about one million per annum; by 1976 it was 2.7% increase per annum. The holding of a census in any country is difficult as there are always people who wish to evade the count but in a developing country where border access is possible by neighbours who are technically foreigners but who ethnographically may be no different, the exercise must not be minimised. People associate it with income tax and political consequences and there is much attempt at wrongful practices. Figures have been published which suggest a population of 93 million in 1977 and 100 million by 1979.

Turning to population density, the land is a patch-work quilt, with above 80% living in rural areas. When Lagos had a federal territory area of 27 square miles the density was 25,000 to the square mile. The average density in Western Nigeria including Lagos was 358, in Mid-Western Nigeria 169 with Benin more dense than Delta where settlement is confined to the waterways. In Eastern Nigeria, Cross River was much affected by the civil war but the territory is the most densely populated at 420 to the square mile. There were twelve provinces and in 1953 Anang had 641, Owerri 645, with Yenagoa at 38 and Abakaliki at 49 at the other end of the scale. Owerri was then the largest province with a population of 1,360,000 and the density in the belt separating Ibo from Ibibio reached 1600. Uyo Division counted 518,938 on Independence Day, 1st October 1960.

By 1964 the densest belt in Nigeria and in the east, stretched from Onitsha to Umuahia and Uyo, reaching 1500 to the square mile, obviously much cultivated land, to drop to 50 towards the Cameroun boundary. In Northern Nigeria the figure is 106, lowest in the Middle Belt, highest in the large towns of the Sudan provinces, which unlike the West, are many miles apart. Twenty per cent of Kano lived in rural areas and in the city itself density reached 500.

Except where otherwise stated, the figures in the previous paragraph relate to 1964 when all Nigeria had a declared population of 55.6 million and a density of 156 to the square mile placing her before Egypt of the same size and the Congolese Republic two and a half times her size. The British figure is 874! For the 1979 elections aimed at returning power to a civilian government, 47,710,680 persons over the age of 18 were registered against a projection from the 1963 census of such category of 39,914,514. It must be concluded that the 1979 population was in excess of 77 million. No one province or state can be followed through from the earliest figures of 1919 given to the present day because of boundary changes but on a 19-state basis the percentage increases over eleven years will have been noted with Lagos and Ondo topping the growth.

West African Ethnology

Several races dot the West African terrain. Some of these are, across the north, the Moor, Tuareg and Arab; hugging the coast are Wolof, Temne, Mende, Kru, Ewe, Yoruba, Ijaw, Ibibio and Balundu; in between are the Fulani, Malinke, Bambara, Mossi, Bariba, Nupe, Edo, Ibo, Ekoi, Tiv, Jukun, Hausa and Kanuri. Of all, the Fulani is to be found inland all the way from Senegal to

Cameroun. Of the ethnic groups named, the Yoruba, Ibo, Hausa and Fulani number 30.6% of the entire population.

Nigerian Ethnology

In 1931, a census established a count of the main peoples as:

Hausa	3.6 million
Ibo	3.2 "
Yoruba	3.2 "
Fulani	2.0 "
Kanuri	0.9 "

but the 1953 census was more informative, the figures coming in thousands.

Group	Lagos	West	North	East	Total
Edo	6	446	12	4	468
Fulani		7	3,023		3,030
Hausa	4	41	5,488	11	5544
Ibibio	2	5	13	737	757
Ibo	32	342	167	4,917	5,458
Kanuri		1	1298	2	1,301
Nupe		7	349	2	358
Tiv	1	2	773	5	781
Yoruba	196	4,302	536	11	5,045
Others	22	931	5,157	1,524	7,634

The "common head" lies between 192.5—195.5 mm long times 144.5—150.5 mm broad placing the people mesocephalic. Many share a common language but not a common culture or religion and here the term "tribe" is a misnomer. Nigeria with its polyglot peoples is entitled to be described as more multi-racial than multi-tribal and many races think of themselves, for example, first as Yoruba, Hausa or Ibo and second as Nigerian. The 1931 census determined over 150 tribes properly so called in the north with individual counts under ten thousand head and no less than 68 of these different groupings were known by names with "B" as the initial letter of the alphabet. At the time of the European penetration the most socially organised were the Yorubas, Binis, Hausas, Fulanis, Kanuris, and Arabs. Ilorin was a great place: because of cattle on the hoof it was the meeting place for Arabs from Timbuktu, veiled Tuaregs, the Baghirimi, Hausa and Fulani, Yoruba and pagans: so the opposing cultures of Christianity, Islam and traditional religion, were to meet.

Masquerades were a favourite in the south. The vertical Egyptian worked loom was found all over the country while the horizontal Asian style worked loom in the north and west, warp sixty feet in front, specialising in togas and women's wrappers. Chastity belts were not worn but the more important girdle between the legs as absolute sign of virginity was not lacking. Kaduna in 1917 sheltered representatives of seven tribes, Bauchi from 1848 no less than eight but excluding Lagos from the count, Jos was supposed to be the most cosmopolitan with well over a dozen tribal factions.

Everywhere the people favoured the use of dyes from indigo, camwood, teak and tamarind, twenty-two sources in all. Twenty-eight per cent of the population was made up to Hausa and Fulani, races like all others accustomed to change. But to describe the people of the country is a difficult task because of migration and the present day extent of "scatterings", and the order in which they are taken reflects, to some extent, a manner of simplified approach.

The Yorubas inhabit a great block of land in SW Nigeria, 100% in the west, 89% in Ondo, between the coast and reaches of the Niger. They are tall, and they embrace the legal, medical and engineering professions. Their townships are large and highly developed and not far apart in terms of African mileage: six were listed at over the hundred thousand mark in 1978. They honour the dead and venerate their ancestors: their women decorate with so many hair styles that they put paid to the patterns of Europe and the States. A great number of them are Muslims and their mosque at Ibadan is the largest in the land. Their language is second only to Hausa. They have their own literature and their dress reflects a democratic outlook and a firm belief in the dignity of man. Long ago, those living around Oyo learnt the folly of too many possessions. Art has followed traditional lines but local patronage is nothing like Europe in the Middle Ages. The Yorubas did not take kindly to the Gold Coast fishermen taking toll off his Victoria Beach, Lagos.

Speaker's Chair, House of Assembly

At the turn of the century, it was said in London that "certain nameless Africans have possessed the power of wood carving to a higher degree... than we as a nation have ever possessed it." The Yorubas were known for richly decorated panels of carved doors and kneeling women supporting *Ifa* trays. At the other end of the scale was thorn carving, one of the best examples being a "British District Officer smoking a pipe in the bows of a dugout canoe proceeding on a tour of inspection with his staff." The famous Ife heads, secret until 1938, were nearer brass than bronze, probably 15th-16th century, and ranked with the finest renaissance works.

At Esie, first seen by a whiteman in 1934, are carvings in soapstone (steatite) of the 17th century in large numbers, of people sitting on stools with their heads on their laps, the faces depicting an expression of humour in the Yoruba fashion. They are the most skilful bead embroiderers of Africa, the making of a crown taking six months and executed by the descendants of the sixteen original Yoruba States. Knee-length boots and fly whips are other such products. Once a year, the Obas don the thirty yard velvet cloak richly decorated.

Oyo and Abeokuta masks do justice with Azrec and Inca. The proof in the south is the tim tim of Oyo. Pattern dyeing has produced the adire cloth, a form of batik, known only elsewhere in India and Japan, worth as a trade £200,000 p.a. in 1938. Every Yoruba village uses a dye named after a British Resident, Lonchocarpus cyanescens Dalziel. The men are excellent cabinet makers and draughtsmen, early learnt by employers of the Railway and Public Works.

According to tradition the Yorubas came from the upper Nile valley and set up in Nigeria under a supreme chieftain, the Alafin of Oyo, originally occupying a larger area until the sack by the Fulanis. An eastern branch provided for a women council of chiefs. Ife became the spiritual head and the Ooni of Ife the custodian of cultural relics. They were not negro and some only acquired such characteristics through marriage.

Going east along the coast are the Itsekiri or Jekri of Warri, good swimmers, pretty girls, lovers of colourful patterned print dresses featuring travel, flowers and animals. Inland are the Urhobos. Their Olu wears a Portuguese crown and the area is the oldest christian community in West Africa arising from Roman Catholic Portuguese penetrations of the 15th century. North of the last in Edo State are found the Bini, speaking the Edo language, seat of the powerful dynasty of the Oba of Benin. They are known worldwide for their work in cast brass ranking among the masterpieces of their time. Such collections, much to the annoyance of present day Nigeria, are scattered in New World and Old World museums. The castings take the form of memorial heads and date from around 1325. Among these people also, women chiefs are not unknown.

Further along the coast in Rivers State are found the Ijaw, the fishermen of the delta, living by the creeks and penetrating the mangrove swamps. Their descendants intermarried with expelled Spanish Jews and provided the nucleus of a population infamous for the history of the Longjuju Aro slavery addiction.

The last tribes on the coast eastwards are the Efik and Ibibio, semi Bantu, of Calabar and well known "Duke Town." In their masquerades the women wear a farthingale skirt and their dances reflect the oldest example of Afro-European synthesis. There too, the mask is much in evidence. Ikot Ekpene is famous for its raffia table mats and baskets, from needlework to portmanteau are everywhere in abundance. After the "prosperity" of the slave days, the people suffered misery. Calabar had one natural accessible hinterland that could be readily raided and drawn upon to fulfil the demand for human bodies. This was the area lying in the bend of the Cross River, an area of something like 5000 square miles of foraging country. Every year a batch of strong young men and nubile maidens could not fail to mature and become high quality goods in a seller's market. But annual yield was not limited to annual increment. Slave dealers, black or white, were not given to long term planning and they soon succeeded in draining the Oban area dry, taking more and more of the breeding stock leaving behind a depleted land from which the place has never recovered.

North of the Efik are the semi-Bantu Ekoi, speaking a language often calling for double interpretation and to the right of them, across the Cameroun border, are the Bamums, brass workers in the lost art of Cire Perdu, employing a guild system of craftmanship that lead to the Kaiser's recognition of their chief as a "King".

An Onitsha lady

The country to the west of the Ekoi is peopled by one of the great races, the Ibo, technically the Igbo, supplier of the first Nigerian Governor General. They are shorter in stature, are called the businessmen of Nigeria or the Nigerian Jew, recognise no higher authority than the village head, and attempted to secede and caused this century's civil war. They have many proverbs:

"A man who knows that his anus is small does not swallow an udala seed."
"The death that will kill a man begins as an appetite."
"A man who visits a craftsman at work finds a sullen host."
When brothers fight to death a stranger inherits their father's estate."

A developed Craft: The Gates of Anglican Cathedral Onitsha

They are experts at tree felling and are fond of a walking stick. They are also stern with their children; the daughters of Onitsha are regarded as the most beautiful girls in the east.

At Uburu there is a salt lake worked by women. The mask is in use, Awka is famed for its iroko wood stool carvings and locally there is produced tree fibre carpets, cloth, the art of the blacksmith in iron, and the potter's glazed earthenware where the left hand rotates and the right hand shapes. The drum cylinder is carved from solid wood. It is a great country for co-operative unions. The former East-Central State was their heartland. They dominate east of lower Niger and occupy what was Onitsha Province, 98%, falling to 90% in Owerri and Rivers. Trade takes them everywhere else, in Nigeria, Fernando Po and Gabon. Having worked amongst them for years one knows that where the example is properly set, the return is undivided.

The Ibos came over from Benin and in their customs can be found traces of Nile basin cultures. They include a diversity of types and were protected from the marauding Fulani by the tsetse belt. They practised the custom of drying corpses over a fire as an alternative to embalming. Onitsha alone with the Obi was unique in a government/kingship/official/hierarchy. Here, unlike the rest of the land, clitoridectomy was not practised. Food for the Obi was prepared only by a virgin. There were as many shrines as in the Republic of Ireland. The people are basically vegetarians cultivating mediocre soils.

North of the Ibo and east of the Niger are the Igala and on the opposite bank the Igbirra, a friendly people under Nupe influence.

North of the Igbirra on both banks of the Niger are the Nupe, good farmers and skilled native craftsmen, whose principal city is Bida, which for long was a crossroads for trade. Silversmiths and blacksmiths are there, the latter deployed to Sokoto State, and weavers produce the 'wadon nupe' (Nupe trousers) highly regarded in Hausaland. Bida is a walled town resplendent with Flame of the Forest and Moorish architecture. Their lineage is partly Hamitic and their head is the Etsu Nupe, first created 1836, 10th in order of precedence of Northern traditional rulers.

Although Bida is the capital, Pategi, where a regatta is held, claimed the first descendant. Mention "Nupe" and the general response will be "potter". Their women potters have created to uniform thickness up to 3 inch diameter and 2 feet high without wheel. The people are glass blowers. Twenty-five miles downstream from Jebba at Tada are 3-feet high brass and copper figures from the lost wax process said to possess a finish equal to Benvenuto Cellini.

Another product associated with the Nupe is hat-making, the broad brimmed headgear being seen all over the Middle Belt. Mats are produced from palm, coloured with the red dye of guinea corn stalk or the yellow dye from rawaya roots. The Nupe in their embroidery employ the difficult double button hole stitch. They produce the deep baskets used by snake charmers, enormous Ndakogboza cult masks, and eleven legged stools carved from the solid. They were a great military power and are excellent horsemen.

Away in the mid north-west are the Borgana, Bariba, and Busa, a reminding alliteration of the prevalent letter "B", all bordering the sparse Borgu country. The Busa derived from the Bussawa, in turn offspring of Arabia, and embraced the Muslim faith later. In 1954 the Emir of Busa was brother of the Emir of Nikki over in Dahomey. North of the Busa live the Kamberi, people of magnificent physique dwelling in small family groups on their farms.

In the centre of the Middle Belt, in Niger and Kaduna States, live the Gwaris, indigenes of Kaduna, former inhabitants of the present Federal Capital Territory. They are non-Muslim. The Emir of Abuja is one of the three descendants of the Habe Emirs, that is purely Hausa Emirs who never gave in to the Fulanis. The Gwari potter produces particularly handsome roulette patterns.

After Idoma country, a land of dancers and ancestor worshippers, travelling east on either side of the Benue is found Nigeria's best soldier, the Tiv. It is only from 1946 that they have had a freely elected chief — Tor Tiv (King of Tiv). Feared by their neighbours for their thrust, they are thought to have originated from South Africa. They are extroverts, dancers of no mean ability, and contortionists. The small township "Adikpo" is called their "London". A Tiv farm can be told by the sheer size of the yam heaps. The Tiv are a tribe because they speak a uniform language and keep within their territory.

Further to the north-east lie the Jukuns with their seat from Wukari through Gongola thinning out towards the Chad basin. In other words they inhabit an enviable pocket of unspoilt country. Jos Plateau shelters a myriad of tribes, pagan, totemistic, polytheistic, believers in the theory that stark nakedness is a necessary adjunct to morality, in which they may well have a point. Their aboriginal ancestors saw the conquerors of other tribes pass by their hillside fortresses. The Plateau tribes numbered one hundred according to a 1900 research. The best known are the Biroms. In 1939 the future Prime Minister, Tafawa Balewa, wrote that shut up and hidden for centuries, farming the inhospitable ground, they were backward and primitive but were wise in their ways and strong with their muscle. Near them live the Angas, origin of Gowon, Head of State 1966-1975, and State Governor Gomwalk who was later executed for treachery.

Chad Republic peoples living in Borno, that crossroads in the heart of Africa, are collectively called "Banana" and they mingle there with the speakers of no less than fourteen languages. But the greatest in number are the Kanuri whose principal chief of the Kanem is the Shehu. With Mr F.A.O. Phillips, Nigerian Chief Mechanical Engineer of the Railway, I assisted the first Shehu of Borno to ride in a train to mount his carriage on the opening of the line to Maiduguri.

The Kanuri are derived from negro and Hamitic ancestors and H.G. Wells, the novelist, convinced the Colonial Office that Kanuri was not the lingua franca of Borno Province but Shuwa Arabic.

The Hausas call the Kanuris Beriberi whose language was Berberci and the translation of the Koran in Arabic was so esteemed that copies were sold for £50 a piece in Egypt. Their women wear long trailing gowns. The people never fell under the Fulani yolk. Chain dress armour of the bodyguard was similar to that worn in the 12th century holy land crusades. Hunters carry a silver ring in the left ear. Amongst the fourteen other peoples are the Bura of Biu and five words of their vocabulary are identical with Welsh. Shuwa Arabs and Tuaregs have long been found this side of the borders of the desert country and the drought of the 70s has driven more of them into Nigeria. The Shuwas who are of Semitic origin live around Gambaru in the Chad basin. The Tuaregs are found further afield having emigrated from Air in 1917 following an uprising crushed by the French. They and their camel pose a picture of statuesque immobility. They wear dark veils. Both the Shuwas and Tuaregs exhibit a tenet of Moslem etiquette, the graven visage.

To the last is kept the intertwined Hausa and Fulani. The Hausas too have their proverbs:

> A seedling is better than a cutting.
> Do what is right and neglect what is desired.
> The dry season does not prevent the silk cotton tree sprouting.

The Hausas are the most numerous in the whole country; Muslim, farmer, trader, soldier, ironsmith from the turn of the century in Sokoto, expert tanner. They produce excellent sandals, riding boots and saddlery: their farms are cultivated for thousands of square miles to an ordered industry. Moroccan leather is Kano leather so called because it was shipped through North African ports: as apparel where weaving is not practised, panniers for the donkey and water bags for the camel. The Sarkin Musulmi is leader of all the faithfuls in West Sudan: Katsina is the ancient seat of Islamic learning: Argungu is the scene of the annual Fishing Festival when a thousand fishermen clasp Giwan Ruwa, the water elephant, or Niger Perch in their arms to a daily catch each of 85 lbs.

Fulani Herd-boys

Bornu Camelmen dressed for a durbar

The Hausas are the people who speak the Hausa language, Sudanic in vocabulary, Hamitic in grammar. Antimony or sulphide of lead adorn the eyelids of the women. Greetings range from "Ranka shi dade" (may your life be long) to the horseback charge Jafi when mount is brought to a foaming standstill.

Pagan Hausas were in the land long before Islam and before the coming of the first Fulani Emir in 1802. At Zaria, the Emir was on his throne before the Norman Conquest, son of a Prince of Baghdad and a Queen of Daura, although the race as a whole inherit today Fulani, negro and Tuareg blood. The seven original states founded through the Baghdad/Daura union were Daura, Kano, Rano, Gobir, Zazzau (Zaria), Kaduna, and Biram. The name for a king in Hausa is *sarki*, an abbreviation for snake slayer. As such, exploit at Daura by the Baghdad prince was his means of introduction to the Daura Queen's hand.

Dye Pits in Kano

The Fulanis, second most numerous in the north, arrived from the direction of Senegal some hundreds of years after the Hausas and are described as "Mediterranean" in type, that is, Hamites, named after Ham, second son of Noah. They are related to the Libyans in consequence. They are a handsome race with their women much addicted to silver ornamentation in the hair.

The Fulanis are most dispersed and are to be found from Cape Verde to the Kodofan, having indeed created an empire. Some remained nomadic and pastoral, owning in Nigeria 90% of the cattle, did not intermarry and exhibit today the purest ethnic features. Other Fulanis became "town" Fulanis, intermarried with the Hausas, and at times spoke Hausa as the mother tongue.

The most hallowed name in northern Nigeria is that of Sheikh Uthman dan Fodio. The Muslim religion had become corrupted by pagan practices and in 1802 the Sheikh quarrelled with the pagan King of Gobir. A Jihad was set in motion and the Hausa chiefs were conquered one by one. A Fulani Muslim Empire was created and the Sheikh took the throne as first Sultan of Sokoto and Commander of the Faithfuls. To his son, the emirates of Katsina, Kano, Zaria, Hadejia, Adamawa, Gombe, Katagum, Nupe, Ilorin, Daura and Bauchi paid allegiance. Fulani estate settles through the eldest son and in 1957 all but two of the Hausa State thrones were held by the race. The Lamido of Adamawa's palace walls have the batter reminiscent of Irish castles. The Emir of Kano's colours are scarlet and green and his bodyguard, the Sulke, wears chain-mail dating from the Crusades. The Fulanis dislike being photographed or painted.

The order of precedence of the traditional rulers in the North is: Sultan of Sokoto, Shehu of Borno, Emir of Gwandu, Emir of Kano, Lamido of Adamawa, Emir Zaria, and Etsu Nupe.

Ocean Passage from Sail to Conference Lines

The natural harbours of Dakar and Freetown only were met with in a 2400-mile coastline stretching from Cape Verde to Debundscha Point. The Liverpool-Lagos sea lane was a distance of 4210 miles. At the African end the transhipment port of Forcados was used and at the British end not the adventurous tobacco port of Bristol, but the Merseyside commercial Liverpool. From 1852 to 1974, a mail boat was to sail and no line was more concerned with the build-up of trade than Elder Dempster. Liverpool it was that had seen the departure on 27th July 1807 of the last British slaver, "Kitty Amelia", trading in, but not the owning thereof of slaves, having become illegal for British subjects. By 1885 slavery was abolished by all nations and on the west coast palm produce became the substitute traffic, not without fighting as crews sought for the best cargoes. Two other issues bore on matters of the day: the expansion in trade following upon the ceding of Lagos in 1861 and the fact that the so-called Oil Rivers were the distributaries of the Niger. Macgregor Laird realised that the channels must be explored to facilitate the trade he realised was there to be won.

The USA flag was first upon the high seas steam-borne, but disturbance of the compass retarded development of the iron clad until the American Civil War provided the impetus and in the 1890s, wood and iron tonnage were approaching equality; water tight compartments were introduced before the turn of the century. The Americans favoured the schooner, the British the square rigged. The first ocean timetable saw the light in 1830 when what became P & O commenced a service from the United Kingdom to Spain and Portugal, a service kept alive by the winning of a mail contract from the British Government.

Macgregor Laird was born in 1809. His father was the founder of Cammell Laird, shipbuilders of Birkenhead. Despite the risk, he sailed in 1832 with Richard Lander in the Columbine, Quorra and Alburka (Blessing), first iron ocean-going ship, five years ahead of the Atlantic crossing by Brunel's "Great Western". He wrote his father "... I have made up my mind... the only chance I may ever have of distinguishing myself, and a nobler one I shall never have." He had much of Mungo Park in him. With 81% of his crew dying, the mission was in one sense unsuccessful. To reduce mortality, the relay scheme had already been adopted of employing two crews, one of which was left behind to take care of what became the trading hulk, no captain but an agent on board.

There followed the 1841 expedition of the vessels "Albert, Wilberforce and Soudan", with the death rate down to 33%. In the National Maritime Museum Greenwich, a painting shows them off Holyhead and in the Oron Museum by the Calabar ferry, a memorial testifies to the dead. Macgregor

Laird was later to found the African Steamship Company for Niger and Zambesi penetrations but he became a leading light in British and North American Steam Navigation Co. whose vessel, "Sirius", became the first in 1838 to cross the Atlantic under continuous steam power. In 1844, he returned to the scene of his earlier interests when he contracted with Her Majesty's Government to send an annual vessel up the Niger. This was the 'Rainbow' — the largest paddle steamer of her day. He died in 1861. Such is the background to the start of the Britain/Nigeria ocean-going history.

European merchants were established in Lagos by 1852, two-way ocean tonnage having reached 82,467 by 1850 and with no systematic evacuation through the exertions of Macgregor Laird, the African Steamship Company received a Charter on 7th August 1852. Laird was Managing Director and Sir John Campbell Chairman; James Hartley, a Director of the P & O was on the board. The ten-year mail contract wrung from His Majesty's Government was worth £21,250 p.a. and return traffic was of course palm produce. The first vessel to set sail was aptly named "Forerunner", 400 tons displacement, engine and sail assisted, and she departed British shores from London on the 24th September 1852 for Nigerian ports, terminating at Fernando Po. The home government was slow to realise the potential of West African trade but "Faith", 922 tons, "Hope", 922 tons, and the inevitable "Charity", 1062 tons, soon followed, using steam in the calms. A fifth vessel, "Northern Light", was intended but was sold while still on the stocks. "Faith" reached 9½ knots and called at Madeira, Tenerife, Goree, Bathurst, Sierra Leone, Monrovia, Cape Coast Castle, Accra, Ouidah, Badagry, and Fernando Po, taking 28 days 20 hours outward and 35 days homeward. Cotton was carried for 1d per 1b.

A British Consulate was built in Lagos in 1855 and an African Commercial Association was formed in 1863 by Europeans because the African of that day was not then the entrepreneur of the 21st Century. In 1857 at Laird's instigation, the "Dayspring" began her Niger voyages of development followed by the "Sunbeam" and "Rapier" establishing amidst native hostility Lairdspoint (now Onitsha) and Lairdstown (now Lokoja). The ending of the Crimean War released five seconded vessels to join the ocean fleet. Laird's death was commemorated by the naming of a new ship in 1862 "The Macgregor Laird" and on the coast, Sir George Dashwood Taubman Goldie, a Sapper, took over where Laird left off. Control of the African Steamship Company moved to Liverpool and their ship, the Cleopatra, in 1859 was the first to the coast to employ superheated steam.

Among the Liverpool office staff of Laird's line were four gentlemen destined to leave their mark on Nigeria for ever. They were Alexander Elder, John Dempster, John Holt and Alfred Lewis Jones. Jones had visited the coast as a cabin boy on a steamer of the ASC. Trade grew and a second company was formed in 1866 in Glasgow but operated from Liverpool. This was the British and African Steamship Navigation Company resplendent with three ships fitted with compound expansion engines built by John Elder whose Liverpool agents were John's brother, Alexander and John Dempster. Alexander Elder who was a shipwright surveyor was present at the fall of Sevastopol and later became associated with the eventual Fairfield Shipbuilding & Engineering Company. John Holt was the son of an innkeeper and he left in 1862 to take up a post in Fernando Po. The investors in the B & ASN Co. included Mirrless the engineer and Coats, of the thread manufacture fame. The seeds were now set for the birth of Elder Dempster and Company in 1868.

Alfred Lewis Jones, a Welshman, was a junior clerk in the Liverpool Agency until he established the firm of Alfred L. Jones Liverpool. Upon purchase of a steamer, he was considered too dangerous to leave in competition with the two steamship companies and he was offered a junior partnership on the 1st October 1879 with Elder Dempster and Company. It was then Jones, rather than the two men who gave the enterprise its name, that built up Elder Dempster to become the Premier Line. He was described as dynamic, far-seeing but charitable. Personality then must have been the answer to the contemporary mystery of why Elder and Dempster each took a back seat.

Over a span of four decades ED & C acquired the interests of the two shipping companies and the first vessel to sail under the ED banner was the "Bonny" of 1280 gross tonnage, 261 feet in length, travelling at eleven knots. She left in January 1869 calling additionally at Bonny and Old Calabar. "Roguelle" and "Congo" were her sister ships except that Bonny and Roguelle were brigs and Congo a schooner. "Liberia", "Loanda" and "Volloc" of increased displacement followed in 1870 and their presence forced the still operating ASC to lower their rates. Bonny, and the contemporary fleet were cargo liners with provision for passengers. If champagne was ordered the day before, it was served at 23p per pint in a voyage that cost the passenger £37-10-0 for the journey to Lagos. Captains were instructed to make the voyage comfortable for Africans who were to be encouraged to travel in every possible way.

John Holt commenced a service, Fernando Po to the Nigerian mainland in 1868 and Jones received the honour of K.C.M.G. In 1891, Sir Alfred Jones became the head of Messers Elder Dempster & Co. which in that year secured the management of the ASC and thus controlled the shipping interests of West Africa. In 1894 they formed a connection with Bristol, acquiring a service to Canada. From that association developed their interests with the West Indies whereby English people were provided with one of the most popular forms of fruit, bananas. Sir Alfred foresaw the importance of this industry. He placed them within easy reach of the consumer and made them one of the cheapest forms of fruit on the market. In the same manner he cultivated the growth of tomatoes (as well as bananas) in the Canary Islands revitalising their declining dependence on cochineal. Las Palmas became the line's bunkering station. Sir Alfred did everything in his power to curb West African traders from unifying so that he could justify an extension from charter in the Niger to charter in the Delta channels and had his way with Lord Salisbury so that Sir George Goldie had to ship by regular lines.

In 1872, the Post Office refused continuation of the mail contract but a year later subsidised both shipping companies to call at Bathurst. By then the two lines had settled down in harmony to sailings every alternate week. A Conference Line was established for the UK-Calcutta run in 1875. Salt was carried to Nigeria for 20/- per ton in ballast. Nigerian merchants came together in 1879 by the merging of the Niger Company with Central African Trading Co Ltd, Miller Brothers, West African Company Ltd, James Pinnock & Co Ltd, and UAC, later in 1882 National Africa Co. The African Association followed later in 1889 with John Holt as Chairman in 1894, but its ships were handed over to Elder in 1896 when ED had a monopoly of British WA trade and with WL's control of European WA carriage. WL was Woermann Line whose predecessors had sent schooners from Germany to Nigeria from 1849.

By 1880 cocoa had greatly expanded in the Gold Coast, cotton rose and fell with the American Civil War, and British exports were put at £584,000. On the 23rd April 1883, the British & African Steamship Co. became a limited company but the ASC returns declined until a joint service from Hamburg to West Africa improved matters along with new ships, 'Winneba', 'Akassa', 'Mandingo' and 'Benin' built over the years 1881-84. In the last year, 1884, respective tonnages co-ordinated by Elders were:

	A.S.C.	B & A.S.N.C. Ltd
Vessels	12	24
GRT	18,284	35,245

The fleet then grew to the following:

	A.S.C.	B & ASNC Ltd	ED-Owned
1896	29	23	3
1909	22	36	11

ED's first ship to be owned and not managed was the "Clare" of 2034 tons, in 1887. This was three years after Elder and Dempster in terms of secrecy had departed the concern leaving Jones to become senior partner. Keeping the Royal Niger Company and the African Association at bay prior to the 1896 handover, and preventing the ingress of tramps forced Jones to follow the Anglo- Indian pattern of approach and he obtained WL of Hamburg's agreement to create a Conference system to regulate the WA shipping trade in 1895. However, Jones was clever enough in home waters to restrict WL to the continent, clear of the UK mainland. In 1891, an interloper, Prince Line, had tried to "horn in", but meeting Crown Agents refusal to negotiate for outward bulk cargoes, diverted its activities to other seas. The combined British and German fleets on the WA run were:

	1893	1907
British steamers	50	61
German steamers	13	47
British tonnage	67,125	97,646
German tonnage	15,741	71,957

The unpopular traffic in mahogany went to WL and Sir Alfred, entrepreneur par excellence, became President of the British Cotton Growers Association which he had been responsible for founding to stimulate the growth in cotton. Eyebrows were raised that one and the same man should be President of the British Cotton Growers Association and Chairman of the shipping lines offering carriage. Around this time he went further and in 1894 established the Bank of British West Africa (BBWA). For such an act it was said, tribute should be paid to his wisdom.

The year 1894 witnessed also another, though dissociated event — the launching of the Turbinia, the first vessel to be propelled by steam turbines. With the assistance of John Holt the General Steam Navigation Co. Ltd. began a service, Manchester Ship Canal-WA, but reckoned that without Sir Alfred and the Crown Agents who left the line no surplus would come from the mail steamers. Within one year the ships had to be withdrawn.

The object of the Conference was to reserve trade to its members accomplished through Sir Alfred's "deferred rebate scheme". All freights were increased by 10% and traffic was only accepted from merchants who signed a declaration to the effect that all their shipments would be made via the Conference Lines for the succeeding six months. Once this period had elapsed the rebate could be claimed, by the shipper, for all outwards cargo and for palm produce for the homeward journey. Payment was however held up during the next six months, exclusive shipment, so that the Conference always had an interest-free loan in their possession. This made other lines wary of entering the trade and little competition existed until the death of Sir Alfred in December 1909. Paterson Zochonis was one of the firms that remained aloof. No merchant really welcomed it but most signed. USA had to come in by transhipment in the UK. Charting came to an end. Sailing frequency with ED was:

	1895	1904
Liverpool-West Africa	Every Saturday & alternate Wednesday	Every Saturday, Wednesday & alternate Thursday
London-West Africa	—	Monthly
Hamburg/Rotterdam-WA	Every ten days	Every ten days
Hamburg-Lagos direct	—	Every three weeks

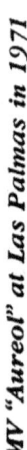

MV "Aureol" at Las Palmas in 1971

Always to the forefront in innovation, the ED's vessel "Lake Champlain", was the first British ship in 1900 to be fitted with a Marconi installation. By 1909 the mailboats called at Plymouth and the LSWR ran sleeping car trains from Waterloo for the White Star to USA as well as the WA service. By 1909 the Royal Commission on Shipping Rings produced its findings under a Liberal Government — the first to be held — and as a result substantial merchants in the WA trade carried more goods in their own vessels. Local branch boats for the connecting Forcados-Lagos service numbered ten and were of tonnages 450-1000; transhipment in heavy seas was quite an undertaking. To improve communications between the two ports, the Secretary of State approved of the use of carrier pigeons trained for the task by Captain Elgee. 1907 saw the mail-boats 'Tarquah' and 'RMS Nigeria'. There was an 'SS Jebba' engaged in the palm oil trade and on the ocean run also were the 'Appam', 'Dakar', 'Burutu' and 'Akabo'.

The first Atlantic liner to be driven by turbines, the 'Victorian', left her Belfast stocks in 1904. The first screw steamer for the carriage of ocean mails was a Royal Mail Steam Packet vessel in 1909 but the most famous was the 'Cunader Mauretania' which for twenty-two years until 1929 held the Blue Riband of the Atlantic. "The Majestic" had been the first large Atlantic liner to be fitted with water tube boilers but a cargo, "Vespasian", was the first to have geared turbines in 1910. Double reduction gearing came to the Somerset in 1918 and diesel propulsion to the Jutlandia in 1912. This latter year also marked the decline of coal as a fuel and the substitute rise in oil fired. The 2-stroke Clyde opposed piston engine as exemplified by the Doxford came to be accepted standard for the ED fleet in post-war years.

From 1900, Sir Alfred operated the West India Mail Service having in the previous year purchased the interests of the Canada Shipping Co. Ltd. and made deeper penetrations into that market by 1903. Shortly afterwards an Antwerp-Congo service was formed by his company and maintained by Compagnie Belge Maritime du Congo. During the South African War, ED & Co. Ltd. helped with the transport of horses, men and materials in securing the victory over the Boers. In 1907 John Holt entered the UK-WA run with their 1272-ton steamer, 'Balmore', carrying their own merchandise and not therefore losing their rebate by Conference Line carriage. Woermann became stronger competitors from the continent of Europe from 1910 and Hamburg-Bremen Line, later accepted by the Conference, began WA sailings in 1907. Rates for produce were certainly not cheap in 1905 at timber 32/6d, machinery 35/-, salt 20/-, cotton 45/- for a ton for which Winston Churchill, in 1907 had to answer questions from the floor of the House. From 1914 the harbour works improvements at Lagos offered deeper passage for ocean-going steamers and the cost of the Forcados leg and the use of the dangerous derrick lowered 'mammy' chair for passenger transference were respectively eliminated.

Jones ran into trouble when a former ED employee, E.D. Morel, ran a campaign against King Leopold's Congo. Jones had accepted the post of honorary consul of the Congo after allying himself with Woermann. But in the atmosphere of the time, Jones' adversaries were commercial and not political. On his death, it may be fairly stated that he was not only a renowned shipper but a man who had taken care to fill his vessels. He even tendered for coal to be supplied to the colonial governments because he could charge his own ships just the freight necessary for the carriage to win the contracts. He also engaged in cement trade in a way that might today be regarded as highly improper.

On his death, the Conference continued as before with Elder, Dempster and Company Limited formed on 31/3/1910 under the control of Sir Owen Phillips (later Lord Kylsant) GCMG, MP, Chairman of the Royal Mail Steam Packet Co., and Lord Pirrie KP, PC, Chairman of Harland & Wolff Ltd. "The properties acquired included the EDC shareholding interest in the ASC, the B & ASN Co., ED Shipping Ltd, the Imperial

Direct West India Mail Service Co. Ltd, shares in the Cunard Co., the African Oil Mills Ltd., the African Association Ltd., the Bank of British West Africa Ltd, a substantial holding of stock and shares in Swan, Hunter and Wigham Richardson Ltd, and twelve steamers directly owned by that firm." The shipping taken over, including management, numbered 109 steamers of 321,924 gross tons.

After 1909, John Holt & Co. strengthened their line by the acquisition of the steamships, Jonathan Holt and Thomas Holt. The British Government did not implement the 1909 findings of the Shipping Ring Commission but publicity did its stuff. William Hesketh Lever (later Lord Leverhulme) bought up W.B. MacIver & Co. Ltd. in 1910 and established palm kernel crushing mills at Opobo and Apapa. Freight by cask was uneconomic and tank chartering refusals by Sir Alfred had incurred Lever Brothers' enmity. The mills therefore lasted only till 1914 in the face of such adversity and palm kernel went unprocessed or to Germany where there was a market for oil and cake. In 1910 the army of branch boats, tugs, barges and lighters belonging to subsidiary companies on the coast were formed into one concern with EDC owning all the issued shares — the West African Lighterage and Transport Co. Ltd.

On the 8th January 1913, there sailed on its maiden voyage the 'Abosso', the largest vessel plying between UK and the coast, built by Harland & Wolff of Belfast to the orders of the African Steamship Co. Ltd. She registered 8,000 gross tons, was 441ft. 6in. by 57ft. beam, and was driven by two sets of 4-cylinder quadruple expansion engines. On board was the Chairman of EDC, Sir Owen Phillips, who paid tribute to the development of Nigeria by her railway and though much remained to be done, he trusted that the Abosso would not prove to have been built to too lavish a scale.

Of the Great War it was stated in 1920 that no line surpassed Elder, Dempster & Co. Ltd. in terms of sacrifice in their share of bringing about the Teutonic downfall. They assisted in the movement of the British Expeditionary Force to France, in the carriage of West African troops to Cameroun and in the Allied Cause in the Mediterranean. The "Nigeria" was employed in the Russian theatre. Thirty-three per cent of their ships were requisitioned by the British Government and the remainder were hard pressed in the conveyance of essential tropical products across an infested ocean submarine. The Woermann Line's eleven ships were sunk or took shelter in neutral harbours upon the capture of Douala and the ninety-two British vessels were unable to cover the loss of 133,000 tons of German shipping.

The Conference system broke down in August 1914. Congestion in England at Liverpool required the opening up of Hull as an import port — all told, British shipping at the outbreak of the war represented 45.2% of the world total. It was not until 1916 that the Ministry of Shipping created a Shipping Control Committee under Lord Curzon to handle the inevitable problems. Convoy protection commenced only in 1917, the worst year for loss of shipping, but was not fully developed on the African run until a further year had elapsed. Then it started up at Freetown, every eight days, eight ships per convoy, common pace ten knots, a different picture to the outbreak of hostilities when the "comfortable" mail boats, well fitted with every detail necessary for a tropical voyage, ran to a timetable unhindered by thoughts of enemy action.

Elder, Dempster & Co. took a dreadful punishment. The 'Nyanga' went down on the 16th August 1914 — despatched by the submarine Kaiser Wilhelm der Grosse. An unfortunate addition to losses was the arrival of the 3987 ton mailboat, 'Dakar', on fire on sighting Forcados in March 1915; beached, she was raised by the Nigerian Marine two years later and steamed to the UK under cargo. The London Brighton & South Coast Railway had enlisted men on board the "Aboukir" and raised a Roll of Honour to those drowned. On the 28th March 1915, shortly after 1215 pm, the U28 torpedoed the "Falaba", the first unarmoured passenger ship to be sunk in the war. There was a great loss of life, forty-nine passengers and fifty-three crew, only the fortunate being rescued by the steam drifter "Eileen Emma" and landed at Milford Haven by a British destroyer. With those that went down was a US citizen causing consternation and furore leading the Imperial German Embassy in Washington to warn American nationals not to sail in the "Lusitania" due to leave a few days later!

The torpedoing of the "Falaba" on Sunday 28th March 1915

The Appam in use as a trooper was captured by the German raider, "Moewe", but was not sunk and later interned USA under the name "Mandingo" to hide her identity. The fine "Abosso" running Bathurst-Liverpool was torpedoed off Bantry Bay on the 14th April 1917 with the loss of twenty-five crew and forty passengers. Defensive armament was fitted to ED vessels in 1917 but did not stop the loss of the sister ship, "RMS Apapa", which went down in November of that year off Point Lynas. The "Umjeni" was lost all hands. The "Oron" was seized in Hamburg, the "Nigeria" lost, and the "Burutu" sunk in collision in November 1918. The "Ebani", almost alone, bore a charmed life as a hospital ship and steamed 200,000 miles in the five years. In all twenty-nine ships of the fleet including six mailboats fell to the toll of enemy action and a further thirteen were lost to other causes. To a watery grave went 487 men and sixty-seven passengers of whom four were ladies and forty-five government servants.

And of the non-warlike events: the French line, "Chargeurs Reunis", was running Le Havre-Matadi but did not call at Nigerian ports. Ships anchored outside the Lagos Bar and passengers were ferried to the Iddo Wharf of the railway to connect the boat train. The mail boat run in 1916 was Lagos-Accra-Sekondi-Freetown-Plymouth-Liverpool with Douala and Lome connections once a month. The Niger Company and African & Eastern Group, like Holts, carried some of their own trading goods and in 1916 the Bromfort Steamship Company was formed by Lever Brothers for the same purpose, six tankers being purchased from Herbert Watson of Manchester, the mills at Apapa and Opobo being re-opened. Three of the tankers were destroyed by enemy action.

The post-war decade to 1930 saw the continuation of the policy of engagement as deck hands of Kroomen for the tropical return cycle of Freetown-Nigeria-Freetown, the purchase of the SS Munshi, the establishment of the African & Eastern Trade Corporation from the African Association, Miller Bros. and F & A Swanzy. Liner requisition ended on 15th February 1919 when tonnage was 40% down on 1913. In the 1920s, vessels were taking three weeks to reach Lagos and the "mammy" chair was still in use at Freetown, Sekondi and Accra. The ports of call homeward were:

Lagos Express Service	Calabar Service	Benin Service	Opobo Service
Lagos	Douala	Sapele	Opobo
Accra	Victoria	Forcados	Port-Harcourt
Sekondi	Calabar	Lagos	Abonema
Freetown	Bonny	Cotonou	Bonny
Grand Canary	Lagos Roads	Addah	Calabar
Tenerife	Accra	Accra	Lagos Roads
Liverpool	Sekondi	Winnebah	Lome
	Freetown	Saltpond	Quittah
	Grand-Canary	Sekondi	Accra
	Tenerife	Axim	Cape Coast
	Liverpool	Assinie	Sekondi
		Cape Palmas	Grand Bassam
		Grand Bassam	Lahou
		Monrovia	Monrovia
		Freetown	Freetown
		Conakry	Bathurst
		Teneriffe	Dakar
		Liverpool	Grand-Canary
			Liverpool

Nigerian external trade by the flag as a percentage of total trade in sterling in shown below:

	1913		1925	
	Import	Export	Import	Export
United Kingdom	64	50	78	55
Germany	13	43	9	21
Netherlands	8	1	3	5
France	0	1	1	4
USA	5	0	7	10
Others	10	5	2	5

Lever Brothers' next venture into ship-owning came in 1928 when the Niger Company acquired the Cunard vessel "Tyria" renamed as the "Ars". In the following year Unilever acquired the African & Eastern Trading Corporation and merged it with the Niger Co. to form the United Africa Co. Ltd. So the A & E which was the main rival and which owned a ship called 'The Nigerian' of 3543 tons was eliminated. UAC took over five ships. In 1919 the Holland West Afrika Lijn NV also began a service to the coast and in 1921 the Woermann Line re-entered the trade at a time of the depreciation of the Mark which was to their advantage.

The West African Lines Conference was re-formed in 1924 with Elders, Woermann, and the Holland Line as members. The terms of the Agreement were never published but renewal was viewed with disfavour by large shippers. The deferred rebate was also reintroduced but only for the outward voyage. At the same time the Bromport was sold to put an end to the rate war. Conference ships then numbered 93 against the 124 of 1914. Lever Bros. were heavily committed in both the West Coast and the Congo which were major sources of raw materials for soap and margarine. UAC then entered into negotiations with the Conference with a view to obtaining special rates but this fell through and they decided to operate their own fleet. The Official Receiver later suggested that the loss of this freight was a factor in the break-up of the Royal Mail Group, owners of a large amount of stock in Elder Dempster Ltd. which led to the complete re-organisation of the latter. However this was held to have strengthened their position, the more so when they received the financial backing of Messers Alfred Holt and Company.

Settlement of all accounts was affected at Liverpool but in November 1922 the Nigerian Railway was prepared to undertake export collection in the country. Settlement in the UK upon reconciliation did provide the railway with local funds for overseas purchases. In the end, the Customs collected import dues at Kano, Naraguta, Jos and Bukuru and the matter was put up by Brigadier Hammond for re-examination.

In 1922 Chargeurs Reunis was reported calling on the coast and the Fraissenet Line a year later. In 1924 the Nigerian Railway timetable showed that Plymouth was again a port of call homeward bound. In 1926 Societe Navale de l' ouest, Chargeurs Reunis, and the Campagnie de Navigation Africaine combined their sailings but did not enlist Campagnie Francaise de Navigation Vapeur (the Fraissinet Line). John Holt added, in 1926, the new Jonathan Holt, the John Holt, and the Robert L Holt, keeping the fleet at five ships to 1938. The Barber Line entered the scene in 1922 as the American West African Line (AWAL) and by 1930 UAC had nineteen palm oil tankers with bulk oil installations at Burutu, Apapa and Port Harcourt. However, the fleet was inadequate to deal with the USA demand and EDL made plans accordingly.

In the period before World War II, 1933 precisely, British tonnage to the coast represented 51% but the depression of the 30s lowered it by no less than a third. Exports doubled imports and at the outbreak of the crisis the number of vessels in the Conference was only sixty-one. It was in 1930 that companies presided over by Lord Kylsant suffered financial collapse. EDL lost 40% of the WA trade and the ASC and BSN Co. had to be wound up and the EDL assets separated from the RM Group and put under the control of West African Lines Co. (WAL). It was said that the basic strength of the trade and efficiency of operation prevented a deeper plunge on the part of EDL. Sir Patrick Hastings presided at the Court of Enquiry. In a few months, in August 1932, WAL gave way to the inauguration of EDL Ltd. the issued capital of which concerned ASC, EDLL, B & ASNC Ltd, Imperial Direct Line Ltd, and ED & Co Ltd.

More foreign lines touched the coast by 1933 after years of isolation. Lever Bros. and Unilever amalgamated in 1937 giving powerful backing to UAC. UAC had acquired G.B. Ollivant and owned 81,916 gross tons of shipping by 1939, being then able to replace charter. In 1938 control of EDLL shipping off WA moved from Accra to Lagos on improvement of cable and wireless facilities.

On the outbreak of the Second World War in 1939, Elders had four liners with a fifth in reserve and thirty-six cargo vessels, and the terminating points of call were either Calabar or Port Harcourt. During the war, the MV Calabar, 2000 gross tons, used as a connecting link from Lagos down the coast, was diverted to a Lagos-Capetown service. At the end of hostilities, Elders had lost twenty-four of their fleet including the mail boats Accra, Apapa, Adda and Abosso. The

Accra was the first to be lost on 26th July 1940, 200 miles west of Ireland. The Apapa succumbed to an air attack the same year. The Adda was torpedoed also in that year, eighty miles west of Cape Sierra Leone. The Abosso, then largest of the fleet at 11,330 gross tons, went down in 1942 on the run Capetown-Liverpool, being torpedoed 700 miles north of the Azores. To share her grave she took with her 251 souls. The Aba, like the Ebani of World War I, was employed as a hospital ship and remained afloat. She was the world's first large passenger liner to be driven by diesel engines.

The Southern Railway named 35,030 of their Merchant Navy class "Elder Dempster Lines" and British Rail later named two English Electric class 40s, No 234 "Accra" and No 235 "Apapa". A further Merchant Navy class was then named "Holland Afrika Line", No 35023, in 1949. In the year before the war, the pattern of trade with Nigeria was:

	Import	*Export*
United Kingdom	55%	51%
Germany	9%	17%
Netherlands	2%	10%
France	1%	7%
USA	8%	7%
Others	25%	8%

The increase in imports to "others" will be noticed. The Admiralty assumed operational control of merchant shipping on 26/8/1939 and ED/John Holt/UAC formed a WA Co-ordination Committee that was to last until 31/9/1947, relaxation being more protracted than in the first World War. The war clouds certainly darkened when Italy joined the conflict and France fell causing diversions round the Cape of Good Hope (magnificent name to those on board a vessel). Panama became a byword on the entry of Japan but Freetown was known everywhere for its vital role in the convoy system. UAC lost nine vessels to enemy action.

The next history spans post-war to Nigerian Independence in 1960. Before deciding to invest in new liners, Elders had to consider air competition but correctly at the time assessed a situation where colonial officers preferred a sea voyage as a health booster after a tour in the Colony. In September 1947 and March 1948, the new Accra and new Apapa, both of 11,600 tons gross, entered services to a three-weekly schedule until the Aureol, the largest ever at 14,083 gross tons, joined them in 1951. Fortnightly sailings were resumed to last until 1967. Six motor vessels of 4,800 gross tons each were commissioned in 1947/48 to join the re-commissioned Sangara. They were the Sherbro, Shonga, Salaga, Sekondi, Sulima and Swedru. The Calabar, built in 1935, was overhauled. The Aureol was named after the hill overlooking Freetown. The Aba was sold in 1947.

On ED books by December 1949 were a total of forty-two ships. Conference total was forty-nine, and had become 129 by 1958. The UK proportion on export traffic dropped from 82% in 1950 to 56% in 1958 chiefly at the expense of Dutch competition. The Korean War and Suez Canal closure brought about a shipping boom but fair rates were maintained to assist in bringing a return to prosperity on the coast where, for four years from 1946, capacity for palm produce evacuation was tight. Marketing boards on the coast replaced private traders except for timber, hides & skins and minerals. In the six years from 1950, turnround time lengthened 25% and the Conference lost 741 days awaiting berths. UAC and John Holt decided to differentiate between shipping and merchant functions and transferred former interests to Palm Line, 1949 and Guinea Gulf Line, 1950 respectively and became Conference members along with EDL and HWAL in January of the latter year.

In 1948 the Hoegh Line of Oslo had entered the WA trade, mainly for timber and the bringing out of stockfish and Danish beer. Palm Line contact on the coast ranged from Mauritania to Angola served by fifteen vessels all named "— Palm". From 1952 Africa Palm and Burutu Palm joined them followed by fourteen more from 1956, two of which were vegetable oil tankers. In all, fourteen of the ships were air-conditioned.

In the 50s Indian Scindia Line ran WA-India and Japanese lines. OSK, Mitsui, and K Line (Kawasaki Kisen Kaisha) came into Nigerian waters. Woermann re-entered the fold in 1952. Between 1952 and 1961, EDL fleet was classified as "E" class: Eboe, Ebani, Egori; "Coasters": Baro, Benin, "Passenger ferry" Eket; "O" class: Obuari, Owerri, Oti, Ondo, and the Onitsha, equipped with 150 ton derricks to enable her to replace the Mary Kingsley. These derricks were the strongest fitted to any British vessel. The "P" class Perang, Patani were of 6,200 tons gross. All these ships were generally of eleven knot capacity. The "D" class were the last, faster at fourteen knots, Daru, Degema, Diccove. Elders pioneered with diesel oil cooling and inert gas fire extinquisher systems. Ocean freight rates came down in 1954 and Elders divorced themselves of all activities other than ocean carriage. SWAL (Scandinavian), on the coast from 1945, became a member of the Conference in September 1955 and Hoegh Line in August 1957, only to leave the Conference in 1963.

National pride saw in 1957 the acceptance of the first West African line to the Conference — the Black Star Line of Ghana (BSL) with one vessel and four chartered grown to thirteen, owned within two years. The Nigerian National Line Ltd. followed on 5th February 1959, one owned and two chartered. There were ten vessels by 1961, 51% owned by the Government while ED and PL, as technical partners, owned the remainder, a total authorised capital. By 1961, it had £2 million wholly owned by Nigerian interests.

The case for a Nigerian line within the Conference had been argued since 1957 but the need for capital had sounded caution. The first Manager and Secretary was Mr L. Passage. Capital had to go round as there were many demands in all fields of the economy and shipping was already taken care of. On the other hand, the existence of a national line satisfied the desire to see some proportion of goods carried under a national flag. The foundations were laid to train Nigerian navigating and engineering officers along with supporting complement. Whilst ED and PL were shareholders there was, as was to be expected, criticism that the line was not a true Nigerian project and it took a little while for time to dispel all fears. The line broke away from the tradition of embarking stevedore labour and tally clerks from Sierra Leone for working their ships along the coast, and instead employed Nigerians.

In 1958 a joint Nigerian/Finnish enterprise was not admitted to the Conference. Popular for a few years until killed off by air was the ED 1957 service with the vessels Wineba and Calabar on a London-WA routing. By 1960 there were five conferences serving the Nigerian trade from the Far East, the Mediterranean, the USA, France, and UK/Europe, the last of which embodied NNLL among the common tariff members, EDLL, HWAL, PL, GGL, WL, SWAL, Hoegh Line and BSL. The tramp went his separate way—bulk trade, highest bidder, under charter, no timetable.

In the decade following Independence, the vessels operated by the WAL Conference in 1964 numbered

EDLL	43
HWAL	12
PL	22
GGLL	3
WL	27
SWAL	13
BSL	10
NNLL	15
Total	145

Just before the stock in 1964 quoted, the EDL introduced their faster 16-knot "F" class vessels: Fourah Bay, Falaba, Forcados, Fian, Freetown and Fulani and along with modifications to its "D" class, equipped them in 1966 for a traffic in motor cars to the extent of fifty vehicles each. The stock inventory for WALCON did not include Hoegh Line which had opted out the year before. In January 1968, the Conference was reconstituted into UKWAL and COWAC, the latter standing for Continent West African Conference. In 1965 Elder Dempster Agencies re-organised and J.C. Lucas, CBE, became West Coast Manager. In 1964 NNLL, PL and EDL formed African Container Express Ltd. to carry containers to International Standards Organisation standards over land and sea to use to the full import and export traffics. The NPA, NRC, NPMC, (Ports, Railway, Produce) boards maintained great interest. Glaxo, National Cash Register, Distillers Company, Longmans Green, and G.B. Ollivant used the service and whisky, sanitary earthenware and record changers flowed in such manner. Laurence Bright of Warrington shipped shirts to Rock City Stores of Port Harcourt.

Twenty lines were regularly using Apapa in 1967, including Farrell Lines, touching Boston, New York, Philadelphia, Norfolk and Jacksonville. Maersk was one of the lines touching the Far East. Independence naturally brought great changes to the passenger trade. Sea travel had been taken for granted. Then came air travel. As time went on more airlines opened services and employers started to write into contracts that individuals should be prepared to fly. Air travel lost its exclusiveness and took over the role of the routine. Inevitably, passenger ship patronage suffered. The two French liner companies merged and reduced the number of mail boats. Compagnie Maritime Belge, because of trouble in the Congo, sold two ships and reduced service to a fortnightly basis. Then the twelve-passenger cargo ships began to go offset to some extent by the retention of passenger accommodation in the two National Lines. There was a conscious bid to attract the tourists but West Africa had a poor start with little help from Travel Agents. Progress was therefore slow although EDL offered a special round trip to Nigeria designed for tourists by the Aureol at a time when Nigeria was still in the sterling block. In this field undoubtedly, Sierra Leone, Senegal and the Ivory Coast led the way. In 1967 and 1968, the Accra and Apapa were sold leaving the Aureol alone to battle on with a 29-day round voyage 42-day cycle now via Las Palmas, Freetown, Monrovia, Tema and Lagos.

The Seaway Car Transporters Ltd. in 1971 chartered one vessel to UKWAL for specialist car carriage Poole-Apapa with a guaranteed berth and a year later Southampton replaced Liverpool as the UK port for MV Aureol in order to reduce the turnround time to thirty-five days. By then ED fleet tonnage had dropped from 293,853 in 1965 to 209,989. In 1973 they had decided that the needs of the future were best met with a combination type vessel and three Polish ships were ordered from H. Schuldt of Hamburg. The Shonga was the first launched in May 1973 and she took up to 410 twenty-feet containers or a combination of containers and general cargo.

In 1960, ED carried 28,107 passengers, in 1971, 5,331. For a long time money was being lost on the service and a four-fold increase in fuel oil prices was the last straw. Aureol, built to post-war standards of austerity, approaching the end of her life, could not compete with the cruise trade, an arm increasingly examined as the few liner services of the world petered out to air build-up, and so the great West African institution of the 'mailboat' came to an end in the Autumn of 1974 upon the conclusion of her 203rd round voyage. There were then no British civil servants travelling left to mourn her loss, certainly a factor in the matter of patronage. Appropriately enough, on her last sortie sailed the Crown Agents representative for Nigeria, Alan Jordan.

By 1973, there was a Ro-Ro 'clearway' and the most modern vessels at work were the 'River' class of the NNLL, the 'Klorte Lagoon' class of the BSL and the Hoegh Beaver of the Hoegh Line. In 1975, NNLL acquired two further River class for a direct service between Grangemouth and Scotland, cutting out rail & road movement to English ports and the West Coast with Nigerian ports of call at Apapa, Sapele and Warri, working to a 28-day frequency. The two ships of about 5,500 dwt each with refrigerated capacity and 80-ton derricks equipped for container/palletised cargo, were named River Gongola and Cross River. The reason for the adjective preceding the noun in the case of the latter has been mentioned in Chapter 2. The year before, EDL had acquired the Sherbro, 12,000 dwt, a semi-container/multi-purpose freighter. She followed Shonga and both were capable of 16.5 knots.

UKWAL deferred until the November 1974 increase in Dublin port premium charges which were necessary then to counteract a deterioration in productivity. In 1975, the berthage problems rising in the main from cement carriage congestion at Apapa forced the African Container Lines of London to cease trading. Two further Ro-Ro services commenced in 1976, African Ferry Services Felixstowe-Cotonou, and Inglesham Shipping and Forwarding/Dicker CL (Contin- ental) Haulage, Avonmouth-Warri, both designed to beat the then bottlenecks of Nigeria.

Poland's link with Nigeria was on the increase. From 1970-75, the General Manager of the NNLL was a Pole and young Nigerians studied at the Polish Merchant Navy Academy. Polish captains were employed as pilots in Nigerian ports. A slightly different new service was the Shoreham-Burutu Nigeria Ocean Ferry granted exclusive use of the Nigerian port in return for investment on its dated facilities. Burutu-Warri was to be by transhipment to catamaran type cargo decks called cargocats of 140 tons carriage pushed in pairs by pushcats. The ferry size was limited to 4000 tons in order to surmount the Escravos Bar. My friend, Colin Riddoch, controlled the UK end. Harbour dues went up in September 1976 because of depreciation of sterling against the cedi and the naira.

The last event of 1976 was the decision of the Nigerian Government to sink $27 million into the NNLL to enable it to operate on a larger scale. Nineteen new ships were to be built to bring the fleet total to thirty-one by 1980. A further half million dollars was to be spent on expanding trade routes and employing consultants to streamline the organisation. Neither Britain nor Japan secured the contract for the building of the nineteen vessels which were shared out between South Korea and Yugoslavia.

Between mid-'75 and mid-'76, world fleet-carrying capacity increased by 8.8% grt and tankers rose by 12%, 46% of the total, In terms of dwt the increase was 10%. Nevertheless trade was not the hive of activity these figures suggest. New services started up in 1977 on the west coast were Genoa/Marseilles-Lagos Ro-Ro by Traghetti del Mediterraneo, Denmark-Nigeria container by Danish East Asiatic Company, Felixstowe/Rotterdam/Antwerp/Rouen-Apapa general freight in minimum parcels of 100 tons by Dipgrove Shipping with special arrangements for discharge at Kirikiri lighterage berth, and Mersey-Sapele by North Delta Lines, subsidiary of Guiness Peat Group operating a monthly schedule.

In 1978, the national shipping line of Zaire, Compagnie Maritime Zairoise, became the seventh member of UKWAL. A Nigerian enterprise, Sea Dantainer Lines Ltd. commenced a container service, Europe-Warri. The East Asiatic Company introduced ventilated containers with five charges of air per hour on the Europe-West Africa run and the BFI Line produced a new Ro-Ro service between the coast and Portsmouth, Virginia and Baltimore, Maryland. They then took on a charter, a French ship built in Spain, the Charles Schiaffino, for a new Ro-Ro service between Sheerness and Lagos, but it was a service with a difference. The vessel carried tugmaster tractors and heavy duty flat-bed trailers on which the load was carried inland — the first venture of its kind.

In 1979, Palm Line placed in service two container/break bulk cargo vessels but the pinnacle of logical achievement was the entry into service, Europe-Lagos/Warri, of the 205 m Baco Liner. In addition to carriage of container and deck cargo, it carried twelve dumb barges floated in and out through special doors in the bows. It could thus be loaded/offloaded at a buoy. Each barge loaded 800 tons. Barges could be offloaded at shallow ports and a further development will be each vessel upon entering service, being equipped with thirty-six barges, twelve en voyage, twelve being unloaded at destination from previous sailing and twelve being loaded ready for the next outward journey. Baco (Barge-Container) operated by Rhein, Maas and See had Westgate Shipping of London as their UK agents and Pan-Atlantic Shipping & Transport of Apapa as their Nigerian agents.

The development was obviously tailor-made to Nigerian conditions particularly for congested or lesser equipped ports but a precedent for such means had already been set, for example, in the American Gulf ports. Much of West Africa's export trade was unsuitable for containers many of which returned empty northbound and if Baco proved successful many a West Coast shipper would regret the too conservative approach to ship design by other lines. The ship's beam was 28.5 m with an overall capacity of 21,000 tonnes and a draught of only 6.65 m. The use of Warri is significant in that access to the port was restricted to vessels of small draught by the shallow depths at the Escravos River entrance to the delta.

As the history closes, the Federation prepared to provide for improved navigational aids, a nautical college, and undertake a National Transport Survey for its Maritime Division. The recorded past shows that the concerned fleets ably catered for the needs of the country and engendered a National Line. As in other modes, the future must provide for more specialisation and there will undoubtedly be a need for the carriage of gas. Turnround on the coast must be quickened. Regulations for ships sailing under "flaps of convenience", the restriction to employ Nigerian marine insurance only, and the like, must be carefully examined by the Legislature, lest such constraints act in a manner detrimental to the overall well-being of the country.

Chapter 5

Inland Waterways

The longest naturally navigable stretch of river is the 2300-mile Amazon, from the Atlantic to Iquitos, Peru. In Africa, the finest navigable river, and at the same time the main highway, is the Gambia, 292 miles to the tidal limit. Collection of data about the Niger Delta began way back in 1841 by Beecroft, the British consul at Fernando Po; the Delta was then known as the "Gate of the Cemetery". The Niger and Benue systems, both of international importance, were firmly placed upon the global map by the Berlin Conference of 1885 which laid down an elaborate set of regulations. Nigeria was so studded with waterways that it was possible to travel by launch from Cotonou in Dahomey to Opobo in Cross River State without engaging the open sea and in all, there were reckoned to be 4200 miles of navigable waterways with another 1000 miles in intermittent use — if only thought useful in 1895 for a few months in the year. Seventeen years later, it was recorded that the Belgian Congo supported 7621 miles of navigable waterways of which 4824 were open to 22-ton vessels, 1959 to 150 ton, and 1051 to 500 tons.

By tradition the inland waterways of Nigeria came not to mean the whole river system but the Niger/Benue, three tributaries, the Cross, and the Delta, associated with the coastal feeding services. Lagos was a lagoon port like Abidjan and Douala and unlike Dakar, Conakry, and Freetown which were peninsular ports. The mouths of the Delta were but vaguely defined. The datum of all Nigeria was settled by the railway which itself in twenty-one years used different figures for the west and for the east, despite lending its services for triangulation. The datum is mean sea level determined by an automatic tide gauge on the east mole of Lagos harbour erected in 1912 and read regularly to 1935.

By 1905, twenty-one waterways had been cleared in Southern Nigeria and by 1909, Coulton Elliot was Marine Superintendent of the Niger/Benue Government Transport. The Marine Departments of the Lagos Protectorate and Protectorate of Southern Nigeria had been amalgamated in 1906 and the origin of the Northern Marine lay in the small naval forces that supported the military and civilian men in the march of pacification. Buoys and coastal lights were introduced from 1923.

Nigerians greatly admired the river works of the Americas but it was to Europe they turned in the 50s for advice, to NEDECO of Delft, Netherlands Engineering Consultants, absorbing a Dutch word "Polder" into their own (English) language in the process. President Theodore Roosevelt said in 1908: "American river systems are better adapted to the needs of the people than those of any other country — in extent, distribution, navigability and ease of use they stand first — yet the rivers of no other country are so poorly developed — or play so small a part of the nation's industrial life. Mississippi once without rival — until railway drew traffic from it."

The West African Joint Group of Engineers (made up then of local members of the three principal British engineering institutions) said of the IBRD Report on

Nigeria: "We consider that the Mission does not sufficiently stress the great importance of the rivers Niger and Benue to the country's economy. If these waterways were adequately controlled they could play an important part in the economy of this country as the rivers Mississippi and Missouri play in the USA." In that continent the barge trains in one form or another developed from the Mississippi to the Caribbean-Newfoundland axis, or Panama-Alaska run and steam tugs hauled log booms to the Fraser river timber mills for a hundred miles. The Mississippi flotillas were pushed in recognition of the more hydrodynamically efficient passage, a fact learnt from oil exploration days. The St. Lawrence Seaway grain route and push traffic over the Great Lakes were further examples of the latest pioneering effort being associated with the Mackenzie River Delta driven on by the grapping needs of the Arctic oil and gas fields.

Europe pioneered great canal projects towards the completion by 1985 of the North Sea-Black Sea link using the Rhine, Main, Nuremberg/Regensburg canal, and the Danube, a seven-country involvement, 1997-mile slice through the countryside ready to take 1500 ton dw craft. Such works dwarf the Rhone/Rhine, Oder/Danube, Lake Maggiore/Adriatic links. The Netherlands has more waterways than freight railway networks, 3473 miles to 2017. In Belgium, water has borne more than the rail. In France rail has declined whilst waterway has increased in terms of traffic moved. German aggregates by water doubled movement by rail. But the serious internal navigation in Europe is on the rivers, free like the Rhine, 385 miles, Elbe, 411 miles, Schelde, 270 miles, the 133-mile Rhone fastest flowing in Europe, or the canalised Seine, 345 miles and Main, 305 miles.

The IBRD Mission, invited by the Government of Nigeria in 1953, recommended that a Federal Department of Hydrology be set up to collect information for the planning of irrigation and flood control and then went one step better. They further said that as the ports were about to be separated from the railway it was essential that such an authority did not concentrate on the seas at the expense of the inland waterways and therefore a distinct arm of the Marine Department should be created to take care of the interior. The Inland Waterways Department commenced to operate on the 1st April 1957 when R.A. Njoku was Minister with the object of development, operation of essential marine services, and clearance of the creeks. River patrols were established followed by radio patrols and maintenance included sea walls and Carter Bridge. In 1975, River Basin Development Authorities were established for the Niger, Benue, Ogun/Oshun, Hadejia/Jama'are, Anambra, Imo, Cross, Sokoto/Rima, Chad, Benin and Delta, and the third five-year Development Plan called for close cooperation from the Lake Chad Basin Commission, River Niger Commission, and the Niger/Nigeria Joint Commission.

By 1980, thoughts of Lugard voiced sixty years before were awakened by, at long last, the decision to spend one million naira on river mapping and eight million naira on river improvement works so that perhaps the country would know as much about the assets of its waterways as it now does about its vegetation. So much by way of introduction to an investment that has been unworthy of a country whose name was called from its principal river.

Niger

The General Act of Berlin of 26th February 1885, Chapter V, Articles 26-34, reflected free access to navigation on the Niger River with identical rules applicable to the Congo River but application of the latter was confined to the ripa-bank powers, and was not placed under the control of an international commission. The General Rules Applicable to African Rivers — International Legal States of Niger, Article 2, provided: "All flags, without distinction of nationality shall have free access to the whole of the coast-line of the territories to the rivers there running into the sea, to all the waters of the Niger, Congo, and their affluents." Under Article 3, "All differential dues on vessels as well as merchandies are forbidden." By the Convention of St. Germain-en-Laye of 10th September 1919, Article 1, the signatory powers undertook to maintain a complete equality in commerce, within the area defined by the Berlin Act, and by Article 5 considered the freedom of navigation of the River Niger "on a footing of perfect equality." The River Niger with its affluents was classified as an International Waterway vide Exclusive Legislative List (International and Inter-Regional Waterways) Order 1955.

The river rises at 2,800 feet at Tembikunda in the Kong Mountains near the Sierra Leone/French Guinea frontiers and tidal influence extends twenty-five miles only up from its mouth. The source to Buram Island is called the upper, Buram Island to Jebba the middle, Jebba to the sea the lower. Outside Nigeria, the name "Joliba" was given; inside, the name "Quorra". At Bamako, it is 1290 feet wide. In the middle reaches, it is much encumbered by rocks and rapids, at Old Bussa "A stone throw across", but at say 700 yards only to the north, it is eight miles wide. The worst rapids were above Wuru and navigation was not really safe above Jebba though steamers have reached Bajibo. The upper reaches are characterised by multi-channels, confined within banks at Timbuktu, three miles wide at Buram Island. In the lower reaches, the Delta is held to begin at Aboh. The expansion and contraction along the course brought about a rise and fall peculiarity whereby the waters of the upper Niger take a whole year to travel to the lower Niger. Bussa was a cosmopolitan river crossroads and the development of Onitsha a mile across from Asaba started in 1857 on the arrival of the Dayspring.

In 1903, the Marine Superintendent was able to maintain a ten-feet channel through the Lokoja-Idah stretch known as "Sacrifice Rocks" and a year later the most dangerous parts were well buoyed. In the upper Niger from 1908, the Messageries Africannes de Bamako maintained a weekly passenger service from Koulikoro, forty miles downstream of Bamako, to Gao, July-December, and Mopti-Gao, December-March, (maintained after Independence by the Mali Navigation Company). Mopti has been called the "Venice of West Africa" (but a Venice without its canals). Gao was once the capital of the Songhai Empire. The Mississippi was improved by suction dredging and a dredger was ordered in 1910 with the object of obtaining the same depth of channel, Lokoja-Baro, as existed between Lokoja and the sea. Along with dredging went clearance and snag busting at low water using blasting gelignite and Bickford fuse laid by divers.

On the Niger up came manatee, crocodile, five feet Niger Perch. A manatee brought up at Omerun Creek, Onitsha measured nine feet and weighed 900 lbs. The staff were Ijaws though many captains were Nupe and the paying off headquarters at each end of season was at Angalabri, not far from Patani. When years later in 1957 river shipping delays were measured, those attributed to shallows or submerged snags were found to average 7.5 per ship per annum; 256 ship-days in the case of one fleet, a witness to the immensity of the task facing the nation.

River distances and 1909 passenger timings were:

Burutu-Lokoja	332 miles	5 days
Lokoja-Baro	70	2
Baro-Jebba	130	3
Burutu-Jebba	532	10

Forcados-Lokoja approach was five miles more at 337 miles; Onitsha was three days distant from Burutu.

The average date for high water on the Niger in Nigeria is the 25th September, often a difference of 35 ft. between seasons, though in 1908 rising 30ft. 5in. and falling 30ft. 1in. Sectionalising the higher level durations:

Burutu-Baro	20th June to 15th December
Baro-Jebba	1st August to 1st December

The tornado months were April-June and September-October and masters of vessels had to allow for a 2-feet fall in twenty-four hours when anchoring on the Niger, Benue or Kaduna in September and October. Specific water level measurements were:

Burutu-Onitsha	Open all the year
Onitsha	12' 41', 12', April, October, February, 1953 8' 41'', 41', May, October, 1957
Lokoja	20' 6''' average depth 1894-1899
	34' 4'' depth 1900
	5', 36' 2½'', May, October, 1957
	33' average depth 1915-1957
Baro	23' 6'' rise October 1908
	3' minimum depth 1910
	Accessible 2½ months by 11' draught, 9½ months by 4' draught, 12 months by 2'
	4' 9'' minimum depth, 25' 4'' maximum depth, July 1st, September 21st, 1955
	23' average depth 1915-1957
Mureji	Lowest level end of June
Jebba	Season open August-February
	15' 6'' rise October 1908
	5' draught available 5 months, 2' draught 2 months

By 1960, there were sixty river and tide gauges on the Niger, Hawal, Gongola, Katsina Ala, Donga, Bantaji, Taraba, Belwa, Ini, Ankwe, Gurara, Benue and the Cross, twenty-two of which read discharge figures, many being read by the Railway, UAC, John Holt and local schoolmasters. In 1955, discharge of the Niger at Onitsha amounted to 9.9×10^{12} cu.ft.; 970,000 cusecs, 9th to 12th October inclusive. During September/October discharge figures recorded were:

Jebba	5,500	cu metres/ second	184,000	cusecs
Pategi upstream	10,000	"	334,000	"
Pategi downstream	7,500	"	250,000	"
Baro	10,000	"	334,000	"

Pategi is on the opposite bank to Mureji at the junction with the Kaduna. Discharge between Jebba and Onitsha, augmented by the tributaries has thus built up to 3.44 times that of the former.

NEDECO of Delft was first commissioned by the Nigerian Government in 1953. They were to look from Baro seawards and the Benue from the French border to the confluence for aids to improved navigation with such divers training works as might be considered necessary. In particular the Escravos Bar, cornerstone of the Delta works, was to be examined. In the 750-page report of February 1959, a major proposal was the multi-purpose dam recommended for construction north of Jebba at Kainji with navigational locks designed to encourage passage as far as the low bridge at Gaya in Niger. In fact, completion of the dam made the river navigable all the year round up to Yelwa, Sokoto State, and the Niger-Benue and tributary 1134-mile network should offer further scope for cheaper transport. The dam cost £68 million sterling.

In 1965, a Niger River Accord Decree was published in Cameroun after signature in Niamey, Niger, by the heads of those States along with Ivory Coast, Dahomey, Guinea, Upper Volta, Mali, Nigeria and Chad. Again, it testified to the Niger and its tributaries being open freely without let or hindrance to trade and exploitation. A Dahomeyan became Executive Secretary, a budget was agreed, once again NEDECO was to study, this time, Gao in Mali to Yelwa in Nigeira, the hope being implied that navigation would become possible, bay to Bamako. Ir 1976, a scheme costing $25 million initiated by UNDP and backed in Paris was put up for the control of the river throughout its length

A year later, NEDECO and Bos Kalis Westminster Dredging were commissioned by the Nigerian Government to develop the 500km stretch, Lokoja/Warri-Port Harcourt, as a shipping route by buoying, and deepening, to transform it into a commercial artery with greater significance than of yore. The 1978 studies suggested that the target was 83% attainable but at least should be able to deal with the Ajaokuta Project lying between Idah and Lokoja. In the 1979 melting pot lies the future of a Lokoja Dam which would impound the Niger and the Benue as a flood water as far as Rabah and Makurdi respectively.

The Niger Delta

Benue

The Benue, called the Tchadda rising in the mountains of Buban-Jidda, Cameroun, and at the confluence with the Niger at Lokoja over a mile wide, forms at its junction a two-mile wide lake dotted with islands and sand banks. Communications remained poor for many years and it was not until 1922 that the first motor car for Yola was delivered by river. Strong winds can blow for the greater part of the year and the harmattan is felt between December and February followed by lesser winds until April. Tornadoes are prevalent from March to October and can be seen approaching from the east, the right bank which is the lee bank being the one to avoid. The worst sandbars are Amagedi-Loko, below Tunga and Ibi, at Amar, and near Jen with notorious flats at Gamadi and Wuro Bokri where barges are pulled over the shallows, and if all were to be eliminated, two weeks passage to each end of the season would be added.

The Niger/Benue Confluence in Lokoja

River distances and journey times were (1909):

Lokoja-Abinsi	165 miles	
Lokoja-Ibi	225 "	14 days by pole canoe
Lokoja-Numan	432 "	
Lokoja-Yola	467 "	12 days. Navigable 200 tons for 3 months
Lokoja-Garoua	547 "	
Burutu-Yola	799 "	17 days
Burutu-Garoua	879 "	21 days
Burutu-Rei Bouba	915 "	Limit of UAC navigation

The journey time by pole canoe between Lokoja and Yola is most instructive in terms of the season:

Season	Up River	Down river
Low water February-April	27 days	24 days
Tornado May-June	29 "	18 "
High water June-November	45 "	18 "
Harmattan December-January	34 "	19 "

The deep water and speed of current at high water times of the year require the canoe poles to be fitted with prongs to catch on and ward off the trees. Garoua traffic in 1913 was guaranteed by lightening loads at Yola. Lokoja was accessible to 1000 tons. In the year, the limit of utilisation was four return journeys to Yola. At the end of the rains, 1500 tons could be taken to Jimeta near Yola, timbers and cotton goods up, groundnuts down. These nuts were Adamawa hand-shelled, fetching the highest prices in 1948. No river compares with the Benue for the variety of its bird life — spur-winged goose, knob-billed goose, pigmy goose, pintail, teal, great white egret, sand pipers, oyster catchers, and king fishers.

In 1911, the French thought of connecting the Benue and Logone systems by a railway to open up Chad and Shari country but the economics were not thought out sufficiently.

The bench mark at Garoua is 600.56 feet and water levels are:

Garoua	Open August to September
Yola	21' average peak water level 1934-1957
	23' record figure in 1959
Ibi	23' 6" rise, 25' fall, 1910
Makurdi	7' 9" May, 31' October
	21' rise noted in 1959
Lokoja	7' June, 37' October 1955
Lower Benue	39' 4" level October 1959

High Water Averages

Lokoja-Loko	Mid June to end of November
Loko-Ibi	Mid July to end of October
Ibi-Yola	20th July to 10th October

Annual Discharges

Garoua	14×10^9 cubic metres 1955
Makurdi	126×10^9 cubic metres 1955
Lokoja	135×10^9 cubic metres 1955

On the 13th October 1955 discharge rate, Lokoja, was 505,000 cusecs.

NEDECO thought that the construction of one or more reservoirs to accumulate water during the floods would assist navigation during the rest of the year. The river was explored for possible dam sites. They carried out a hydrographical survey Garoua-Numan. The Joint Group of Engineers following upon the IBRD survey believed that the use of the Benue could be considerably extended if access were provided to loading facilities during the wet season by the construction of raised access roads and the use of small shallow draft power barges. Tests had shown that suitable groynes could be built up by driving stakes into the river bed causing the flood water to deposit its silt and provide the basis for the raised road access to the river sides. Such device had been practised on the Nile.

In 1973, Government decided to dredge to facilitate transport between Nigeria and Cameroun. In 1978, the lower Benue River Basin Development Authority planned to construct two dams at Mada village on the Mada tributary to the Benue to irrigate 10,000 hectares of farm land.

Kaduna

The junction with the Niger at Mureji is 122 miles distant from Lokoja, and the Bari-Juko limit of navigation 85 miles up-stream is 207 miles from Lokoja or 539 miles from Burutu. High water to Bari-Juko lasts from 5th August to 30th September and at Wushishi higher up the level in 1955, recorded 21 feet in September and 9½ feet in December. Zungeru, farther up still and much rock-strewn, was three days from Lokoja or eight days from Burutu. Steam canoes were employed in early days taking twice as long.

Gongola and Donga

In August 1903, Lt. Moran ascended the Gongola in a steam canoe and found depths of three feet between mid-September and the end of October for up to 150 miles from the Benue junction. The opening up of the waterway was a principal task of 1904 when navigation was accomplished with difficulty to Ashaka at mile 130. There was no navigation by Government vessels in 1910 and much of the antics of the river remained to be explored until the building of the Borno Extension for the Nigerian Railway.

The Gongola is a right bank river of the Benue but the Donga, a left bank tributary, came into more prominence in 1977 when Sir M. MacDonald & Partners, Consulting Engineers, in association with Hunting Technical Services, was to carry out a pre-feasibility study of irrigation and water resources over an area of 8000 sq. miles in the Donga River Basin under an agreement with the Nigerian Government and MRT Consulting Engineers (Nigeria) Ltd. Hunting Technical Services were to be responsible for soils, agriculture and economic studies. Dams, barrages and pumping stations, for the full development of irrigation and hydroelectric power, were to be explored.

Delta

It was Capt. William Allen who steamed through a delta approach in 1841 and the export of palm oil from the Oil Rivers that gave the name to the first British Protectorate on the coast. The Oil Rivers ports became Akassa and Brass on the coast, Degema up the Sombriero, and Bonny on an inlet. Ships of all nations knew the multi-mouths with otherwise no idea wherein the maw lay. At one port, the locals imported European pans so it was an easy step to call this Brass on the river Brass. This river gave an entrance to the Orashi, a main distributary, and Ndoni Creek leading to the largest lake in Southern Nigeria, Oguta, 24½ miles from Owerri and 42 from Onitsha, the waters being 2½ miles long by one mile wide. The lake contained crocodile, manatee, turtle, and at one time the hippo, Bush cow (buffalo), tortoise and boas abounded.

That continuous line of mouth, creek and lagoon that mirrored the delta apex, Aboh, was never really specified and so here it is, west to east, twenty-one main distributaries and rivers.

Benin
Escravos and Nana creek
Forcados and Warri
Ramos
Dodo
Pennington
Middleton
Kulama
Ikebiri
Fishtown
Sengama
Nun, a main entrance
Brass
St. Nicholas entrance
Santa Barbara
San Bartholomeo
Sombriero
New Calabar
Bonny
Andoni
Imo

Inland Waterways

Borassus palm dugout canoe on River Sokoto, Argungu

Port Harcourt lay forty-one miles up the Bonny with 24 feet at high water and denoted the limit of the mangrove. Sudd was cut back from the Benin from 1909 and fifty-two miles of the Imo cleared in 1910. The Debin was formed from the Jamieson and Ethiope and the latter was cleared as far as Umutu in 1911. The Escravos makes a 120° bend before it reaches Koko, fifty-three miles from the bar. Escravos means "slaves".

The Nun entrance, almost in a straight line with Aboh, was the most important but subject to silting, was not commercially used and pride of place was taken in 1910 by the Forcados which followed suit for the same reason particularly after branch boat cessation to Lagos. The Escravos then became the main channel. The Aboh people were known for the best of yams and Onitsha for marking the sight of the first hill. The people developed a bicycle canoe for taking children to school by water; balance was required because the child sat on them and not in them. The Forcados bar was two miles wide, in the forty-eight years to 1947 widening seven times whilst the navigable channel decreased from 21 feet to 13 feet in the same time. It had given direct access to Burutu and Warri, the latter the old 15th century settlement. Forcados has however been redeveloped as an oil terminal.

The Escravos too had its sandbar and the NPA (Nigerian Ports Authority) had the responsibility for dredging eventually, Government having left the removal of deposited alluvia in the hands of private enterprise not wanting this line of communication to compete with the railway but deteriorating conditions after World War II brought about a change. A clearance scheme was outlined to give a minimum depth of 22 feet. This channel was now longer for the Burutu and Warri approach but shorter for Koko port's bulk oil palm and plants, and Sapele port's plywood and veneer factory. Twenty feet at all states of the tide was reached by 1964 so the export of faraway Chad came down the Benue and Niger through the ports of Warri and Burutu and out to the sea, via the Escravos. The original Oil River ports carried on with Opobo taking the place of Bonny whose channel had been dredged for the Port Harcourt approach.

The WA Joint Group of Engineers took the IBRD to task for not suggesting improved methods of creek transport for bulk timbers, the long passage of which through the creeks led, in their opinion, to recession in the export market through deterioration. Creek depths varied between 4½ and 40 feet and the Marine Department's main work was to maintain at least one channel continuously open. The Nun, left alone by shipping may become Madam Bountiful in terms of fish supply. Twenty-two million raffia palm trees grow in the swamps and may prove a source of alcohol.

The 1961 Niger Delta Development Board was set up to advise on physical development of the delta in an area where major occupations were farming, fishing and timber extraction. BG 79 was the rice best suited to the swamp, the land remaining fallow September through December. A 300-acre polder near Pevemabiri will support a 3600 ton per annum rice mill. Agriculture has otherwise made no progress because of the problems posed by the physics of the delta.

Depots

The Government of Northern Nigeria Marine (NNM) workshops were at Quendon, 25 miles downstream of Lokoja, installed by 1st January 1900, but as the administration became centred on the latter, the facilities were moved there on Lugard's direction. By 1904, NNM had repair bases at Burutu, Lokoja, Mureji and Bari-Juko, the last linking the tramway. In 1909, the Crown Agents ordered from Vickers, Sons & Maxim of Barrow a 450-ton capacity floating dock of sectional pontoon type for Lokoja to deal with the river craft. With the opening up of the BKR, Baro became an export port and of course had facilities for offloading of heavy materials. Forcados, transhipment port for Lagos and centre of stern wheeler traffic for Niger and Benue, became a marine shipyard. Burutu was also a transhipment port for ocean going and became a customs station.

There were privately-owned fleets. UAC established Niger River Transport Company

(NRTC) early in the present century with two ocean berths at Burutu. Burutu port became owned by UAC although it was open to other vessels and was one of the most comprehensive repair yards in Nigeria. In later years, inshore and offshore oil exploration plants were serviced there. Warri Transport commenced operations at the turn of the century becoming Holt's Transport Ltd. after the Second World War. They were the operators of Warri Wharf and maintained well equipped workshops and described the location as "a modern ocean and river terminal", designed to deal with ocean going and their river fleet. The terminal developed into a 600-feet affair and the dockyard was able to accommodate all craft offering. One thousand two hundred Nigerians were employed afloat and ashore.

To take petroleum into the Camerouns by 1952, a substantial storage depot was created at Garoua and a relay depot at Lokoja with Makurdi as flood season headquarters. The Inland Waterways Division created navigation branches at Lagos, Lokoja, Forcados, and Port Harcourt and transferred their Lagos headquarters to Lokoja in late '59. In 1958, a hydrological base was set up at Lokoja. In 1959, the Marine dockyards and slipways were at Apapa, Forcados, Lokoja, Calabar, and Port Harcourt. Lokoja set into a pattern of decline and in 1979 it had the peaceful air, and how welcome, of the early century. The new Warri-Kaduna road may set it up again and the steelworks at Ajaokuta should certainly give a boost — in fact it was Government's intention in 1980 to develop Yelwa, Lokoja, Onitsha and Ajaokuta. Yelwa is north of the Kainji dam.

Fleet

In 1900, NNM employed lighters, stern wheelers, tugs, launches, barges, canoes of all sizes, and small ocean-going steamers with funnel aft. After the rains, people liked the view they saw over the river banks from the deck. In 1904, Weir of the BKR survey team described the fleet at fourteen vessels, two twin screw, two single screw, one independent paddle, and nine stern paddle capacity ten to 100 tons, draft empty 8in. to 3ft. 6in., beam 8ft. 8in. to 30ft., length 54ft. 43in. to 160ft., quite a range. There were also four launches, five steam canoes, eleven poling canoes, and four lighters along with the High Commissioner's craft.

Down in the south in 1905 there were nine launches and a very fine lifeboat, "Moseley", based in Lagos. In 1906, the northern fleet had grown to thirty-three vessels two of which were capable of ten knots under 150 ton loads and the southern fleet to thirty-nine steam and motor craft.

Three rates of carriage were offered in the north. advertised in 1909 as first class cabin, first class deck, and deck, passengers providing camp equipment and provisions. Steel poling canoes had sun decks and screens and required a helmsman and six polers.

The 1909 NNM fleet consisted of six mail vessels 75ft. to 160ft., 15 to 200 tons, first class accommodation ranging from six to twenty. The largest was the TS Corona of 200 tons, the remainder being stern wheelers such as the "Empire". There were then stern wheeler steam canoes 60ft. in length with second class accommodation for five named after wading birds such as "Stork", three tugs of 100ft., 20 tons, Egbom, Egori, Etobe, the 75ft. launch Zaria, and three lighters of 45-90 tons capacity. The following table in that year shows the cargo that could be lifted in one bottom by the type of vessel permitted (stern wheeler SW, ocean steamer OS, steam canoe SC, native canoe NC) at five Niger stations, one Kaduna station, and one Benue station:

Station		Low Season Draught Tons			High Season Draught Tons	
Onitsha	SW	3'	30	OS	11'	1500
Lokoja	SW	3'	30	OS	11'	1500
Baro	SC	3'	10	OS	11'	1500

Station		Low Season Draught Tons			High Season Draught Tons	
Mureji	SC	2'	5	OS	11'	1500
Jebba	SC	2'	5	SW	8'	500
Bari-Juko	NC	1'	1	SW	7'	200
Yola	NC	1'	1	SW	10'	600

Government river steamer circa 1912

On the advent of the BKR, Government river traffic declined although it was designed that it should stay level at least with past performance. In 1913, total northern lifting capacity was 1800 tons gross, 600 tons net, giving a lift at four trips per vessel of 2400 tons paying traffic, insufficient to lift over 7000 tons produce from Yola without releasing SWs for the Benue and chartering branch boats for the Niger. In 1914 on the amalgamation of North and South, it was stated that Lagos took charge of the NNM fleet in poor mechanical condition. The evacuation problems of the Benue were perennial; only by sufficient boats at the peak, laid aside low season, could the service cope and the economics did not justify such arrangements. A railway was not considered except through Cameroun to Douala.

The stern wheelers, pleasant sight, lasted till 1926. The close of the Second World War saw a fleet of forty-four vessels. In 1955, excluding dumb craft, the Nigerian inland fleet were deployed as follows:

	Western Division	Northern Division	Eastern Division
Touring launches	18	8	15
Ferries	2	1	7
Motored barges	3	—	2
Pinnaces	4	1	—
Dredgers	1	—	—
Sounding dinghies	—	3	1
Towing craft	—	—	1

Among the 1958 vessels ordered were the 83ft. launches Dawn, Daphne and Diadem from Phillips of Dartmouth and the 40ft. cabin cruiser "Jebba" built locally by the Opobo Boatyard. In 1974, the survey of the upper Niger into the Republic of Niger was taken care of by purchase of a suitable craft and in 1977, Riverine I and Riverine II, passenger ferries, built by the Delta Boatyard Co. at Warri began to ply between the riverine areas of Bendel State.

The Niger River Transport Company operated the largest river fleet in Nigeria. Starting off with stern wheelers, they had twenty-seven powered craft and a number of barges by 1953 and shortly had twenty-eight PC and sixty-one barges with a total life capacity of 19,000 tons. They were the first operator, in 1950, to introduce the "push-tow" principle and its two latest units, "Gongola" and "Yola", were each capable of pushing 3600 tons up river and 4500 tons down river in eight specially integrated barges. The fleet complement is some 250 Nigerians, twenty-three of whom were captains of the vessels. By 1968, diesel with screw propulsion was replacing steam, late, it might be said, and in 1969 the Flagship "Lord Trenchard", not new to the coast, had in train six barges, 2600 tons. Holts too commenced with stern wheelers and had a lift capacity of 4000 tons spread over ten boats in 1969. They embarked upon a policy of diesel push tugs and employed thirteen tanker barges as well as a pontoon barge of 350 tons capacity. Back in 1953, their fleet had been eight stern wheelers, two screw tugs and two stern wheelers adapted for creek service. Barges were up to 150 tons capacity.

Socony Vacuum Oil Company with Shell and UAC after research replaced the Garoua petroleums in 44-gallon drum canoe traffic by an eight tug barge train on the lines adopted on the Mississippi driven by twin screw. The dumb carriers came from Clelands (Successors) Ltd. of Wallsend on Tyne, 8 × 200 ten barges and the motive power from Yarrow & Co. Ltd. of Scotstown Glasgow, 2 screw 130 ton diesel tug, 2 × 425 hp 400 rpm Crossley engines, draft 4ft. 3in., named Adama after the Fulani Emir of Adamawa. The propellors were shrouded in tunnels because of the sudd.

In April 1949, the canteens proposed that a river fleet be set up under a public transport service but the scheme was not acted upon. The capital employed by the canteens based on a 25-year life was £2,750,000 with assets taken at replacement cost. They saw the future with depreciation and interest at £355,000 per annum, receipts of £175,000 and an annual deficit at £159,000. In fact in 1949, they saw a future no different in terms of viable working of the rivers than that foreseen in 1910. Obviously, dredging of such vast lengths to achieve all-the-year-round services was out of the question and the future, if it was to mean something, lay more in the direction of solution by impounding at strategic points. This future has yet to be resolved.

In 1953, the combined NRTC, Holts, and CFAO (Compagnie Francaise d' Afrique et Occidentale) was put at 50,000 tons, 300-400 hp propulsion and 150-350 ton barges with new units of 600 hp TS push-tow under construction. In 1956, "Susie" of Compagnie de Transport et de Commerce joined them and Zircon luxury motor cruisers from Reliance Marine of Salisbury were ordered by Allens Marine of Port Harcourt for offering to the Nigerian market.

Services

During the 1906 high season, a weekly mail service ran Burutu-Bari-Juko and Niger/Kaduna to connect the tramway and in addition in 1909, a Burutu-Lokoja-Baro service ran weekly, augmented every three weeks on a Thursday to connect the new BKR terminal. The latter grew into Forcados-Burutu-Patani-Aboh-Onitsha (Asaba on the opposite side on the return journey)-Idah-Lokoja-Baro-Egga-Mureji. When Zungeru was opened on the LGR link to the BKR, it was intended to abolish river traffic on the Kaduna to Bari-Juko but the intention was postponed due to washouts on the line and the last steamer actually left the Kaduna river on the 15th October 1910.

Southern Nigeria ran 1911 services Lagos-Siluko (on river Siluko) — Sapele, Forcados-Burutu-Warri, Forcados-Koko-Sapele, and Akassa-Bonny-Opobo. There was also, from 1899, a weekly Lagos-Porto Novo run in Dahomey. Many of the services were connected with the ocean mails but low water incidents often meant the missing of the connection — quite a disaster with the then facilities for wait over.

During the 1914-1918 World War, a Marine Contingent was sent with the Nigerian Forces to the Camerouns and Lagos-Sapele had to close down. By 1916, absence of officers who were at the front had reduced all services to ferries across the Niger and Cross and mailboats across Forcados-Warri and Bonny-Degema. In 1917 from July, this was improved to fortnightly Forcados-Warri-Akassa-Brass-Degema-Port Harcourt on the opening of the eastern railway line, Bonny-Opobo. With ten officers lost and the vessels laid up, later that year, there could only be seen priority to Udi coal ex-Port Harcourt for Lagos and the river ferries. In January 1918, the Lagos-Sapele service recommended for botanists started again and a year later, all services were coming back to normal, a new normal however because river patronage was declining with the spread of rail and road.

In 1927, Government decided that river mail boat services should no longer be their concern and in the 30s, EDL put their MV Calabar on a connecting run on the arrival and departure of their Liverpool services, serving Lagos-Forcados-Warri-Port Harcourt-Calabar-Victoria (Camerouns). Traffics in petroleum in 1952 saw the commencement of the Apapa-Niger-Benue-Garoua and Yola on the one hand, Baro, rarely Jebba, on the other hand, contracting in the low season to Lagos Delta Port shuttles. In 1955, the Marine was running the long standing Lagos-Apapa ferries, vehicle ferries across the Niger, the Ethiope at Sapele, Lagos-Warri-Forcados, Port Harcourt-Akassa, Port Harcourt-Opobo, and supplied the colliers for the coal and Port Harcourt-Lagos.

In 1957-1958, Government services were the ferries Onitsha-Asaba, Sapele-Benin road crossing, Lokoja-Shintaku (a most important cross country route), Mamfe-Atimbo Calabar road crossing; the Lagos services on the 1st and 15th of each month, motor barges Rover and Robin to Epe, Ajijero, Arogbo, Youngtown, Forcados, Burutu, Warri, Frukama, Bomadi, Patani, and Tropari, that is, an approach using the Lagos Lagoons. The Raven left Port Harcourt on the 1st and 15th for Kiama, Odi Creek, and Vixen and Egret ran the Port Harcourt-Bonny Creek mail services.

In 1973, the scene went international. Societe Nigeriane des Transport Fluviaux et

Maritime of Niamey in association with Central Water Transportation Company of Onitsha ran a cattle service, Niamey-Onitsha, made possible by the Kainji improvements. The CWTC was State-owned but in late 1976, it was taken over by the Federal Government. It had a growing fleet. In 1979/80, an Idah-Agenebode ferry was to start linking Auchi in the west with a number of routes in the east. Farrell Lines ran a tanker service to Garoua, Holt's Transport Ltd. covered 1700 miles of inland waterways, NRTC covered the hinterland and neighbouring Republic of Cameroun and Chad. Holts diversified into oil and their round trip Apapa-Garoua clocked 2300 miles.

The Niger South Channel and Juju Rock at Jebba

Traffic

In 1904 cargo amounted to 3500 tons brought up from Burutu together with the following passengers:

	1st Class	2nd Class	Deck
Lokoja-Burutu	295	106	1796
Burutu-Lokoja	264	95	796
Lokoja-Zungeru-Lokoja	456	180	3457
Lokoja-Ibi	58	22	374
Lokoja-Yola	29	7	459

The breakdown is extremely interesting when seen from the view of contemporary events. The 1905/1906 report for Northern Nigeria stated that 114 privately-owned vessels of 7591 tons carrying capacity, produce carried not stated, entered the territory from the south whilst there were 128 government vessel movements out of Lokoja whilst the Southern Nigeria report said 15,937 passengers were booked, 137,598 miles sailed, 5081 tons cargo were carried. From 1909 there was much concentration on the BKR construction material and on the coast, 1911 saw the carriage of 4493 passengers from Lagos to Porto Novo and 11,548 passengers Lagos-Sapele. Elder Dempster Limited and the Niger Company raised Bills of Lading in Europe for through destinations in the creeks and rivers in 1911 and with the BKR established from Baro, there were high hopes of traffic stimulation.

Total traffic carried in 1913 over the Niger was 13,209 passengers and 18,704 tons of goods, so that up to the war, traffic had been intensifying. There was then a gap to 1947/49 when the statistics for freight was altered to a ton mile basis and an imbalance was revealed, 50 million TM up and 30 million TM down. The trade pattern was timber into Sapele and palm produce into Burutu, Abonema and Port Harcourt. But the pattern was not consistent because in 1947, Warri received 52,000 tons and despatched 124,000 tons. Lagos-Okitipupa in Ondo State through the lagoons, took 15,000 tons up, 17,000 tons down, 1948 figures. In 1949, the Niger and Benue produce figures were:

up	salt	18,332 tons
	cement	9,029 tons
down	groundnuts	24,432 tons
	beniseed	5,547 tons
	cotton lint	8,765 tons
	palm kernels	31,553 tons
	palm oil	11,392 tons

In 1948/49, the average length of haul on the Niger/Benue systems was 342 miles and by 1952/53 this had increased to 438 miles on the movement of 217,000 tons, the increase being due to greater use of the Benue.

	Up Benue	Down Benue
1950	13,696 tons	25,088 tons
1952	27,143 tons	32,813 tons

In the 60s, Holts loaded directly from Marketing Board Stores on the banks of the rivers.

Rates

In 1903 to reduce monopoly, Government accepted trade by their own launches. Burutu-Lokoja passenger rate was £4, £2 and £1 by the three classes of accommodation and cargo up, 30/- per ton wet season, £2 dry season, down, 15/- and £1 respectively. In 1909, a rate of £6 per ton was charged to the French for the Garoua-Forcados run, of 804 miles and that year marked a clear publication of the rates prevailing.

Passenger

	1st cabin	1st deck	deck
Lokoja-Baro	17/-	14/-	3/6
Lokoja-Mureji	30	23	8
Lokoja-Bari-Juko	60	43	18
Lokoja-Loko	22	15	7/6
Lokoja-Ibi	60	43	19/2
Lokoja-Yola	117	80	40

Specimens of goods class rates:

Class I: silk goods at owners risk, wearing apparel, bicycles;
II: cotton goods, cement, kolas, machinery;
III: salt, rice, coal, railway & medical stores;
IV: rubber, tin, skins;
V: palm oil, shea butter;
VI: palm kernels, peppers, groundnuts,

country produce specials ivory, gunpowder, petrol.

Specimen rates during high water:

	I & IV	II & V	III & VI
Burutu-Baro	40/–	32/6	27/6
Burutu-Jebba	47/6	38/–	35/–
Burutu-Bari-Juko	70/6	56/–	45/–

Downstream was up to 22% cheaper. Makurdi on the Benue was not then of course quoted as no railway had been built and the nearest point for comparison was Abinsi. Up and down rates were:

| Lokoja-Loko | 20/– | 18/– | 15/– |
| Loko-Abinsi | 26/– | 26/– | 20/– |

A special rate of 25/– per ton applied for ginned cotton between Baro (brought down by rail) to Burutu and there was a special rate for bricks but with no quote to a railway point. Livestock were carried at double deck rate per head. Towage was quoted at 2/– per mile and demurrage was raised per 24 hours of daylight at the rate of 2/– per ton capacity of the lighter. Low season rates were up 50% approximately. All rates tapered with increase in mileage. Cargo to and from the tributaries of the Benue was excessed at over 25%.

It was always thought that the Niger would offer formidable competition to the BKR but in 1913 the matter of rates to be charged had to be reassessed. Years later the Joint Group of Engineers commenting on the 1953 IBRD Mission thought that insufficient attention had been given to river freight rates "which should have been much cheaper." Until such time as there is an all-the-year flow, seasonal imbalance precludes any such possibility.

Cross River

No study is complete without a reference to the Cross River farther east, an international waterway also, the only other river navigable by large steamers as in the delta, always open in the high season the 200 miles to Itu. It rises in the Bamenda Highlands and flows into the Bight of Bonny, never surveyed, by a channel that changes yearly. Its mouth is shared by the Calabar river. Calabar is thirty miles distant with Duke Town, the centre of trade for a century and the equally famous Creek Town lying across the swamp. The low and the high water times in Nigeria are:

	Low	High
Itu	1' February	19' September
Afikpo	Dry January	21' August
Obubra	Dry December	26' 6" October
Ikom	5' February	32' October

These highly remarkable figures were taken over in 1957/58 and reveal a completely different pattern to that described for the delta rivers. In the May-September navigation season of 1948, traffic moved to the following extent from Oron in the mouth, 32,000 tons up 94,000 tons down with similar tonnages at Nwaniba farther up. Seasonal traffic flows between Mamfe in Cameroun and Calabar despite the existence of a road, and much produce came down from what was Ogoja Province. Both EDL and UAC ran tugs, barges, and palm oil tankers on the water and moved 150,000 tons in 1953.

The Marine started a mail service in 1911. The wreck of the Seamaid, out of Birkenhead in 1874, was still visible in 1920 and doubtless remains to be seen. The clearing of the river of snag and sudd was an annual formidable enjoyable business. Little water could be carried for washing and bilharzia was always a threat. The Marine Officer was provided with a house boat of five compartments consisting of living, sleeping, toilet, stores and cooking, and had no means of propulsion. Each end had two poling platforms. Lighting was provided by kerosene burning lamps and kerosene ran the refrigerator. Enyong Creek, off Itu, was a terrible spot calling for much explosive to rid trees massed with aerial roots.

The Cross was never what it might have been. Creek Town and Duke Town languished after the death of the powerful Eyo II in 1858. Then when steam came on the WA coast, the Sierra Leoneans competed with the local Efiks. Finally, in the end, no railway served that part of the country although by 1978, it was again on the cards.

The main highway to Calabar from the west is via Uyo and Oron (although a new road is to be driven from Itu) requiring the assistance of a ferry. Elder Dempster had their ferry "Eket" there, a Cross River State ferry, "Pioneer I", was built locally and eventually a hovercraft appeared on the scene. An ocean service operated Calabar-Victoria

Lagos-Apapa, the Lagoons, and Elsewhere

In 1898, Coode, Son & Matthew considered dredging of the Lagos lagoon for a stretch of sixty miles premature and expensive. Algae grew in the harbour which was first really cleared of sudd in 1909. A Lagos-Apapa ferry was also a popular and quicker alternative to the way round by land and in 1958 there were five vessels on the run — Kelt, Kail, Kite, Karen and Kathleen. A new vessel joined them in 1974. To combat the appalling congestion on the roads, a hovercraft service was due to be inaugurated by the State Ministry for Information between Badagry, Lagos, Ikorodu and Epe. They were to be called water buses and the order was on Hover Marine in England.

The water lettuce that grows in fresh waters is called Pistis stratiotes. The Yewa flowing into the lagoon was cleared in 1910 although launches had penetrated from 1894. The Osiomo, tributary of the Benin, was cleared for 155 miles in 1909. The beautiful Ogun still sported elephants north west of Ilugun in 1950, and, it is said, lion, was a regular highway between the lagoon and Abeokuta until the railway diminished its importance as a carrier. In 1980, feasibility studies were to take place on the far north Komadougou Yobe Basin Project by the Nigeria/Niger Joint Commission. Financed by UNDP and FAO the aim was defence against the approaching Sahara and encouragement to produce more food.

Road Networks

One quotation said "Next to religion, roads have been the most civilising influence in the world and in what we term progress they have outdistanced religion." Nigeria saw railways built before roads and so the pace of the latter, financed in the closing decades of the 20th century by oil revenue and never by taxation practised on the scale of the American turnpikes, fell into line with the quotation, despite a civil war, peacefully. But in some countries, roads have furthered the march of armies and of tranquillity there is little to be seen.

Goods were moved by camel — Clapperton recorded no less than five hundred in a single salt train — donkey, oxen, or mule brought over from India, the mule and the camel both being priced at £5 a head but the donkey at £1-5-0 fared best, heavy mortality taking its toll of the others. The transformation of Benin from 1898 to an orderly town with wide roads by 1910 was quoted as a justification for British rule but road developments in a sense paralleled the lines of Cuba where plantations were connected to nearest seaports by ensuring that the first Nigerian roads were feeder roads to the two railways, accomplishing the same end.

In 1903, Weir of the BKR reported that in the Protectorate of Northern Nigeria, the Nupes were the most businesslike in the preservation of paths free from foliage suitable for horsemen but that there were no tracks for wheeled traffic and it was not until 1904 that 6¼ miles of road were laid out in Zungeru township and a cart road-driven through Zungeru-Zaria via Birnin Gwari, the first oxen-hauled carts pioneering the distance in 1905. The first motor cars to travel the route came along in July 1908 and were used for the conveyance of invalids Part of the route is in use today as the A125 but the public had to wait till 31st December 1909 for the convenience as the Baro-Kano Railway construction had absorbed all labour.

Down in the Protectorate of Southern Nigeria, the first road was Ibadan-Oyo driven in 1905 to connect the interior with **Lagos Government Railway** railhead quickly followed by four feeder roads to stations on the Oshogbo extension. The palm oil trade in the south east generated the first road from Itukabong with exit via Aba, the Bonny replacing the Cross.

In August 1900, thinking the LGR would take a long time to reach Kano, Sir William MacGregor tried to prevail upon Colonial Secretary Chamberlain to authorise the first long distance road from Ibadan to Kano but the attempt to duplicate this means of penetration fortunately came to nought. In the meantime, officers in the north got around on horseback, a 1912 journey, Loko on the Benue to Borno taking thirty-seven days and Zaria across to Yola in Gongola taking twenty. The Government decided that sleeping sickness demanded that it was roads and not waterways, harbourer of the fly, that should be opened up. A decided fillip to road construction was the decision of the LGR to realign its track north of Agege a good deal of which was laid out to standards of "Roman" straightness, the original formation and bridges becoming much of what was the first **Lagos-Abeokuta road**.

Little was done however to develop a road system until 1925, planners being put off by the expense of tackling swamps, the extent of the bridging, grading the climbs into plateau areas and providing for the spate in the rainy season. Mr Bunning, General Manager of the Nigerian Railway, emphasised the cost of wasteful competition in observations on the different natural assets of the Gambia and the Gold Coast. Here and there, there was community effort; egged on by horn blowers, native authorities accomplished much in Ogoja Province, brought to light by P.M. Riley, the Resident. The Marina had become the first decent road in the capital where the sandy track to Victoria Beach was the only road in Nigeria to go down to the sea. The first bituminous surface to a road outside a township fell to the honour of the Lagos-Abeokuta route in 1926.

In the long distances involved, refreshment gaps were provided by the Government rest houses where for 1/– a night an officer had the use of shelter and hot water. Jos-Bauchi was described as spectacular along with Bukuru-Jemaa. For beauty however the Nigerian Field Society gives the accolade to Gombe-Yola. At the opposite end to the kaleidoscope lay the mushrooming of the slums of Lagos abruptly brought to a halt by the 1924 outbreak of bubonic plague giving rise to the need to exercise population control, a control exercised by the creation of the Lagos Executive Development Board in 1929 whose first works were to be seen in the new Yaba Estate on the mainland outskirts.

In 1946, Cameroun links with Nigeria from Kumba were proposed and in 1950 an important West African Conference on Surface Transport took place at Dschang in Cameroun. In May 1972, orientation of the road axes laid to the colonial pattern came under very close scrutiny and from 1974, pan-African considerations were at the forefront. Fifteen African States attended the ECA Conference in Niamey and heard that it was still quicker to travel from Bamako to Brazzaville via Paris. Two trunk routes were born, 5500 km west-east, Dakar-Fort Lamy (now Ndjamena) through Mauritania, Mali, Upper Volta, Nigeria and Cameroun and; 4500 km Dakar-Lagos through Guinea, Sierra Leone, Liberia, Ivory Coast, Ghana, Togo and Dahomey. Three years earlier, Algerians had completed 470 kms of the trans-Saharan highway projected to connect their country with Nigeria. Contract with the Niger border was due in 1978 and construction through Niger was to be financed by Nigeria who was building upwards from the Atlantic coast to meet the south bound team. Bituminous surfacing had by no means extended to the whole length of the highways towards the close of 1977. Dakar-Lagos had become Nouakchott (Mauritania) – Lagos.

Forty-five per cent of the land area of ECOWAS (Economic Community of West African States) was held by three landlocked members — Mali, Niger and Upper Volta (now Burkina Faso). A further highway was reccognised — Lagos-Mombasa but was never realised.

This introduction to the subject of Nigeria's road networks is concluded by a quotation, in part, from the 1979 Chairman of the British "Railway Development Society" in connection with British motorways and the call there for still further investment.

> Motor tax revenue from all vehicles using 80% of our motorways is about £100,000 per mile per annum. The cost of police patrols, accidents, gritting and general maintenance is roughly £37,000. The retail value of the agricultural products which are lost is about £40,000, leaving only £23,000 to service a capital debt ranging from £2 million to £4 million per mile. In strict commercial terms, motorways are very uneconomic. The Department of Transport emphasises the social and economic value of the time savings that they provide. A few do, but the majority transfer the time delays to the bigger towns and cities much to the annoyance of local road users.

In any analysis the parallel in Nigeria must be borne in mind.

Distances between Towns

It is essential to appreciate the size of the country if a grasp is to be gained of the distances involved. To that end a typical distance chart in kilometres is produced based on a Federal Survey information of the routes open 31/12/1978. In order not to cloud the issue with too many figures I have designed the aid to reflect Federal and State capitals only.

cantonment. By 1926, the Public Works Department (PWD), as distinct from Native Authority (NA), had become responsible for 2,970 miles in the whole country and it was 1930 before there were 3,775 miles of bituminous highway. In 1927, plans were drawn up for a rate of trunk road expansion

```
Abeokuta
283   Akure
1150  816   Bauchi
317   171   891   Benin
767   621   1004  493   Calabar
574   428   742   257   278   Enugu
77    206   1070  303   520   560   Ibadan
84    343   1204  324   774   581   134   Ikeja
240   200   911   401   851   658   159   293   Ilorin
1017  684   132   760   872   610   938   1170  779   Jos
837   799   412   788   1036  774   758   891   599   280   Kaduna
1088  1048  303   1051  1298  1035  1007  1141  848   420   262   Kano
102   304   1213  333   784   591   143   19    303   1082  901   1151  Lagos
1598  1280  464   1355  1467  1204  1534  1667  1374  595   876   576   1677  Maiduguri
993   582   470   509   534   272   922   822   865   358   502   758   887   933   Makurdi
665   634   591   608   861   599   594   727   434   459   299   505   737   442   443   Minna
560   415   880   243   201   148   555   566   669   748   912   1175  576   1344  410   737   Owerri
673   526   977   356   198   251   658   679   846   845   1009  1271  689   1440  507   833   113   Port Harcourt
972   932   779   1022  1527  1274  892   1025  732   647   483   549   1035  1125  1118  676   1413  1509  Sokoto
1561  1280  418   1109  1134  871   1545  1614  1321  542   822   713   1442  439   676   1126  1010  1107  1189  Yola
```

The most central capital in terms of distance from other capitals is Kaduna. The longest capital to capital journey is 1677 km, Lagos-Maiduguri. The longest road journey in the country would be Badagry on the coast west of Lagos to Kukawa, a place of historical importance in Borno, 1922 km.

Growth of the Network

Few are gifted with the opportunity to use the cipher in the commencement of a chronology but that this is possible is because in 1900, motorable roads in Nigeria were recorded as zero in extent. In the north, 374 miles of cart roads had been completed six years later and on the outbreak of the First World War, the road mileage, to quote some examples, was:

Sokoto Province	"	2,060
Ilorin	"	1,286
Kano	"	1,197
Bauchi	"	1,069
Niger	"	432

The end of that War recorded nine miles of township metal finish roads in Kaduna

of 400 miles per annum and all officers were mustered, including three Royal Engineers, but the depression of the 30s put an end to the scheme.

In 1946, there were 0.07 miles of road per square mile or 0.92 miles per thousand head of population; twelve years later the figures had become 0.10 and 1.07 respectively. Mileages maintained took on the shape:

		1947/48	1949/50
PWD	bitumen	688	906
	gravel	5,958	6,159
NA	bitumen	17	20
	gravel	18,987	20,660
Township	bitumen	97	98
	gravel	198	192
	total	25,945	28,035

so that in the last year, bitumen finish accounted for 3.7%, a reminder that whilst construction was progressing, quality was not. Little further progress had been made by 1952. Regional Development Boards participated in extending the roads to 40,000 miles at a cost of £8.5m on a ten-year period. Regional Development Boards took a hand.

In the first year, it was stated that Nigeria had attained a high density figure, for Africa, by achieving seventy-seven miles of road per 1000 square miles of territory and in looking at other African figures for 1977, this was no exaggeration. In the same year, route mileage became classified and the 1953 figures were:

	North	West	East	Southern Cameroun	Total
Trunk Road "A"	3,496	672	710	329	5,207
Trunk Road "B"	4,232	1,038	536	264	6,070
Local	9,631	1,336	6,383	118	17,468
Total	17,359	3,046	7,629	711	28,745

Although the North had the lion's share, it was the East that was to develop faster.

By 1958, maintained roads were PWD 11,420, NA 25,300, total 36,720 miles, of which 10.6% were tarred. At the time of hand-over by the British to the Nigerians, total mileage had reached 41,065, 13.2% tarred. The main tarred routes were Lagos-Ilorin, Ibadan-Port Harcourt, Onitsha-Abakaliki, Gusau-Sokoto, Jibiya-Katsina-Kano-Wudil, and Kano-Potiskum-Maiduguri. Mileages in the early 60s, now without Cameroun, were:

	1961	1963
Lagos	182	204
Western Nigeria	10,539	10,550
Eastern Nigeria	14,032	17,539
Northern Nigeria	20,166	21,135
Total	44,919	49,428

and the percentage tarred had risen to 15.2%. Trunk "A" roads connected Lagos and State capitals and ports and were PWD maintained; trunk "B" roads connected Provisional and Divisional centres and were maintained by the State. All other roads fell to the lot of the local authorities. By 30th September 1974, "A" roads stood at 6,541 miles and on the following day which was of course an anniversary, the Government announced that they would take over and reclassify 10,000 miles of "B" roads. In 1972, total mileage had stood at 50,000 so in the last twelve years of British rule, route length had grown 58.3% and in the first twelve years of Nigerian rule, 21.8%.

The Nigerian Government must certainly have appreciated that work remained to be done as in their Second Five-Year Plan they announced that their intention was to legislate for a total of 30,000 km of "A" roads. They had however gone metric and the new total was but an increase of the order of 13%. They therefore geared themselves up faster and at the conclusion of the Third Five-Year Plan in 1980, aimed at a total of 96,500 km, 60,216 miles, an increase of 20% spread over eight years. Twenty-five per cent of the latest total was to be tarred. By July 1996, "A" roads had assumed 18,750 miles of the target.

The meaning of "A" roads was now to embrace any road joining two or more state capitals. The expenditure incurred in the previous Five Year Plan had amounted to ₦4500 million and there was no doubt that the look of the country was being changed. But in her endeavours, how did Nigeria shape with other African nations? Twenty-three African countries reported-up-to date statistics from which it was possible to arrive at road length per unit of area. In 1977, Nigeria had 0.1050 km of road per square kilometre of territory. Only six of the twenty-three nations had a greater density. They were Ghana, Ivory Coast, Rhodesia, South Africa, Tunisia and Uganda.

Vehicles

It is not the intention to produce a history of the vehicle upon the Nigerian roads but merely to make some reference to the increasingly heavy user. There were already thirty car manufacturers in the United Kingdom by 1901 and within the decade, Lugard in the north experimented with bullock carts while Egerton in the south got up to 35 mph to Oyo. Cars appeared after the First World War and the Emir of Kano, Ooni of Ife, Alafin of Oyo, and Alake of Abeokuta each possessed Rolls Royce or Daimler by 1930.

Private cars including taxi exceeded commercial vehicles in new registrations in later years:

	Commercial	Car/Taxi
1937	1,819	822
1948	1,993	2,199
1953	4,159	3,783
1958	7,220	7,459
1963	5,490	11,559

Total commercial vehicles numbered 2,829 in 1931, 5,113 in 1937, and 10,600 in 1953. Total cars numbered 12,300 in 1953. Vehicle life was around 2½ to 3¼ years. New registrations were taken out evenly round the country for trucks but were concentrated in Lagos for cars and taxis. Traffic surveys in 1938 showed that the heaviest traffic passed via the lagoon to the Ejinrin-Ibadan road whereas the intensity had in 1951 shifted to the Lagos-Abeokuta road. A 1940 census revealed 10,000 cyclists a day plied Uyo-Calabar, usually laden with palm oil. Motor traffic over the only bridge to the north from the Lagos coast, the Jebba railway bridge, averaged 26/day in 1951, 85 in 1955, and 248 in 1959. The decade prior to Independence showed the manner of the leap:

	Commercial	Car/Taxi	Total
1948	8,107	6,626	14,737
1959	24,561	28,593	53,154

At 23.7% increase p.a, the rate exceeded that of Great Britain or USA. Little wonder that the "omolankes" (wooden hand carts) were driven off the streets of Lagos. Specific permits were requested for trucks over 8 tons gross weight but from the late 50s lorries were classified in accordance with the bridge classification of the roads over which they were to operate and it became possible to run 25 ton vehicles. By 1979, Government had very wisely decided on the installation of road weighbridges.

To help the Lagosian find his way into the right bus, Zarpas employed a large "A" for Apapa and "Y" for Yaba for his destinations. This is not a new idea because Glasgow trams had a similar principle using a colour code. Nigeria drove like Britain — on the left but on the 2nd April 1972, without fuss or bother, she became right hand drive in company with her neighbours. When the Expressway was opened between Lagos and Ibadan, a toll tariff was rightly raised so that the user could contribute to upkeep. The single deck buses with destination "Nigeria" are an inter-State service. British Leyland were to supply Marathons and trailers for a National Freight Company.

In 1973, vehicles on the road numbered 232,000, a far greater increase than the increase in the road network and people reading this statistics and familiar with township congestion and the traffic on the north-bound highways from Lagos think that the country is congested. They are quite wrong. A vehicle is met once only in every 650 metres of road.

Technical

The Public Works Department was created out of the Department of Surveyor-General in 1896 and a Road Division with one officer was created in 1905. A good laterite road cost £750/mile and a good metalled surface £1000. Among the first steel bridges in the north were those pitched across the Koriga and tributaries on the road to Kaduna in 1906, lengthy jobs of 118ft. and 80ft. span. By 1907, there were seventeen road engineers in Southern Nigeria and among them was A.R. Milliken. No "Old Coaster" needs to be reminded of this name; a road up an escarpment out of Enugu was accomplished in safety by the European but the object of demand in the late 70s by the Nigerian for improved grading was because of the death and destruction resulting from their driving.

In 1915, the Director in the north was P.H. Lamb soon nicknamed by the Hausas, Dan Mahaukaci — "Son of a Madman" — because he called for everything to be done at the double. In 1939, Taffy Jones came on the scene as the first Town Engineer and his name became a legend as he earned the highest memorials on his death in 1949. All that was good in Ibadan, buildings and roads, was built by him.

In 1917, Government decided that the roads were not wide enough so they coined the new construction "Broad Gauge". In 1929, the Colonial Development Fund was instituted. In 1930, half the cost of road maintenance went on brushing. This simple reference needs explanation for the uninitiated.

In the dry season, problems of corrugation

arise with earth roads. Longitudinal waves are born from movement of gravel particles after fines have been blown away and a special brush in the form of a delta drawn at waist level was designed. In 1953, scarifiers wore down their teeth 50% in the first 24 hours in dealing with corruga- tions.

Roads had been classified trunk "A", trunk "B", and NA from 1927 and in the 50s, the first assumed more and more the meaning attached to "main sketal". The Provincial Engineer was the responsible party, direct or as agent. The technical specification, as distinct from the administrative "A" and "B" classification, was:

	Class I	Class II
Minimum distance inner edge sidedrain to road centre line	20 ft.	20 ft.
Top width of embankment	32 "	22 "
Bottom width usable road formation in cutting	32 "	22 "
Width of carriageway	22 "	12 "
Width of verge	5 "	5 "

These dimensions were governed by the volume of traffic and not the permissible loading which was determined by the bridging enroute. An intensity of 100 vehicles per day warranted Class II and 300 per day Class I.

The soil conditions varied from pest in the southern swamps, through stable sand clays of the forest area, to laterites of the middle belt, and sand-silts of the more northerly regions. A gravel pavement 4 to 6 in. thick provided the base course. In the south, hard surfacing soils were not easily come by but a sand-clay, after weathering of dry density 115 ibs/ft^3, will accept a bituminous coating. In the north east jigalin pavements, white limestone were used but this area held the black cotton soil, less easily susceptible to solution. Black cotton soil from Gold Coast, Rhodesia, India and Israel had been examined at the Rothampstead experimental station in Hertfordshire. Bituminous carpets took the form of two-coat dressings, 0.3 and 0.2 gallons per square yard and there was little need to employ the more expensive premix type. Work had been completed on a 60-mile premix carpet contract laid by Barber-Greene equipment in the south in the late 50s and the excellent results had suggested a further 193 miles of such treatment.

Sir Hernert Walker, a Director of the PWD, laid it down in 1948 that earth roads would bear a traffic of forty vehicles a day, gravel up to a hundred, bituminous in excess of one hundred. A single carriageway was suitable for five hundred vehicles a day. Seen from the light of transport running costs, there was another picture; 6d/ton mile was an average expenditure for a truck over gravel and 3d/ton mile over bituminous. Work on classification of agricultural soils had commenced in 1952 and forty-four soil types had been distinguished in an area of Southern Nigeria subject to the same rainfall. Specifications for grading by sieve size based on A.S.T.M. were laid down and California Bearing Ratio (CBR %) measured for gravels, hard pan laterite and quartz gravels, the maximum CBR varying from eight soaked to one hundred unsoaked.

Moisture content on the Ibadan-Ife road varied between 2.8 and 14, Secretariat-Bodija-Aerodrome road had a minimum depth of water table of 1ft. 3in. and moisture content lay between 2.8 and 11. CBR was devised by the American Corp of Engineers following airfield operation during Word War II, much like the hardness number adopted by physicists and engineers and the Western Region specified 80% CBR after 24 hours soaking. CBR falls with increased moisture content in typical nodular lateritic gravels.

The term "laterite" is little understood. It was first used by Dr Buchanan in 1800 to describe red/yellow clay-like soils of India. The word today is understood to embrace a range of soils containing hard concretionary ferruginous materials. The best binding materials were the Dendrital quartz gravels found in Ogun, Oyo and Ondo States. Where the material did not match up more expensive alternatives of soil cement, soil lime, or sand bitumen were used as stabilisers. Over the 100 vehicle/day mark the bituminous standard was:

100-300	vpd	12" bituminous surface
300-1000	"	18" "
1000-2000	"	22" "
over 2000	"	a bituminous carpet

The Onitsha Bridge over the Niger on the Benin-Enugu road opened in 1965

Jamaica was an example of costly roads because of the inferiority of the soils.

New bituminous work in 1949/1950 cost £1181/mile, risen because of the cost of materials, to £1676/mile in 1952/1953. These figures were cheaper than in other tropical countries. Cost of government-maintained roads outside townships in 1953/53 was:

Bituminous surface	£156.5/mile
All season gravel	77.5 "
Dry season earth	8.3 "

Opening of the 2nd Carter Bridge in 1931

Twenty-five years before, the first figure had been £40. 1953 had seen a great fillip to maintenance with the aid of the Colonial Development Corporation (CDC) because of fears of cocoa crop evacuation not being possible over the then state of the highways. In the nine years 1945/46-1953/54, highway expenditure on capital and maintenance averaged 4.67% of the national cake. A 3½ month survey based on the American practice of awarding points under designated headings to arrive at priorities for improvement attention was carried out in the early 50s; such a survey, it was said at PWD HQ, removed the matter from the heads of the politicians!

Bridges were single carriageway on the grounds of economy and not so designed simply to try out the patience of later day Nigerians when competing for position. Trunk roads in 1949 included 2,200 bridges from 20 to 1,200ft. in length with an aggregate length of 85,000ft. Only 10% exceeded 100ft. in span. Up to 50ft. span superstructure was probably reinforced concrete, medium spans prestressed, or longer spans steel. It was realised from 1955 that where density was over 300 vpd over, there would have to be expansion.

When steel bridges came into use in quantity, Nigeria adopted the standard designs of steel spans for light loading recommended by the Crown Agents. This loading was for a train of 4-ton axle loads 10ft. apart with allowance for impact and permitted the passage of vehicles of 8 tons gross. With the introduction of longer vehicles, the aftermath of the War saw a policy change in favour of twelve units of British Standard "A" loading. This loading is a train of axles at 10ft. intervals in the order of 4.2-12-5.4 tons. In due course, all the more important road bridges needed strengthening to take 20-ton gross loading. Costs of standard type bridge work varied considerably from £40 to over £100 per foot of length, depending on the bridge parameters. A Crown Agents Bridge Team visited the country and prepared schemes for strengthening and by 1955, 200 bridges had been brought up to standard.

When the IBRD reported on the roads, the West African Joint Overseas Group of Engineers pointed out that it was incorrect to think that Benin sand could only be stabilised with cement and that roads in the north required watertight seals just as much as those in the south. They added that road overseers should attend maintenance schools, that bridge abutments should be built with double carriageway in mind, but they agreed that more work should be let out to contract because of the shortage of skilled personnel.

In the mid 1960s an African Road Transport Symposium held at Lome proposed a standard width of nine metres. The Crown Agents ordered from Redpath Brown & Co. Ltd. their standard 100 ft. through girder trussed bridge for Western Nigeria. In 1977 they sold £391,000 worth of Bailey bridges to Nigeria and one of them went up over the Imo River. The Callender Hamilton unit bridge first erected at Dulas, Montogomeryshire, made many sellings in Africa of from 50 to 200 ft. spans. The heaviest single component was the gusset plate at 164 lbs. The Government's Second Five-Year Plan put more money into maintenance plant and voted £27.57 million for on-going projects, £6.55 million for feasibility studies. In March 1977, the Federal Ministry of Works was controlling 144 separate contracts involving 11,250 km.

In the last quarter of the century, the most spectacular works have been those now to be described. First proposed as a transporter bridge but killed off by tests in the UK when it was found that the platform "took charge", some device had to replace the ferries between Abakaliki and Ikom to open up communications with Cameroun on what was to become the through route from Algiers via Lagos to Leopoldville and Mombassa. The Cross River had to be bridged and the site chosen was Ajasso on the borders south of Ikom where a wind of 50 mph had to be tolerated. A suspension bridge of 350ft. with approach spans of 48ft. 9in. right bank and 95ft. 9in. left bank had all the advantages. The superstructure included a Warren truss as a stiffening girder in bays of 16ft. 3in. and each main cable took 170 tons breaking stress being pre-stressed in England to avoid take up on accepting the load. Dorman Long contracted and the Crown Agents appointed Coode & Partners as the Consulting Engineers on behalf of the PWD. The bridge took a live load of 5.4 tons at 10ft. spacing and was completed in October 1952, a Blondin Cableway easing erection problems over the two banks. The Ajasso bridge added to the few Nigerian suspension bridges, one of which was my unfortunate responsibility to prepare for demolition in World War II.

7.30 am on Carter Bridge in 1956

In 1958, the Maiduguri-Fort Lamy road bridged the river Gambaru 143 km on the way by a single carriageway structure of nine 40ft. spans. In the following year, the river Taraba was bridged by 26 spans of 1,100ft. total in Adamawa Province. At Independence, the Five Cowrie Creek bridge in Lagos took upon itself the name "Independence Bridge" but the public went on calling it by that name which had survived from the days of the Sanitary Tram. The Niger was bridged at Onitsha linking herself with Asaba by 8 × 420ft. + 8 × 140ft. with a designed carriageway of 36 ft. and centre truss, the opening at Christmas of 1965 being one of the last public performances by Alhaji Tafawa Balewa, the Prime Minister, before his assassination in January 1966. In 1967, the bridge was damaged in the civil war.

The Apapa Road/Ijora Causeway complex, designed for the level but built as an elevated 8-mile carriageway and ramp with 7-mile service roads, was opened by General Gowon on 6th January 1973 construction having started in 1967 and carried on despite the civil war. All restraints to the 32,000 vehicles per day movement were removed by the provision of flyovers. The elevated portion consisted of table tops alternating with suspended spans and around 4000 piles were driven, an average of 112 ft. The depth was expected because roads had settled 8ft. in eight years in the area and was simply the railway experience of the 1920s all over again. Scott Wilson Kirkpatrick & Partners attended to detail design, Guffanti of Milan erected the complex to supervision by the Federal Ministry of Works (FMOW). The cost was ₦23.658 million. The project was a sister project to the Eko bridge.

The Eko bridge was erected in 1968 by Julius Berger Nigeria Ltd. with German aid and required much displacement of the local inhabitants. Ten years before, the Road Research Laboratory, England, carried out a survey designed to relieve congestion on the only mainland bridge, Carter bridge, by the building of a second bridge across the lagoon from Lagos Island to the mainland. Of the sites suggested, the Apongbon/Adeniji Adele road, Lagos, to Ijora carrying over Ebute Metta Creek was the one chosen with 25ft. clearance above high water, running onto Western Avenue. The bridge was designed for 2 × 24ft. carriageways with central reservation and cycle and pedestrian provision and was to be carried by 200ft. spans eight in number on 150ft. driven prestressed concrete piles.

The Lagos-Ibadan Expressway became the first modern high speed motorway cutting short the distance covered by the previous routes through Shagamu and Abeokuta. Tenders were invited in 1972 and contracts were awarded in May 1974 for a start to be made on 1st October 1974 with scheduled completion date of December 1977. The route was designed to reduce journey time between Apapa ports and Ibadan and, to expedite construction, was let in three stretches:

Ikeja to near Shagamu	43.5 km
Near Shagamu to Alapako	38.6 km
Alapako to Ibadan	27.4 km
	109.5 km

The three contractors were Berger, Strabag, and Dumez. Six points only gave interchange by clover leaf or flying junction. Reinforced concrete box or pipe culverts took care of drainage and there were twenty-five major structures in the design. The longest river crossing was the Ogun. Because of very poor soil conditions, it was found necessary to construct a bridge of almost 730m on piled foundations. The superstructure was a box girder beam prestressed in both planes 3.7m high, 16.24m wide at the top and 5.52m wide at the bottom. Instead of employing falsework, taktschiebeverfahren (cast and push) was employed to project the sixteen spans onto their piers. Other major structures included the 7-span Olowoira Viaduct, the 90m Ojota interchange, the 109m box cell culvert at river Ibu Ogere and the 25m span at the river Ona.

The geometric design of the expressway provided for dual two-lane carriageways each 7.32m wide with a paved shoulder each of 3.05m, the whole set off with a central median. The arrangement is such that in the future, a dual three-lane carriageway can be made. Both horizontal and vertical curves and the gradients have been designed to allow for a safe operating speed of over 100 kph. Designed by consultants, the three contracts were supervised by the Federal Ministry of Works. Three thousand five hundred and sixty-two acres of land had to be acquired and the cost escalated to ₦175 million on the discovery that soft peat soil required a concrete deck on piled foundations.

Wimpey secured the Jos-Bauchi road contract 7.3m carriageway, 2.65m shoulders which had 150mm deep laterite sub-base covered with 50mm dust crushed rock base placed on wet mix. Julius Berger completed, ahead of schedule in 1977, the two-lane dual carriageway Niger bridge at Jebba, cheek by jowl with the railway bridge, valued with approaches at ₦15.8 million, supervised by the FMOW. The work consisted of two bridges across the north and south channels. The north was a five span of 45.72m each and the south a fourteen span of 45.72m each. There was provision for walkway and cattle track.

The Crown Agents supervised the 90-mile Funtua-Mando road construction followed by the Manchok-Lere road which required back-up services for bridging design. The Stevin Group in 1977 tackled the 50-mile plus 3-bridge Zaria-Pambegua road not far away from the old Bauchi Light Railway. Nigeria continued to be short of planning engineers and much development work had no choice but to be put out to foreign contract. The Ogun was again to be bridged at Abeokuta. The South-eastern States were to have the longest dual carriageway in Nigeria — Enugu-Port Harcourt.

The Murtala Muhammed bridge on the new route, Okene-Kaduna over the Niger at Jamata, right bank, Edeha, left bank, just short of Koton Karifi, ₦36.3 million, is 1.754 km long and has a dual carriageway two-lane 7.32m wide each way with a concrete partition in the middle Both sides of the bridge make provision for pedestrian and cattle traffic. The concrete guard separation is 47.5 cm high and 35 cm thick. It cost ₦38 million in the end and was supposed to ease use of the Makurdi bridge but to me, there is no connection. The road is to traverse Abuja.

Inter-State Routes

An efficient road transportation system is an amalgam of many factors and here will be measured the success or otherwise that Nigeria has made of it. Fifty years were to pass before the stamp of modern planning was first to be seen so that early history is modest and isolated. In 1894, contact with Ijebu-Ode was established by road from Epe and Ejinrin on the Lagos lagoon. Township roads were constructed in Otta, Ibadan, Iwo and Oyo, all in the south-west in 1898 and a year later Ejinrin was linked with Ibadan and a connection, Otta-Ilaro, was in hand but was hampered by the absence of quarries.

In 1903, the Zungeru to Kano bullock cart road over an old trade route was put in hand with the aid of traction engines, ramping lesser streams, trestling the larger. Road making in "dead level" Borno was known to be easier but ballast was lacking though the oxen were a fine breed. To aid tin evacuation, Loko to Keffi was driven in 1906 along with Bida to Bari-Juko to connect the tramway but in 1908, BKR construction was given the go-ahead and the road out of Zungeru was stopped. In the south, they thought of wheeled traffic and built the first trunk road from Ibadan railhead to Oyo in 1905. The Warri area was "touched" and the Ebute Metta road got as far north as Agege with Ibadan as the ultimate destination.

Remetalling was done in 1908 and a formation was completed Ebute Metta to Apapa. Awka-Udi, in the east, was culverted and Oyo-Iseyin in the west was bridged. Ilesha "reached" Oshogbo and Benin "dropped down" to Warri but thereafter there was little progress for three years as the railway attracted all the labour. To pave the way for the Bauchi Light Railway, Rigachikun was road-linked with Naraguta and then tin took a new exit. In 1911, the Zungeru road was reopened to mile 22 and a survey commenced from Zaria on the beginning of a

Sokoto artery. In the south, the only developments were Abeokuta-Meko designed surely to assist smugglers or hunters. The introduction of Iju waterworks stimulated Lagos-Abeokuta by 1911 and Ibadan by 1922 with Oshogbo and Benin connections. In 1912, a visitor from India said "in the north you overburden your carts and the bullocks die and in the south you provide an inferior surface and your cars die."

The Road to Keffi near Abuja

At the end of the first decade, you could reach Sokoto or Maiduguri from Lagos, Kabba from the delta regions and Ogoja from Calabar. Only the rivers flowed through Gongola and the Benue remained untapped along with Chad. Kano was shut off from the south east and Lagos to the south east was by water carriage. No roads penetrated international boundaries. In other words, construction was modest in great areas and non est in areas larger still. The moment you wished to travel beyond Zungeru you were in for horse and hardship.

By 1914, "surgery" had been carried out at Kaduna and the most important artery was to be the railway feeder, Sokoto-Zaria via Gusau. In the south, Ibadan-Ijebu-Ode was completed. Through communication established, Benin-Asaba, by the bridging of the Osiomo and an Onitsha-Itu route, developed. In 1915, passengers still took railway or river out of Lagos. In 1916, Owerri-Okigwe-Afikpo road was opened for motor traffic and good progress was made on Ibadan-Ilesha-Akure, having got to mile 74 by 1917, which aimed at an Ibadan-Cross River trunk. 1917 saw Milliken Hill and a year later, Kaduna-Zaria whilst Jos-Bukuru was remodelled. 1919 became a year of achievement as it became possible, just, to motor from Lagos to Port Harcourt. Jos-Bauchi went on slowly along with Udi (Enugu)-Abakaliki. The road north from Lagos remained the only exit for thirty years until 1946 when the Ikorodu alternative was constructed.

Through the early 20s, the railway maintained the road across the swamps to Apapa. It is astonishing that when the Apapa Wharf was built in 1926, there was to be no bypass until 1953 to relieve the combined Lagos and Apapa traffic where they met at Ebute Metta. Clearly, the increased traffic that had generated an Apapa substitution for Iddo was not taken to its logical conclusion and this was because the railway had its finger in the pie; right through the 30s care was to be taken not to parallel the railway with roads. The worst offspring of such a policy was Kano to Zaria where one sets off north-west instead of south-west to reach the destination.

In 1926 there was a scheme for improvement. There was to be a north/south via Jebba and three west/east, Shaki-Bamenda, Kishi-Yola, Bida-Yola, as well as a north lateral Sokoto-Dikwa with links from Lokoja and Keffi. A 1929 review added the needed Port Harcourt-Jos. Then came the slump and only the best of intentions remained as a memorial. Ilorin pioneered on within its own provincial boundaries. On the 13th May 1929, the first pile for Carter bridge No 2 was driven; the official opening took place on the 22nd October 1931.

Before 1933, the Kano-Maiduguri road ran to the north from Wudil through Azare and Misau where it joined the second attempt but then ran on as an all-season miserable track through Dikwa to the Cameroun border. A 22ft. tarred road led to Bama. In 1933, all season roads were advertised as Lagos-Ibadan, Ife-Onitsha-Port Harcourt; Benin-Warri, Owerri-Uyo-Oron Ferry-Calabar; Onitsha-Abakaliki, Enugu-Makurdi-Lafia; Ibadan-Shaki, Oyo-Ilorin- Lafiagi; Owo-Lokoja, Dida-Kontagora, Argungu-Sokoto-Zaria-Kaduna; Kaduna-Jos-Potiskum, and Kano-Katsina-Niger border.

In 1937, the plans of 1926 were brought to the forefront again; there were to be six major routes the newcomers reaching Biu, Jalingo, Yola and Bamenda. The Kaduna was ferried at the Mokwa-Bida axis. Someone went Umuahia-London over the desert and clocked it at 4213 miles. East of Ogoja, not even the bicycle could make it. Adamawa was expensive with bridging needs. Flooding east of Maiduguri in 1940 required a battery of 12,000 men at work. The collapse of the French in World War II precipitated a demand that key routes be all season, notably, Birnin Gwari-Kusheriki. In 1944, Gombe-Biu and Wukari-Jalingo were planned but failed to get off the ground so a ten-year Trunk Development Plan was devised the main ingredient of which pudding was the entirely new Lagos-Benin, via Ikorodu, Kano-Zaria direct despite railway objections, and the Calabar-Mamfe, in abeyance for twenty-three years. The 1940 map however still showed great communication gaps NW, NE, and through the "Middle Belt".

In 1951, the ECA provided £700,000 to improve the Kano-Maiduguri road the decision having been taken, much to Woodward's annoyance, not to build a railway branch line. Date palms grew in the region. The 104-mile Calabar-Mamfe road had but five miles of gap left. Potiskum became a crossroads, camel by day, hyena by night. The World Bank came on the scene in 1953 and proposed heavy traffic arteries which on examination turned out to be railway feeders, the only really new designation being Sapele-Ibadan. They recommended a stop to the 200-mile Bamenda-Yola road because a route from Takum would become available. They mentioned the 12-unit BS bridge and concentrated more beyond railway terminals. They foresaw three S/N and five W/E arteries as being the real requirement. The canoe, reminder of Hugh Clapperton's second expedition, was replaced by a 600ft. bridge over the Oli, present day principal river of Borgu Game Reserve, between Kaiama and Bussa. By 1960, the map was much more dense but only south of latitude 10° north. Carter bridge number two had a facelift to its approaches.

In 1959/60, everything necessary was again emphasised with accent on the Onitsha Niger bridge and the Shagamu-Benin road. With only eighteen miles to go, the latter had been stopped two years before but was to go ahead under a new scheme of contractor finance. Tegina-Daura was to be bitumenised giving a proper surfacing to the A1, Lagos to the northern border.

By 1963, despite the building in the end of a railway to Maiduguri, tardy recognition had come to the problems of fish evacuation from Lake Chad and a survey was in hand from Kukawa to Baga on the peninsular strip. In January 1965, Ove Arup & Partners were instructed to make a feasibility study of the road networks of Western Nigeria expected to take two years, financed by the UN, IBRD, and the Western Regional Government. By March 1965, the Onitsha bridge was nearing completion and work was to begin on Sokoto-Yelwa and Bauchi-Yola improvements. Thus the basic pattern of two N/S and four E/W trunk routes had been established. With the building of the rail, Numan was in touch with Gombe instead of "a weary 500 miles from Jos via Damaturu". By 1969, Lokoja and Idah, both on the Niger, had a laterite connection with Enugu.

Benue has always thought of itself as neglected and the Second Five-Year Plan of 1970-74 provided ₦78 million to iron out existing trouble spots. The east-west Nigeria part of the International Highway, with USAID, Ajasso-Lagos via Onitsha, was divided into six sections plus the Onitsha bridge. Italians in 1972 tackled Birnin Gwari-Funtua which would lop eighty miles off the Lagos-Katsina route and in 1974, Borini Prono Company (Nigeria) Ltd. commenced reconstruction of a 70-mile length of the Zaria-Gusau road which included at the Zaria end, a 4-mile bypass. Rivers State, haven of waterways, in September '74 planned a Port Harcourt-Ahoada-Patani shortened route to Lagos. Anyone with knowledge of the delta would know that this was unnecessary competition with coastwise shipping.

Two projects of Freeman Fox & Partners interested me. The first was Ilorin-Kishi improvement. This route via Kaiama links across to the Republic of Benin and to my mind taps the wildest of Oyo country; one trusts that in the interests of conservation it will be a link and not a tap. The second was Gusau-Jibiya. This is right on the Niger Republic border.

Other roads in the 1970-74 Plan included Calabar-Ikom-Katsina Ala, Warri-Benin-Auchi-Kaduna, and Kwoi-Kafanchan-Manchok in Birom country on the edge of the Plateau. The projects required the new Niger bridge near Koton Karifi and duplications of the railway bridges at Jebba and Makurdi. The last two provide grounds for both amusement and education. When erected by the British in 1916 and 1932 respectively, there was much British criticism to the effect that better sites could have been chosen. Nearly half a century later the new structures paralleled the old!

A fine new road that came out of the 1970/74 hat was the Ilorin-Kabba twisting and turning between the inselbergs. Benue bridges at Numan and Yola were also required. With all this accomplished and the ports of Warri, Port Harcourt and Calabar developed, pressure it was said, would be reduced on the port of Lagos. At least six years would pass however before there would be any evidence of this. The Lagos-Badagry dual carriage expressway built by Julius Berger would reduce terminal distances from eighty to thirty-six miles at a cost of ₦18 million and was opened in June 1974 by Governor Mobolaji Johnson.

Stirling Astaldi (Nigeria) Ltd. were much concerned with road development in the last two decades to the four points of the Nigerian compass. It was in the 70s that the most intensive construction was to be seen in the country although much of it got away to a slow start and there was much repetition of programmes and much vociferous dissatisfaction with rate of progress. The programme started off in early 1975 in Rivers with the east-west road to link Cross River, Rivers, and Bendel States (but this time no further) from Opuoko through Ahoada to Patani with six linking roads making much of Ahoada as a focus. The cost was ₦104.5 million with more to follow and the length under construction was 480 km. West of Degema, the Orashi had to be bridged, two-lane, and such was the nature of the terrain that sixty-five bridges and 1,585 box or pipe culverts were required in all, short of the survey of one remaining route. Design was apportioned out between Deltaconsult, Guffanti and Dumez, and construction undertaken by Monier, Guffanti, and Dumez.

At the end of 1975, the Republic of Niger was seeking tenders for the construction of Maradi-Nigeria (Katsina link) and Zinder-Nigeria (Daura link) and in 1977 the most go-ahead of the International Highways was the Mfun-towards Enugu from Cameroun but by 1979 Nigeria was financing 366 kms of such roads in Benin, Niger and Cameroun, the longest being from the Kongolan terminal from Algiers bordering Zinder.

The dual carriageway Falomo bridge linking Ikoyi with Victoria Island, one kilometre in length, was opened in the second half of 1976. In Sokoto State, Illela-Gada bordering Niger on the north and Kaingiwa-Kamba bordering Niger on the west, were awarded in 1977 along with the Gummi bridge over the Zamfara, to Taylor Woodrow. In early 1978, the Dutch Group, Stevin, were entrusted with the 110km, £25 million, 30-month task Koko (on the A1) west and north to Bunza. The ₦43 million task structure in concrete to replace Carter bridge number two was awarded Julius Berger for commencement in September 1976 against March 1980 completion. The "noble" steel structure of CB 2 would be used at the Steel Reduction Plant in Warri to be used all over again.

In May 1977, it was reported that funds had been set aside in Niger State for Bida-Kataeregi-Minna and Lemu-Kataeregi, at long last penetrating BKR territory. A month later, the Federal Military Government awarded the Ilorin-Bode Sadu A1 cut off in Kwara to Plisson Fisko (Nigeria) Ltd who were to construct the Ilorin township carriageways for completion within 2½ years. In Benue upstream of the railway bridge, the new road bridge was built by RCC (Road Construction Company (Nigeria) Ltd., a joint Nigeria/Italian company, due for completion in August 1977 at a cost of ₦28.56 million, 1170m in length and 20m wide, a concrete structure on concrete piers carrying the A3. A further ₦37 million was spent in 1977 on Benue networks built by Singhai Construction Ltd., Shinco Nigeria Ltd., and Gyado & Steers Nigeria Ltd. Two years later, Makurdi-Yandev cost £16.3 million and Lafia-Shendam tapping little known country cost ₦29.9 million. Still in Benue, the Katsina Ala bridge, ₦21.8 million, built by Borini Prono, was opened by Major-General Muhammed Shuwa towards the end of the 70s; 1200m in length and 20.12m wide 4-lane carriageway with provision for cattle and pedestrains.

The ₦29.6 million Ogoja-Katsina Ala highway was due for completion by December 1979. The Katsina Ala-Mutum Biu road — the other way — was completed in June '78 at a cost of ₦42.7 million. In 1977, Sokol (Nigeria) Ltd; Mensa Construction Co. and

George Wimpey & Co. (Nigeria) won contracts for the Gombe-Darazo, Dindima (railway feeder)-Mainamaji and Magama-Gumau roads respectively, in all worth ₦40 million. The last road had been designed by Ove Arup & Partners (Nigeria) and included bridges over two major rivers. The first improved penetrated territory, the second led to the Yankari Game Reserve, the third tapped rural presserves.

In Kaduna in 1977, Abee Engineering & Construction Ltd. won a ₦12 million construction of Kabau-Dutsin Wai-Makarfi road, oil Bauchi Light Railway (BLR) country. The only all weather road tapping Federal Capital Territory is the Bida-Keffi through Abuja and the Emir and his horse is often forced to the forest path. The Okene-Kaduna road will solve the N/S axis but there will have to be one east/west. A London/Nigeria partnership, Fawcett/ Okeke, was in September 1977 designing a £50 million 106-km Warri-Benin as trunk road A2 including an urban bypass and eleven bridges, two over major waterways feeding the delta.

Stirling Astaldi was to finish the Benesheikh-Kari road in Borno in July 1978 at ₦61.4 million (Kari is on the A3) and was to finish in 1980 the ₦45 million 150 km Potiskum-Gasua across the Komadugu Gana. The latter road required a hot sand bitumen base course with a premix overlay.

In Gongola, the ₦30 million Jimeta bridge by Yola over the Benue was due to be opened in October 1978, again a concrete massif but with uniform depth side panels. This provided passage for the A4 between Gombi and Jimeta, a latter construction priced at ₦17.8 million. Also to be bridged to the NW is the Numan bridge over the Benue with a contract value of ₦12.4 million, a junction for five routes. The Numan bridge replaced the single truck ferry in 1979. Further bridges in Gongola over the Benue were to be provided at Lau and Ibi and of these the second was the most important. ₦113 million went on auxiliary roads in 1979, two years after W.S. Atkins & Partners had been asked to design a 75 km bituminous trunk road, Takum-river Suntai, a continuation from Katsina Ala in the direction of Jalingo.

1979 ended with seven major criss-cross highways planned and 1980 started with the President taking a personal interest. It was realised that maintenance provision had not matched the required proportions and that the new highways, because of a lack of understanding of the forces of inertia by drivers, had become a graveyard for vehicles and a temporary cemetery for human beings. Education was as much required as the artery if the ₦4500 million spent in the last Five-Year Plan was not to be a part investment for bereavement. One hundred and ninety roads in nineteen States were to be rehabilitated.

But whether built, planned, projected or maintained, plans do at some time come to fruition. So what has been accomplished in eighty years? First the ferries: ferries are still necessary at Lokoja to cross the Niger west to east, at Oron-Calabar to cross the Cross, at Sapele to cross the Ethiope. In such a vast country, time can surely be spared by the Nigerian for this as he maintains his heritage. And of the routes other than the expressways, there are:

A 1 Lagos-Sokoto-Niger Republic
A 2 Warri-Kano-Niger Republic
A 3 Port Harcourt-Maiduguri-Cameroun/Chad Republics
A 4 Calabar-Maiduguri
A 5 Lagos-Abeokuta-Ibadan
A 6 Jc A 232-Owerri-Aba
A 7 Ilorin-Kaiama-Benin Republic
A 8 Gembu-Toungo
A 9 Kano-Katsina-Niger Republic
A121 Jc A 1-Ijebu-Ode-Benin
A122 Ibadan-Benin; A 232 Benin-Enugu; A 343/342 Enugu-Abakaliki-Ajasso-Cameroun Republic
A123 Jc A 2-Ilorin
A125 Kontagora-Kaduna
A126 Zaria-Sokoto
A234 Abuja-Akwanga
A235 Jc A 3-Jemaa-Kaduna
A236 Rigachikun-Jos
A237 Kano-Kari
A344 Aliade-Gboko-Katsina Ala-Takum-Jalingo
A345 Jc A 4-Bauchi-Gombe-Jimeta
Unnumbered Jc A 7-Abeokuta-Iseyin

It is clear that the forest states are well provided for and equally clear that the Sudan states are less well serviced. The Niger state capital, Minna came to be served by a trunk road of "A" classification. The Benue State capital, Makurdi, suffers from no extension direct trunk road western approach. The ports are well taken care of but can the same be said of the food-producing areas in the north?

If trunk "A" roads only are produced on a map, it is seen that Niger State has insufficient provision to the south; Akure in Ondo has no north/south axis. Gongola, Borno and Sokoto require feasibility studies and when it is all over, the numbering system, a legacy of Colonial Lagos, should be scrapped in favour of a new system with reference to the compass, and continuity of direction.

The problems have been highlighted but there remains one more. The Nigeria Police are too preoccupied with customs evasion and should be trained to be more on the alert for overcrowding and overloading of vehicles. Careless driving should call for licence suspension and poster aids should call attention with graphic detail to the daily loss of life on the roads.

Chapter 7

Ports, Harbours and Terminals

The port farthest away is Shanghai, 13,517 nautical miles from Lagos. In Africa, Alexandria is 4895, Freetown 1148, Pointe Noire, 838, Cape Town, 2566 and Dar-Es-Salam 4912 nautical miles from Lagos. The distances separating the ports within Nigeria where a sea voyage is undertaken were in 1972 put at:

	Escravos Lt	Forcados	Burutu	Warri	Koko	Sapele	Akassa	Bonny	Degema	P. Harcourt	Opobo	Calabar
Lagos	126	153	158	184	171	192	221	288	330	315	315	394
Escravos Lt		36	40	46	48	69	119	186	228	213	213	292
Forcados			5	27	59	80	149	216	258	243	243	322
Burutu				32	64	85	154	221	263	248	248	327
Warri					86	107	175	242	284	269	269	348
Koko						21	167	234	276	261	261	340
Sapele							188	255	297	282	282	361
Akassa								83	125	109	109	190
Bonny									42	27	27	136
Degema										69	69	178
Port Harcourt											84	163
Opobo												101

The first "ports" were Akassa, Forcados, Calabar and Victoria and by the middle of the 19th century the order of importance was Forcados (including Burutu, Warri, Sapele), Bonny, Degema, Calabar, Brass, Akassa, Bakama and Buguma. The ports to be described fall into the following modern terminology:

Lagos Complex	Iddo, Customs, Ijora, Apapa, Tin Can Island
Delta Complex	Warri, Sapele, Koko, Burutu, Escravos, Akassa, Forcados, Benin, Pennington, Brass
Rivers Complex	Port Harcourt, Bonny, Okrika, Degema, Abonemma
Cross River	Calabar, Opobo
Cameroun under British & French Mandate	Victoria (Bota), Tiko

In 1912, fourteen "ports" were in use, without wharf or jetty. They were Obokun, Calabar, Bakama, Bonny, Buguma, Degema, Forcados, Koko, Ikang, Brass, Akassa, Lagos, Sapele and Warri. "Lagos" meant riding in the roadsteads. Ports served by ocean steamers in 1923 were Lagos, Forcados, Burutu, Warri, Sapele, Koko, Akassa, Brass, Bonny, Port Harcourt, Degema, Opobo and Calabar. In 1953, Lagos and Port Harcourt were described as "National", Sapele, Degema, Abonemma, Calabar, Victoria (Bota) and Tiko as "Regional", and Warri and Burutu as "Ocean Niger Transit".

In 1955 upon the formation of a Ports

Authority, a statutory corporation, Lagos and Port Harcourt were described as general cargo quays and Calabar, Akassa, Bonny, Burutu, Degema, Forcados, Koko, Sapele and Warri as harbours. In 1975, Lagos, Port Harcourt, Calabar, Warri, Burutu and Koko were described as sea ports. In terms of jetty, wharf, quay, dock, harbour and port, the correct term to be individually applied will become apparent as this work unfolds.

The history of the ports of Nigeria is a sage of struggle from the arrival of the first hulk through the battle against bar and silt to the need in the 1980s to assess total facilities against the country's balance of trade aspirations. There were no land depots, the river hulks doing justice as warehouses. The coast was harbourless; Lagos, the least important for years, being but a break in the coastline. In terms of physical hardship and hazard, neighbouring Accra furnished a good example as a "surf boat port" where in 1961 no less than 1.2 million tons were manhandled. Of natural harbours like Bathurst, Freetown and Douala, there were none. Envy turned to Rio de Janeiro and Genoa with their 50ft. depths and to England's best, Southampton's 31ft. at LWOST and 15ft. tidal rise; to Sydney, the largest natural harbour in the world and to Poole in England, the second largest. Lagos was to become a protected harbour like Haifa, Malta and Plymouth.

On the West Coast, mineral exploitation was often the driving force — the Marampa-Pepel of Sierra Leone, the Tarkwa-Sekondi of the Gold Coast and the Enugu-Port Harcourt of Nigeria. Admiralty Sailing Instructions described the Nigerian coastline as so "infinitely low and flat that not a single inland eminent is visible from the offing." Casuarina trees were planted for just such a purpose but in the 50s the new Apapa railway station surpassed all such aids as its tower floodlights were, by chance, in direct line with the Lagos harbour entrance.

During slaving, the Royal Navy exercised control over the ports. A Harbour Authority was formed in 1862. The Lagos Harbour Department was similarly formed in 1885 and a Northern Nigeria Marine with headquarters at Lokoja in 1900. The Southern Nigeria Marine formed at Calabar in 1893 moved its headquarters to Akassa where the main engineering works were established in 1902. A Lagos Marine Department started up in 1903 and in 1906 became, with the Southern Nigeria Marine, a combined Southern Nigeria Marine; Akassa headquarters then moved to Lagos and Forcados took over the ship repair function. In 1908, a Port Division was created to deal with civil engineering work. In 1913, anticipating 1914, the Customs and Marine of Northern and Southern Nigeria were amalgamated. The buoyage of Nigerian waters from inception was carried out by Elder Dempster Lines until the Marine took over the task in 1923 using the steamer "Pathfinder". On this service the 1102 ton NMS "Dayspring" served from 1928 for twenty-five years.

The position of the ports in 1923 was that the Nigerian Marine was the Harbour Authority and was responsible for dredging, buoys and lights. The Port Department was responsible for engineering works in Lagos and Port Harcourt and the Public Works Department for government wharves elsewhere. The Railway was responsible for the wharves at Apapa and Port Harcourt and the Customs Department for Customs Wharf Lagos. The railway effort was managed by the Superintendent of the Line from February 1926. In 1934, the Railway reported on ports and quays separately from railway functions; post World War II saw Marketing Boards, and Tanganyika's railway administration of that country's ports was hailed as the example to follow.

In 1951/52, the Federal Government decided that there must be an autonomous statutory corporation to take over as Ports Authority so from December '52 the Railway no longer reported and on the 1st June 1954 a General Manager Ports was appointed and the NPA (Nigerian Ports Authority) was constituted on 23/9/1954 but with the railway in control until Vesting Day on 1/4/1955. All railway personnel on the quays were seconded. The Nigerian Railway retained control of coaling at Port Harcourt and Ijora and its Baro Port of two tracks and water edge shelf berth. They also continued with operation and maintenance of railings within port areas at Apapa and Port-Harcourt.

Port controls bear the name Commissioners, Trust, Commission, Board, Authority or Conservancy with ownership as varied, but for Nigeria the term "Authority" was chosen by C.A. Dove, the first Chairman who defined the word as a responsibility for both wharf and harbour services, financially self-supporting, adding that in the case of Nigeria, control was stretched over 400 miles of coastline and was responsible for more functions than any other in the world. He referred to the division of responsibilities set out in 1923 unchanged and added dockyards under Marine, cargo handling under shipper and importer, accounts under the Accountant General and some staff work handled by the Secretariat.

With the formation came the inauguration of the Inland Waterways and the Nigerian Navy whilst the NPA assumed the mantle of Pilotage and Light House Authority. Assets were transferred at a valuation repayable over forty-one years at an interest rate of $4\frac{1}{2}\%$ p.a. It was hoped in due course to float a loan. Facilities meant approach channels, buoys, quays, transit sheds and warehouses; services meant pilotage, mooring, receiving from and loading cargo to hook, delivering to or from shed, discharging or loading, warehousing, hauling, labelling, coopering and craft repairing.

Dove defended the so-called monopoly by reference to the three dockyards which depended almost entirely for their financial justification on marginal work obtained from outside sources. Here they were in direct competition with dockyards run by other interests. Although the NPA was the Harbour Authority for Warri, Sapele and Burutu, these quays were operated by private interests in direct competition with the Authority. One result of the creation was the rehabilitation of the neighbouring port of Cotonou which sought Niger traffic through Dahomey as an outlet.

Containerisation, Ro-Ro, side loaders and fork lift hardware were to come, but for the start the quotation: "for almost four centuries Fort and Port were synonymous in West Africa" will introduce a period of learned argument that was as protracted as that suffered by the two railway systems before their construction was put in hand. In fact, at the time, the three formed an inseparable triumvirate.

1863-1918

Ninety-nine ships, 58% British, called on the Nigerian coast in 1863. Thirty years later, the total had grown to 446 of which 53% flew the British ensign. Nigeria was growing, the palm produce trade pushing her, and by 1900 her total trade had reached £4,033,770. By 1870, Customs Wharf Lagos had appeared on the Admiralty charts but steamers drawing more than 9ft. 6in. were unable to come alongside.

In 1890 Coode, Son and Matthews (CSM) wrote the Crown Agents (CA) about Lagos whose lagoons at 29ft. deepest extended west fifty miles and east 200 miles with a bar entrance depth of 12 ft. restricting passage to 1000 ton branch steamers from Forcados ocean transhipment station. Mr. Nagel and Lt. Buckland RE surveyed the scene. The fairway in the middle channel off Greslie Point was 23-28 ft. Training works would require stone and the nearest was sixty miles away at Aro on the Ogun, protected by a native fetish and the site as then untapped by a railway.

Down at the water's edge, Europeans died at the rate of 10% a year and sharks were a constant menace. The training works would take off from Wilmot Point, Greslie Point and Beecroft Point, the bar being distant $1\frac{1}{2}$ miles from Greslie Point. The harbour was some six miles in length with an area of four square miles, 2.7% 3-5 fathoms deep but with a well defined channel of 23-30ft. Outside, the waves driven by the west to south west winds rarely exceeded 8ft. but travelled with great speed — as many a person had found to his cost on meeting a watery grave.

Some $88\frac{1}{2}$ million cubic yards of water were discharged during spring tides and 128 million during neap tides; if this discharge could be trained to pass wholly through the middle channel it would bring about the desired scour. With this in mind, Sir John Coode set out his recommendations for training moles. The works were costed at the vast sum of £830,000, "disproportionate to the benefit they would confer," and further development of the country should be awaited, a view with which the Government concurred.

A period of quiet ensued for five years. CSM was then asked to investigate bar dredge, canal outlet, graving dock, floating dock, slipway and a tramway. In connection with the first, they had now discovered that the rock on the Ogun River at Aro acted as a dam in the dry season and removal would be very much taboo but good quality granite two miles in extent was found to the east, close by, but not on the river, with no opposition to removal, site of the future 1901 rail quarry. Conveyed in skips it would be tugged across the lagoon from Iddo wharf to Wilmot Point jetty and there railed to tipping point on a line laid on the harbour with steam propulsion. They thought they could deal with 100,000 tons p.a. at both ends and skip it at 3/4d per ton. They produced an estimate that stood for a long time:

3000 feet east training bank	£78,000
7000 feet east mole	£324,000
4800 feet west training bank	£66,000
7000 feet west mole	£329,000
Total	£797,000

There was a more expensive version designed to accept "European" steamers paid for by savings arising from the elimination of the Forcados tranship. The west training bank was intended to bring about wave dissipation in the outer harbour. Thirty-six thousand pounds would purchase a Dutch type suction dredger to work on the bar but there were doubts of the safety of operation in these turbulent waters.

The recce for the canal was approved on 17/4/1896 and mercifully ran into difficulties. Exploration was difficult, there were invalidings, there were marine disasters but eventually they came out with a canal design 85ft. wide × 24ft. at HW × 7500ft. long lined with rubble from the Aro quarry. They put the final price at £670,000, cheaper than the breakwater scheme of £797,000, but fortunately not favoured although Sir Gilbert Carter suggested a tramway extension on the lines of Cotonou terminating in a 750ft. iron pier and starting from Elegbata Creek after a reclamation of alluvial mud, 6½ acres in extent. The tramway would have added £109,000 to the canal cost, or £10,000 less if it started from Customs House.

The graving dock was out of the question due to the nature of the bed. A slipway was best located 900 yards north west of Apapa Point opposite Customs House. His Excellency preferred proximity to the railway workshops north of Iddo Island close to Denton bridge but was told a firm "No" — no secure foundations. Twenty boats needed to be taken care of and the EDL said the "Ilorin" was the largest at 795 tons so a decision was taken in favour of 1000 tons with entry slope at 1 in 20 and power provision as at East London by steam and hawser. Cost was put at £45,000. Commander Paget Jones, Master at Lagos, stipulated floating dock lift of 900 tons in a frame 163ft. 9in. times 40ft. beam accomplishing the manoeuvre in eighty minutes. Because of the nature of the local currents and the inability of the dock to take a dredger, the slipway stood out for first preference. No decision on any of the schemes was taken although recurrent expenditure of £25,000 p.a. on bar works was not forgotten.

The Crown Agents discussed with Col. Sir Henry McCallum and in July 1898 advised the Colonial Office that a tramway would never have the capacity and was out of the question and that a canal would provide the traditional width of access for such schemes only, and was equally out of the question. Harbour works now revised to £800,000 must be the sole aim. Interest and sinking fund charges on such a sum amounted to around £30,000 p.a. and should be found from £24,000 annual savings on completion of the works, the levying of harbour dues and an inescapable loan by the Treasury from

Admiralty funds. The progressing railway up the west coast called for thinking ahead since it would be disastrous to parallel the line with a further line from Forcados. If their visions were sound then the works should be put in hand. Joseph Chamberlain thought the issue not one to be viewed from the Lagos aspect alone, so he invited Sir Ralph Moor, Brigadier General Lugard, Sir William MacGregor and Sir George Goldie to think of Warri/Sapele/Akassa as an alternative port complex for Nigeria. He needed more background knowledge.

Lugard replied in June 1900 and dwelt on "had it been *ab initio,* before railway was afoot, then strong arguments in favour Warri/Sapele, but it was no longer *ab initio* because the railway was at the foothills of Ibadan." It was compounded of Hausa States, export route, site for the railway crossing over the Niger, railway too far to the west, only one port to deal, and "Empire might have cause to regret half measures."

Shelford & Son (S&S) wrote the Crown Agents the same month on the basis of information from ships' captains to the effect that Warri was superior for access to the interior with 22ft. HW entrance through the Forcados river to a good harbour; Sapele, head of Benin river, small and unhealthy with but 12ft. headway; Akassa an island surrounded by swamp and creek, 15ft. was unsuitable. The Bonny gave 23ft. over the bar at HW navigable for forty-five miles to Dyama through tortuous creeks which would require heavy outlay. The town of Old Calabar where a government wharf was being built was thirty miles from the Cross River bar with a promising hinterland and explored for eighty-five miles. "If Western Nigeria is to be given prominence in civilisation then Warri is the suitable port." Later they said "we stand on virgin soil so the question of labour is paramount." West of the Niger was better known; this was no excuse to neglect east of the Niger, thought to be rich in rubber. Sir William then advised Chamberlain that Lagos harbour could not be developed at the expense of the Colony.

The railway, somewhat fed up in 1901/02, put in hand construction of their Iddo terminal wharf on the Lagos Lagoon and extended it in 1903. Sir Walter Egerton who had assumed office in Lagos wanted a second opinion on the mole suggestion and got the Crown Agents to ask the Colonial Office for a dredge master to come out and report. This time it was Mr Secretary Lyttelton in command and he concurred. Egerton had found it difficult to understand how a decision on bar removal should be so long delayed with steamship companies paying 5/- per ton on transhipment, brooking an extra two weeks delay in the process.

Meanwhile, Customs wharf remained small and fragile, CS&M felt it essential that in the carriage of stone for a national enterprise the railway should make no profit. There was a report that sand accumulation at the east horn of the entrance had largely disappeared and drew the conclusion that part of the ebb tide escaped over the lowered sand bed. The only permanent remedy was to build a bank of rubble and the first effort would take three years. Sir William Matthews suggested that deepening of the sand bank formations confirmed CS&M contentions that east mole will deepen the entrance and lessen the work of a dredger. He looked upon the removal of the Lagos bar as even more important to Lagos than the railway. "Once the bar had been removed no longer could it be contended that access to Northern Nigeria by way of the Niger was easier than by railway." Moreover, much Dahomey trade passed through Lagos via the lagoon and Porto Novo. "With every extension of the railway the absence of Lagos port will be increasingly felt."

In August 1906, CS&M estimated stone tonnage at 1,317,750 but latest information indicated that the east training bank could commence 2000ft. farther out seaward so a saving should result. A time scale of twelve years was agreed for the completion of the works. At last the Lagos Chamber of Commerce was told by the Governor in 1906 that the Secretary of State Lord Elgin had authorised: (1) 3800ft. east mole at £150,000, (2) strengthening of Customs wharf at £50,000, and (3) purchase of a dredger.

Meantime, the railway, mindful of their

own troubles, charged realistic rates for the stone and the £797,000 became £897,000. The dredger was named after the Governor and the TS 1200 ton 27in. pump hopper suction dredger capable of lifting 2500 tons/hour from a depth of 35ft. was driven by 2500 IHP triple expansion engines fed by two 180 lbs/sq.in. Scotch boilers was launched by William Simons & Co. Ltd. on the 3rd April 1907 arriving off the Lagos roads in the following May. In April 1908, stone left Aro and by June was in position. At this time they said Lagos resembled, to a marked degree, the conditions of Durban harbour. "Egergon" dredged 5 feet in the first year of operation. Four vessels were lost off the bar in two years.

In January 1908, the Crown Agents addressed the Colonial Office with firmness. No extension to Iddo wharf could accommodate the railway's future carryings and a grievous error had been committed in settling upon Iddo island as the railway terminal. It was too far or too short. The decision should have favoured mainland or Lagos Island but not the Iddo Island in between. The whole question of the terminal must be faced and whilst Mr Wilson, Resident Engineer Harbours, was in the Colony, CS&M should look at the whole thing again.

A second dredger, "Sandgrouse", was ordered. This was an improvement as she had increased hopper capacity, and started work in 1909. The Aro stone had been sampled by a geologist as porphyritic biotite granite, surrounded by areas of graphic shist. Lord Elgin agreed to the CA's request and said that while the railway was thinking of extension to Lagos Island and tapping Apapa to save Iddo wharf from being crushed under the weight of stone, CS&M should think also of extending Iddo wharf along the deep water line to make a complete railway circuit.

Ordinance No 7, Lagos, of 1908 provided for the £3 million loan. In June, His Excellency sought permission to spend £200,000 on an iron pier at the harbour mouth signal station together with provision for barges, tug and cranes at the signal station and Iddo wharf. The sum also entertained expenditure on locomotives for the mole, the opening up of Aro quarry and the purchase of rolling stock for the carriage of stone. Quarters for staff were not neglected but the financial provision was directed solely towards plant and structures and made no provision for labour.

Tipping of the first stone took place on Monday 8th July 1908 and was obviously a gala day as it was witnessed by members of the Legislative and Executive Councils, the Bar, Chamber of Commerce, White Cap Chiefs of Lagos and all Heads of Departments. Everyone was told that the 3800 ft. mole would be ineffective until it reached the sea at a distance of 2400 ft. If all went well, the railway would be supplying four trains a day to the Iddo crane by 1909.

Soon the Resident Engineer thought part of the west mole should be put in hand and His Excellency asked for an additional £13,000 in order that they could look forward to the sight of an ocean-going steamer. Trade through Lagos was worth £2,926,764 and transhipment cost at Forcados had gone up to 12/6 per ton. These figures justified an expenditure of £3,890,625 on a 4% calculation — so £13,000 should hardly have raised eyebrows. But it did because they now had the conservative Earl of Crewe to deal with and he cautioned those sweltering in the tropical heat by admonition and the language "proceed by the use of well marked steps."

In September, CS&M weighed in with the essentiality of west mole construction — there were heavy seas and the sand was in constant motion. They even descended to use the expression to His Excellency "get a move on". They wanted wharf, sidings, crane, loco, sixteen wagons and the stone skips and reminded one of the 18-month lead time. His Excellency passed this on to the Secretary of State and indicated that work should commence latest March 1910 to achieve proper coordination. Ocean freight UK-Lagos was at the exorbitant rate of 35/9d/ton and as the bar deepened, a saving of 10/- a ton should be evident. The railway (with the BKR) was nearing Kano and it was now useless not to pursue the entire scheme to its planned end. He again asked Lord Crewe to dip his hand into his pocket, this time with the desired response.

At the same time, CS&M expounded on railway expansion to Apapa wharf, a rail connected wharf at Marina Customs and a rail connected wharf between Signal Station and Wilmot Point. Apapa was killed because the merchants would have no direct land access although it obviated a railway bridge. Marine & Railway favoured the scheme between signal station and Wilmot Point but it found no favour with merchants because it was far from the town and lacked land for development.

Most commended was Marina Customs erection. Detailing the three schemes, there was provision for reclamation, sheds and lattice girder railway bridge of 120ft. spans over the lagoon. There was further provision for an 800ft. turning circle for 20ft. draft loaded mailboats, grain elevators for the future and utilisation of Lagos Steam Tramway for spoil removal. Finally came the need for Wilmot Point coaling depot and floating dock. They put these work at:

Elegbata Point Wharf	£260,000
Railway lines	19,000
Sheds	48,000
Cranes and lighting	15,000
Drainage	10,000
Railway bridge	125,000
Coaling wharf	50,000

a total of £527,000.

His Excellency held a follow up meeting with the representatives of seventeen merchants, shippers, bank and everyone, except Mr Osborne of Patterson Zochonis was in favour of Customs Marina. Four hundred and fifty feet sheds, elevated ropeway, and canoe approach for vital post office traffic were all examined. Five days later, His Excellency went through the same exercise with the Legislative Council where an expression of regret was sounded that the floating dock proposal had been scrapped in favour of the private dock at Forcados. He then recommended the Customs Marina scheme to the Joint Committee of London, Liverpool and Manchester Chambers of Commerce. He wrote the Secretary of State in October, asked that CS&M carry out a detailed survey and then assured their Lordships that Lagos could bear the annual charges involved.

On learning that 27ft. would be procurable, the Secretary of State in August 1909 sanctioned the whole of the harbour training works. The Ebute Metta-Apapa branch line, to relieve Iddo of the stone traffic, was commenced in 1910, the screw pile jetty on termination of the mole work later becoming the Lagos-Apapa ferry landing stage.

Heigh-ho! SS Abeokuta, first ocean steamer to enter the harbour, dropped anchor inside on the 10th December 1912. Until 1928, tugs then took in tow all ships of size over the bar In 1912, the west spit channel was moving east and navigation had to keep clear of the Egga and Kittiwake wrecks; in fact erosion was noticed because the west to east littoral drift was interrupted and by 1950 Lighthouse Beach had advanced 1500 ft. and Victoria Beach receded 2300 ft. Iddo wharf with seven sets of railway tracks by 1915 would hold five branch steamers in 1912. The first mail boat entered the harbour on 1st February 1914, the 8000 gt Abosso. Later that year, Lugard took the personal decision to scrap the Wilmot Point scheme. Further works to direct the channel by a west training bank were put in hand in June 1915 but stopped in March 1919 for fear of adverse consequences.

1914 saw the sanction of Customs Wharf extension by 400ft. to 1183ft. and 180ft. extension to the limited Apapa facilities, both at 20ft. depth, the Apapa branch line being well advanced by then. The congestion of 1975 was mirrored in 1915 albeit on a tiny scale and was solved by the diversion of prize (war) ships captured at Douala brought in to pick up produce.

Apapa had three sidings, coal road and weighbridge and the wharf extension was completed by March 1916. Iddo in the same year received an extra 3400ft. of sidings, goods shed, explosive shed and police barracks. Customs quay extension of 401ft. 6in. in ferro-concrete on screw piles was completed in 1918 and the need for transhipment at Forcados at last ceased. Three suction dredgers were now at work and their accomplishment is shown by the following figures at the bar:

1907	11ft.	maximum	depth	of water
1910	15ft.	"	"	"
1913	18ft.	"	"	"
1917	20ft.	"	"	"
1918	21ft.	"	"	"

Progress of the moles, counting the northern extension of the east mole "proper" as part of it was, in feet:

	East Mole	West Mole	West Training bank
1907	988		
1910	5,571		
1912	8,009	1,072	
1914	10,043	2,772	
1915	10,423	3,154	413
1918	10,423	4,266	2,516

Commodore Channel between the east and west mole was 2300 feet. The mole had started before the first Aro stone was tipped but the total tonnage tipped from 1908 to 1918 was:

East mole including northern extension	528,972
West Mole	581,968
West Training bank	256,669
Total	1,367,609

The maximum tonnage moved in a year was 185,804, in 1913

Lagos Port Complex 1918-1954

In 1919, Apapa and Iddo were finally decided upon as the cargo and coal wharves of Lagos but it was not really Iddo but next door at Ijora and here work was put in hand on the attainment of peace. Iddo still dealt with cargo and in 1920 two buildings for export went up and later moved to Apapa. A canoe wharf, steps down to the water's edge, also went up at Iddo and lest anyone should be taken back at such an archaic device, let it be known that in 1929/30, a further one followed at Apapa and fifty years later the canoe still had its uses. In 1923 a 720ft. screw pile wharf was constructed at Ijora and some eighteen acres of land were reclaimed. The wharf dealt with unloading of coal for railway, Ijora power station and ship's bunkering, and was taken over by railway in 1924/25.

Training Works

By 1919, the east mole was reported at 528,214 tons stone but it had not been lengthened, only consolidated. The west mole had become 4,580ft. and eastern another 1,558,660 tons and the west training bank had become, 2,562ft. after over 8,792 tons of stone. Coode, Son and Matthews become Coode, Matthews, Fitzmaurice & Wilsen (CMF&W) and they still felt in 1920 that the west mole should become 5,236ft. (It became 5,175ft.) After 1924, dredging was only required along quay walls so the harbour entrance scheme, with the removal of 17 million tons of sand, was judged to have been successful. By 1926 the bar depth was 24ft., the intentional depth of 27ft. being reached in 1937. A 4-fathom contour map in June 1928 clearly showed the need for pilotage. Extensions to the west training bank were put in hand in September 1926 to bring it to a length of 3,575ft. by 27th August 1928. The "Lady Clifford" (wife of the then Governor) was the dredger at work but west training bank activity had to be suspended whilst attention was given to the effect on south west point of the eastern spit causing a reduction in the deep water channel. In 1930, the west training bank became 3,682ft.

Expenditure, Trade and Early Works

The total harbour works expenditure by December 1918 stood at £862,285, very close to estimate, with a total December 1921 at £1,123,285, excluding dredger costings. The spit at the mouth of Five Cowrie Creek worried them. All construction on the works ceased in September 1922. In this year the railway contracted with Nigerian Transport Co. Ltd. to handle all sea-borne cargo at Iddo. Trade through Lagos was valued at £13.4m in 1913 and £19.2m in 1922. Customs wharf with no rail connection could not be extended and new works had to be placed at Apapa since the business on offer was to the limit of capacity. Three screw pile wharves for the Marine Department were constructed in 1925 at Apapa upstream of the original stone jetty. At least a 600-ton slipway was constructed and on the land to the rear was set up the Marine dockyard. A 4000-ton floating dock did come later, but was replaced in 1961.

Apapa Developments

The decision had been taken to build 1800ft. of deep water wharf on the Apapa side of the harbour with a capacity for four ocean-going vessels, each berth to have a double-storey transit shed. The wharf wall was constructed of 15-ton precast concrete blocks set in sloping bond on a rubble base with a dredged depth alongside of 32 ft. at Lagos Wharf. Iddo was put onto cheaper maintenance as a consequence of this and the proposed wharf for Ijora. The Apapa works including a railway terminal were authorised in 1920. The transit sheds, 350ft. × 600ft., of capacity 5000 tons, were of reinforced concrete columns on reinforced concrete piles with steel roof trusses sheeted in corrugated asbestos. The works which were the first to be carried out by contract in Lagos harbour were awarded in 1921 to Sir W.G. Armstrong Whitworth & Co. Ltd. and construction started in November 1921.

A King's warehouse went up 300ft. × 60ft. In 1922 the railway laid 2200ft. of sidings for the contractor and in 1924 proposed to re-route the connection to the mainline from Ebute Metta to a new station at Ebute Metta Junction farther north. The first berth was completed in April 1925 and was taken over by the railway in the December. The first ship to berth at the new quay was the EDL "Cochrane" on 13th December 1925. Upon completion of the port, Lagos would accommodate at quay and mooring a total of twenty-five vessels. The wharf was in a handover state by April 1927 and had cost £700,000. At last the railway was on the mainland. Unit cost of the sheds including foundations was 29/- per sq. ft. and the wharf wall excluding dredging £146-10-0 per foot run.

Both "port" and "railway" offices at Apapa were let out to merchants on rent on completion. The first floors of the transit sheds were opened for import traffic on 1st April 1927 and the RMMV "Accra" was the first to discharge, before the official opening, on 22nd January 1927.

1927 brought its problems: post surface water bound macadam breaking up and portal cranes developing structural defects on the luffing gear. Brigadier Hammond, back in 1924, could not recommend the elevators for palm kernel and groundnut flows that had been urged by Lord Lugard. He recommended that on completion of the works there should be only one authority — railway or ports — and he favoured the South African solution of a Department of Railways and Harbours.

E.M. Bland, GM Railway, wrote the Chief Secretary to the Government in May 1929; the previous financial year had seen $2\frac{1}{2}$ ships and 2 and $\frac{2}{3}$rds lighters alongside Apapa every day and further berths were a "must" within five years. On February 15, vessels awaited accommodation and 300 tons produce was stacked in the open. Railway had asked merchants to make more use of Port Harcourt as Customs Quay (CQ) without rail was useless. The Customs & Excise said there had been an 80% increase in traffic in 1918/1928. The continental and US Lines urged that any development cater for single storey sheds only in line with USA practice of some fifteen years later. Customs Quay handled only imports except gun powder and petroleums which went to Badagry Creek and Ijora magazines respectively.

With more vessels changing over from coal to oil, burning oil companies began to erect bulk oil storage tanks and in 1930 a bulk oil wharf of steel sheet pile construction was completed at Apapa upstream of the Marina dockyard. This was unsatisfactory for in the event of spillage all vessels lying at Apapa would be at risk, particularly bearing in mind that the ebb current at Lagos always flows for a longer period than the flood. Investigations were later carried out as to the feasibility of constructing an oil wharf immediately upstream of the west training bank in what was known as Atlas Cove.

Bewildering Statistics

Statistics follow later but with reference to Bland's 1929 analysis, elucidation of the available data would task anyone of little patience and local knowledge; the following figures have been got together to demonstrate the complexity of movement in Lagos harbour in 1925/26: all figures are in terms of tonnage:

Landed at Customs Quay	147,983 tons
Landed at private wharves	142,906 "
Landed at gun powder magazine	170 "
Landed at kerosene magazine	7,780 "
Landed at petroleum magazine	7,786 "
Landed at Iddo Wharf	55,454 "
Railway materials landed at Iddo Wharf	7,167 "
Landed at Ijora Wharf	2,362 "
Coal brought in at Ijora Wharf	106,219 "
Imports brought in through Iddo railway station	49,886 "
Exports through Iddo Wharf	195,603 "
Exports through Apapa Wharf	55,786 "
Aro stone traffic through Apapa	21,730 "

Coode said the delays were due to insufficient cranage but this was not a problem after July 1930 upon receipt of Stothert & Pitt cranes to an equipment total of 26 from 1 to 25-ton capacity. Then there were shippers ignorant of the vessel by which produce was to be lifted.

Further Proposed Development at Apapa

It was agreed that Apapa needed extending by projecting the line of quay outwards. In January 1930, Coode was asked by the Nigerian Port Advisory Committee and the Lagos Chamber of Commerce to give his advice. Apapa was 29% more effective in handling cargo per lineal foot of quay per annum than Customs Quay and he thought a 2-berth extension would be sufficient including provision for the fortnightly mail boat then indifferently handled.

A build on the design used by Armstrong Whitworth would be recommended. They had two schemes but put their faith in the second at £559,000 with 32ft. FAS and double-storey transit sheds 420ft. × 70ft. although not liked by the shipping lines. They estimated three years to construct. The railway thought that with development at Port Harcourt and the Oil Rivers ports, this should suffice for Apapa so long as a straight line quay was preserved allowing cranes to work ship to ship. A scissors crossing should be put in between existing No 4 and proposed No 5 sheds.

The Customs wondered why Ijora, now used for the new Carter bridge materials, could not be more used for railway materials. The new Benue bridge materials were going through Port Harcourt without detriment to the commercial use of the port. Over there, there was but single-storey sheds and there was no quay cranage. "Any WA shipper would tell you PH was the port for expeditious handling." "Why not use Iddo wharf for lighter traffic?" The Controller suggested that the Durban Port Manager came out, collaborated and reported. "Stop looking at the problem as if it was a railway matter."

Elias, Railway's Superintendent of the Line, thought with considerable foresight that twenty berths would suffice all time. Coode agreed to 13,000ft. of quay including existing — much on the lines of Capetown — but there should have been more consideration in earmarking land behind Badagry Creek. Coode thought that there was space for thirty-seven berths and 22,000ft. of quay. The railway scheme would cost £460,000 and Coode could not agree with the Controller of Customs' remarks about Port Harcourt in view of the figures quoted for handling per lineal foot of quay at the two ports.

But what happened? The trade recession of the 30s happened and fifty officers and 1500 men were retrenched with good-bye to all improvements until the 50s. The best they did was in 1935 to reallocate transit shed space and increase export capacity by 25%. The old stone jetty cum ferry wharf a year later became allocated to lighters. In 1938, a Director of Transport, G.V.O. Bulkeley, the Railway GM, was appointed to collate all transport matters with particular reference to port working, the railway being left with quay working but this did not help and in 1940 the post was abolished. The railway's Chief Traffic Superintendent then operated through Senior Port Traffic Superintendent A.P. Masseey. In 1939 the port became part of the Marine Department. The war "made" the ports into a 24-hour affair and additional sheds went up. Congestion again reared its head and the enemy succeeded in sinking a modern suction dredger at the harbour entrance. After the war surge, it was seen in 1945 that traffic through Lagos had increased nearly 60% since 1927. Customs facilities were expanded.

The Government moved in 1947. They anticipated a throughput through Lagos of 1.5 million tons p.a. by 1960. Wharves would handle 350,000 tons so Government had to find additional capacity of 1,150,000 tons. At 300 tons per lineal foot of quay, this meant 3830 ft. of deep water quay. Customs Wharf, time expired in 1960, was to be neglected and therefore the Apapa extension would be 3,830 less 1,800 existing that is, 2,030ft. and Coode and Partners were instructed to prepare the contract documents for a wharf prolongation downstream. Transit shed storage would be required for a further 750,000 tons.

Between 1936 and 1945, the storage accommodation had handled an average 3.75 tons per sq. ft. of floor area; therefore 200,000 sq.ft. would be required provided by four transit sheds, each 480ft. × 120ft.

Work started in May 1950 but in the following August Messers Pauling & Co. Ltd., the contractors, found it necessary to withdraw. With but slight delay Richard Costain Ltd. stepped into the breach. The existing four sheds at Apapa were expected to handle 375,000 tons p.a. import & export. In 1950/51, they had to handle 455,000 tons. In 1953, the World Bank placed Apapa Port annual capacity at 1.4 million tons on completion of the works and as adequate for near future.

Nigerian Ports Authority

In 1949, a Commission comprising Mr. A.N. Strong, Barrister-at-law, Chairman of the Colombo Port Commission and Mr. W.A. Flere, of the River Division of the Port of London Authority was invited to Nigeria to report on the ports and to submit its views on future control. It was said that the report was so biased that the best thing was to ignore it. As a result of many meetings it was recommended by Professor Gilbert Walker that the easiest way of working out an executive organisation for control of the ports was to recruit a chief executive officer and charge him to produce the necessary organisation.

Up to 1952, the handling of cargo had been railway's responsibility with the Marine Department being responsible for maintenance of the channels and berthage. Within the Marine there was a Port Engineer seconded from the Public Works Department who was responsible for quay maintenance up to cope level. Then there were Customs, Legal, Land and accounts. This was a cumbersome arrangement and "there was inevitably a tendency for the port to be run for the benefit of the railway to the detriment of the port and road traffic, instead of the railway being run for the benefit of the port." The IBRD referred to this pot-pourri in 1953. The railway was of the view that Lagos and Port-Harcourt were more dependent on the railway than vice versa. It did not think the Controller of Customs should administer Customs quays, and neither should the Marine be a port managing body. But an autonomous authority had to come — the writing was on the wall for those who could detach themselves from the contemporary scene.

On 3rd March 1952, the Council of Ministers approved for an expert to be recruited and on the 10th October, Mr. C.A.

Dove was appointed General Manager (Ports) to plan the organisation. The Nigerian Ports Authority was eventually to "control" all the ports but in the first place, it was to take over the ports of Lagos and Port Harcourt. A later Permanent Secretary said, "while Government did not get Ports Authority as they thought, Mr. Dove got the one he thought best suitable to Nigeria and so Government gained in the end."

The Ports Ordinance came into force in August 1954 with Vesting Day as 1st April 1955. The Nigerian Railway transferred to the Authority assets and renewals fund contribution, the two amounting to £378,903 but retained control of Ijora coal wharf. A chairman assisted by ten appointed members (including GMR) and six elected members ran the Board subject to directives of a general nature by the Federal Minister for Transport. The officers on formation were:

Chairman & General Manager	C.A. Dove
Secretary	H. Jackson
Chief Traffic & Commercial Manager	L.E. Taylor
Chief Engineer	D.H. May
Chief Harbour Master	F.W.J. Skutil
Chief Accountant	P. Tamini
Personnel Manager	E.S. Williams
Stores Manager	A.S. Balman
Estates Officer	A.M. Storey

The task was to operate the ports of Lagos and Port Harcourt, and to regulate Akassa, Bonny, Burutu, Calabar, Degema, Forcados, Koko, Sapele, Tiko, Victoria and Warri. Excluding dock labour, they employed 6000 men in 1956. They operated the Government collier of 4000 tons and maintained three dockyards on the seaboard and two in the rivers of the hinterland. They were responsible for dredging, lights and buoys.

On 1/10/1959, a Government Coastal Agency to take care of government stores and personnel was started up with the assistance of the Crown Agents and in 1957 the Authority gave birth to the Inland Waterways Department and the Royal Nigerian Navy. In 1959 when S. Davis was the Railway's Chief Superintendent, by agreement, the post of Railway Ports Representative was created to put the railway back on the port map.

Lagos Port Complex 1954-1980

The NPA soon put their own blueprint into the Apapa extensions under construction. The extension was not quite in a straight line with the quays of the 20s. It consisted of 2565ft. quay wall behind which an area of land 100 acres in extent was reclaimed, contained within a rubble bank. Four transit sheds were built; the upstream shed had two storeys and was 487ft. 6in. × 100ft. with a ground floor for cargo and upper floor for passengers. The other three sheds were single storey, 150ft. clear span × 350ft. in one case and 425ft. in the other two cases covering railway loading platform in the rear and lorry loading platform at one end.

Design facilitated use of mechanical handling equipment. In addition there was a warehouse 450ft. × 150ft. with loading platforms in the front and rear. Provision was made for future conveyor equipment to transfer bagged produce to a ship berthed downstream. A Queen's warehouse, Customs, Fire House, Police Barracks and Ambulance Station went up. In addition, mechanical workshops and fumigation chambers for infested produce were provided.

The shed edge to quay edge sloped at 1 in 40 — a standard practice. The whole layout was well provided with ten miles of tracks and a turning circle at the bull nose and exchange sidings were built at the point of handover to railway. A 370ft. lighter berth to handle pool and creek traffic was built to the rear. Borings showed that the bed consisted of fine and coarse sand, with some silt and pockets of clay consistent with the subsoil encountered in other parts of the harbour. It was therefore decided to use the same type of construction as had proved successful for the original Apapa Wharf, namely, concrete blockwork set in sloping bond on a rubble base. Crane wheel load was taken at 50 tons. The wall lay upon a trench suction dredged-filled with the Aro stone rubble base and took 11,564 concrete blocks of between 8 and 15 tons. With an 8 to 1 mix concrete cube tests gave 1930 lbs/sq. in. average crushing strength after twenty-eight days. Lagos sands used for reclamation were essentially quartz and made first class materials; 2,105,640 cubic yards were required.

Stothert & Pitt supplied twelve level luffing portal cranes of 3-5 tons capacity and one goliath transporter at the stacking grounds covering 1.4 acres of lift. Power was supplied by the Electricity Corporation at 6600V. Structural steelwork weighed 2765 tons, mild steel reinforcement 1642 tons, the labour force was 2300 and fifty expatriates.

The 5-berth extension was built for £5 million, the first block in the wall was set in position on 15th October 1951, the fifth berth was completed on 26th October 1955 and the whole was opened by HM Queen Elizabeth in February 1956. The Resident Engineer was G.H. Farleigh. Preece, Cardew and Rider were the Consulting Engineers for the electrical works; the rail tracks were laid by Thomas Summerson & Sons and the dredging was carried out by Blankevort & Zoon NV of Holland.

In 1953, a newspaper correspondent described the 1926 build as a grandiose misuse of funds. What was apparent in 1956 was that the extension would not prove sufficient. There was more sense to the argument that despite the facilities laid on, Burutu was in advance of Apapa and Port Harcourt in handling methods. A residential, industrial, commercial, trading estate from reclaimed land off Porto Novo Creek for 12,000 workers was the child of the Lagos Executive Development Board. From 1960, Lagos began to deal with over two million tons of imports per annum; so the estimates were again wrong and customs quays with its three berths had to remain. They had introduced night pilotage from 1957. The Authority realised that further deep water berths would be required but thought that construction could be left until 1965. Again they were wrong; ships were awaiting fourteen days for a berth. This forced the Authority to issue instructions for the next 2500ft. of wharf extension to be put in hand. Berths, moorings and anchorages, accommodated thirty-five ocean-going vessels. Apapa quay itself was either described as nine or ten berth according to the length of vessel but "10" was the generally assumed figure around 1962.

Preparation of the necessary documents commenced in June 1961. This second extension similar to the design of that opened in 1956 would be continued downstream and was due for commencement in 1962. From the model maintained at Delft it was thought that nineteen berths could be accommodated at Apapa. Whilst the construction of deep water berths on the Badagry Creek side was perfectly feasible, that such berths would not prove popular to ships' captains was thought obvious as the prevailing wind was from the south west. Consideration was therefore given to an alternative site and this was in the centre of the harbour on the Apapa shoals with deep water channels of sufficient width on both sides. A road and rail bridge to connect up with Apapa would have been necessary so it is fortunate that such a bottleneck came to nothing. Meantime it did not help shippers who treated Apapa and customs quays as separate ports in their Bills of Lading so that a vessel might await a berth at one quay when there was room at the other.

Sixty-one Lines and Agents were using Lagos Port. Two bulk groundnut oil installations to the rear of Apapa quay handled through pipe line 46,000 tons p.a. on behalf of six Northern Nigerian companies and three Niger companies. Number nine berth became connected to a flour mill via a 200 ton/hour bulk grain discharge plant, a much needed addition to the country's welfare, with its "Golden Penny" products. Warehouses were allocated to cocoa, cotton lint, groundnuts and palm kernels for export through Nos 6-8 berths, mostly controlled by the Nigerian Produce Marketing Company. Such produce, except ex-French Niger territory, was not stemmed against a nominated ship. The Ijora coal wharf handled 70 tons/hour. The petroleum wharf handled 750,000 tons plus 100,000 tons reshipped coastwise per annum. Eleven thousand tons of palm oil were handled through the privately owned bulk oil wharf.

Iddo Wharf 1906

Ports, Harbours and Terminals

Iddo Wharf 1917

The 1962 extension, started in 1964 and completed in 1967, catered for two warehouses, four transit sheds and a quay extension of 2810ft. for four berths, providing for a total of fourteen Apapa and three customs quays. Number 10 was the lighter berth. This brought the prolongation close to the Badagry Creek entrance but despite this a further four-berth extension was scheduled to start on completion of the 1964 extension, providing Apapa with eighteen deep water berths. The 1969 "call" was a capacity for 4 million tons p.a. The 1964 extension formed the subject of the NPA Christmas Card for 1965. The new 4000-ton floating dock for Apapa arrived in 1961. In 1963/64, harbour sand was used to reclaim Victoria Island where embassies and ministers' houses were to go up and removal of this spoil lessened the perennial question of blockage by the west mole with consequent build up.

The further four-berth extension did not come off. The NPA issued a "glossy" handbook in 1973. It described the harbour moles then as, east 1.35 nautical miles, 8193 ft.: west 0.45 nm, 2731 ft.: training mole 0.25 nm, 1517 ft. Obviously a new datum for measurement had been taken. Berth Nos 1-14 occupied a quay length of 7687ft. (2343 m). This excluded the lighter berth on the other side but included berth 7A as well as berth 7. Maximum draft was 8.23 m or 27ft. at all berths. Floating crane "Kainji" could exert a lift of 101.61 tonnes. Berth 14, 220 m, was then in use as a container berth handling 365 units a month. By January 1976, there was a queue for this berth. In March, the Government acquired 7.09 hectares of land for a container terminal near Lillipond. Earlier, they had placed container movement port to inland site in the hands of Container Terminal Company which got up to a figure of 4500 units a month. Jones Cranes supplied 2 × 30 ton mobile cranes and from Europe, ordered by the Crown Agents, came £12 million worth of tugs, barges and handling equipment. Preference had to be given to berth allocation to the Conference Lines. A master who entered Nigerian waters without a Ships Entry Notice risked two years jail — that was an edict of 1976 repeated in April 1978 to reduce congestion, although no such penalty was ever incurred.

In 1973, the IBRD provided a loan of $55 million to help finance a $83 million Apapa extension project, the main Nigerian ports, capacity being then put at 5.2 million tons, although in 1975 the realistic figure of 3.56 million tons was used. This was to be a comprehensive scheme based on over 1000 metres of face for six berths. There was to be a container terminal and berths were to be made available at the rate of one per year with a contract let by August 1976. In March 1976, they were thinking of a thirty-berth complex "near Lagos". In May, they announced a ten-berth addition to Lagos to start the following November. In July, "near Lagos" was defined as Badagry or Epe/Lekki on the lagoon and in the same breath this scheme was shelved. They referred in the Press to four container berths and two ordinary berths for Apapa but on the worsening of the situation at the end of November 1976 by the closure of Customs Quay (which went the way of the mail boat it has so long served in the past), the Government awarded, on 19th July 1976, a ten-berth complex road served to Julius Berger on Tin Can Island in Porto Novo Creek for $320 million. Customs Quay went in the end to make way for a Lagos Ring Road. The quaint name, Tin Can Island (TCI), originated from the former use of the island as an open garbage depository for Lagos. The contract of over 2500 meters perimeter was to house eight seagoing berths and two lighter/barge berths. The NPA announced that dredging would maintain 11 m depth at Lagos.

Meantime in May 1977, what was to become known as the Apapa third wharf extension had been let for the 1979 completion for container terminal and conventional berths plus the others which later however included Ro-Ro and straddle carriers. The "yoyo" planning post World War II described, reminiscent of the Irish "off again on again off again gone again", must have induced the thought that planning was the last exercise contemplated. It is therefore pertinent to remember that the country had gone through a civil war, one port only operating, and had to taste its aftermath.

A noticeable improvement to traffic flow came about through the appointment of the "Black Scorpion", retired Brigadier Benjamin Adekunle, civil war veteran, as Ports Commandant charged with the message: "Clear up the mess within six months." And then, of course, no one could have failed to be cognisant of the congestion in the world, although Nigeria was not an isolated example — Port Sudan was much a brother in misfortune.

Mailboat & Boat Train at Apapa Quay in the 30s

Congestion may be said to have commenced in December 1974 with thirty ships at anchor, worst sufferers being the non-Conference Lines, particularly tramps. Delays were anything from ninety to two hundred days although Calabar and Port Harcourt remain at around fifteen days. The trouble arose through lack of facilities and became aggravated by the so-called cement scandal with rogues outside Nigeria as well as within. Bulk carriers in Lagos roads assisted along with ports of immediate neighbours who however soon discovered they could not cope. By August 1975, no less than 455 ships stood off outside Lagos, but within twelve months, the figure was down to 138, only to start up again in minor fashion in 1978.

Tin Can Island Port was described as the first of its kind in West Africa; access was via service road connecting the new Outer Ring West, Badagry Road, and the Apapa-Ikeja Expressway. Replacement pontoons for the 1961 floating dock were towed to Nigeria in 1976/77 from the works of Swan Hunter. Peter Fraenkl & Partners were appointed consultants in 1978 for a £10 million tanker jetty at Atlas Cove which was to replace the old jetty and reduce the port fire hazard by its further distance from the quays. Ro-Ro traffic from Britain, USA and Italy by February 1977 was through its local teething troubles. A year later, UMARCO was appointed as coordinator for these services. The third Apapa extension had been let to Julius Berger who sub-contracted the track to Henry Boot Engineering of Sheffield and in 1977 the news that a thirty-berth complex would after all be built was leaked to the Press — erection was to be at Sea School Island near Apapa.

Julius Berger, in the building and designing of the Tin Can Island Port, 5000 kw power station and road access, had the backing at Wiesbaden, Germany, of its parent, Bilfinger and Berger. They aimed at fifteen months which perforce included removal of 4-5 million tons of rubbish and the clearing of 181 hectares. Over nineteen million cubic metres were dredged, 10 million cubic metres of sandfill for reclamation were handled, 180,000 of the same units of concrete were used and 106,000 metres of piles were driven. The port was commissioned by Brigadier Shehu Musa Yar'Adua, Chief of Staff Supreme Headquarters, in October 1977 and the first vessel alongside was, of course, a ship of the NNLL — MV River Niger. The port was designed to handle three million tons p.a.

Thirty feet harbour depth was reached in 1979. The third Apapa extension was opened on 24th April 1979, a year ahead of schedule. Built on 50.8 hectares of reclaimed land on the southern side of the existing wharf, the new extension as built added 1600m of quay making a total of 3573m. The quays were designed to provide 1005m of container berths holding four to six ships at a time, 525m of general cargo berths holding three conventional ships at a time and one Ro-Ro berth usable from both ends and four jetties for tugs.

Required then were feasibility studies for the dockyard — a ship turnround of three weeks in 1978 possible for a Ro-Ro in one day in 1979, and anchorage for seventy discharge points quay and pool.

Port Harcourt

It is a relief to turn from the complexities and uncertainties of Lagos to the other ports. The discovery of coal and the discovery of a port for its export evacuation, Port Harcourt, Rivers State, are treated elsewhere. It was treated as the second port of the country. It was forty-four nautical miles up the Bonny River from the Fairway Buoy, past Okrika at nm 25, past Dawes Island at nm 34, point of pilotage. In 1960, the sheltered harbour was described as 500 to 800ft. wide and 19 to 60ft. deep but the Bonny bar governed entrance was 19ft. in 1979.

Lugard opened the port after dredging to colliers in 1913, three years before the railway drew on the Enugu coal fields. In 1914, a temporary 900ft. jetty was built under loan funds to handle traffic generated by the opening of the first seventy-two miles of railway line and in 1916 a coal tip lowerator was put in hand to discharge 10 ton net 4-wheel railway wagons over the hatch. A

500ft. permanent quay wall to replace the temporary jetty was begun in 1917 after dredging a protuberant toe of land but on the advice of Coode of CFW&M that it was wrongly laid out, it was abandoned in favour of two steamer berths upstream on steel screw piles. Whilst Iddo had used ekki timbers, Port Harcourt, coded PH by the railway and known by everyone in the land by the same, used the expensive mangrove.

It was thought in 1919 that with reclamation there was potential for twelve berths. The thought was generated because PH was then at the limit of capacity for business on offer. A Railway District Engineer, H.W. Lawson, became seconded as a Resident Engineer PH in 1920 to examine the question of wagon standage and facilities. As a result of this, two import goods sheds 300ft. × 70ft. went up in 1920 followed in 1921/22 by a contract with Nigerian Transport Company to handle everything but coal.

The piles were completed in December 1922 and by March 1923, steel structures were up and 75% of the trackwork using 62,000 tons stone from Ovim Quarry for the quay was completed. Railway Open Lines took over the first instalment of the completed works on 22/10/1923 and the new goods shed on 1/3/1924. The temporary jetty fell into disuse and was partly demolished in 1924/25. Up line, a concrete deck canoe jetty was brought into use at Imo River. In 1924, a wharfage increase of 975ft. was recommended to the Secretary of State in London. When it was sanctioned, two further berths were constructed and the quay became 1,920ft. in length at 24ft. low water off spring tide (LWOST) by 1927. But the quay was not straight and included two bends giving the basin 630ft., 420ft. and 870ft.. The first two figures related to the addition. 1928 saw the completion of the necessary offices. Earlier, the lowerator had become eclipsed by a concrete bin high level loading cellular structure of 2500 tons capacity conveyor fed to ships able, of course, to take 4-wheel or bogie stock. Discharge, electrically powered, was at the rate of 400 tons/hour. There were two conveyor belts at right angles to each other, one tapping the cell bottoms, the other ending in the chute to the hold.

Brigadier Hammond in 1924 thought the quay would be too short as the "Ebani" measured 420ft., coincidental with one of the three quay dimensions. Five ships were in harbour and more stood at Dawes Island waiting permission to come up. When Nigerian Eastern Railway reached the north, the port inadequacy would become more apparent as it was estimated that 125,000 tons p.a. would funnel through the port. He ruled against the practice of East Africa in dedicating one shed per ship's bottom and was more instrumental in securing the two-berth extension than the Railway's General Manager. Hammond would have put first priority on double storey sheds and quay cranage instead of expenditure on a Minna-Kaduna relay. The second extension included transit sheds of 55,800 square feet. Hammond was right; by 1929 shipping tonnage had trebled.

The Lagos Customs in 1930 criticised the poor use to which a new 620ft. × 90ft. shed was being put when it had been designed to relieve Apapa of its groundnut load — otherwise the port with no cranes was being handled better than the Capital. Fairways Buoy to Dawes Island Buoy were lit by gas for night navigation and then the depression of the 30s halted further improvement. After the war, PH was taxed to the utmost handling in addition the Chad traffic. Relief was given by a new dump for awkward cargo and plans were made for a King's Warehouse and back stage storage sheds and Arcon produce sheds. Road evacuation was encouraged but met with difficulties because the low level port was designed for rail movement. The World Bank found fault with the original design and lack of mechanical handling equipment and this observation was, of course, thoroughly deserved. Port Harcourt was brought up on the cheap. The three lengths of jointed quay were only effectively occupied to full extent by a right combination of steamer lengths appearing on the Nigerian horizon. The worst month was

August 1955 with fourteen ships awaiting berths. For some reason, the English and Ibo/Ibibio voices were not heard until Dove saw a PH Port Advisory Board Report in 1954. A £4 million 1600ft. extension with portal cranes was commenced in 1957 and opened by Her Royal Highness Princess Alexandria on 12th October 1960 providing for seven berths in all. Dawes Island-PH Buoys were lit so that night navigation now became possible Fairway-Port Harcourt. The coal tip area was converted into a palm oil wharf.

Port Harcourt Wharf 1915

Port Harcourt Harbour Works 1921

Then the original wharf began to sink. The area around the port, being in the Niger Delta swamp, is overlaid by floating silt and mud to a depth of forty feet and more. There were plans to extend the wharf two berths upstream and two berths downstream to bring the total number of berths to eleven. Similarly, there were plans to develop another port on a site three miles away on the Okpoka River where the soil was more favourable. There would have been provision to build up to about thirteen berths. Port traffic in was building materials and foodstuffs, and out, palm kernels, groundnuts, cotton lint and cotton seed, benniseed, tin, columbite, soya beans, scrap iron and piassava. There were facilities for petroleum discharge.

In the mid 60s, PH assumed or should have assumed a new importance. The railway extension to Bauchi, Gombe and Maiduguri gave an outlet to these towns shortened by 214 miles if PH was used instead of Apapa. So in 1964, the Bonny bar was dredged to 35ft. LWOST over a channel width of 700ft., involving a lift of 20 million cubic yards of sand and silt but at PH, depth remained at 27ft. LWOST. At the time of the civil war, an annual throughput capacity of 1½ million tons was credited to the port.

In 1965/66, PH handled a total of 873,460 tons, in 1968/69, nothing! In the civil war, the Imo River railway bridge was destroyed and there was therefore no rail passage. The port channel was littered with sunken debris; there was a blockade and the Annual Report of the NPA said of 1969/70, "a shambles" The only rail movement was shunting to local merchant's sidings. Tonnage got moving again at a healthy rate only by March 1974, 98000 tons total, although port reactivation had commenced in April 1970. Dutch Consultants recommended a container terminal by 1980 but local NPA favoured, as more urgent, over 2 berths for general cargo. As can be imagined after such a setback to the country's progress, there was much fault to be found by the unions in staffing and promotion.

In 1972, the port was officially described as three berths of 158m each, one of 110m, one of 128m, two of 134m, all at 7.92m draft. Number 8 was the 137m coal berth and No 9 the 143m bulk palm oil berth, both at the lesser depth of 7.62m. Numbers 10 & 11 were 137m, 6.71m draft, at Kidney Island (Shell/BP) and timber buoy respectively and No 12 was pool anchorage at 6.55m. Pilotage was compulsory. There were four import and three export transit sheds with the ARCON sheds used for road born palm kernels. Four warehouses with a 37,086-tonne capacity vegetable oil tank, supplying berth 9 outside the quay area by pipeline, completed the picture. Container traffic had shown a slow start. Tankers up to 243m in length discharged ashore by pipeline. Aside from the one mooring, berth vessels with import tied up at Dawes Island.

In 1975, plans for four more berths were revived but this time thought was concentrated on a Bonny extension as more worthwhile because there was deeper water and improved roads were in contemplation. Fortunately, this view did not persist, hazarding the PH infrastructure, and provision was made in the 1975-80 Third National Plan for "massive development".

In December 1975, the PH element was put at ₦65 million for a four-berth complex but in the new location of Trans-Amadi, as land by the port was exhausted. Trans-Amadi was the post-war II PH Industrial Estate. The idea was sound but would require separate approach through the Amadi Creek. By this time, the existing PH considered capacity of 1.5 million tons p.a. had been reduced to 1 million.

In July 1976, it was said that a new port "up to" thirty berths would be built. The dockyard was definitely to be expanded as an integrated project. In February 1977, a tender was under preparation for four to six new berths and in 1978, six berths, quay length 1000m, were in hand on the new site. In 1979, the berth figure allowing for increased ship length was put at five instead of six but plans were then announced for a new complex at Onne, the location of a lighter terminal of 1366m in 1976. The first phase of the fifty berth was to cost £110 million. It was destined to be the deepest port in the country, a long term project to handle the raw material imports for Ajaokuta iron & steel project and export of coal. The contract was placed with Royal Voeker Stevin of the Netherlands in late 1979. There was strong competition but not from Britain, prevented from tendering because of the British Petroleum furore.

Onne lies in farmland off mangrove creek fed swamps of the Bonny River, 10km south east of Port Harcourt and the complex will cover 12 sq. km, six quays bulk, three quays harbour services, container and Ro-Ro. A power station will be provided, and this time, railway lines.

Port of Warri

Warri, a Delta port in Delta State, is a sea and inland waterways port. The town is 20ft. above the sea level. The approach is not through the direct access, Forcados, but through the Escravos River and Chanomi Creek to the Forcados River in line for Burutu, but with a turn to port up the Warri River to Warri Port. The Escravos Light is 46 nautical miles to the port.

Warri was a serious competitor to Lagos at the turn of the century for the country's No 1 port and railhead. Instead, it developed under John Holt as a river port and dockyard with ocean-going facilities but was always turning round some overseas trade, timber, cotton lint and palm kernels out, and merchandise in. It went quietly on until the World Bank reported its facilities in 1953 as three ships moorings of 1750ft. to short wharves pontoon connected in a parcel of twenty acres. Thereafter in the 60s, it began to handle trade for the oil companies with their expanding requirements of rigs, stores and pipe racks, and Holts Transport Ltd. found it necessary to enlarge by a further 100 acres with a new 500ft. ocean berth and improved dockyard facilities, including a slipway of 600 tons for building 700-ton steel barges, for they had the Kainji Dam in mind. The channel was to be dredged to 21ft.

The Authority from inception regulated Warri Harbour, that is, maintained the channel and provided navigational aids but by Decree 55 of 1969, the facilities were taken over and vested in the Nigerian Ports Authority for operation with practical implementation from the following January 1st. The new Inland Waterways Department was responsible for the dockyard which was actually at Igbudu. Holts extension later required dredging and the 1969/70 NPA Report gave the berthage as:

1	Buoys fore and aft	525ft. limit to berth at 21 ft.
2	Buoys fore and aft	625ft. limit to berth at 21 ft.
3	Single Buoy	No limit to berth at 21 ft.
	Holts Wharf	525ft. limit to berth at 21 ft.
	Holts new Deck	1000ft. limit to berth at 17 ft.

In the Second Five-Year Plan 1970/74, the Government determined to spend £4.7 million on two new berths for Warri with modern cargo handling equipment. Dutch Consultants had thought that the facilities would require placement by 1990. Shipping sources thought that the future hinged on the health of the oil industry. It was known that there would always be a commitment to heavy dredging of the Escravos bar (whose entrance however served three other ports). However as the plan went by, the Warri intentions remained unaltered and in January 1977 it was stated that the quays would be reinforced and the port rehabilitated pending full redevelopment. "Importers must learn to use the port nearest their base", said Brigadier Godwin Ally, the Chairman, in a message that would have to be increasingly learnt.

By February 1977, the two berths had grown to four, then to six. By April 1977, newspaper sensationalism over Warri had been publicly condemned. The port was not built for the traffic it was now handling; it had grown from a private port; rehabilitation was necessary before development. In October 1977, it was again announced that additional berthage was to be put in hand, and later that month, that the berths were to be increased from two to eight and that Raymond International had been awarded a £6 million contract for the concrete cylinder pile foundations.

In January 1978, the Federal Military Government earmarked ₦84 million for a new port development at Warri. The six "standard" berths were given priority because of the Ajaokuta project. Later that year, trade journals carried the advertisement, "Warri is Nigeria's fastest developing port and it's not hard to see why. It suffers very little from the congestion that is found at other major ports. And with six modernised berths already operational and another six berth complex with full container facilities under construction, Warri is going to be

Nigeria's most efficient port for years to come. Warri also enjoys excellent road connections with all major towns of Nigeria..."

The work was commenced in September 1977 by Julius Berger. In fact, the development cost ₦142 million and was opened by Major-General Yar'Adua. Along with the six berths was a Ro-Ro on a quay of 1950m and, of course, everything that went with it. It is the intended port for the present capital, Abuja, and dredged depth by 1980 was 11.5m accepting 15,000 ton laden vessels. Like Tin Can Island, it has a control tower.

Port of Calabar

Calabar on Cross River in the State of that name is treated as a river port under "Inland Waterways". It was once the seat of the British Consul, 40 nautical miles from the Fairway Buoy and 5nm from the main entrance channel where Tobacco Island and Alligator Island are to port as the channel turn is made. It has a least depth of water of 15ft. in Duke Town Crossing. The port was a serious contender for a railway terminus. It was however bypassed by Lagos and then Port Harcourt, and having no roads, it lost importance. By 1935, it was the fourth Port, handling 11,400 tons of ocean shipping and in 1951 ranked fourth in import and export by value. It was therefore always important to the economy despite the drawbacks mentioned. Twelve miles below lies Oron, the former port often thought of as suitable for rail connection to Aba. Calabar's sheds are at right angles to the quay face. The port suffered in the civil war. It has always despatched coastwise shipping.

The World Bank in 1953 reported a 20 feet high tide in the estuary and said there were nine berths including buoys and storage capacity of 40,000 tons, but the equipment allowed for the working of three hatches at one time which slowed work. The other two berths were used only by coastal vessels. There were facilities for three ocean-going ships to work to lighters in mid-stream. The NPA maintained a dockyard and was responsible for navigation aids the port being run by Palm Line Agencies of Nigeria Ltd. But by virtue of Decree 55 of December 1969, operation of cargo and port was vested in the Authority. So Warri and Calabar fell into line with Lagos and Port Harcourt. In the civil war, ocean going hove to off shore and used lighters.

The 1970/74 second Five-Year Plan voted £2.6 million for two further berths and four transit sheds and modern equipment upstream of the cement wharf having already set aside £1 million and rehabilitation after the war. It was said that the Abakaliki palm kernel mill and resumption of rubber plantations would improve the port's potential although outlook must remain modest. Nevertheless pressures on Lagos would have to be watched. In 1972, the NPA categorised the port as:

Identity	Specification	Berthage	Draft
Pool	3 ocean going	—	—
Jackson Wharf	1 coastwise	27 m	5.79 m
Millerio Wharf	1 ocean going	61 m	7.32 m
Ivy Wharf	1 ocean going	41 m	4.27 m
Cement Wharf	1 ocean going	75 m	5.79 m

There were mobile cranes up to 10.16 tonne capacity, nine transit sheds, four warehouses and an air inflated warehouse. Shell leased a 305-tonne gas tank and Mobil had five bulk oil plants.

The intentions of 1970/74 were transferred to 1975/80. The postponement of roads, ports and the like was not due to finance shortage although the cash flow did give rise to problems in the latter plan but solely because the pace was geared faster than the country could plan and mobilise, a lesson fully appreciated by 1980.

In 1975, planners had doubts because of Calabar's isolated position and plumbed for the west bank of the Cross River. In December, the vote had increased to £16.5 million and the berthage to four. However in July 1976, it was recorded that tenders were out for two berths in a new location entailing much dredging of mud flats. Seven months later, "four berths were under construction" and later still, "contracts to build six berths were due to be awarded to a timetable of twenty-two months." In October 1977, the plan was described as modernisation of existing facilities and letting of contract for new works.

By August 1978, the work had been phased and costed. Phase 1 of the new £85 million project had been completed with a 250m quay and resulted from the 1976 award given to Royal Netherlands Harbourworks Ltd, a 1000-day project completed on schedule with a workforce of 2000, including seventy expatriates. It was further extended to 38 hectares able to handle thirteen ships at a time at a four-berth quay 860 × 40-60m wide, three transit sheds, two warehouses and plant of all kinds. Channel was dredged all the way from the open sea to 7m in LWOST. But when the final phase was completed in May 1979, seventeen ships were taken care of, alongside and in mid-stream and it was thought that the needs of six States of the Federation had been catered for, obviously Cross River, Anambra, Benue, Gongola, Borno and Bauchi.

The port was commissioned in July 1979 on movement of staff from old to new site by the Chief of Naval Staff, Vice-Admiral Adelanwa. The Norwegian Government made a grant of ₦4 million towards the cost of the project. The Head of State put the completed Phase 1 works, including dredging, at ₦72.34 million.

Sapele Harbour

Sapele, in Delta State, is now approached through the Escravos River, Nana Creek and Benin River to a point just below the confluence of the Jamieson and Ethiope Rivers, some 58nm from the Escravos entrance. Cargo facilities were on the south bank, a ferry being required for traffic offering from the north. The port lies in the riparian forest and is surrounded by rubber plantations. Rubber was started in 1905 by Miller Brothers, and sawmill, veneer, and plywood factory, one of the largest in the world, was started by the African Timber & Plywood (Nigeria) Ltd, a company of the Unilever Group, in 1935. It was the first commercial town in Mid-Western Nigeria and was an important point for shipment of agricultural produce. It was a private wharf (AT&P) with five mooring berths and the timber wharf at 20ft. draft and was described technically as a harbour on the formation of the NPA which was to regulate it by responsibility for navigational aids.

As Sapele required the use of a ferry, it was proposed in the early fifties to construct a port at Koko, reached before Sapele on the Benin River, for all traffic other than timber. But on economic grounds, this did not have the support of the World Bank. Two hundred and forty three ships used the port in 1969/70. In that same year, the berths were listed as ten in the pool and two at the private AT&P wharves and the description remained unchanged through 1973. Clearly, Sapele was a harbour with wharves.

In 1977, it was announced that additional berths would be provided and in March 1979, the ₦42 million contract had been shelved due to poor soil condition. This was known at the turn of the century. However in his 1979/80 speech, the Head of State gave the impression that they would persevere with construction and in February 1980 the Minister of Transport said that necessary steps were being taken to establish another port complex at Sapele. It is however the only location to have stood still, as a harbour with wharf facilities.

Port of Burutu

Burutu is a delta island harbour in Delta State, a point of transhipment, now approached over the Escravos Bar and through the Chanomi Creek to Forcados River alongside mangrove, 40nm from the Escravos Light. The site was picked in preference to Forcados in 1903 as the main port for Northern Nigeria upon the revocation of the charter of the Royal Niger Company continued in use by the Niger Company until the disastrous fire of 1921 and rebuilt to become the headquarters of NRTC as described under "Inland Waterways". Covering 135 acres, it was the largest privately owned port in Nigeria. The World Bank described it in 1953 as a private wharf for the then UAC river fleet together with a dockyard, four berths and ample storage facilities.

The dockyard had four slipways taking up to 610 dwt maximum, was equipped with an extensive machine shop and was powered by local generating plant. The wharf frontage was made up of 750ft. and 300ft. and there were seventeen transit sheds and a bulk oil plant. The four berths could accommodate two ocean liners, one coaster and one smaller craft. The port was ideally suited to the needs of the oil exploration companies, casing, mud and cement. By 1967, the channel was at 21ft. and in 1969 provision by Decree was made for the port to be taken over by the NPA but by 1973, entrance was still controlled by the Burutu flats, 3.96m Chart Datum. Cargo was handled by ship's derricks.

In 1975, Burutu was earmarked for the repair of larger vessels at a cost of ₦10 million with improvements to the berthing facilities and the Head of State's 1979/80 speech referred to the dockyard feasibility study. By February 1980, plans were at an advanced stage.

Bonny Terminal

Bonny Terminal is in Rivers State on the east bank of the Bonny estuary, a place of great history which lived to see more history recorded in the International Press. The first African independent nation to raise an amphibious force, in the Nigerian civil war, federal forces in July 1967 captured the port, already an oil port, from the secessionists. Bonny, an island in the swamp, is 16nm from the Fairway Buoy. It lies 27nm below Port Harcourt.

A crude oil terminal was opened in 1961 and in 1966, storage capacity increased from 330,000 to 3.5 million barrels. By the mid-seventies, the Government was negotiating with Shell/BP for LNG plant at Bonny to place Nigeria with her natural gas reserves in line with Algeria. A tanker of petroleum products can leave up to 39ft. draft. But Bonny was a port long before — it simply lost out to Port Harcourt and found itself again in 1961. In the Second Five-Year Plan the terminal had to have funds voted for rehabilitation after the "troubles". In 1969/70, 567 tankers took on crude despite difficulty over the provision of pilots. The loading of super tankers was in mind.

The facilities consist of Bonny shore terminal, three main berths and a standby berth each of five mooring buoys taking up to 78,236 tonnes, movement taking place at turn of flood tides, loading by submarine hose at 3048 tons/hour average. There is a jetty. A Bonny off-shore platform at $4°\ 11N \times 7°\ 14'E$ (off shore 8-9 miles) with 22.86m draft for two single buoy moorings fed from the Bonny shore storage tanks was due to come into operation. Forty hour turnround loading rate was envisaged. In June 1975 there were high hopes for Bonny, now the principal port for crude oil with storage for five million barrels on-shore, and mooring for 200,000 tonnes off-shore.

The first shipment of palm oil to the Western world was made from Bonny in 1806.

Koko

Koko is on the Benin River in Delta State. It is also approached through the Escravos and Nana Creek, 48nm from the Escravos Light. In 1953 because of the impediment of a ferry at Sapele, there was much talk in the Western Region of building a further port at Koko, 21nm below Sapele, to absorb all but the Sapele timber traffic. Draft was adequate but building area was limited and the World Bank did not recognise the justification and called for re-examination. However, it was built six years later for the export of palm oil with one deep water berth of 450ft. and a warehouse. There were plans for two transit sheds and a further warehouse. 1966 depth at existing quay was 24ft. Finance was voted to put right the damage from the civil war. The port handled 13,567 dwt in 1969/70 when the NPA certainly had misgiving for the future as a toll on the new bridge over the Ethiope lessened the vehicular traffic in the wharf. The port was NPA operated and the entrance gates proclaimed "Port of Koko"; technically correct only since Customs was there to handle the imports.

Only nine vessels, other than those of the Navy or fishermen, used the port in 1972/73 but in 1974, timber was certainly being handled and floated to the ship's hook. In December of the following year, it was announced that Koko was to be the base for government-sponsored fishing fleets and there was to be over 300m deep berthage and over 300m shallow berthage costing ₦14 million. This intention was re-expressed in October 1977. The expression, "the possibility of developing new berths at Koko" was significant in the Third National Plan. In February 1980, again it was read, "financial constraints have bedevilled completion of the Koko Port."

Forcados (Port)

On either side of the estuary, the coastline shelters the palm whilst over the bar is extensive mangrove. The 1899 bar depth favoured the "private dock", an island, well established by 1905 and until 1909, had Liverpool-Lagos ocean/branch transhipment and virtual control of Lagos import/export. The last vessel on the service, SS Dakar, stood off bar on 12th January 1909. That was the first death knell of the port; there was a second; the depth of 20ft. in 1899 slowly disappeared to 11ft. by 1960. At Government request, NEDECO studied the situation and recommended Escravos as the entrance. Finally, the railway killed it and by 1930 it was point on the map and by 1960 it had dwindled to nothing. The port was 153nm from Lagos.

In 1913, stern wheelers were connected with the BKR at Baro. In 1905, Nigeria Dry Dock & Engineering Co. Ltd. installed the only dry dock of its kind in West Africa, 2700 tons, but moved it to Wilmot Point, Lagos, in 1917.

In 1966, Forcados was described as virtually defunct; but the oil writing was on the wall. It might have made it in 1898 when the Royal Niger Company sought a port superior to Akassa HQ. They anchored in Forcados but a typhoon blew them further up to Burutu. Shell oil terminal was developing rapidly by 1969 and by 1972, there were two single buoy moorings 5° 10′ N × 5° 10′ E at 19.81m depth fed by a 7.3 million barrel tankage with a loading rate of 86,250 b/h. A total of 31,203,328 tons of crude were shipped in 1972/73. Despite the silting up history, an access channel, Warri-Forcados, was constructed.

Escravos Estuary & Terminal

One of the problems of shipping in the delta ports was the existence of sandbars in the entrance to the ports, reducing significance and threatening use. Access to Sapele, Warri, Burutu, and of course Forcados was via the Forcados estuary with a 1899 depth of 20ft down by 1934 to 12ft. In 1938, Government decided to open the estuary with a dredged channel in the direction of the prevailing wind and swell but the war put a stop to such schemes. In 1952, they decided they must come to grips with the problem; so long as nothing was done, economic progress was retarded. Professor Thijsse of Delft Hydraulic Laboratory was invited and he asked NEDECO to survey the area. This took place between June 1953 and December 1954. Coode & Partners as the Consulting Engineers examined this and the Dutch Consultants were instructed to carry out experiments in scale, a task completed in November 1958. Anticipating this, the Government in September 1957 instructed Coode to prepare working documents and the Crown Agents invited tenders in June 1958. A contract was awarded in April 1959 to Richard Costain Ltd. due for completion by October 1963 at a cost of £7.65 million.

The Consultants said that selection of the best entrance lay between a choice of Benin, Escravos, Forcados and Ramos openings and they produced the following figures:

	Benin	Escravos	Forcados	Ramos
Width, miles	1	1.3	2.2	0.7
Direction of channel	sw	wsw	w	nw
Distance to Sapele, miles	50	79	102	116
Distance to Burutu, miles	78	38	20	33
Distance to Warri, miles	98	58	40	53

Length of channel between bar and coast, miles	3.0	3.5	6.5	4.0
Depth of bar, feet	8	12	11	10
Max sand discharge per tide, cu. yds	nil	nil	nil	5000
Max river discharge per tide million cu. yds.	negligible for Benin & Escravos		120	300
Length of bar, miles	2.7	0.5	1	0.8

Of the water carried by the Niger, the Nun took 45% and the Forcados 55%. Of the 55%, 13% went down leaving 42% for the direction of the Ramos but of this, 16% was diverted down Bomali Creek leaving 26% only for the Ramos. This 26% petered into 14% for Ramos and 12% to the Forcados but was again reduced to 7% for Forcados, the remaining 5% going up the Warri. Unquestionably, the Escravos offered the best approach and to deal with littoral drift, a mole of breakwater at right angles to the coast should be built. As to the justification, the following total annual tonnages in thousands were quoted for 1953 as carried in ocean steamers:

	Burutu	Warri	Sapele	Total
Ocean going	110	63	249	422
Coast wise	56	39	45	140

Thus, $\frac{140}{140+422}$ = 24.9% had to be transhipped in Lagos and, at 13/6d per ton, this was an annual sum of £94,500 to be saved by deepening the bar to 20ft. They recommended stone from Otu near Okitipupa, Abeokuta or Idah-Lokoja stretch, or reinforced concrete caissons on the lines of the Normandy beach landings, or Peine & Krupp sheet steel piling for the first 11,000ft. of main mole. It was desired to use the first and last in combination but the tender exceeding the estimate, one million tons of stone from Otu was signed up. The main mole became 5.5 miles and was to take care of coastline creep for the next 200 years. The waterways to the ports had to be dredged in turn to conform. The cost crept up to £13 million. The work was described as of the first importance and required the building of complete townships at Ore and Escravos.

Escravos however became more than an assured estuary. In April 1965, it was discovered to be sitting on the first off-shore oil field, two years later running at 1½ million tones a year. Gulf Oil had a tank arm at Escravos by 1969. Two single point mooring buoys were provided at 5° 29′ × 4° 55′, N and E respectively and at 5° 31′ × 4° 59′ N and E respectively in the case of the first at 32m and in the case of the second at 21.95 m. They were fed from 2.8 million barrel capacity of 25,000 b/h.

In 1972/73, 16,374,473 tons crude were shipped and 287 tankers were entered. Dredging up the estuary was still a problem to be faced in 1975. In 1979, it was still on the cards along with a "straightening" of the river. A few years before, the Government was negotiating with Agip-Phillips for the siting of a LNG plant at Escravos. Such installations require most careful thinking and in the end, a decision in favour of Escravos was abandoned.

Okrika Refinery Jetty

The low sulphur content oil is found in Delta, Imo and River States. There were seven producing companies; in 1974, Nigeria was the largest producer in Africa; in 1974, the seventh producer in the world. In 1975, they stepped up Port Harcourt refinery from sixty thousand to eight thousand bpd and as a short term measure, the building of a new refined oil jetty at Okrika up the Bonny pipeline, connected to the existing jetty which, in 1972/73, had handled 1.8 million tons refined. This "L"-shaped jetty with a square dolphin at the end of the arm, accommodated tankers of up to 33,530 dwt on the outside, coastals on the inside. A 600ft. wide channel at 29ft. LWOST had been dredged. In 1975, the facilities were to be capable of taking two main and two coastal tankers and a ₦6-8 million contract was awarded to Nigerian Dredging & Marine Ltd. but a year later, Rendel, Palmer and Tritton were retained by the Federal Government and the National Company to design the new jetty. The intention to expand was again expressed in 1979. Okrika is full circle; when of Marine took, as his jumping off point, the Bonny River and sent Robert Hughes in the yacht "Ivy" to recce. They had decided upon Okrika before they found Iguocha, the future Port Harcourt, further up.

Pennington Platform

The Pennington, one of the delta mouths, lies just over on the Bendel side of Rivers State. Here there is an off-shore platform holding 36,700 barrels and loading at 18,000 bph. 465,382 tons were shipped in 1972/73.

Ancient and Modern

Akassa, with trading hulk from 1856 on the broad but shallow Nun sandy beaches, was in 1886 the first to receive a land-based depot when it became the HQ of the Royal Niger Co. and Southern Nigeria Marine. The silting up of the bar caused Colonel Ratsay to move to Forcados and quickly to Burutu in 1898 and the Southern Nigeria Marine followed suit so that after 1906 it was of no importance although ocean-going steamers called until the 30s. The lighthouse alone remains together with the remarkable fact that the bar is now deepening. Brass on the river of that name was a "port" from the time of the Portuguese. It later became a consular headquarters and later a submarine cable station. With the bar silted to 6 ft., it was abandoned until Agip established an export oil terminal.

Opobo, ten miles from the mouth of the Imo, was a most important palm oil centre approached over 13ft. bar. I was on one of the last 5000 ton vessels to berth the port in 1939 whose 18,000 ton trade was taken over by Port Harcourt with railway facilities. The bar was not dredged after the Second World War and the port was closed in 1950. Degema and close-by Abonnema on the Sombriero but reached through the Bonny, Boler Creek, New Calabar River and Kra-Kra Creek, forty-two miles at 16ft. provided mid-stream anchorage for palm products. The NPA's responsibility was limited to dredge, light and buoy. Degema is now defunct but at Abonnema the United Africa Company of Nigeria Ltd. has a bulk palm oil plant and a small "T" shaped wharf alongside on which sea-going ships berth for the purpose of loading. Bakana and Buguma were "ports" on the New Calabar whose trade has been absorbed by Port Harcourt.

The NPA provided a pilot service for Tiko, twenty miles from the sea. Bananas, to the tune of 5.7 million bunches per annum, were produced in 1953 by a system of irrigation that yielded six tonnes of fruit more per hectare than elsewhere. On the territory in the south joining Cameroun in 1961, responsibility ceased. Douala was named by the Portuguese Rio dos Comaroes (River of Prawns) and Victoria was named after Queen Victoria by the Reverend Alfred Saker of London Baptist Mission, proclaimed British on 19th July 1884 by British Consul Hewett who was tipped to the post by Dr Nachtigal in his rush for Douala. The Germans took it for Germany.

The area of the German Cameroun was administered by Nigeria from 1916 to 1922 and as a British Mandated Territory from 1922 to 1960, when Ambas Bay, Bota and Victoria went the way of Tiko. Seventy years before, 10ft. of foreshore were eaten up by the violent surf arising from a wind and current continually in the same direction, and Ambas Bay with submerged rocks was certainly no harbour although four ships could anchor if they got within the protection of Bota breakwater. Imports increased in 1953 because of Colonial Development Corporation's investment. Bota remained unchanged from 1914 and nearby Mondoleh Island harboured kindly memories of Roger Casement.

Turning now to the "modern" of the sub-title, Eket, east bank of the Qua Ibo River has two crude oil berths at off-shore terminal. Warife, on the Benin near Sapele, is used exclusively by coastal tankers for the import of petroleum products in bulk from Lagos.

Lights

The first lighthouse, a fixed light, was built in 1891 by John Stuart to the design of Ritchie of Smethwick, common to 67% of the world's light. The tower still stood in 1954. The second lighthouse was Palm Point, Akassa, Nun entrance, built 1907, clockwork driven rotating, kerosene burning; again to Ritchie's design. Akassa is the most southerly point and there is no land mass before Antarctica. Due to erosion, it was later moved to the eastern bank.

The Germans erected lighthouses in 1904 at Debundscha and Cape Nachtigal in the Camerouns, looking like Rhine Castles. Up till 1926, the scene covered the two Cameroun lights, Escravos, Lagos, Bonny and Akassa. There was no need at "Murder Point" governing the Ramos! In 1977, the NPA called for tenders for six further lights, 30-mile range, at:

	Latitude N	Longitude E
Ebute Lekki	6° 23'	4° 08'
Benin Entrance	5° 46'	5° 01'
Bilabri	4° 51'	5° 28'
St Barbara	4° 19'	6° 37'
Opobo Entrance	4° 27'	7° 33'
Tom Shot Bank (off West Point, Cross River	4° 37'	8° 21'

Survey & Buoyage

Survey and Buoyage was the responsibility of the Harbours Department, and the year 1969/70 marked a real low. Survey ships were laid aside, the acknowledgement that surveys did not tie in with National Triangulation. 1923 saw NMS Pathfinder, jack of all trades — collier, buoyage and survey. Destined to become a beacon in the Calabar River, she was replaced by a new Pathfinder in 1954 followed by a new Dayspring. The laid-aside vessels in 1969 were the Aba (not the EDL of that name) and the Agege. In January 1977, the much needed NMS Lana was commissioned in Lagos. She had a crew of sixty-four.

Port Locomotives

The Nigerian Railway supplied Apapa and Port Harcourt with quay locomotives and cast off flats until the formation of the authority. The maintenance work of Lagos moles and PH harbour (under the Harbour Department) had been entrusted to steam shunters, 0-6-0 ST, Hunslet works numbers 1159 & 1171, ex LGR 1 class Nos 2 & 4 and Hunslet works 655 & 810. In 1955, the moles acquired the use of NR 0-6-0 ST Nos 61, 63, 65, 66, Hunslet Nos 1159, 1170, 1171, Bagnall works Nos 1869 & 1920 and ex Hawthorn, Leslie NR No 42, 0-6-0 ST. For the construction of Carter bridge No 2, Bagnall supplied 0-4-0 ST works No 2373. For the construction of the 1922 Apapa wharf, Armstrong Whitworth used LGR No 7 which was a Hunslet 0-6-0 ST makers No 939. Lagos Harbour Works also supplied the power for Aro quarry and Bagnall supplied 0-4-0 ST works No 1940.

The Authority purchased 5 MAK six coupled diesel hydraulics of 400 hp to man Apapa and PH quays on take-over and by 1965, NRC, which had almost similar machines, obligingly purchased them, the writer being the NRC negotiating officer along with the Chief Mechanical Engineer, so that the Authority could in turn purchase ten Hunslet 268 hp C class diesel hydraulics with centre cab, 28ft. 2in. length over buffers employing Voith L203V transmission coupled to Rolls Royce C8SFL pressure charged engines. Axleload was 12 tons and maximum tractive effort put at 24,430 lbs. The locomotive could negotiate a 160ft. curve and haul a trailing load of 1320 tons on the level.

To build the Escravos 6-mile breakwater, Richard Costain Ltd. acquired locomotives similar to the Associated Portland Cement Works fleets at Abese between Lagos and Abeokuta. These were F.C. Hibberd & Co Planet LC-TC 20-ton 4-couple diesel hydraulics, 3ft. 6in. gauge 25 tons weight, powered by Dorman 6LC 152 bhp engine.

Rates

Harbour dues were levied from 1910 on all passengers, livestock, cargo, shipped or unshipped, in connection with a sea voyage, but only in respect of the port of Lagos. The Forcados/Lagos 10/- per ton transhipment was absorbed as a harbour due from 1917.

Port Harcourt was otherwise treated, but in order that ports should not compete with each other, Hammond suggested in 1924 that on completion of the NER, PH should fall into line with Lagos. Light and buoyage were levied per ton of NRT on first entry into a port and were in force everywhere by 1924. Anchorage dues per ton of NRT for all ships remaining in port after thirty days tied up were in force in 1962. Mooring per ton of NRT was levied on every ship making fast and for every 48 hours thereafter. Berthing dues were payable on all ships exceeding 500 tonnes.

Berthage in force in 1924 was at the rate of 1d per ton per 48 hours Lagos. Elsewhere it was 5/- ton, terminals and handling. By 1962, it was 3d for the first 24 hours; by 1973, on any ship alongside wharf, ₦0.025 per tonne of NRT per 24 hours, and thereafter per half day. Pilotage covered ship changing berth and from the start was raised per foot of draft. Towage rates were calculated at under 0.4 or over 0.6 nm. Storage rates always favoured exports but the fondness of shippers for translating transit into warehouse forced, from the 50s, penal action as necessary to accelerate throughput. In 1962, import free period was 72 hours; tin and produce export 14 days; export others 7 days. Revision rates in 1973 were not severe.

Wharfage rates were levied if shore handling charges had not been raised, 2/- per ton in 1962 and ₦0.2 per tonne in 1973. Except for coal, shore handling was reduced in 1927. Eight years later, Conference Lines raised 2/- per dwt. Railway became responsible at tide water terminals in 1934/35 but on the formation of the Authority, entries ceased on railway waybills. In 1962, the Authority treated exports and imports of flour, stockfish, salt, sugar and milk at the same rate, 15/- per ton. All other imports were 17/- per ton.

In 1917, Elder Dempster Lines introduced through charges, Liverpool to any railway station and vice versa.

Crane hire was always kept low as an encouragement to masters to use the facility and not their own derricks. In the sixties, the Authority introduced the entirely new charge of conservancy, bar to berth and back but in 1972, the Government listened to the grumbling of the oil chaps and "slashed" terminal handling from 3/4d to 1/2d per ton. The Authority used 1016 kilos to the ton and treated volume as 40 cu. ft./ton and 50 cu. ft./ton for timber. In 1924, the Port Harcourt Chamber of Commerce complained about the cost of transhipping a ton to Opobo and Degema, 10/- transit, 5/- import terminal, 2/6d export terminal, 2/6d haulage.

Statistics

Statistics is a most difficult subject because of constant contradiction and change in meaning. Even 1980 was no help. Quotation veers more to the historical. The first yardstick is overall country-wide trade. In 1894/95, Niger Coast imports totalled £739,864, while exports was £825,099. In 1896, a separate Lagos appeared with £901,475 imports and £975,263 exports. Until 1904, Porto Novo was included in the more comprehensive figures published by the Colonial Office from 1901 — £:

	Imports Merchandise	Specie	Exports Merchandise	Specie	Total Trade
1900	1,735,244	210,809	1,886,883	131,834	4,033,770
1910	5,122,370	734,965	5,258,452	45,734	11,161,521
1918	7,423,159	895,240	9,511,970	52,888	17,883,256

At the time of Independence trade had taken on the following pattern in £000's:

	1958		1960		1962	
	Import	Export	Import	Export	Import	Export
Sterling area	86,215	77,564	105,441	82,469	88,196	72,931
Dollar area	12,101	9,060	14,035	17,866	19,531	20,954
Europe	29,676	41,901	42,187	31,221	39,225	56,477
Others	38,282	7,025	54,228	34,063	56,265	13,651
Total	166,274	135,550	215,891	165,619	203,217	164,013

Dealing in country-wide traffic but in tonnage in 1900, the export of 85,624 tons palm kernel and 45,508 tons palm oil dominated the scene. The First World War with its shortage of stemming depressed export although the demand for oleaginous products remained high. Right up to Independence, palm kernels led the way with significant tonnages of groundnuts, palm oil, cocoa and hides and skins, until everything was dwarfed by the petroleums. In 1909, Southern Nigeria cleared 749,016 tons; in 1912, 380,000 tons. The following years taken from three decades include Victoria and Tiko: 000's of tons:

1935		1945		1954	
Import	Export	Import	Export	Import	Export
401	985	343	1037	1654	1972

From 1955 to 1963, cocoa led the way, groundnuts for two years with palm kernels second in 1960 and otherwise the runner up. In 1900, the principal import was cotton goods always beloved by the fashion conscious indigene. From 1937, for twenty-six years, the most important food import was always fish except only for the four years, 1947-'50, when salt eclipsed it. Sugar and flour were imported from 1952, milk from 1958. From 1955 to 1963, manufactured goods averaged 62.9% and machinery 37.1%. At the close of the 70s import control became rigid with emphasis on plant and consumer goods were only brought in where there was no local substitute.

By 1976/77, import and export total had reached 7,591,553 tonnes. In 1978/79 export was 2,622,959 tonnes, import 16,357,008.

Eight ports were at work, namely, Apapa, Tin Can Island, Port Harcourt, Okrika, Warri, Koko, Burutu and Calabar, an imbalance which was a cause of national concern. In fact, the imbalance had persisted from 1969 and had been building up.

Coastwise traffic in 000's of tons reached the proportion:

	Loaded	Unloaded
1949	321	312
1956	453	353
1958	368	508

Lagos took the lion's share of export and Port Harcourt/Lagos the import. Turning from £'s and tons to ships as a unit, entering Nigeria:

1910	557	vessels	
1918	286	"	(worst war year)
1928	1,029	"	
1958	2,112	"	(1st year to top 2000)
1966/67	4,632	"	
1976/77	5,432	"	

Taking nominated ports, Lagos grew from 526 in 1922/23 to 994 discharged, 340 loaded, 282 loaded/discharged in 1968/69. Port Harcourt in 1965, its peak year, handled 1230.

Turning to the flag fluttering at the mast 1904 saw 425 British and 211 German. Other nations were recorded only as "others" from 1910. The French and Norwegians were recorded from 1937 and the Nigerian flag from 1969. In 1972/73 vessels, excluding fishing and naval, reported:

British	593
Liberian	412
Danish	365

Greek	293
Nigerian	264
Norwegian	245
French	180
Dutch	106
West German	95
USA	70
Senegal	44

Others, the flags of forty-eight nations made up 1067, made a grand total of 3734.

The greatest total tonnage handled by the railway was 534,379 Apapa and 379,296 Port Harcourt, both in 1952/53. In 1955/56, stirring times, the railway handled 76% of Apapa import and 54% of Port Harcourt import, in 1956/57, 81% of Apapa export and in 1958/59, 68% of Port Harcourt export. Indeed the mighty have fallen; in 1972/73, Apapa rail shared imports ten per cent. The railway ran a "C" and "D" service, mainly the "collected" end, clearing 13,508 tons in 1960/61, the maximum since the first service of 1936 with a Z.N. Zarpas lorry and 4-wheel trailer.

Turning to individual ports outside Lagos, Forcados was the most important in 1904. 1930 was the best year before the depression and figures in £s for the scattered ports were:

	Import	Export
Burutu & Forcados	856,764	1,879,943
Calabar	854,231	1,040,759
Warri	644,468	647,139
Opobo	232,136	540,545
Degema	219,633	645,658
Sapele	1,77,764	396,244
Koko	33,353	169,151

Considered next are tonnages dealt with at individual ports: Calabar did not exceed 54,000 until 1962. Warri handled 81,000 total in 1935 but in 1972/73, it reached 205,422 total. Imports through Sapele grew to 104,000 by 1960. Imports at Burutu was 72,000 in 1957. Thereafter, it dwindled. Figures for Victoria and Tiko when controlled by Nigeria, were:

| | 1935 | | 1945 | |
	Import	Export	Import	Export
Victoria	4,000	6,000	2,000	4,000
Tiko	4,000	43,000	—	—

The case of Port Harcourt:

	Import	Export	Total
1918	12,778	13,422	26,200
1919	23,384	27,600	50,984
1920	41,955	38,480	80,435
1935	41,000	99,000	140,000
1945	23,000	314,000	337,000
1954	309,000	423,000	732,000
72/73	470,833	169448	640281
78/79	2,444,735	180,915	2,625,560

In the case of Lagos, exports was 787,285 in 1895 but war year 1917 saw but 167,807 total; 1927/28 import, 346,384, export, 281,304, total 627,688. Lagos total 1935, 607,000, 1945, 809,000, 1954, 2,027,000. Import climbed to 2,290,000 in 1961 and import and export 2,936,646 in 1972/73 went up to 4.8 million tons in 1974.

There were 8,867 staff on the payroll in 1955/56. This grew to 10,834 by 31/3/1970. In the fifteen years between 1955-1970, the number of expatriate staff dropped from 191 to 51. By this last year, indigenes were in control to the extent of 90%.

Post World War II import figures, £000:

	Lagos	Sapele	Warri	Burutu	Degema	Port Harcourt	Calabar
1951	60,273	1,663	2,257	1,462	98	13,338	2,185
1955	96,217	2,266	2,751	1,851	160	24,239	2,747
1958	112,926	2,558	2,247	2,239	84	37,259	2,260
1961	158,020	3,747	3,229	2,589	58	47,759	1,405
Export £000:							
1951	69,434	9,853	1,397	1,790	4,682	21,777	7,083
1954	87,233	9,852	1,866	3,351	3,338	30,266	8,014
1959	87,319	18,450	3,066	3,691	1,941	32,095	7,905
1861	88,472	20,535	3,164	3,820	1,071	38,405	5,677

Containers were planned from the late 50s but first saw the Apapa statistics horizon in 1968. From 1968 to 1972 in dwt metric metric, growth was from one thousand to just under twenty-eight thousand. By 1974, 50% of Apapa trade was in containers, 6000 twenty feet equivalent units p.a. with expansion put at 24,000 units by 1980 for which the ports were gearing themselves.

The Making of Records

Baro was a railway river port tied to seasonal flow and operation by head porterage, a port where the railway retained its wagons and should have offered shippers an inducement rate. But what records did the railway achieve? Maximum imports was 22,357 tons in January 1945; maximum exports was 8,115 tons in December 1946. In 1959/60 the annual imports was 44,320 tons. In 1934/35, the exports was 43,429 tons.

Port Harcourt, the port without its own crane for years, reached a discharge rate of 55 tons per hour in 1922. In September 1946, maximum imports reached 6,415 tons; in July 1978, 310,133. Everyone is aware that with the discovery of oil, agricultural produce leaked off and the best month for exports was, as long ago as March 1946, at 18,775 tons. Iddo railway wharf loaded 102 tons per hour but Apapa reached 144, or, in 1933/34, 25.1 tons per crane working hour. It is to be remembered that we are dealing with bagged produce. Maximum monthly export in the old days at Apapa was 60,326 tons in December 1944. Imports reached 18,295 tons in August 1945 and the excellent figure of 533,009 tonnes in January 1977. This last was a "Lagos" figure but it did not include Customs Quay which had been closed two months before.

From the foregoing, it is instructive to turn to efficiency, measured by cargo handled in tons lineal foot of quay per annum, and one can only compare the two old railway ports because, of the others, no statistics were ever published. Port Harcourt's best figure was 208 in 1952/53, Customs Quays 144 in 1927/28 and Apapa's 296 in 1952/53. So the World Bank, for future projections, used a figure of 300 but Charles Rooke of the railway said 324 was possible when Nigeria would be on par with Bombay and Calcutta. The Authority came near the target figure in 1969/70 with 299.

Conclusion

Oil at 2.4 mbpd was near the capacity of the infrastructure. Other global forces at work obtruded. Tin Can Island was hailed as Nigeria's second port; second because shippers preferred Apapa with its better connection to the hinterland. Nevertheless, it was later to become the supreme of the two in use. Way back in 1970, shippers had wondered why mandatory instructions had not been given to spread the load there and elsewhere. In February 1980, the Transport Ministry at least said just that; Warri and Calabar would be forced down shippers' throats.

In 1976, the Government planned six fishery terminals — Lagos, Badagry, Aiyetoro Ibidauda, Koko, Port Harcourt and Orun Idua. Trawlers had long been playing around in the highly lucrative sea and the move was welcomed. In December 1977, a National Lighterage Company was to be set up. In 1978, invitations were sent to the USA, Poland and Italy to submit proposals for construction and management of the Lagos, Port Harcourt and Burutu dockyards of which the Nigerian National Shipping Line would take full advantage. Nigeria asked the Netherlands to accept trainees at the rate of 100 p.a. in harbour administration, carried out in Rotterdam, an idea born of the Lagos congestion of the late 70s. In February 1980, the Government said they were interested in providing a passenger service by NNSL along the coast without such facilities since the withdrawal of the EDL Aureol. In all these moves, thinking was in the right direction.

A port is as efficient as its basin inside and mode of evacuation outside allow it to be. By 1979, the latter was in hand, but, far too late. Co-ordination between port construction and port evacuation was lacking until the late 70s.

The 1962/68 National Plan allocated

₦47.2 million, and spent ₦48 million. The 1970/74 Plan allocated ₦37.5 million mainly for civil war rehabilitation. Main improvements fell into the 1975/80 Plan and at the end of it all, 120 deep water berths would be projected for a 1990 throughput of 9.7 million long tons. Then there was the "curse" of documentation, the good and the bad of it, overdue for revision. Every new Government control provides a possible doorway to corruption. Before there is further port expansion, documentation with inherent ship delays or cargo imprisonment must be examined.

Once upon a time, ships from Europe called all the way out at other ports but now they are quite often express to Lagos, beating the airmail and the necessary paper work.

Finally, there is the most difficult hurdle of all — trade imbalance; with her wealth, Nigeria imports every conceivable shipment but there is no exportable surplus to make up for the loss of foreign currency. This is the most important long term consideration in the matter of berthage utilisation.

Chapter 8

Aviation and Airports

On 17th December 1903 in North Carolina, an aircraft was borne aloft; on 25th July 1909, an aircraft flew the English Channel; on 25th August 1919 the British commenced their first regular airservice, between London and Paris. But, it was said that air travel came late to West Africa. By 1980, every State wanted a prestigious airport to international standards. It was realised that the world was shrinking and that this was due to air explosion and no other media.

The western states of Africa lacked international highways and railroads and for reasons of history trade lay with the continent of Europe and hardly at all with neighbours. African land-locked countries had to depend on the facility of air once it was within their financial grasp. The East African Community engaged consultants. Most countries realised that tourism was just not on without an airline. The first most successful multi-state venture was Air Afrique. Europe led the way with Air France, Lufthansa, Alitalia, Sabena (forming ATLAS) and KLM, SAS, UTA, Swissair (forming KSSU) and pointed to the benefits of standardisation, a lesson unheeded by Nigeria for too long.

The history of Nigeria in the air is a compote of the Royal Air Force, Imperial Airways, World War II supply route, an international corporation, a national corporation and refuge in a foreign airline, with planes in use from converted bombers to large subsonic planes and plans in mind for the reception of supersonic planes.

Royal Air Force

"Bud" Carpenter, a private individual, not infrequently flew a de Havilland Moth from Kano to Lagos in the 20s using the Nigerian Railway as his "radio" aid, keeping it in sight mile after mile, as did British Royalty when flying years later. In the early 30s Herr Blaitach, Cameroun Plantation Manager, flew around with Focke Wolfe training craft. Then there was the pilot who flew Lagos-Warri with a sea plane. Dakar was on the French airline map from 1925 when planes made four hop stops to cover the Sahara.

The Imperial Airways was formed in 1924 and by 1929 was flying Egypt-South Africa via East and Central Africa. It had opened up routes to West Africa, West Indies, Malaya and Hong Kong by 1939. For the West African route, it had prepared a survey of the coast from Guinea to Khartoum in 1925. In the same year, the Royal Air Force had a particularly active squadron in the Sudan whose commanding officer decided to fly Khartoum-Maiduguri-Kano. The flight of Bristol fighters landed all right — on the race course — and a report of the sortie said it would be necessary to have emergency landing fields every twenty miles. When the RAF flew Cairo-Khartoum they used wheels or floats as the case appeared to demand! The Kano landing became the subject of a water colour now in the safe-keeping of the Department of Civil Aviation.

The maiden issue of the Nigerian *Daily Times* was published on Tuesday 1st June 1926. The front page carried the news: "Aeroplane flies over Lagos". It was a French plane piloted by Monsieur Landrich carrying a passenger from Elizabethville to Dakar. Forced down at Opobo for want of fuel, replenished by local merchants, she next made it to Cotonou and everyone who heard the noise rushed to the Lagos race course to see her overhead at 1000ft. Further history of early flights coming down in the Niger at Jebba and Lokoja is recorded in the "European" Club at Lokoja.

In 1932, the Imperial Airways commenced a passenger flight, Cairo-Cape of Good Hope; in 1934, Chargeurs Reunis operated a flying boat service along the west coast from Dakar to Pointe Noire; in 1936, the Imperial Airways flew West Africa-Britain via Khartoum with a 14-seater de Havilland 86. The first administration to cater was the Harbour Department whose Apapa Marine Officer in charge of dockyard became Control Officer Apapa Airport.

The need for aerodromes in Nigeria was realised in 1930 and a representative of the Air Ministry in London came to inspect sites for a chain of landing grounds. In the meantime, flights of the RAF continued until Imperial Airways took up their 1936 service. Sites were selected by the RAF at Maiduguri, Kano, Kaduna, Minna, Oshogbo and Lagos (Apapa). In the beginning it was thought necessary to construct several runways oriented to avoid cross wind landings and take offs as the older type of tailwheel aircraft was more prone to swing than later nosewheel types. The Imperial Airways flying boats touched down in the lagoon off Ikoyi and provided a fine sight from Carter Bridge.

In 1934/35, Elders Colonial Airways and Imperial Airways, 50% share each, proposed a Takoradi-Accra-Lagos service running in conjunction with the mail boats. There was to be a three-stage implementation of the scheme; the first step was Khartoum-Kano air and Kano-Lagos rail; the second was Khartoum-Kano-Kaduna-Minna-Oshogbo-Lagos air while the third step was to extend the service to Takoradi. If ever there was a useless exercise, this was it and attention was soon diverted to Lagos-Khartoum to link in with Johannesburg-London. The chosen airfield sites became a reality at Lagos (Apapa), Kano and Maiduguri in 1935. Because of a fear of yellow fever, however the Kano site was moved five miles to the north of the city and the Emir cut the first sod. The first scheduled arrival, in 1936, at Kano, that 1000-year old central market of the Sudan and future air junction, was heralded in a spectacular fashion by the Emir and people who staged a full scale "FAFI". A hundred horsemen clad in chain mail and black ostrich feathers in their helmets, thundered across the airfield to halt at the nose of the plane to deliver their welcome.

The Governor, Sir Bernard Bourdillon, flew in the October 1936 DH 86 first ever commercial flight from Lagos calling at Oshogbo, Minna and Kaduna. Flying in Nigeria was mainly military, up to 1935.

Airways from 1936

The Imperial Airways operated Handley Page 42 "Hannibal" 4-engine biplanes on their route, Cairo-Kisumu, and one of their pilots was Wing Commander E.H. Coleman AFC, later to become Director, Civil Aviation, Nigeria. The de Havilland 86 named "Daedalus", "Delia", and "Dione" on the "Horseshoe Route", Khartoum-Kano-Lagos, run once weekly from 15th February 1936, was a biplane powered by four small engines stationed at Khartoum, transhipment to the "Hannibal" being effected at that base. The return circuit took seven days. The plane took off from Apapa leaving a cloud of laterite dust in the sky. The 1200 feet polo ground in Kano, still in use up to 1936, called for great judgement in landing and flight across Northern Nigeria during the harmattan, with the primitive navigational aids in use, called for every skill from the pilot. The route had been proved by Captain O.P. Jones who had reached the Sudan from London on the 1st February 1936. He chose El Obeid-El Fasher-El Geneina-Abeche-Ati-Fort Lamy-Maiduguri-Kano.

The outbreak of war prevented implementation of the plan to build twenty-four aerodromes in Nigeria at the rate of two per annum, a facility then seen as inevitably required. The weekly service was extended to Accra in 1937 and later on to Takoradi, Freetown and Bathurst. The service continued till 1940 still connecting Khartoum when it was withdrawn.

More people used the London-West African service and for some years, the trunk arm was way ahead of the patronage up the west side of Nigeria at the three intermediate aerodromes of Oshogbo, Minna and Kaduna. Due to soil erosion, much grass planting was needed before touchdown could be made. The essential backbone to the trunk was the tie in with air junctions, Khartoum in the past, Kano in the future. For Empire routes, Imperial Airways laid down 1400 yards. Apapa airport, apart from the dust nuisance, lay in the direction of heavy line squalls.

World War II

At the outbreak of the war, the general practice was 1000-1200 yards main runways and 800 yards secondary runways. Between Egypt and Cape Town, there were twenty-seven main airfields, thirty intermediate and seventeen wireless stations; on the 2150-mile hop Khartoum-Lagos, there were ten airfields not counting the terminals.

During the early days of the war, it remained peaceful in Nigeria but with the collapse of France and the entry of Italy, affairs changed rapidly with the virtual loss of the Mediterranean. With few aerodromes, those planned and more besides, including Yola, were completed soon after the close of 1940. Much extra work was entailed with the construction of buildings and accommodation for crews as Lagos had become an important staging post for the ferrying of aircraft to the Middle East and India. The RAF used the old Empire mail route out of Lagos to Cairo via Khartoum and called it the "Middle East Reinforcement Route". The first sortie began on 14th July 1940. Long range fuel tankers were used as the three Nigerian intermediate airports were closed as fuelling points. The aircraft to be assembled came into Takoradi in packing cases in their thousands. The new aerodromes of which Kano and Lagos were the most important meant urgent compliance with Customs, Immigration and Health, to World Health Organisation's standards.

In 1941, the USA started to take an active interest, building large camps at Kano and Maiduguri. Pan American Airways started to operate in conjunction with British Overseas Airways Corporation (BOAC), the Corporation formed from Imperial Airways early in 1940 on the Kano-Maiduguri route. The number of aircraft ferried increased and at one time, over 100 planes a day were passing through Nigeria for the Burma Campaign, the norm being eighty.

Apapa as an airport was killed by the long term enemy — not the short term enemy, Germany, but the mosquitoes luxuriating in the nearby swamps and the alternative airport, Ikeja by the railway line, was brought into substitute use in April 1942. (The mosquitoes of Apapa were finally put paid to in 1949 when reclamation works for the port included the old airfield.)

Elders Colonial Airways was taken over by the British Government from 1940 for the duration of the war — in fact, in a sense, for all time, as in due course they decided to nationalise the London-West African route and this precluded further Elder activity in that field. During the war, the Atlantic was not only used by the UK/WA personnel, but also by those posted to the Middle East and India who then changed from afloat to aloft. The de Havilland 86s were replaced by Lockheed 14s but they took the new route, Takoradi-Lagos-Douala-Bangui-Arusha-Juba-Khartoum-Cairo. Towards the end of the war, the route Lagos-Bathurst-Lisbon-London was introduced and sometime after the war Khartoum, with its appeal, was abandoned.

Meantime, the future "milk round" was born. Before the end of the war, RAF Transport Command operated a twice weekly "bush" service, Accra-Lagos-Port Harcourt-Enugu-Jos-Kano-Kaduna-Lagos-Accra. The service ceased when RAFTC was withdrawn in the middle of 1946. By the end of the war, the heaviest aircraft employed had been the USAF Liberator of 90,000 lbs requiring a 2000 yard runway. Kano had become 8900 feet.

West African Airways Corporation (WAAC)

After the Second World War when the RAF and the USAF had withdrawn from Nigeria, the main responsibility for civil aviation was vested in the Public Works Department with the Department of Posts & Telegraphs providing aeronautical radio facilities using obsolescent war-time equipment. Air traffic control required re-organising on a civilian basis and an adequate fire service was needed. The British Ministry of Civil Aviation conducted an aerial survey in 1945 and the Nigerian Government re-opened the "bush" service under the name "Nigerian Air Services" using DC3s on charter from BOAC. This time the route was Accra-Lagos-Benin-Port Harcourt-Enugu-Jos-Kano-Kaduna-Lagos-Accra thrice weekly whilst BOAC undertook all servicing.

In May 1946, legislation was signed by His Majesty the King setting up a West African Air Transport Authority consisting of the respective Governors of Nigeria, the Gold Coast, Sierra Leone and the Gambia with the Governor of Nigeria as President; and the formation of the West African Airways Corporation (WAAC) to develop air services "in and between the West African territories." The Corporation was subsidised by the four member states and Nigeria, in which two thirds of all the flying took place, had to pay the greatest proportion; it was 1948 before the Corporation was self-supporting.

The first scheduled flight operated by WAAC in its own aircraft was on October 28th, 1947 in a de Havilland twin-engined 730 hp "Dove" flying Lagos-Benin-Calabar-Enugu-Port Harcourt. Eleven of these craft were purchased by 1948. It was considered best suited to the Corporation's commitments, seating six; of them it was said that most of the operating cost was in the nose of the aircraft — a reference to the highly paid captain.

The Doves were named after members of the Air Transport Authority. "Sir Beresford Stooke" was one example. It was a serious problem obtaining suitable aircraft. In the developed countries, there was a preponderance of military aircraft; in the developing countries, the economics of what was suitable had not been worked out. Overseas, they used de Havilland 86 and 89, Dakotas, Vikings, Lodestars, Doves, Herons, Bristols and Beavers. Outstanding was the Dakota, at one time 75% of civil aircraft — indeed the model Ford T.

In view of the considerable delay in the delivery of the six 18-seater Marathons ordered in 1948, the Corporation had to charter two Bristol Freighters from the West African Command and to hire-purchase two Bristol Wayfarers from the British Ministry of Civil Aviation. The Corporation flew the Doves on Nigerian and Gold Coast internal services and the Wayfarers on the coast route as far as Dakar, having taken over this route from BOAC. Wayfarers also went to Khartoum once a fortnight. On international routes, BOAC continued the service introduced after the war from the UK over the Sahara to Kano and Lagos at first with modified wartime-built Haltons and Yorks such as "Manton" and then with the comfortable Hermes design of civil airliner carrying forty passengers. This route brought one down at Tripoli to a breath of fresh air northbound and to hangars studded for years with wartime bullets.

Kano and Lagos were international airports but Calabar serving Tiko was not until Cameroun ceased to be under British and French Trusteeship. Yola became linked with Maiduguri and everywhere they called the Dove "Jirgin Sama" (Canoe of the sky).

There were other difficulties. In 1948 a Director of Civil Aviation was appointed to advise the President of the Air Transport Authority and the individual West African Governments but the post was without executive authority until 1950 when it may be said that the Department of Civil Aviation was truly formed in Nigeria. The Meteorological Department supplied data about the weather at destination and along the route. The Posts and Telegraphs provided telecommunications between aerodromes and maintained radio navigational aids at internal aerodromes but not at the major airports. The Department of Civil Aviation administered the aerodromes in Nigeria which were placed in four categories: Grade 1, Kano and Lagos; Grade 2, international aerodromes of less importance; Grade 3, internal aerodromes to which scheduled traffic operated but enjoying less traffic than Grade 2; Grade 4, points to which non-scheduled traffic operated.

Early Biplane landing in Nigeria

Altogether there were two major airports and twenty-six aerodromes in Nigeria. In general the largest aeroplanes in use by the British, French, Dutch and Belgium Lines on long range international routes could land and take off from the two major airports but at the internal points, size of craft was restricted to about twenty-eight seaters. In the Eastern Region and the Camerouns, there were landing strips and helicopter pads and there were at least thirty landing strips of about 1800ft. in the Northern Region to which light aircraft could ply.

Herald on the approach of an aircraft to Kano Airport

Air Traffic Control had three functions: Flight Information Services, Approach Control, and Aerodrome Control. There was a Flight Information Centre at Kano and a Sub-Flight Information Centre at Lagos. In Nigeria, the students selected for this professional training had nearly all been Air Traffic Control Assistants. Nevertheless on arriving overseas they carried out fifty hours in a synthetic training aeroplane before starting the course.

It became evident in 1951 that specialist staff were necessary and an Aeronautical Signals Branch was set up in the Department of Civil Aviation working very closely with the engineering staff of the P & T. This was in marked contrast to the aids used in the early days of aviation when manually operated direction finders worked by a wireless operator in a hut somewhere near the aerodrome sufficed during daylight. There were fifteen radio navigation beacons throughout Nigeria.

Arriving at Kano during the harmattan could be hazardous and the approach lighting system consisted of a series of searchlights, two hundred feet apart, sunk into the runway with the beam directed towards the approach by mirrors. Aircraft were segregated in flight, vertical, by the observance of 1000ft. between planes. Up to a ceiling of 29,000ft., when double that distance, was required; lateral, by adherence to different routes, longitudinal, by laid down time intervals for departure or holding in the air.

The Police, Local Government Authorities, Military, Nigerian Navy, Nigerian Ports Authority, Nigerian Railway and the National Airline had important parts to play in air/sea/ground rescue and the demarcated areas coincided with the air space controlled by the two Flight Information Centres. Kano was responsible for north of, and Lagos, south of, the following line: the Dahomey/Nigerian boundary at $10° 00'$ N $\times$ $03° 38'$ E to $08° 00'$ N $\times$ $08° 00'$ E thence alone the 08 parallel to the Cameroun boundary at $08° 00'$ N $\times$ $12° 07'$ E.

Elsewhere, war had stimulated demand and a few African countries were without an ex-wartime aerodrome. Robertsfield in Monrovia was built entirely by the Americans for military use. The showing of the national flag overseas began to mean something. The oldest African airline to take wing was the United Arab Airways closely followed by South African Airways, both in the 30s. From the newly independent states, Ghana, which set a high standard for the customer, was the first away in 1953 in association with BOAC with a fleet of four — Doves and DC3s. After Nigeria came Air Guinea and Air Mali, both aided by Russia. BOAC assisted Kenya, Uganda and Tanganyika to form the East African Airways. Sierra Leone entered into agreement with British United Airways, Gambia acted as handling agents. Ghana, Guinea and Mali however had difficulties with the Ilyushins designed for servicing at 300 flying hour intervals as they had been used to a figure more like 2000. By 1965, Aeroflot had four routes into Africa.

One airline deserves its own place in history as it was in the course of time to become a truly international affair, conceived by four airlines and fostered by twelve ex-French colonies in Africa. That airline was Air Afrique.

Before the war, Chargeurs Reunis' Aeromaritime coastal service was extended inland coupled with Regie Air Afrique to sub-Sahara to become UTA — Union de Transports Aeriens. Then followed a 15-year competition between the Line, the independent TAI and the state-owned Air France. Before 1965, TAI and the Chargeurs Line had fused and shared routes with Air France. Air France came to retain Dakar for Latin America and Nairobi for Madagascar only. No other airline in Africa represented a responsibility to twelve independent states.

Back to Nigeria where in 1948 Sir Hubert Walker had laid it down that one aircraft per day called only for a grass runway. Whilst the Khartoum service lingered, it remained a west coast-east coast link, a link later restored but only by a foreign airline. Passengers carried by WAAC were:

1947/48	1948/49	1949/50	1950/51
1,804	12,813	15,149	32,089

The railway lost first class passengers only to the airline. Bida strip was laid down in 1950. In 1951, an Aerodrome Fire Fighting service was started and by 1965 the establishment had grown to 400 officers, non-commissioned officers and men. Kano headed the list with 120 men, a very up-to-date fleet of rescue vehicles, fire tenders and first aid.

In 1951, sixteen aerodromes were manned by African Superintendents and the need for training of West African pilots was appreciated. Both Ghana and Nigeria sent their students to Air Services Training Ltd. at Hamble in the UK. In 1955, a site of side 3000 feet for a flying training ground was picked out from the air seven miles west of Apapa and ten miles south of the airport.

In 1951 also the WAAC fleet was listed as ten Dove, three Bristol Wayfarers, two Bristol Freighters and six Marathons on order. The Marathons were 4-engined Gipsy 70 of 340 hp each and provided seating for eighteen. The Handley Page Hermes on the Lagos-London BOAC flight were replaced by Argonauts by March 1952, more robust, an earner of an excellent reputation for time-keeping. The Hermes, such as RMA Hannibal, would leave Lagos 12 noon for Kano, Tripoli, former Castel Benito, London, arriving 8.00 a.m. the next day and what a first class journey it was after a 15-month tour in the tropics. The preprandial refreshments took as long to serve as a main meal and there were many who raised no cheer for the faster jet of later years.

The WAAC Doves on the busier routes were replaced in 1952 by four long overdue Handley Page Marathons. The Marathons were not however made for the rough aerodromes of the times, they had a short life span, and in turn were replaced by de Havilland Herons, 4-engined, 12-seater, very much a larger sister of the Dove. It was in this year that the WAAC Khartoum service known as the Blue Nile route, was withdrawn for lack of patronage.

In 1952, aerodromes in Nigeria had grown to thirty with twenty-one in use by scheduled services. WAAC carried first class mail at 1½d per oz, the cheapest rate in the world, some two years after they had pioneered second class flight using 56 sear Bristol Wayfarers. This idea was the father of the tourist class on other airlines. The Bristol Freighters, ugly planes in the skies, carried many cars in the wet season. The 2-engined Bristol flew the coastal routes and all services were known as "Fliers". There was the Coastal Flier Lagos-Accra, the Ashanti Flier Accra-Kumasi, the Eastern Flier Lagos-Benin-Port Harcourt and the Hausa Flier Lagos-Jos-Kano, both Marathon and Dove cruising at 160 mph. It was possible to connect with Senegal from Freetown using the "Intercontinental" service. Lagos-Accra cost £4. Ikeja-Tiko, the latter then a grass surface in the banana plantations, ran four times a week. Ikeja-Port Harcourt was 2° 20' flying, Port Harcourt-Calabar 45' and Calabar-Tiko 35'.

The craft were based at Accra, Lagos and Kano. The camel-mounted trumpeter that heralded the approach of the caravan to Kano romped over to the airport to sound like warning. He was busy; Kano handled more long distance traffic than any other in the British Empire and paid tribute to the four corners of the world whence it came by its famous signpost. Certificates of airworthiness were issued by the Ikeja Engineer licensed by the British Ministry of Civil Aviation and the British Air Registration Board kept a surveyor resident in Lagos. In 1952 Kano was designed for a maximum of 100,000 lbs weight and Ikeja and Maiduguri up to 80,000 lbs each.

In 1953, the World Bank gave its views: extend runway lighting and make all runways suitable for the landing of Bristol planes, at a cost of £173,000. This meant "take the Marathons out of service." They said the cost of operation was high because of low aircraft utilisation, 1200 hours per annum or 14% brought about by the absence of landing lights for night flying.

The staff in 1953 numbered 1092 and the recorded take offs and landings on Nigerian fields were 16,000 in 1949/50 and 26,444 in 1951/52. The average distance between airfields was 170 miles and the Bank felt that Nigeria was adequately covered except in the area of the delta where the terrain did not permit the use of conventional craft. Rates averaged 1/- per passenger mile first class and 4½d second class. The Bank recorded that the Corporation viewed a future based on the success of the second class fare associated with the use of large capacity aircraft. The Joint Group of Engineers felt the recommended runway improvements did not go far enough.

An additional Wayfarer was purchased in 1952 and later the Freighters were converted into 56-seater passenger planes, Tiko becoming a point of call on this service. The Airline had adopted the symbol of the Flying Elephant and the slogan " You Too Can Fly". In 1951 elsewhere, it was stated that the first successful fixed radial engine was the Bristol Jupiter and the Armstrong Siddeley Jaguar and that the turbo-jet had no competition over 500 mph. The 1952 Nigerian route map showed Dakar in the west and Khartoum still in the east Tamale was an extra in the Gold Coast and there were seventeen aerodromes in Nigeria which included Sokoto, Gusau and Yola.

From 1953 on, the world screen the Handley Page Herald and the Avro 798 became serious contenders for purchase. Aircraft registered, all types, to make some comparisons, were Nigeria 30, Federation of Rhodesia and Nyasaland 136, East Africa 144 of which latter 90 were privately owned. By 1954 all British Colonial territories were served by air except St. Helena, Seychelles, and the Falklands.

Flights within Nigeria and international travel therefrom were not marred by accident but in 1954, a WAAC Wayfarer crashed near Calabar with the loss of all thirteen on board, the casualty being put down to metal fatigue. In 1956, a BOAC Argonaut crashed on take-off from Kano in heavy rain killing twenty-four people. Among those saved was the Railway's Chief Mechanical Engineer, R.K. Innes. The Sudan Interior Mission flew three light aircraft with safety and Shell D'Arcy operated Hiller helicopters over the Owerri oil fields without incident. On the withdrawal of the Wayfarers, service continued with chartered Vickers Vikings and later chartered Douglas DC3s until seven of the latter were acquired by purchase in 1957.

The BOAC Argonauts were replaced by the much larger Boeing Stratocruisers which had been originally designed for the North Atlantic crossing. Jalingo and Mubi airstrips were laid down in 1955 and the route to Freetown via Gambia was reopened as a coach class service by Elders Colonial Airways. On the purchase of the DC3s the Doves were sold except for two which were retained on survey and charter.

In 1957 the WAAC fleet was eight Herons, seven DC3s and two Doves. Monthly flights out of Kano in 1957 numbered, as destinations, Rome: 92, Tripoli: 56, Nice: 8, Algiers: 12, Lisbon: 10, Casablanca: 2, Accra: 60, Lagos: 80, Leopoldville: 49 and Fort Lamy: 8. In 1957, the WAAC commenced to fly to London to show the flag and chartered BOAC Canadair Argonauts and Stratocruisers, first once a week and then twice a week from April 1958.

In 1954, Kano's runway became 8610 feet and by 1960 it had been used by over thirty thousand large aircraft at a yearly average by the last year of 8800, bringing in yearly landing fees of £85,000. Ikeja became 7600 feet. With little change in the scale of landing fees such revenue with increased landings went up from £39,600 in 1949 to £222,500 in 1959, all Nigeria.

Aerodromes

The Federal Public Works 1955/56 Annual Report inventorised runways maintained for £126,979; the order of presentation has been selected based on aircraft movement.

	Length of Runway (yards)		
	No 1	No 2	No 3
Kano	2,870 & 3,000	2,200 & 2,400	
Lagos (Ikeja)	1,800	2,200	
Jos	1,200	1,700	
Kaduna	2,290	1,090	
Calabar	1,002	813	1,705
Port Harcourt	2,000	1,530	
Enugu		1,270	1,270
Benin	1,350	1,350	
Tiko	1,500		
Maiduguri	2,000	1,600	
Ibadan	1,000	1,000	
Zaria	1,700	1,400	
Gusau	1,500		
Yola	2,115	1,670	1,230
Ilorin	1,900	1,100	
Sokoto	1,300	1,100	

Aviation and Airports

	Length of Runway (yards)		
	No 1	No 2	No 3
Minna	1,906		
Makurdi	1,860	830	
Lokoja	1,000	800	
Oshogbo	4,744	3,000	
Bauchi	1,300	2,000	
N'guru	1,350		
Yelwa	1,000	800	
Potiskum	1,500	800	
Bida	1,100		
Katsina	1,300	1,100	
Mamfe	1,500	800	

The order in which locations 3-21 find themselves is surprising in places. Bituminous surfaces were to be found at Benin, Calabar, Jos, Kano, Ikeja, Maiduguri, Port Harcourt, Sokoto and Tiko. Light aircraft only were received at Bauchi, Bida, Katsina, Lokoja, Mamfe, Minna, N'guru, Potiskum, and Yelwa so that eighteen aerodromes only were in use by registered airlines in the country. Herons touched down only at Gusau, Ilorin, Oshogbo and Sokoto. International lines called at Calabar, Kano, Ikeja, Maiduguri and Tiko.

Traffic

The Department of Civil Aviation's return of numbers of passengers and total freight handled in kilos for 1956/57 was for the eighteen aerodromes in receipt of scheduled services:

	Embarked	Disembarked	Transit	Freight
Ikeja	27,438	27,418	6,568	580,947
Kano	17,853	17,541	42,351	453,887
Jos	5,754	5,408	6,247	109,634
Port Harcourt	4,375	4,027	4,792	83,215
Kaduna	3,578	3,391	1,510	47,179
Enugu	3,176	2,951	4,429	56,655
Tiko	2,761	2,237	9	96,739
Calabar	1,463	1,809	2,199	36,523
Benin	1,302	1,259	5,661	12,706
Maiduguri	857	913	926	81,731
Ibadan	726	793	2,942	12,214
Yola	436	380	nil	6,583
Sokoto	341	345	39	5,747
Zaria	226	179	581	3,515
Gusau	164	179	505	4,040
Makurdi	145	121	1,702	1,690
Oshogbo	18	34	344	208
Ilorin	no return			

If transit passengers are ignored, then terminal stations of importance numbered nine at the most and agreement is expressed with the IBRD view of three years earlier that further airports in Nigeria at that time were unnecessary and would be uneconomic.

Aircraft

Seven of the aircraft seen in Nigeria during the WAAC period are described in more detail.

The Douglas DC3, thirty-five years after its December 1935 first flight, was still in the inventory of more than two hundred airlines. At the end of World War II the number in commercial service outnumbered all the other commercial planes in service put together. No other craft ever earned such recognition. It was built in the USA and under licence by USSR and Japan. So reliable were they that developing airlines grossly overloaded them. Later models were a structurally strengthened version of wartime Dakota. A South American model employed 2 × 1200 hp Pratt & Witney 14 cylinder radial engines, 95ft. span, 64ft. 0½in. length, cruising 178 mph at 10,000 feet, 660 mile range with 5000 lb payload.

The Avro York was flown in July 1942 as a military transport modelled on the Lancaster bomber and produced from 1945 by A.V. Roe with BOAC, the first commercial airline to use them, as 12 seater/cargo on the run to Cairo. The 1955 model in use by Skyways Ltd. had 4 × 1610 hp Rolls Royce Merlin 12 cylinder Vee type engines, 102ft. span, 78ft. 6in. length, cruising at 210 mph at 10,000ft., 1400 mile range with 20,000 lb payload.

The Handley Page Marathon was designed by Miles Aircraft to meet the requirements of the Brabazon Committee and the 14/18 seater prototype made its maiden flight in May 1946 with a triple tail assembly, with production model in flight by 1951. WAAC did not use the standard power plant and they were really Mark 1As with seating for twenty-two. In 1954, the WAAC machines were purchased by Derby Airways of Great Britain. Roomy fuselage made them popular with passengers in their short life span. As used by WAAC — VR-NAN — 4 × 340 hp de Havilland Gipsy Queen 70 Mark 4 six cylinder inline engines, 65ft. span, 52ft. 1½in. length, cruising 201 mph at 10,000 feet, 720 mile range with 4172 lb payload.

BOAC 'York' aircraft at Ikeja Airport

The Handley Page Halton was a conversion of the Halifax bomber, the first sold to Australia, and it was the Halton 1 used by BOAC on the West African run. These planes were used in the Berlin airlift of 1949. The machine as used by British American Air Services had 4 × 1675 hp Bristol Hercules 14 cylinder radial engines, 103ft. 8in. span, 73ft. 7in. length, cruising 260 mph at 15,000ft., 2530 mile range with 8000 lb payload.

The Vickers Viking made its maiden flight in August 1946 and remained airworthy till 1962. It utilised geodetic pattern outer wing panels and a majority were used by BEA on Scandinavian services. A later model was the Viking 1B used in Africa; only the French used them after 1970. As used by Indian National Airways 2 × 1690 hp Bristol Hercules 14 cylinder radial engines, 89ft. 3in. span, 65ft. 2in. length, cruising 210 mph at 6000 feet, 520 mile range with 7240 lb payload.

The Handley Page Hermes was the first new post war plane to enter service with BOAC and most comfortable it was. It received a setback when the prototype crashed on take-off on maiden flight December 1945. The BOAC production design — G-AGUB — was first flown in development stage in September 1947. The in-use model had nosewheel landing gear and rectangular windows and commenced service to West Africa in 1950 carrying forty passengers and five crew. The Hermes was meant to be an interim measure until the Argonauts were on the scene and after two years they became the property of Airwork Ltd. London. In all, four independent British lines used them until they ceased to be operational in the mid 60s. As used by Airwork, they had 4 × 2125 hp Bristol Hercules 14 cylinder radial engines, 113ft. span, 96ft. 10in. length, cruising 270 mph at 20,000ft., 2000 mile range with 14,125 lb payload.

The Boeing Stratocruiser was a descendant of the American B-29 Superfortress and came out with two deck "double bubble" fuselage, fully pressurised. First flight was in October 1945 of a future family of nearly 900 off before the prototype civil model was flown in July 1947. The first customer was Pan Am. BOAC later ordered six, finally ten in all, and first entered the air on 6th December 1949. We all liked the cocktail bar! She carried either 89 or 112 high density passengers. BOAC added seven to its fleet but had dispersed all by 1959 and four years later, the design was off commercial routes. As used by Pan Am 4 × 3500 hp Pratt & Witney 28 cylinder radial engines, 141ft. 3in. span, 110ft. 4in. length, cruising 340 mph at 25,000ft., 2750 mile range with 23,930 lb payload.

WAAC (Nigeria) Limited

In March 1957, the Gold Coast became an independent State, Ghana, first with BOAC then with Alitalia going it alone with a major stock of Ilyushins and the West African Air Transport Order-in-Council no longer applied; the Authority was dissolved and WAAC terminated on 30th September 1958. On 1st May 1959 WAAC (Nigeria) Limited came into existence with the name Nigerian Airways used in all publicity and markings, and the Flying Elephant still used as its emblem, to take over the internal services in Nigeria previously covered by the old Corporation. The main routes taken over from WAAC were maintained — Lagos-Northern Nigeria, Eastern Nigeria-Northern Nigeria, within Northern Nigeria, Lagos-Eastern Nigeria-Camerouns, Lagos-Ghana-Senegal. It also ran Lagos-Leopoldville; in fact it ran 3986 Nigerian unduplicated route miles plus 1800 route miles to Dakar.

Financing was Federal Government 51%, Elder Dempster 33%, BOAC 16%, a relationship criticised on the grounds that it gave Elder Dempster too much monopoly. In March 1961, Minister R.A. Njoku, then in charge of aviation, announced that to meet the desires of the Nigerian people the two companies had offered to surrender their shareholdings and in the following April the airline became the baby of the country. Nigeria Airways took over seven DC3s and four Herons as its share of the assets. In April 1963, they acquired five F27 Fokker Friendship aircraft from Holland. They then had a fleet of the five Fokker, seven DC3, and two Aztecs. Towards the end of 1958, BOAC in charter with Nigerian Airways withdrew the Stratocruisers and replaced them with Britannia 112 turboprop on the London-Lagos run via Kano. Imperial Airways D86 had taken a day Lagos-Kano, the Argonaut 2½ hours, the Britannia 2.45hrs.

In 1958, BOAC issued the 35,000lb payload long range specification that was to lead eventually to the VC10, a Vickers product although at the time part of British Aircraft Corporation (BAC). In 1956, there were thirty-three aircraft on the Nigerian register and 157 professional pilots' licences issued and renewed. A federal review pictured Warri as an airport in 1960 whilst Tiko and Mamfe remained federal responsibility. Soil mechanics entered the scene and it was discovered that Kano laterite base plus two coats surface dressing was stronger than Prestwick in Scotland. Runways were progressively tested. Lagos airport was extended 1000 feet by March 1960 and new terminal buildings went up at Kaduna, Ibadan, Enugu and Port Harcourt. An engineering base workshop went up, "second to none in the whole of Africa".

A Nigerian Flying School was in the making in 1961 to grade students so that rejection before more costly training was embarked upon could be determined. After aptitude tests, forty hours dual and solo flying earned Private Pilots Licence and overseas training for Commercial Pilot's Licence of 200 hours, day and night flying. Senior Commercial Pilot's Licence was 700 hours. Airline Transport Pilot's Licence, the summit, was some seven years away from initial training, or 1200 hours from SCPL.

Independence in 1960 saw the local need for improvements in navigation and communications and, in association with larger turboprop craft, the need for more skill in all forms. Tribute was paid to the Sudan Interior Mission planes on mercy flights between missions and leper colonies and recognition paid to the special skills in connection with crop spraying and helicopter oil exploration.

In 1962, the airport inventory was two main, two customs, thirteen aerodromes in regular use, ten aerodromes in occasional use and eighteen landing strips; thirty landing strips were planned. Capital expenditure in 1962/63 amounted to £2,011,732, mostly on Fokker planes and the engineering base. The older airlines BOAC, UTA and BUA did much to assist growth among the emergent states. After independence, a horde of airlines entered the country or increased their activities — Sabena, Lufthansa, Air France, Swissair, Alitalia, KLM, Air Liban, Ethiopian, United Arab, Air Afrique, Pan Am, Air Congo and UTA. Pilgrimage traffic rose but tourism could be given no fillip.

In 1962, annual take off and landing figures had reached 5364 at Lagos, 3736 at Kano and 568 at other airports combined. The total cargo carried in Nigeria had grown:

	Inward	Outward
1958	336 tons	335 tons
1960	726 tons	442 tons
1962	1019 tons	767 tons

Lagos handled the bulk.

BOAC, like other airlines in Africa, had to recognise the parameters, high speed long range demanding long runways, or the adaptable plane. They chose the DC10 and the first African port of call, in April 1964, was Lagos. They flew a courtesy flight Lagos-Dahomey-Lagos, not coming down over the border. Everyone liked this plane and people loved to come down to Ikeja airport and hear the zoom. The plane flew London-Lagos non-stop in 6 hours 10 minutes. After that, the VC10 took over all the BOAC African routes and captured the first class market on the route to the Nile. Nigerian Airways shared in the VC10 run but in the same year inaugurated DC8s with Pan Am. to New York

In 1975, the Nigerian Civil Aviation Training Centre, put together with the aid of UNDP and ICAO, cast off the parent yoke and became Nigerian. On a typical Saturday in 1964, Lagos had departures for ten international destinations. In 1965, Air Afrique celebrated its fourth birthday among the twelve forming states which were Cameroun, Central African Republic, Congo, Ivory Coast, Dahomey, Gabon, Volta, Mauritania, Niger, Senegal, Chad and Togo. With route kilometreage at 96,000, the airline surpassed all others on the continent.

Civil War

The war lasted two and half years; The Air Force with HQ at Kaduna had only training aircraft. The Federal Government had to call on the domestic airline for craft and transport. The Biafrans had one Fokker that had been high in the air when hi-jacked out of Benin, some helicopters and Col. Ojukwu's "executive" jet. There was also a converted civilian craft called the B-26 said to be of the kind the Americans used for heavily armed counter insurgency combat. The nearest airport to the frontier some 70 miles distant was Makurdi, capable of taking internal flight aircraft only. On Biafra's side they had the use of major airfields at Port Harcourt and Enugu and landing grounds at Calabar, Owerri and Ogoja.

Owerri fell on the 11th January 1970 and a $3.4 million loan was necessary after the war to rebuild the shattered Enugu Airport. It was 1975 before Nigeria Airways was able to resume night flying throughout the country.

Light Aircraft

Aeronautical Services West Africa which provided the only maintenance on the West African coast, and which was directed solely at the light aircraft industry, was developed out of Air Stock West Africa, the new name retaining the same initials. Formed in 1959, it provided the industry with spares. The major shareholder was Britten Norman of Great Britain and the local director was Brian Partridge who had been OC 7 Valiant Squadron, Royal Air Force. The company had Lycoming, Piper, Bell and Dornier franchises. Piper and Cessna had the lion's share of the light plane market. Lagos Flying Club was equipped with Pipers, a Colt and a Cherokee. Other Piper sales included a Colt to Arno Kieschke, a Lagos timber exporter, an Aztec to the Nigerian Ministry of Aviation and an Aztec to the Northern Nigerian Government.

The company sold a Bell helicopter to Aero Contractors for oil exploration in the delta and leased a Dornier demonstrator to Cameroun Air Transport. The Nigerian civil aircraft register in 1965 showed ninety aircraft. No less than seventeen Cessnas were sold in countries between Brazzaville and Dakar. On the charter side, Pan African was expanding. It replaced DC4 with DC6, opened a branch at Kaduna and was considering a branch at Ouagadougou in connection with possible manganese deposits. Aero Contractors Company of Nigeria Ltd. by 1965 comprised six Aztecs, one Dornier, three Otters used to counteract smuggling on behalf of the Government, one Bell helicopter, one Sud Aviation Alouette helicopter and one Dove. It was 1966 before aerial survey really got going.

Second Five-Year Plan

The airline was to play an increasing part in the economy. Ikeja and Kano runways were to be extended and apron extensions made to other airports. The investment was to be £25.6 million, £17.3m on aircraft and £8.3m on runways, communications and a hangar. At this time free world carriers were recording a growth rate of 13% p.a. Britain being ahead at 14%. The Nigerian money was put to use by the purchase of a Boeing 707 and two 737s by January 1973 for routes then unannounced. A year later the Government denied that it had abandoned a scheme for TWA to collaborate in management.

BOAC and BEA merged in 1974 to become British Airways. The London-West Africa route went to British Caledonian and Nigerians were highly affronted, saying that the loss of the British national airline to the coast was to be taken as a mark of lessening British respect for her erstwhile colony. They were wrong and came to realise this. No doubt the fact that the adjective "British" persisted before the Caledonian "noun" had something to do with this.

In August 1974, it was announced that Jos was to have a new ₦5 million airport and a month later, it was known that there would be technical assistance from the Netherlands. There was to be a 3-phase development concerned with six international and eleven domestic airports. Two parallel runways with modern equipment would be provided at Ikeja while Kano airport, scene of one of the world's worst air crashes two years before when landing with pilgrim traffic, would be reconstructed. A new international airport was to be built at Ilorin for diversion from Lagos-bound flights during poor weather. The contracts for Ikeja and Jos were awarded to Strabag-Bau AG and Nigerian Dredging, Roads and General Works respectively.

In February 1975, the purchase of five Fokker F-28s was arranged. This would bring such craft up to a total of seven and allow flights to Niger and Chad. Bonny and Brass had airstrips laid out by Monier Construction Company. The airline had its fair share of overload from the dock congestion crisis and a massive concentration of freight at Ikeja was the result. Cargo flights built up to four a day and were well handled. British Caledonian thought it had 51% of the UK-WA market.

Third Five-Year Plan

The Plan was extended to 31/12/1980 and marked the greatest step forward by the Government with the domestic airline. It started off with the 1975 contract to Dumez for ₦8.86 million for earthworks and pavements at Benin airport. The Jos contract already awarded in the earlier Plan became ₦6.5 million with completion within sixty-four weeks to take Boeing 737 aircraft and provide airport buildings. However, the airline seemed to be running before it could walk — in facility and patronage — with plans for services to the Caribbean and South America. Consequently, a Times Supplement of July 1976, after making reference to plans for seventeen modern local airports, had to refer to a lack of audit of accounts for seven years and a lack of direction and of plane sufficiency for such grandiose plans. A government that allows a state concern to go without annual audit must expect nothing but condemnation. IAS Cargo Airlines was now handling hides and gum arabic from Kano for export — the first all-cargo Nigerian airline.

In September 1976, a new body was set up — the Nigerian Airports Authority which functioned from 11/7/1977. The management of aerodromes by the Ministry of Aviation was thus removed to the Authority which also assumed responsibility for the handling by the domestic airline of services to airline operators. Aircraft recovery equipment was acquired. Handling of baggage and cargo of all airlines was to become the responsibility of Nigerian Airways and Nigerian Aviation Handling Company. The Authority did however allow one concession; a foreign carrier could still advertise his image at the check-in point. It reminds one of the 1946 UK legislation in parts. The Chairman was appointed on the recommendation of the Commissioner for Aviation and there were to be nine members, representing Defence, Economic Development, Finance, and Civil Aviation; four members were to represent the Commissioner; the General Manager was given a place. Unfortunately, the NAA was soon in disarray.

In 1975 the airline carried:

on domestic routes	479,017 passengers
on West Africa route	31,728 "
on international routes	26,821 "

In November 1976, two Fokker F28s and one DC10 brought the fleet to nineteen aircraft. They were employed as follows:

Domestic routes	14
West African route	2
International routes	3

Shortly afterwards, the fleet grew to twenty-one with American additions, one of them a further DC10. Nine Nigerian pilots had been trained to man the Boeing 707s, eleven for the Boeing 737s, and eight for the Fokker craft. To make full use of the assets, this was far from sufficient and meant reliance on foreign airlines.

The Chief of Staff, Brigadier Yar'Adua, opened the new Enugu airport in November 1976 and said "that the Government was making continuous efforts to ensure equitable nationwide distribution of amenities", and "₦550 million had been voted to develop air transport. Every State capital would have a modern airport. Sixteen airports would be developed and improved to take medium range jets. Those in Lagos, Kano, Port Harcourt, Ilorin and Maiduguri would be capable of handling long range jets."

Everyone pointed to the success, as an example of cooperation, of Air Afrique, now reduced to ten sponsor countries with the hive off of Cameroun and Gabon but still an outstanding airline. But the British colonies, for those who wonder at the French success, lacked the extent of contiguity left to Africa by France. The two main ex-British colonies in West Africa had to go it alone and there is no doubt that Ghana was the more respected of the two; in Nigeria there were too many incidents of bad landings for the reputation of the airline.

The Government then awarded contracts for the construction of new airports at Yola, Sokoto and Kaduna. Kaduna Airport, valued at ₦22.18 million, was awarded to Dr. Ing Trapp and Company for the construction of earthworks and pavements for the runway, taxiway and apron with access road and lighting to meet requirements for the operation of a Boeing 747. A start was made in September 1977. Sokoto went to Stevin Construction for ₦18.26 million. Designed also for 747 operation, there were to be two connecting taxiways, a cement concrete apron, terminal roads and lighting. The contractor was also to maintain the existing airport for F28 use while the new one was being built. The construction of earthworks and pavements for Yola was awarded to Amey Roadstone Construction Ltd for ₦12.57 million and was designed round the Boeing 737 with a runway of 2400m × 45m. Parking facilities in the terminal area plus lighting was included.

In January 1977, Ibadan came in for its share of attention. It was to have a 2400m runway, to take 737 aircraft and the work valued at ₦11 million was entrusted to Strabag Bau AG.

A competitor in the freight business in August 1976, the British Seevar, in partnership with Algerian Societe Nationale Transports Routiers, then started up eleven 20-ton trailer weekly convoys from Europe to Marseilles, ferry to Algiers, desert trucks to Kano, taking 15-18 days UK to Kano customs' clearance. It was held that it successfully competed with air traffic but later examination showed that insufficient provision had been paid to depreciation for such a journey over the Sahara.

In March 1977, Civil Aviation announced that ₦200 million had been spent in the previous two years and that the revised figure for 1975/80 was ₦700 million. New works then mentioned included Port Harcourt, Maiduguri, Warri, Ilorin and Gusau. In all, thirteen contracts had been let. On the register were:

Boeing 707	2
DC10	1
F27	7
F28	7

and one DC10, two 727, one 707 were awaited. Nigeria had signed bilateral air service agreements with Belgium, Mali, Ivory Coast and Niger and agreements were to be negotiated with Denmark, Sweden, Norway, Ethiopia, Angola, Pakistan, India, Sudan, Liberia, and Iraq.

The domestic timetable in force from 1/4/1977 is worth detail examination:

Route	Flight(s) per week	Aircraft
Lagos/Accra/Abidjan/Robertsfield/Freetown/Banjul/Dakar	2	B727
Lagos/Kano/Rome/London	9	B707 & DC10
Lagos/Abidjan/Robertsfield/New York	1	B707

Route	Flight(s) per week	Aircraft
Lagos/Cotonou/Lome/Accra	1	B737
Lagos/Accra/Abidjan	2	B737
Lagos/Accra/Robertsfield/Freetown	1	B727 & B737
Lagos/Douala/Luanda	1	B737
Lagos/Port Harcourt/Calabar/Douala	1	F27
Lagos/Enugu	14	B737 & F28
Lagos/Port Harcourt	29	F28
Port Harcourt/Enugu/Kaduna	4	F28
Lagos/Enugu/Port Harcourt	3	F28
Lagos/Port Harcourt/Enugu	1	F28
Lagos/Benin	43	F27
Lagos/Benin/Enugu/Calabar	2	F27
Calabar/Port Harcourt	4	F27
Lagos/Calabar	7	F27
Lagos/Ibadan	13	F27
Lagos/Ibadan/Benin/Port Harcourt	2	F27
Lagos/Kano/Niamey	1	F28
Lagos/Ibadan/Kaduna/Jos/Kano	2	F27
Lagos/Kaduna/Kano	21	B737 & F28
Lagos/Kaduna	7	B737
Lagos/Kano	3	B737
Lagos/Kaduna/Kano/Sokoto	3	F28
Lagos/Kaduna/Kano/Maiduguri/Sokoto	4	F28
Kano/Maiduguri	3	F28
Kano/Maiduguri/Yola	3	F28
Kano/Sokoto	4	F28
Lagos/Jos/Kano	5	F27
Kaduna/Jos	5	F27

The majority of the flights provided first and second class accommodation and used twelve ports of call within Nigeria. There was no service to Ilorin, Minna, Katsina, Bauchi or Makurdi.

A heavy loss was incurred by British firms engaged at work on Maiduguri airport arising from bad pricing with inadequate knowledge of local conditions. In June 1977, Government approved of a new Board of Directors for the airline headed by J.A. Orshi as Chairman. In Kano a conference was held for the first time to consider one airline for West and Central Africa. In 1976, air freight to Nigeria reached 26,680,000 metric tons, it was recorded. In 1976, passengers carried by the domestic airline numbered:

internal	529,212
international	125,172
Total	654,384

This was an acceptable return.

In October 1977, the Nigerian Airways announced an inaugural flight to Kenya due to start on 1st November with flights to Gabon, Congo and Zambia to follow. This followed the receipt of the second Boeing 727 and agreements with the countries concerned. Routes were to be Lagos-Douala-Libreville-Brazaville and the "peculiar" Lagos-Nairobi-Luanda. Lagos-Luanda, already in service, had flown empty for weeks. To cut the future story short, only Nairobi appeared on the flight map. Undaunted at the time, agreements were also signed with Brazil and Liberia whereby "Nigeria" could also touch down at Monrovia as well as Robertsfield and in the case of the former, fly to the famous Rio. Lagos-Athens was also to commence in December 1977. Lagos-New York got off to a slow start.

The 1975/80 plans were spelt out more carefully. Lagos was to be in a position to accept supersonic craft; Port Harcourt, Maiduguri, Kano, Kaduna, Sokoto, Ilorin (Lagos alternative) were to accept Jumbos; Calabar, Enugu, Jos, Benin, Ibadan and Yola were to accept 737; Zaria, Gusau and Warri, the last offering quick approach to Sapele and the oil industry, were to be improved but with no specification as to craft. The *Financial Times* described Lagos as "one of the most uncomfortable terminal facilities in the world". Although this was being put right, the Government was most deplorably lax in that they permitted touts unrestricted entrance, corruption was allowed to flourish and officials were allowed to preen themselves as if they were a race apart and above. The African came to dislike the Nigerian. It came home to one that the courtesy of the rural Nigerian was too often absent in his city cousin.

In February 1978, British Airways, British Caledonian and the domestic airline were to meet to consider a Concorde service, London/ Lagos. It is no secret that in the old days, BOAC's London/Lagos run was the cream of the traffic. On their London/New York run, they had a super first class booking as well as the ordinary first class. Meanwhile, the new Federal Commissioner told the airline to treat passengers with respect, not to overbook and to get away on time. To show that he meant business, he had 125 employees retired, terminated or dismissed, the third purge in two years.

The Government was again asked to admit private carriers to the domestic routes. Long-suffering internal travellers questioned the wisdom of half-empty flights to a growing number of international destinations. They forgot that this was prestige, like the supply of electricity to Niger when the local demand cannot be met with regularity.

The airline was suspended by IATA for failure to pay $1.4 million owed and reinstated on payment of the same. *En passant*, it may be remarked that the Nigerian scene, so far as corporations go, is one where bills remain unsettled and the accounts and balance sheet are often unaudited. This is but one direction where the axe must fall. *The Sunday Times* of Nigeria stated that ₦1 million had been lost to the airline in three months due to embezzlement and theft.

ILS (instrument landing system) was to be installed at Kaduna. Nigeria House in London advised in March 1978 that Nigeria and the Federal Republic of Germany had initialled a draft agreement for Nigeria to fly to Frankfurt and Lufthansa to fly to Lagos. Once again, Lufthansa was no stranger and Frankfurt had often been a point of call by BOAC. The USA agreement which now turned out to be provisional was ratified and a third kick-off was proposed for the New York service — on 7th April 1978. Nigeria in March took possession of her third Boeing 707 from Seattle. Ikeja Airport had been renamed "Murtala Mohammed" Airport in 1976 after the assassinated Head of State and it was now proposed that Aviation Planning Services of Canada drew up a master plan for maintenance of the Nigerian fleet now housed in a hangar big enough to take four jumbos. The shed was 300m × 100m. The move would save foreign exchange on part maintenance carried out overseas.

By April 1978, passenger growth was becoming more noticeable on the domestic sector than on the international sector and this was surely in the right direction. They had corrected figures of previous carriage, put carriage at 4000 passengers per day, and given passenger revenue for 1975 as ₦30 million, ₦45.6 million for the following year which gave an average fare paid of ₦66.8. On the 17th October 1978, the first Jumbo Jet landed in Nigeria. She was a UTA flying Lyons-Kano in connection with Peugeot car plant erection.

With modern airports about to come on stream, qualified management staff in the numbers required were not available. Fares went up 25-40% and customers wondered if improved services would match the increased outlay. A foreign newspaper said that the cabin staff should be sent to a "smile school", normally an unheard-of requirement for the Nigerian man or woman. Again the *Financial Times* said that Europe-West Africa was one of the most lucrative routes open and it was hardly surprising that so many airlines had jumped on the bandwagon. The prominent charter companies were now Pan African, Aero Contractors and Bristow, mainly used by the oil companies. At least they were not required, as on the other side of the continent, for dealing with the locust menace. The airline fleet was now recorded as two DC10, three B707, three B727, three B737, eight F27 and six F28, with two F28 on order. An aircraft had to be chartered to fly Vienna-Kano with parts for the Steyr-Daimler-Puch factory at Bauchi. Nigerian Airline would have liked the business but was already overloaded.

In 1979, administrative divisions were flight operations, finance, marketing, administration and technical services. There was a Controller of Audit. The airline flew regularly to thirteen airports in the country and wished to cover the nineteen States of the Federation. The States without airports then were: Ogun, Niger, Bauchi, Gongola, Benue, Imo and Ondo. Minna in Niger State was nearest to the proposed new Federal Capital Territory Abuja and a Board was set up to plan an airstrip there. The airline started to call itself "Skypower". Staff numbered 6000 of whom nearly 600 were expatriate and in April, British Airports International was engaged to send a team of seventeen to train staff at the Murtala Mohammed Airport in five disciplines.

The airline put 1978 passenger traffic at 1,444,436 or 3963 per day, an increase on the previous year of 38.4% and over 80% were carried on the domestic sector. July 1978 was the peak month, recording 140,733 passengers carried at the rate of 4540 per day. International sector traffic in 1978 varied between August, 24,921 and December, 13,923. There was a decline in the West African coast sector from 71,956 in 1977 to 63,091 in 1978. Pan Am was flying the Jumbo Jet on the Lagos-New York route in 1979, calling at Dakar, Monrovia and Abidjan.

The new Lagos Airport was designed by the Netherlands Airport Consultants (NACO BVO) and was modelled on the "best" of Schiphol in Amsterdam. Strabag constructed the buildings, Julius Berger the access roads. It was commissioned on the 15th March 1979 by the Head of State, Lt-General Obasanjo and was operational from 1st April. The new airport was used by international flights only, the old airport covering the domestic sector needs with 2316m runway and 424m extension planned. Undeniably, the new building is magnificent, so magnificent that it immediately focused attention on three things — the need for a management in keeping with the new image, the unenlivening introduction to the Capital over the twenty kilometre distance to Lagos, and the lack of inadequate access. The airport cost ₦240 million. The associated architects were Nigerian — Messers Egbor & Associates. Capacity had been designed round 1985 estimates, i.e., 2.5 million passengers p.a. and 100,000 tons cargo p.a. In 1979, twenty-two airlines used the new base — Aeroflot, Air India, British Caledonian, Ghana, Lufthansa, Scandinavia, Air Afrique, Iberia, MEA, Sabena, Swissair, Alitalia, Egyptian, KLM, Nigeria, UTA, British Airways, Ethiopian, Kenya, Pan Am, Varig and Balkan, but the design can take care of a future 200,000 aircraft movements per year.

The complex is the largest in black Africa with accommodation for four aircraft at the fingers. Earthworks measured 2 million m^3 60% of which was cut and borrow and the area occupied by the pavements reached 1.1 million m^2. The terminal occupied 1500 hectares. Departure was at first floor level and arrival at ground floor level so far as the passenger was concerned. Movement to the finger was via an axiobridge. Other floors were provided for passenger facilities. Local artists decorated the interior lounge walls. There was a substation for the necessary power which has taken care of all eventualities in the event of failure.

Thirty-one check-in counters were provided. The runways, one on each side of the terminal building, were 2743m × 45m and 3900m × 60m.

The ₦30 million Maiduguri International Airport was due to commence operations at the end of February 1979 taking B727 and F28 flights from Lagos although its 3000m × 60m runway was designed for 747 and DC10 aircraft. The existing site was used but new terminal buildings were erected.

Port Harcourt International Airport, a new site, was completed in September 1979 after a 1975 start, the interim having had to take care of the 747 acceptance decision, the sacking of the first contractor, and constant interruption to the supply of essential services. It had received an allocation of ₦35 million for the works.

The Chicago disaster of 1979 saw the temporary grounding of the two Nigerian DC10 planes at a loss to the airline. A 707 replaced them. By July 1979, the airline had ordered further craft, the two F28 and three Airbus 300 at ₦30 million each to be delivered in 1980/81.

In June 1979 the Government, fed up with listening to and experiencing the ills of the airline, dissolved the Board and did a "railway" on Nigerian Airways inviting a none-too-willing KLM to take over the management. KLM was the first airline in the world. It started operations on 7th October 1919. Sixty years later, it flew to 118 cities in seventy-three countries and had trained pilots for twenty-six foreign lines.

In March, 1980, the airline announced passenger traffic for 1979 as 213,042 on international routes, 1,308,243 domestic, total 1,521,285. As usual, they had altered the 1978 figures and said 1979 represented an increase of 9.8%. The fleet was put at:

F27	8	
F28	8	
B707	3	
B727	2	
B737	3	
DC10	2	Total 26.

In December 1979 under KLM, the airline created the new monthly record of 176,411 passengers carried, despite Christmas memories of long queues and longer frustrations. On the other side of the coin, Air Afrique made its first loss, attributed to the civil war in Chad. In January 1980, the Government awarded a ₦6 million contract for Yola Airport, complete with power station, equipped for night flying and reception of F27/F28, to an indigenous contractor, Alhaji S. Ribadu & Sons Ltd. The contract included the buildings, apron and access road.

Ilorin became a touch down in 1978 and the airline put Jeddah on its map. They called ports of call along the west coast "The West African Connection" using 727s for Conakry, Banjul and Dakar, 737/F28 to Accra, and 707 to Abidjan. For the 1st April 1980, additional flights were introduced for Enugu-Yola, Jos-Yola, Lagos-Yola and Jos-Ilorin. Makurdi was brought into a schedule after much political pressure from the State.

KLM found some overstaffing, some hands too old in the job, and considered that a total of twenty-six aircraft should not be represented by as many as six types, headaches alike to engineers, stores, operators and, of course, training. One of the first decisions therefore was the declared intention to sell the F27 craft. In March, a crisis developed in the Nigerian Association of Aircraft Pilots and Flying Engineers as members jockeyed for position, said in the past to always lead to executive appointment with the airline, But KLM was reported unperturbed.

The new Ibadan Airport on the Ife Road at ₦22 million, designed to take 727 × 737 but to be used for local flights only, was completed in 1980. The 2500m Calabar runway and terminal buildings had been completed. The new "Jos" on the Bukuru Road was opened in September 1979 and the works included a dam to ensure a long term water supply. Kano with its two non-parallel runways had been upgraded in all directions for the sum of ₦55 million. The new Sokoto was designed round the 747. The new

Kaduna off the Lagos Road, ₦40 million, with separate cargo building, planned for 747 reception, had become operational. Enugu in use had been well planted with grass to check erosion in the areas susceptible and its 2400m runway would take the 747. Benin was upgraded at a cost of ₦18 million and provided with a new apron.

The new Warri ₦30 million airport was to have a helicopter pad and work commenced in 1979. Gusau at ₦15.4 million designed round the F28 awaited site determination. A Site Planning Committee was considering the best location for Zaria. Makurdi was thought of in the context of a military base. Airstrips were on the cards for Katsina, Oshogbo, Lokoja, Bida, Bauchi, N'guru, Gunnel, Kontagora, Mubi, Shendam, Yelwa and Zuru. In terms of scheduled flight airports, the third Year Plan catered for eighteen in the country.

The aircraft in use by Nigerian Airways from 1959 were typically to the following general characteristics:

Craft	Engine	Span	Length	Cruising	Range
Fokker F27	Rolls Royce 2 Dart Turbo-prop 2050 ehp	29.00m	23.50m	483km/hr	1468km
Fokker F28	Rolls Royce 2 Spey Turbofan 4468 kg	23.58m	29.61m	843km/hr	2093km
Boeing 707	Rolls Royce 4 turbo fan 7938 kg	43.41m	46.61m	954km/hr	7830km
Boeing 727	Pratt & Whitney 3 rear mounted turbo fan 6577 kg	32.92m	46.69m	977km/hr	3260km
Boeing 737	Pratt & Whitney 2 turbo fan 7030 kg	28.35m	30.48m	927km/hr	3815km
Mcdonnell Douglas DC10	General Electric 3 turbo fan 18597 kg	50.39m	55.54m	940km/hr	4353km

The last described is the basic US domestic model. The long range intercontinental was the series 30 with plus 3.05m on the wing span and pro-rate.

Twenty-three African countries reported their air traffic in 1978. The place of Nigerian Airways in the three traffic statistics is as shown.

Total km flown by craft	Passenger km flown	Freight net ton km
10th place	10th place	14th place

Nigeria has a good aircraft fleet but for the utilisation factor. Her airports are worthy and serve for seen needs. Flight frequency is generous. It remains to manage free from jealousy and corruption and to return the reported lost smile to the visage.

Electricity Undertakings

The first British ship, "City of Richmond", was lit in 1881 and London's first public power station at Holborn Viaduct produced illumination from 1882. It is astonishing that electricity should have been available in Nigeria from as early as 1896 though it was said to have been for the benefit of Europeans only.

First Nigerian Power Station

At a cost of £6000, the first power station was erected by the Public Works Department (PWD) on the Lagos Marina on the exact site years later taken by the Electricity Corporation of Nigeria (ECN) as its headquarter building. The plant consisted of two 30 kW 1000V 80-cycle single phase EEC alternators belt driven by two compound double-acting Davey-Paxman engines fed by Davey-Paxman boilers. The Marina was lit between 6pm and 11pm by series connection from early 1898, Government House and the Colonial Hospital following in the September. A year later, all streets were illuminated by 250 CP glow lamps and the maximum demand had reached 24 kW. A third unit of identical manufacture was put down by 1902 and by 1909, 120 kW installed with 65 kW demand was registered, supply having reached Iddo and Ebute Metta by installation of some 10,000 yards HT underground cable feeding thirty-one transformers of which the largest was 5 KVA capacity. The cost was 10d/unit and the overall charge to the PWD amounted to £4604-15-9d in 1905

Not to be outdone, Lugard in 1901 pinched a searchlight dynamo from the Niger Company and illuminated Government House in Zungeru. Development in early days however was very slow as the only need arose for lighting, the country being basically agricultural and supporting no industry of a size to justify an economical power supply. When an industry was projected, there were then no funds available. The Lagos Railway workshops at Iddo and later at Ebute Metta were the notable exception and supply thereto was largely responsible for the replacement of the Lagos steam plant by diesel engines after 1910 at the new distribution of 2-phase 40 cycles. The 1914 World War put a stop to further development, cannibalisation of generating plant was necessary to provide spares to keep sets at work, and in 1918, street lights had to be turned off.

Post World War 1 Developments

By 1920, the Lagos Marina station had an installed capacity of 420 kW but the load was spreading northwards and it was decided to look for a new site with reserve for expansion. The obvious place, as coal was to be burnt, was close to the railway terminus at Ijora on Iddo island and sidings were laid to facilitate erection. The new undertaking called Iddo Power Station was commissioned on 1st June 1923 and the Marina site was shut down on 28th November 1923. New installed capacity was 3.6 MW and the station was described as the first landmark in the development of electricity in Nigeria. To achieve an improved load balance, 3 phase 4 wire 50 cycle was adopted in 1924. The station grew to 13.75 MW comprising four Babcock & Wilcox cross tube marine boilers generating 40,000 lb steam/hour each at 260 lb/sq. in. pressure 650° F temperature with a feed water inlet to the economiser at 175°F. The boilers were fired by travelling grate stokers and supplied two 5 MW and one 3.75 MW Bellis & Morcom turbines producing at 6.6 kV with an overall station thermal efficiency of 19%.

Kurra Falls Power Station on the Plateau

The next developments were obvious: on the Plateau to serve the tin mines and at Enugu to serve the new Nigerian Eastern Railway (NER) Enugu workshops and Enugu coal mines. The Plateau supply was a high head hydro-electric installation which meant that it was using a clean source of free indigenous energy, available after use for other purposes, employing quick start up low maintenance water turbines. It also meant inaccessibility constraints with remote location and power transmission costs coupled perhaps with non-continuous flow in dry seasons calling for both storage and run-of-river elements. In fact, on the Plateau, the disadvantages were little with storage of eight months available from the rainfall of April to October.

The Plateau supply derived from the Kwall installation and the Kurra/Jekko No1/Jekko No 2 installations. The former derived from the river Ouree, 150 square mile catchment, and the latter from the Kurra, both in foothills lying on the 4200ft. contour. The Ouree rose south of Vom and the Kurra 30 miles further to the south. The works were privately owned by a British company, Nigerian Electricity Supply Company (NESCO), established in 1922 and planned after the NER had been planned to supply the Plateau with coal for a steam station! Ouree reservoir was at RL 3800ft. and used an open canal to join with a diversion weir/canal to a balance reservoir RL 3480ft., the outflow being pipeline-fed to the 2MW Kwall power station at RL 2745 under pipeline head of 698ft. The station comprised four Pelton wheels driving 500V 50 cycle generators stepped up to 2.2 kV on the 12½ mile transmission to Sabon Gida supported 70% on pole, 30% on lattice mast.

The second installation collected at Tenti reservoir, RL 4322 and fell over a river bed to Kurra reservoir, RL 3849, thence over river bed/diversion weir/open canal to the head of the pipeline RL 3774, feeding RL 3020 8.4 MW Kurra power station under pipeline head 754ft. comprising three 1.4MW Pelton wheels and one Francis turbine 4.2 MW transmitting 33 kV to Bukuru. The outflow fell by bed, weir and canal to RL 2855ft., the head of Jekko No 1 pipeline with the 4 MW station at RL 2212ft. under a head of 643ft. This station was in hydraulic series with Kurra and comprised one Pelton wheel and 4 MW alternator. Remaining in hydraulic series was Jekko No 2, 410ft. head, one Francis set, 4 MW, RL 1814, the civil works from No 1 being pipe in tunnel to surge chamber and descent pipeline. Total installed capacity was 18.4 MW. From 1931 to 1945, there was a six-fold increase in the number of units generated at 1d/unit sold, reaching 71.8 million units to the minefields by 1955.

NESCO made bulk supply to ECN for the townships of Bukuru 1936, Jos 1937, and Vom 1944, in all, with mines, an area of 600 square miles. Peak load was 12 MW with an annual load factor of 60%. Between April and September, the Plateau is reputed to be the second highest risk in the world for lightning attack to man and installation. Away across the border into Cameroun, the risk is put at eight times that prevailing in the United Kingdom. Conical thatched roofs are more at risk than corrugated iron roof tops. Ardo Sunda was struck by lightning on four separate occasions, left alive but numbered — surely a statistic for the Guinness Book of Records.

The Enugu building was just off the railway workshops. Engines, dynamos, boilers, and a riveted steel chimney were in position in 1922 at an audited eventual cost of £103,389. From this, plant power was made available to the mines from 1924. Naturally, the station was coal-fired and comprised 3 × 350 kW Bellis & Morcom vertical reciprocating direct condensing engines steamed by Babcock & Wilcox boilers, the typical grand sight of steam at work. The township was lit from 24/12/1924 the plant being commissioned on 24th June 1924. But the station was never a part of the railway capital works being separately funded against NER capital works although it was controlled by the railway.

In 1924/25, the annual cost of the Enugu working was £4021 of which no less than 66.2% went on general superintendence.

Interest and sinking fund amounted to £5680 and as sales only amounted to £499, the total loss on working came to £9202. It is to be remembered however that the set was installed to provide power for the railway workshops and not for PWD purposes and in any case the township had no further funds to purchase additional points. The electrical balance sheet for 1924 was:

Units generated	161,560
Units consumed by power	139,905
Units consumed by lighting	4,297
Units lost in transmission	338
Units surplus to consumption	17,020
	161,560 161,560

In 1925/26, a further 111.5 kW was connected to the Enugu mains. In 1926/27, an extension was given to the European Hospital whilst further extensions in the mines had increased the load by 40%, 860 kW for power and 110 kW for lighting. A 150 kW AC set with condensing plant and auxiliaries was added in 1928/29 and power was extended to the Secretariat, PWD, Coal Camp and Roman Catholic Mission. Units generated had become 936,342 and a 3.3 kV line connected the residence of the Lieutenant-Governor and was intended to reach the barracks of the Royal West African Frontier Force. Units topped the million by 1932/33 when the Electrical Engineer-in-Chief of the PWD took over the Enugu Electric and Power Plant from the railway from 1/11/1932 and its accounts from 1/4/1933.

Later, Enugu was to have 2 × 600 kW Harland & Wolff diesel generating sets, the station reaching an installed capacity of 3000 kW by 1953. But strangely, despite background and location, Enugu never grew to eminence, becoming a stand-by station upon linking in with the new Oji station, and it was to be 1955 before thoughts again turned to Enugu.

The railway at Ebute Metta converted the 3300 AC Iddo supply to 440V DC power and 220V AC lighting at cost to themselves on top of a 60/- coal cost at Iddo which, according to Brigadier Hammond, on every scene in 1924 should have been 40/-. The conversion plant was 3500 kW rotary converters and 3550 kVA transformers supplied by Metropolitan Vickers Ltd. In fact, the railway purchased at 13/4d per unit which worked out at 11.7/- per kW per quarter for a demand of 800 kW.

The Nigerian Railway installed tandem sets at Minna and Zaria in 1926/27 for its workshops there. The next plant to go up featured the second port, Port Harcourt, 28th March 1928, commissioned by the PWD. This was a 2250 kW steam station generating at 3300V and 400V to which, as demand increased, various makes of diesel sets, unfortunately, were added of total capacity, 6280 kW, making a grand total of 8530 kW.

Next came the provision for Government headquarters Northern Provinces, Kaduna, commissioned by the PWD in December 1929. It was a diesel station, destined to become the largest diesel station in the north, generating at 3300V transmitted at 11 kV AC. The power plant by 1961 was to comprise:

5 × 900 kW Crossley RMO8
3 × 600 kW Harland & Wolff TR8
2 × 990 kW English Electric skid sets, an installed capacity of 8.28 MW.

Next on stream came a steam station run by a Native Authority, Kano, in 1930, providing for the most important commercial centre in the north. It arose from a report by Sir Alexander, Binnie, Son and Deacon dated 24/3/1928 concerning future water supplies for that station which would require power for sunk pumps. The PWD Chief Electrical Engineer, Mr Pickworth, decided on a location for the generating station fed by a siding off the railway in section worked by Subsidiary Electric Train Staff Instrument on the main line between Challowa and Mundadu. Wagons were propelled round a curve off the reception into lines feeding coal dump, conveyor, cooling towers and water tube boilers. Mr Pickworth asked for 40,000 gallons water per day which Sir Alexander thought excessive.

By 1962, Kano station was to comprise:

- 2 × 15000 lb/hr Babcock & Wilcox boilers
- 2 × 25000 lb/hr John Thompson boilers
- 2 × 2400 kW Brush Ljunstrom turbines
- 1 × 1500 kW Allen turbine
- 1 × 750 kW Bellis & Morcom turbine
- 2 × 600 kW Harland & Wolff diesel sets
- 1 × 990 kW English Electric diesel set
- 2 × 3 MW S.I.G.M.A. free piston gasifiers and gasturbo alternators

The English Electric set was used for peak load requirements and the S.I.G.M.A. sets burning bunker "C" fuel, maximum viscosity 3500 secs Redwood No 1, were employed from installation in 1962 as base load machines. Power was generated at 11 kV and 400V.

Water power, the oldest after air, had been put to use on the Cameroun plantations from 1929 by the German fraternity. Lack of other use and therefore allocated funds locally saw the policy continued by the Cameroun Development Corporation for the port of Victoria, 1470 kW capacity, and Tiko, and extension plans were afoot in 1955 at Njoke, second 750 kW set. The three existing hydro-electric plants were Malele, 720 kW A.E. Co. turbine, Luermann Falls 350 kW Echerwyss turbine, and First Njoke, 750 kW alternator coupled Francis turbine running at 300 rpm. Victoria supply was to be taken over by the ECN but meantime, it had supplied the township. Njoke, fed by the Njoke river at 37.4ft. head, had water lettuce problems requiring clearance at half-hour intervals. Screen intake water level was 98.2 and the design provided a forebay to accommodate a hairpin bend before introduction to twin 69in. pipes to the 3.3 kV station transmitting 22 kV on single tubular steel poles over the twenty-eight miles to Victoria. The station was near the junction of the Njoke with the much larger Mungo which, when in flood backed up the former, causing trouble to the station tailwater.

Njoke station was interconnected with the older Malele station, later CDC-owned, a storage station artificially created off Malele Lake, with sufficient head to feed the turbine for four hours at a time transmitting at 23 kV as a reserve station.

Stations in Nigeria then came on stream as listed with the installed capacity shown for 1953:

Station	Authority	Year	Capacity
Katsina	Native Authority	1933	100 kW
Maiduguri	PWD	1934	210
Abeokuta	Native Authority	1935	600
Yola	PWD	1937	75
Zaria	PWD	1938	1,438
Calabar	PWD	1939	570
Warri	PWD	1939	330
Ibadan	Native Authority	1940	4,515

There were therefore a total of fourteen public undertakings plus the Cameroun stations by 1940. Calabar had been discussed way back in 1912 as a potential source from a hydro-electric supply in the "bush" but the scheme was abandoned.

Ibadan was a coal fired steam turbine station to which diesel plant was added. The boilers were four in number, Babcock & Wilcox coal and wood fired 250 lb/sq. in. at 650°F, and the generating plant grew by 1961 to:

- 2 × 500 kW Allen turbines — peak load only
- 2 × 1500 kW Allen turbines — used as base load
- 2 × 600 kW Harland & Wolff diesel sets — peak load only
- 2 × 2000 kW Crossley diesel sets — used as base load
- 2 × 1250 kW Mirrlees diesel sets — used as base load
- 1 × 990 kW English Electric diesel set — peak load only

Steam was generated at 400, 3300, 6600 volts, diesel at 3300, 6600.

Abeokuta, Warri and Zaria were medium size diesel stations, by 1961 generating 400 and 3300V with installed capacity between 1765 and 3400 kW. Katsina, Yola, Calabar and Maiduguri were small diesel stations, by 1961 generating at 400V with installed capacity between 255 and 1050 kW.

Because of the impact of World War II, Ibadan was the last undertaking to be put on stream, efforts being turned to maintaining the existing plant during the emergency, a plant increasingly overloaded with 19 million units consumed in 1938 rising to 38 million by 1945; inevitably this burden took its toil.

Nigerian Government Electricity Undertaking

After the Second World War, problems of supply continued and it was time for Government to create a new department out of the PWD to take care of an essential growing development and remove inevitable government restrictions — the Nigerian Government Electricity Undertaking (NGEU). This was to pave the way for a later corporation planned from the start. NGEU was set up in 1946 and was to last five years. During this time, no further undertakings were commissioned but orders were placed and hydrological studies put in hand. It took over the nine Government undertakings in Nigeria and it was said of the NGEU that its *raison d' etre* owed as much to an increased political awareness as any other factor. The NGEU was contemporaneous with the 1946-1956 £1.7 million Ten-Year Plan designed to increase capacity by 200%.

NGEU was charged with the task of putting the undertakings on sounder financial basis and, in reviewing, development reminder must be made of handicapping factors. Though Nigeria is a typical agricultural country, the basic resources required for industrial development were available. There were raw materials, fuel, water, labour and a reasonable home market but the lack of capital hindered growth. Almost all undertakings were running at a loss due mainly to absence of load. Hence, it became necessary for a large industrial company like the African Timber & Plywood Factory (AT&P) to generate its electricity at Sapele. "The staff situation was critical: it was difficult to obtain experienced African craftsmen and operatives, there were hardly any African engineers, and it was difficult to recruit experts from Europe, so that up to 1947 only thirty-five European engineers were available," wrote Mr Manafa. Finally, there was the low population density; over 33 million people were scattered over the country making it most uneconomical to supply electricity to a great many.

Electricity Corporation of Nigeria

The Electricity Corporation of Nigeria was created on 6th July 1950 under Ordinance No 15 of 1950, to plan the development of the country's electrical potential in such a manner as to provide the cheapest form of energy consistent with continuity of supply. NGEU's undertakings were taken over on 1/4/1951 and Native Authority undertakings on 1/4/1952 at a time when eighteeen townships only enjoyed the facility in Nigeria and the Camerouns, the two additions being Sokoto and Abakaliki, both commissioned in 1952. Much hard work was necessary because of the poor physical condition of the plant taken over and the Corporation expected to run at a loss for a number of years. The Corporation was an autonomous commercial enterprise responsible for generation, transmission, distribution and sale of electricity and had a part-time Chairman and Board appointed by the Federal Minister of Mines and Power to cover policy, with administration left in the hands of a Chief Executive Officer.

By 1952, 57 million units were being consumed annually. Then the IBRD Mission arrived in the country. They found that in 1952/53, 165.2 million units were generated, double the output of 1944 but amounting only to 5 units/capita. 40.3% of all power was generated by NESCO, ECN plants being small and widely separated, selling 55% of their power of Lagos, 12% to Enugu, and the balance of 33% to eighteen towns. The AT & P factory at Sapele was the largest of the industrial undertakings, selling power in bulk to the ECN. Stations were:

ECN	17
NESCO	1
AT&P	1
Planned & under construction	17

Power generated was:

ECN	89.1 million kW
NESCO	66.6
Industrial undertakings	9.5
Total	165.2

The number of consumers was 43,659. The considerable distance between generating stations in the opinion of the World Bank called for independent undertakings without a national grid since a policy associated with the latter would have been uneconomical. The pattern of consumption, according to the Bank, for 1953/54 was:

Domestic	50.3%
Power	33.1
Commercial	12.7
Miscellaneous	2.2
Public lighting	1.7

The largest projects under construction were the second Lagos plant, 2 × 12500 kW steam turbine station with provision for doubling, the first Lagos plant to go on standby as a diesel station and the new Oji River Project, 2 × 5000 kW steam turbine station, to come on stream for Eastern Nigerian industries.

The Joint Group of Engineers had plenty to say, and in this discipline, tore the Bank to pieces. The bank advocated the encouragement of industry but counselled restriction on electrical growth. Industry would find its own economic feet in the right place; it was cheaper to transmit electricity than to move raw materials thereto or finished products therefrom. Groundnut processing and textile preparation surely called for the Shiroro Gorge hydro scheme for power and irrigation. Was electrification of the Enugu-Port Harcourt railway line to be dismissed — in an area also of the densest population? Light industry must be given aid at the expense of the Government machine. The Bank dealt in five-year forecasts; those with experience knew only a ten-year basis was sound.

The Joint Group set out station growth at fourteen stations to show that the IBRD forecasts were off beam. Port Harcourt was a good example of what had actually taken place in demand:

1952/53	1953/54	1954/55
650kW	960kW	1353kW

The average annual increase at the fourteen stations was at the rate of 23.78% against the Bank's calculation of 16.5%. The Bank estimated Lagos peak load in 1954 as 11,000 kW but in fact it had become 12,150. The Joint Group felt that the second Lagos plant should be of the order of 75,000 kW as demand would be in excess of 50,000 kW long before the life expiration of the proposed plant. Large sets were more economical in capital cost and they were more efficient. The Joint Group agreed that a 300-mile transmission line, Asaba-Ibadan-Lagos, was unrealistic but Lagos-Ikorodu-Ijebu Ode-Abeokuta-Ibadan merited closer examination. They referred to the increasing efficiency to be obtained by employing oil fired over coal and drew attention to developments in grade "C" bunker fuel oil.

They did not agree that the Oji power station would render further development in the Onitsha/Enugu area unnecessary for the next ten years and pointed to the demands of the Nkalagu Cement Works and the fact that the old Enugu plant was being renovated to chip in. They thought capital development in the region of £9 million was nearer the required figure. Shortage of skilled personnel should not restrict growth as it could be imported and used on the job as a training medium. Finally, they said in what was a useful document ..."The endorsement in the report of the policy that the Electricity Corporation must function on a strictly commercial basis, that is must support its own expansion out of profits, is unsuited to the present stage of development of Nigeria unless the proposals to create a permanent capital fund are followed."

In the Gold Coast, the Volta Dam hydro station, bauxite smelter and Tema Harbour came into being with much help from the geologist, the dam established at 275ft. OD (235ft. above river level) and the reservoir flooding 2000 square miles, a major work in Africa. In Nigeria, thoughts were turning in 1954 to the Shiroro Gorge in the Kaduna River but the load to take care of the projected 10,000 kW was not there. Similar considerations applied to the Jebba hydro-electric station. Nevertheless, Lagos was to have 75,000 kW and Oji was to go ahead and by the end of 1960, there were to be fifty-five towns with a supply. A year later, in connection with the "New Towns Development Programme", this was to rise to seventy-six towns.

Oji station at mile 25 on the Enugu-Onitsha road was commissioned in July 1956 at a cost of £2.45 million. It had 2 × 5000 kW turbo generators with coal fired boilers fed by the 16-mile Hayes Mine aerial ropeway delivering at 55 tons/hour. Power at 11 kV generated was transmitted over what was then the longest high voltage system in West Africa, ninety miles of 66 kV to Onitsha, Enugu, University of Nigeria Nsukka and Nkalagu. By 1960, the plant was extended by 10,000 kW with a further 10,000 kW anticipated by 1963 fed by 120,000 lb/hr boiler, a total capacity of 30 MW. Thermal efficiency was 21.5% and cost of fuel per unit generated was 0.55d.

Oji had stoker travelling grate feed coal fed by rotary feeders to water tube boilers pressed at 425 lbs/sq. in. at 740° F to Babcock & Wilcox manufacture, four with a continuous rating of 27,000 lb/hr and one with a continuous rating of 120,000 lb/hr. Feed water at economiser inlet was at 250° F. The design made provision for the boilers to burn natural gas. Two turbo alternators were 5 MW each to Allen & Sons Ltd. manufacture and one was rated at 10 MW supplied by Parsons. This comprised the generating plant by 1960.

Iddo Power Station was renamed Ijora "A" and the addition to the Lagos supply, one of the most handsome buildings in the environment, was called Ijora "B". It lay 350 yards east of Ijora "A", closer to the railway terminus on an eleven acre site remarkably ill chosen, nine feet above low water off spring tide datum Carter Bridge on land reclaimed in 1923 from mangrove swamp of 25 to 40ft. depth. This added to the cost of commissioning as 125ft. piling was required and the whole was built on buoyant foundations. K.P. Humpidge was the ECN Chairman and the Resident Civil Engineer was W.G. Wheatley. Consulting Engineers were, civil, Coode and Partners; electrical, Preece, Cardew and Rider; and the contractors were Richard Costain Ltd. and Messers Tileman to whom the reinforced concrete chimneys were let. A total of 1650 tons of structural steel work, by arrangement with the Crown Agents, came from Baume et Marpent, Belgium.

Ijora "A" went on standby when Ijora "B" Low Pressure Section was commissioned in 1956. This section had four Stirling boilers each with a maximum continuous output of 75,000lb/hr at 425lb/sq. in. pressure and 825° F. The chain grate stoker boilers were later converted to burn heavy residual oil. The turbines were Brush Lungstrom rated at 12.5 MW each and generation was at 11 kV. The High Pressure Section had two Babcock & Wilcox water tube oil fired boilers rated at 250,000 lb/hr at 625 lb/sq. in. pressure and 865° F with water temperature at economiser inlet 340° F. The two turbo alternator sets were supplied by Parsons and were capable of continuous output of 30 MW each at 8 Power Factor lagging when running at the normal operating speed of 3000 rpm. Regenerative feed heating in three stages to a final temperature of 325°F was provided. The turbine was of single cylinder impulse reaction type and turbine and generator shafts were rigidly coupled together.

Both LP and HP sections were provided with James Gordon automatic pneumatic boiler control, the essential features of the system being a master steam pressure regulator maintaining correct balance between steam and air flows and a furnace pressure regulator maintaining constant suction in the combustion chamber under all conditions. Overall thermal efficiency was 24.5% and the average cost of fuel generated per unit, both sections, worked out at .58d; before conversion of the LP section to oil firing, it had been .65d. Ijora "A" and "B" stations were interconnected by 2 × 7500 kVA feeder interconnectors and 2 × 7500 kVA generator interconnectors.

The installed cost for the LP system was very high at £72/kW but the HP corresponding figure was low at £16.6. The sub-soil spring water supply had the following characteristics:

Chlorides as Cl	470 ppm
Total alkalinity as $CaCO_3$	25
Total hardness as $CaCO_3$	151
Total iron as Fe	7
Total solids dried at 180° C	1080
Total solids after gentle ignition	548
pH	5.7
pH after 20 minutes aeration	6.1
Total acidity	6.6
Total acidity after 20 minutes aeration	2.2

Considerations of the Sixties

Around this time, Nigeria was concerned with her electrical standards — the proportion of fires in Lagos due to electrical faults was relatively high — and the principles that governed the choice of prime mover. Except in industrial undertakings, installation was not in accordance with the best practice. House wiring was often exposed because of high humidity and the fact that breeze blocks in wall construction did not favour concealed wiring. Much work was done by the Tropical Testing Establishment at Port Harcourt — a station well chosen for this purpose because of the town's incessant rains.

In the United Kingdom, lighting and power circuits had been separate because of requirements arising from electric fires but in Nigeria, confusion had arisen with the term "power" where lights and fans came off from a common circuit. Starting current determined motor choice. Single phase 230V was used for fractional hp motors, three phase for larger. Totally enclosed motors, with small provision for escape of condensate, were always recommended because of the protection they afforded from vermin access. (The extent to which vermin burrow has to be seen to be believed.)

For years there was much trouble in finding suitable earthing; in the south of the country these figures were obtained:

Clay	2,000-6,000 resistivity ohms/cm^3
Sandy clay	8,000-20,000
Marsh peat	15,000-30,000
Laterite	Average 30,000
Sand	25,000-50,000
Rock	Up to 100,000

An early revision of the out of date Electrical Wiring Regulations was clearly called for but enforcement would be another matter as into the 80s, deaths from electrocution were tragically common and installations were often put together in poorer quarters by "bits of boys".

The smallest standard generating set used by the UK Authority was 30 MW but except for Ijora "B", Nigerian sets were envisaged over the following ten years as being of lesser capacity. England was dominated by a grid, large sets, a pool of specialised labour. In Nigeria, the issues were capital cost, maintenance, avoidance of complexity, accessibility and availability of cooling water. Hydrological data gathered over thirty-five years was usually a prelude to the siting of a hydro-electric station and such information was lacking in Nigeria. Run-of-river applications were not commonly found and storage potential took even longer to determine. A Hydrological Survey Department had been recommended by the IBRD. Steam reciprocation was competitive with turbine up to 750 kW but fell below CI engine yield at this figure. "Wood fuel should have been considered more", but only from the waste products of the African Timber and Plywood factory. Much more attention should have been directed at the question of reducing the cost of coal at point of use, and the mechanisation of the mines delayed to the late 70s could only be of use if the pit head price had been materially reduced. Oil firing appreciation too came late on the Nigerian scene, its advantages and disadvantages, one of which was an exhaust gas rich in sulphur with its problems of corrosion. Natural gas at this time was out of sight round the corner, and if anything was to be learnt, it would be from the hands of Shell D'Arcy. There was no question, fortunately, of nuclear power; "fortunately" because in 1960, conclusions based on the experience of other countries would have been inconclusive.

Diesel sets posed maintenance problems.

Gas turbines were thought profitable from ranges of 25,000 kW upwards when civil engineering works were no longer pro-rata with steam turbine size for size. Steam turbines enjoyed a lower cost per kW for sizes of 1500 kW installed. In Northern Nigeria, scarcity of water for cooling purposes favoured the diesel engine. The first matter for consideration was, of course, the load factor. Diesel engines were readily available from many manufacturers but they were noisy and fuel cost might be subject to political decisions. Derating of gas turbines takes place with ascending altitudes. The steam turbine enjoyed a long life but boiler maintenance costs were high.

Statistics of the Sixties

In 1958/59, ECN generated 80% of the units, generally distributed at 50 cycle, 3 phase, 400V to 11000V. ECN installed capacity, under construction, and units generated as at 31/3/1960 by type of plant were:

	Installed capacity	Under construction	Generated
Steam	93,050 kW	40,000 kW	252,019,378 kWh
Diesel	38,940	4,085	102,234,794
Hydro	1,720	750	6,453,650

When the Jebba and Shiroro Gorge schemes went ahead, "Under construction" added 225,000 kW to the hydro-electric category. Number of consumers were graded:

Year	Residential	Commercial	Industrial	Miscellaneous	Total
1955/56	49,600	10,663	1,596	503	62,362
1957/58	65,231	15,252	1,373	259	82,115
1959/60	74,245	17,977	1,040	1391	94,653
1964/65	144,728	40,069	2,540	4764	192,101

The increase in income brought revenue to a figure in excess of £10 million in 1964/65. Growth had been:

	By 31/3/49	By 31/3/58	By 31/3/61	Planned by 31/3/1962
Towns supplied	14	31	63	80
Power stations	13	25	36	39
Generating capacity	22MW	98MW	185MW	215MW
Aggregate MD	9MVA	58MVA	95MVA	114MVA

Growth from 1900 had been:

	1900	1910	1920	1930	1940	1950	1960
Installed capacity MW	.06	.105	.36	4.2	12.7	23.1	135.7
Units generated million	.018	.145	.36	6.85	18.5	61.1	360.7

British and Indian figures for million units generated in 1960 were 100,000 and 1408 respectively.

In terms of demand, Lagos topped the bill with Ibadan, Kano, Enugu and Plateau following in that order. Power stations on 1/4/1961 comprised:

Steam	Lagos (Ijora) and Oji River
Steam and diesel	Ibadan, Enugu, Port Harcourt, and Kano
Diesel	Remaining stations

Units generated in thousand kWh by source and region were:

	1954/55	1956/57	1958/59	1961/62	1963/64
Lagos	69,138	91,180	125,220	264,488	428,104
Western Nigeria	15,592	28,408	39,873	56,595	46,179
Eastern Nigeria	21,602	34,222	68,638	127,947	187,000
Northern Nigeria	20,811	32,025	50,550	96,236	131,890
NESCO	71,825	82,461	46,639	100,990	121,221
AT&P	10,173	11,530	15,601	16,044	14,665

The increase in 1960/61 over 1959/60 was no less than 43.5%!

The fuel used by the ECN was:

Year	Coal 000 tons	Oil 000 gallons	Bunker C Fuel oil 000 tons
1954	130.6	1,124	
1956	160.7	2,486	
1958	203.0	4,410	
1959	167.9	5,687	27
1960	128.3	7,002	65
1961	136.0	8,202	84
1963	148.8	7,827	

Growth in capacity, demand, units generated and sent out, was:

Year	Installed capacity 000 kW	Max demand 000 kW	Units generated 000,000 kWh	Load factor
1954	42.93	29.10	139.5	
1956	85.39	44.02	201.4	.45
1958	102.42	65.70	302.5	.47
1961	185.37	109.86	522.9	.53
1963	229.6	152.58	750.2	.57

The figures show a marked similarity in the decade at 435%, 424% and 438%.

Undertaking at 31st March 1964 was:

Thermal	Diesel	Hydro-electric	Grid
Kano	Sokoto		Jos
Enugu	Katsina		Nsukka
Oji River	Maiduguri		Nkalagu
Afam	Bichi		Onitsha
Port Harcourt	Gusau		Sapele
Ibadan	Funtua		Ondo
Lagos	Gombe		Idanre
	Bauchi		Ado-Ekiti
	Zaria		Ikere
	Kaduna		Owo

Minna	Ikare
Bida	Ilesha
Yola	Ife
Abakaliki	Gbongan
Owerri	Ede
Umuahia	Iwo
Aba	Oyo
Calabar	Ejigbo
Warri	Ogbomosho
Koko	Ilorin
Makurdi	Ikirun
Benin	Offa
Akure	Shagamu
Oshogbo	Ijebu-Ode
Abeokuta	Epe
Badagry	Papa Lanto
Lokoja	Ilaro
Asaba	Ifo
Omoba	Otta

The largest of the stations were Lagos (Ijora "A" and "B"), 100 MW; Oji River, 30 MW; Afam, 20 MW; Kaduna, 18.1 MW; Kano, 14.1 MW; and Ibadan, 10.9 MW. Units were purchased from AT&P at Sapele to boost the Warri ECN station network. UAC produced at Burutu, the Nigerian Sugar Company at Bacita, Shell at Bonny and Dunlop Rubber estate near Calabar. The railway closed its plants at Minna and Makurdi in 1961 and took on the ECN supplies.

Undertaking proposed at 31st March 1964

Thermal	Diesel	Hydro-electric	Grid
Ughelli	N'guru	Kainji	Ikot Ekpene
	Bacita	Jebba	Awka
	Okitipupa	Uyo	
	Oturkpo		

This brought the installed capacity by 31/3/1965 to:

Steam	142,050 kW
Diesel	63,475 kW
Gas turbine	32,000 kW
Free piston	5,000 kW
Total	242,525 kW

Transmission Lines

In units of miles:

	31/3/1949	31/3/1958	31/3/1961	Planned 31/3/1962
132 kV	0	0	40	187
66 kV	0	91	121	121
33 kV & cables	0	127	301	740

Small sizes of stations and long distances between them militated against construction of power lines on the grounds of economics except where the station was not at the load centre as was the case with 66kV Oji River/Enugu/Nkalagu/Nsukka and 33kV Oshogbo/Ede/Ilesha/Ife. By 31/3/1964, there was also 33kV Warri/Sapele/Benin, Akure/Ondo/Ado-Ekiti/Ikare, Lagos/Ibadan/Ede/Ilorin, the 33kV Shagamu/Ijebu-Ode, the 132kV Afam/Aba/Port Harcourt, and the planned Kainji/Jebba/Shiroro Gorge at 330kV with Kaduna/Zaria/Kano at 132kV. Also planned were the Kainji/Jebba 330kV link to Oshogbo and Lagos/Oshogbo/Akure/Ughelli double circuit 132kV, Benin/Asaba/Onitsha 330kV, Onitsha/Aba 330kV with the Aba/Ikot Ekpene/Uyo/ Calabar at 33kV and Onitsha Awka at multi voltage.

Prestressed concrete, wooden poles and steel tubular poles, were the norm for the power lines with lattice towers for higher voltages and over swampy coastal areas. Extensive high and low voltage cable systems were laid in Lagos and large towns. The conductor was mainly stranded aluminium, copper being replaced on factors of weight and cost. Switchgear breaking capacity was between 75MVA to 350MVA. Distribution voltages were 3.3 kV to 33 kV primary, 400V secondary, phase to neutral 230V domestic. The policy was to operate at 33,000V when the load was within sixty miles of the station.

Station Developments of the Early Sixties

Due to much power failure, the railway had standby plants for Ebute Metta, Zaria and Enugu. They had their own power stations at N'guru, Offa, Kafanchan, Jebba and Zungeru with installed capacity of 560 kW, later 770, with 1215 kW at the Chief Engineer's Eziator Quarry until this was shut down in favour of ECN supply, and the same capacity on the Bornu Extension. The railway had plans for Mokwa and Kaura Namoda.

In the north in particular, the large distances between towns favoured the creation of more stations rather than a network of transmission lines and where employed transmission was at 11kV, they were standardised only from 1956, with provision for older conversions to 6600V to save expenditure until the end of the power plant life. A major problem with transmission lines lay in obtaining access to the valuable land in the vicinity of a town. Provision was increasingly made for maintenance by connection of load at installed total capacity less the output of the largest set. Based on coal cost, a connection Lagos-Ibadan was not justified until the Ibadan MD reached 12 MW, and on the conversion of Lagos to oil burning, on Ibadan reaching 9 MW.

In 1959, the average consumer consumption was 8384 kWh p.a. This was 69.9% used less than 100 kWh per month, 4.3% were in the range 501-1000 kWh and only 1.2% used over 5000 kWh. Two years later, whilst it was realised that consumption per consumer had increased over ten years from 1460 kWh p.a. on the basis of the then 1961 population, it was still under 10 kWh per capita. This last figure compared with 1958 returns:

Spain	500
Colombo	200
Algeria	100
Egypt	70
India	40
Pakistan	20
Indonesia	15
Nigeria	10

Nigeria was therefore very low in the global scale with what she had to offer. It brought to mind the old adage of what came first, chicken or egg, industry or electricity.

The Afam station, sixteen miles from Port Harcourt, was powered by 2 × 10,000 kW open cycle Brown Boveri turbines designed to run on natural gas or gas oil but in practice fed by the former from the Afam gas fields. The plant was commissioned at the end of 1962. A third set was contemplated but in 1964, 2 × 17500 kW sets were instead under commission bringing the installed capacity to 55 MW. On transmission reaching Port Harcourt, the steam plant and part of the diesel plant there were written off, the remaining diesel plant coming into use as a standby. The gas was ample and the surplus went to flare waste. Afam cost £1.5 million. A great stride had been taken in utilising national resources. With a minimum calorific value of 950 B.Th.U's/cu ft. and with operating efficiency of 15.5%, guaranteed full load figure 18.5%, cost per kWh generated was reckoned to be 1d, all in aim of the government's effort to produce cheap electricity.

After 1964 and Afam, it was natural to turn attention towards Ughelli where a first generation plant came on stream in June 1966, and a second generation, six months later. Ughelli was in Mid-Western Nigeria and the 2 × 36 MW natural gas turbines took their fuel from the nearby fields. Not only did power stations consume natural gas; the Michelin tyre factory and the Port Harcourt glass industry used the gas of the Apara fields. Tenders were out for a new 2 × 5 MW Sapele station designed to draw natural gas from Ughelli, twenty-eight miles away. The Ughelli plans were fathered by the wish to produce cheap and quick electricity.

Kano was another case in point. Without previous experience in the country but on the estimates of 32%, overall efficiency orders were placed for a 6 MW free piston plant using bunker "C" fuel. In Lagos, they created Ijora "C" before 1965 was "out" by the commissioning of a 30,000 kW high speed aircraft type gas turbine plant to bring the "A,B,C" total to 134 MW. This was peak lopping until the Kainji grid came in parallel. The trouble with Lagos, if trouble it was, was that there was almost no such thing as a peak load.

When the 132kV line (Lagos-Ibadan) was commissioned, the Ibadan steam plant was to be put out of use and the diesel plant kept on standby. Three years later, however, the thoughts were of an expansion in generation from local centres. A free piston plant was earmarked for Kaduna in 1960 but the tenders of 1961 called for 2 × 3 MW diesel driven alternators using bunker "C" fuel whilst the conversion of one plant there and at Zaria and Aba to this fuel were to take place. In 1964, a new station, Kaduna "C" comprising 2 × 10 MW gas turbine sets, was quoted, designed to operate on heavy residual fuel oil.

Before the Niger dams came on the scene, augmentation of the supply was necessary at Sokoto (a new station) to cover the load of the cement industry, at Jebba to cover the paper mill and a 460 kW diesel alternator set at Bacita for the sugar plantation. The water works power plant at Lokoja was taken over and expanded and the Shell Development plant at Owerri was taken under ECN wing. Standardised sets were established in towns such as Bida, Minna, Funtua and Gusau. To achieve some flexibility, skid mounted semi-portable diesel sets were purchased.

Rural supplies were considered using gas turbines of 40-80 kW range with heat exchangers. There were no plans for nuclear plants because of the difficulty of staffing and removal of radio-active waste but the possibility was not written off. This left the future hope in the shape of hydro-electric schemes on the Niger and Kaduna with every prospect of materialisation of 225 MW at a cost of £57 million with commissioning not later than 1967.

Tariff

For the first time, the tariff of 1953 took into account maximum demand in kVA, requiring elaboration of the meters. In 1956, a tariff was introduced based on a fixed charge related to floor area of domestic premises or installed load of commercial premises, and a running unit charge based on energy consumption. The unit charge domestic rate at the most viable undertaking was 3d/unit for the first 200 units and 1.5d for units in excess. At the other end, the less viable undertakings charged a flat rate of 5d. A concessionary rate was available to an industrial consumer able to show high demand and load factor and favourable off-peak characteristics. The monthly charge per kVA was graduated in seven scales from 27/6d for 11-25kVA to 13/4d above 1000 kVA. A consumer with an installed load above 5 kVA willing to bear the cost of MD metering could elect to be charged on measured demand. Measurement was certainly normal practice where demand exceeded 25 kVA.

Niger Dams Authority

The Niger and its tributaries drain more than 50% of the country. It was the "Mississippi" of Nigeria. Preliminary work on the Kainji Dam estimated to cost £68.1 million was put in place by the Federal Prime Minister on 31st August 1964 with the aid of a loan of £29.3 million from the IBRD and £14.7 million from other foreign sources. The project aimed at an eventual installed capacity of 960 MW in stages of 4 × 80 MW turbine installations and navigation of the river possible throughout the year and was due for completion in 1969/70. The Chairman of the Authority (NDA) was J.H. Ings of Canada and the Secretary was S.O. Wey of Nigeria. The lowest bid for the civil engineering works was put in by Impresit-Girola-Lodigiani, an Italian partnership otherwise known as "Impregilo" in the sum of £35,728,151. They had obtained West African experience on the Volta Dam in Ghana. The Nigerian contract was awarded to Impregilo in February 1964 and comprised concrete dam, power house, left, right and saddle fill dams, navigation works, roads and construction camps.

Kainji island was about sixty-four miles north of Jebba and was chosen as the first of the three hydro-electric schemes in mind to be put in hand, being described as the "cornerstone" of the then National Plan. The dam was to store flood waters and ensure continuity of passage over the Niger. Kainji was one of the many villages bordering the Niger on its travels through Yauri and Borgu Emirates, sparsely populated land except close to the river where the soil was fertile. Bussa would be submerged and Yelwa protected by a 25ft. wall and resettlement in New Bussa would be necessary upon the creation of the 480 sq. mile, 85-mile long lake from dam to Yelwa, capital of Yauri Emirate. The relocation was done excellently.

Land in the neighbourhood was very flat, no hills lent their support, with the concrete dam 215ft. high by 1800ft. across and the rock fill dams on either side nearly five miles long. The ECN had commenced a survey in 1958 and in 1959 the two major consultants, Balfour Beatty of England and NEDECO of Holland, had produced first reports. A special UN fund allowed of an instruction to both consultants to produce contract documents and supervise first stages.

Merz & McLellan of England then became Consultants in addition for the transmission system survey to determine substation sites. Contracts were awarded to English Electric for the turbines, Voste of Austria for intake and spillway gates, Provincial Engineering of Canada for overhead cranes, ASEA of Sweden for generators and transformer, and GIE of Italy for electrical equipment. Other contractors were Mather & Platt of England and Haydn of Nigeria.

Kainji was associated with a national grid, and was expected to be sufficient until 1980 when other dams would feed in, namely Jebba ten years later, followed by Shiroro on the Kaduna, bringing total potential to 1730 MW. But Kainji creation was not without criticism from within. There were those who thought that expansion should be met on the lines of Afam/Ughelli where the effect on the human environment would be less glamorous but less severe. However, Kainji would, where Afam/Ughelli would not, provide 10,000 tons of fish a year and by its two lock gates, basin, and 1½ mile canal, put the Niger in touch with the Republic of Niger and Baro in touch with the delta all the year round.

Impregilo arrived on site in March 1964 and commenced the camp and mobilisation of equipment and stores. By May, the river's left channel had been diverted by coffer dams in order to permit of main dam foundations on dry soil. Temporary bridges over river channels and a 16½ mile access road from Wawa had been completed by June. The Federal Ministry of Labour established a Labour Office in October to advise on the control of a labour force of

6700 of which 800 were technical, administrative, hospital and master artisans, 1770 skilled workers, 450 semi-skilled and 3680 unskilled. Balfour Beatty and NEDECO consultant staff numbered 200. A second access road, the fifty-two miles from Mokwa, was ready by April 1965 along with the Awuru-Kainji road and Kainji airstrip.

Concrete founds were commenced in May 1965 using silo side loading carriers to 10-ton capacity buckets suspended from 300ft. high aerial cableways controlled from a look-out tower in radio contact with the man directing operations. Eight hundred thousand cu. yds were to be required, the base width of the dam being 300ft. The cement, low heat, and ordinary Portland, was imported from Norway and at times ice, instead of water, was added to keep the concrete mix low in temperature. The cement came out at five-weekly frequencies in specially built ships of 12000 tons capacity being moved by rail to Mokwa and thence in cement tankers over the new access road. The crushed aggregate came from the banks of the Niger and was graded ¾in., 1½in., and 6in. Sand and water came from the Niger. The sand is of very fine quality around this area. A flow of 400 tons concrete per hour was obtained.

The power house was situated immediately downstream of the intake dam with eight penstocks and provision for four more. Fill dams had a compacted sandy clay core introduced by crushed rock and transition materials and took 6¾ million cu. yds of material. The clay came from borrow pits on site. The saddle dam was 2½ miles long, 1½ million cu. yds of fill, maximum height 45ft. Reservoir level/tailwater level difference was 135ft. maximum, accommodated in the navigational channel by 80ft. upper lock, 55ft. lower lock. Each lock was 650ft. × 40ft. and would accommodate a 600ft. pusher Gongola type barge train taking an hour to pass through the two locks and basin. A two-mile canal bypassed the Awuru Rapids eleven miles downstream of Kainji. The Niger was bridged over the left tailrace by a reinforced concrete road slab deck 22ft. wide in a structure 616ft. × 32ft. This, at the time, ranked as the third bridge over the Niger, the others being Jebba rail/road and Onitsha. The right tailrace was bridged later.

Model tests were carried out at the Hydraulic Research Station, Wallingford, at the University of Wales, and at Delft in Holland. The University of Ife arranged for biological studies to be completed before the dam was closed and the Kainji Biological Pilot Research Station at Shagunu near Bussa, Universities in the United Kingdom and Nigeria, took part along with the British Museum.

A factory inspector was posted in December 1965. It was thought better to construct the camp nine miles from site. It had to cater for the 2000 workers and their dependants, no mean figure, and for this shops had to be provided on a non-profit basis, as well as schools, street lighting, sewage disposal, a most modern hospital, clubs, lawn tennis, indoor sports and a cinema. Even an orchestra was laid on. There was a handsome Roman Catholic Church. Eighty security guards assisted the police and there was a thirty-man fire brigade. Of course there was a maternity ward. Altogether 50,000 people had to be resettled to 150 new villages but Bussa was the principal new town.

From May 1966 to August 1968, the Niger at Kainji had to be closed to all forms of river traffic so that the second stage river diversions could be carried out.

The dam was closed on the 2nd August 1968 and held back 1120 sq. kms of water. Construction bridged a major political crisis in the land. Around 1250 workers from the East left after the coup of 1966 and many Italians panicked and got as far as Lagos before deciding that the troubles would not affect the safety of expatriates. Northerners and Westerners replaced the Ibos. To move the transformers from Apapa to site, a 150-ton rail/road vehicle on four 5-axle bogies was built by Head, Wrightson & Co Ltd. of Thornaby-on-Tees. Maximum load dimensions were 28ft.× 12ft. × 13ft. 9in. high. When on the road from Mokwa, the 20-ton two-road bogies which were Crane Fruehaf built were 30ft. × 11ft. 6in. wide. Tare weight was rail, 120 tons, road, 81 tons; suspension, Timken tapered roller bearings.

1970-1974

The tumult and the shouting died and this period was but an interregnum until further activity in the 80s. There was civil war damage to repair but capacity was considered in excess of demand. The main stations of the NDA and the ECN were classed as:

Kainji	hydro-electric
Afam and Ughelli	natural gas
Kaduna	diesel
Ijora	steam and gas
Oji River	steam
Kano (Challowa)	steam and diesel
Ibadan	diesel and gas

By 1974, 34% was consumed by the residential sector but overall demand was but 20% of that of India and it was necessary to plan realistically ahead and not stay with eyes glued on water power beyond a new scheme at Kano's Tiga irrigation dam with a 20 MW capacity. The Made River in Benue State also lent itself to development.

Third Five-Year National Plan

Guidelines said in part, "Infrastructural bottlenecks are becoming binding restraints on the pace of economic activity and the need for reliable power supply cannot be over-emphasised. Hitherto the nation's energy requirements have been met, for the most part, from hydro-sources, but with the growing availability of gas and fuel oil, it has become necessary to examine our past commitment to hydro-power. A study is soon to be commissioned to examine Nigeria's long term energy requirements and to formulate a strategy for an overall development programme."

Public installed capacity in 1975 was 690 MW, operational capacity 519 MW and rated firm's capacity 358 MW. By 1980, installed capacity was to be 1740. One hundred and fifty million naira was to be set aside for rural electrification against a background knowledge that the North West State with an area of 65,143 sq miles, for example, had only four towns with water, roads and electricity. African returns in 1975/76 included the following:

	Hydro-Electric Installed cap. MW	Total Installed Capacity MW	Total Production Million kWh
Nigeria (public)	320		
Nigeria (all)		860	3216
Algeria		1110	3120
Cameroun	197		
Ghana	925	995	4050
Zambia	759	1031	6192
Egypt (public)	2445		
Egypt (all)		3893	10421

National Electric Power Authority

The Niger Dam Authority and ECN became merged for the public benefit as National Electric Power Authority (NEPA). In March 1975, Alhaji Danbaba was made Chairman. That year, capacity remained stagnant whilst demand was increasing at 20.5% p.a. NEPA became a lasting target for consumer and press criticism by not having realised the impact the oil boom would have on the national demand. In five years, there would be much load-shedding. The public at large had of course no appreciation of the meaning of lead time. Additional plant for Kainji and the natural gas stations remained to be commissioned. There was poor maintenance at the thermal stations and transmission facilities were inadequate.

Despite what had been said, emphasis was to be placed on hydro-electric and small undertakings were to be phased out. Early candidates were Funtua and Gusau in February 1975 when the Zaria-Funtua-Gusau transmission line went "live". New proposals were:

Sapele	4 gas-fired steam turbines 480 Mw ₦115.5 m;
Afam	capacity increase from 55 to 100 MW;
Ughelli	second gas unit of 120 MW to be installed;

Kainji	units from 4 to 8, power from 440 MW to 760;
Jebba/Shiroro/Gongola	3 new hydro projects of 830 MW to be built;
Ikom/Makurdi/	hydro potential estimated at 400, 600 MW;
Lokoja	1950 MW potential to be examined.

Five hundred rural communities were to be supplied with power from the grid. Transmission lines were to be extended, 330kV by 3144km, 132kV by 2272km, a principal additon to the former being Benin-Lagos.

NEPA's operating revenue for the year ended 31/3/1976 was ₦83 million, a return of 4.2% on fixed assets despite failure of the gas turbines at Ughelli, now called the Delta power station. Eight additional gas turbines were installed at Afam and Delta and 100 MW at Kainji. A further 100 MW for Kainji and two gas turbines for Afam were due. Customers new totalled 503,022 and would have been more but for shipping delays in bringing in transmission materials for Sokoto, Jos, Bauchi and Gombe. The Benue/Plateau project had been arranged by the Crown Agents financed from a UK £2.8 million loan. Inflation and the provision of two further units at Sapele caused the five-year budget to be increased from ₦928 million to ₦1250 million. The tariff was by now inadequate. The II kV network grew by 546 route kms. Feasibility study contracts were awarded for Jebba and the Shiroro Gorge now put at 500 and 400 MW respectively. The contract was let for investigation of the Niger/Benue below Lokoja and Makurdi, and the Cross at Ikom but the potential had been revised to 1900, 500 and 500 MW respectively. NEPA staff totalled 13,142 and the first grumbles of discontent with service conditions were to be heard. This was to increase and cause anxiety. The Training Schools at Kainji and Ijora were strengthened and, among the overseas despatches of Nigerian operators, figured Sapele to the Irish Electricity Supply Board.

In April 1976, a Swedish Trade Mission visiting Nigeria was anxious to assist in the field of mining but was informed that electrical issues would be a more helpful gesture, particularly in the setting up by a partnership, local manufacturing resources thus reducing Nigeria's dependence on imports of electrical goods. A twenty-year old railway problem shifted to NEPA with alarming proportions, theft of conductor materials from Onitsha and Enugu. Bush fires caused their havoc. The national grid operated as a single system. New gas turbine sets were of General Electric manufacture. Kainji carried 75% of the base load but was not in such a healthy position that Lagos/Ijora could draw its requirements from. The 330kV line from Kainji and Ijora standby thermal units were in continuous use.

In August 1976, negotiations were commenced in Bonn between Government and Kraftwerke Union AG for a nuclear reactor purchase, 450MW, one thousand million Deutsche Marks, Germany having no objection to the transaction as Nigeria had signed the Nuclear Non-proliferation Treaty. A month later, Nigeria set up an Atomic Energy Commission for all matters relating to the peaceful uses of atomic energy with powers to prospect for and mine radioactive minerals and to construct and maintain nuclear power plants. The Commission of eight members required the approval of the Head of State to implement any decision reached. Per capita consumption in Nigeria had reached 29 kWh.

Contracts awarded in 1976 were the Jebba Dam project, design, manufacture, delivery, erection, supervision of emergency and spillway gates to Mitsubishi of Japan, ₦4 million; phases 1 and 2 soil investigations Lokoja Dam site to Radio Nigeria Cementation & Drilling Co., ₦1.02 million; phases 1 and 2 soil investigation Makurdi Dam to Warren George/Nigerian Foundation Services & Soils Research Co. Ltd., ₦0.73 million; phase 1 Ikom Dam to the same company entrusted with Makurdi, ₦0.4 million. Three MW was under construction at Makurdi and the transmission lines would take in Ankpa and Oturkpo.

NESCO pre-tax profit for 1975/76 was £619,553, up in such figures but down after tax. Control of tin export depressed the mine's requirements and called for revision of the power tariff. In the last quarter of 1976, work was due to begin on the Chad Basin Development Authority in Borno at the new Marte station situated on the Dikwa-Kukawa road designed by Mott, Hay and Anderson International, associated with the MRT Consulting Engineers (Nigeria) group Also in the group was Sir M. MacDonald & Partners who were Consulting Engineers for the electrical power and telecommunications. Irrigation water was planned to flow from the lake in the Autumn of 1978 and the complete works come on stream in 1979.

The Shiroro Gorge 115m dam on the Kaduna in Niger State was re-advertised in November 1976 by Charles T. Main International of Boston. The work involved 2 × 13m tunnels 430m long for river diversion purposes, a power station of four units producing 600MW, access roads, construction camps, and a permanent village to house the station operatives. It was hoped to award the contracts from November 1977 with completion target set at July 1982. The Sapele installation became steam turbine and the four units were awarded to Deutsche Babcock & Wilcox AG with the George Kent Group being responsible for instrumentation and control. In December 1976, Montreal Engineering was instructed to design the $400 million Jebba hydro-electric project and to provide for training of the Nigerian construction supervisory team.

The first hardware contract for the Marte station valued £6.5 million went in the latter end of 1976 to Hawker Siddeley Power Engineering for the first stage plant provision. Marte was twenty kilometres south of Lake Chad and was to provide electricity for the full needs of the 425 sq. km. Chad Basin irrigation scheme and a number of outlying towns and villages from an initial output of 13 MW eventually boosted by four further sets to a total capacity of 30 MW.

In February 1977, further contracts were awarded. The 700 km. drainage channel using 633 structures went to a Greek/Nigerian Consortium, Edok-Eeter Mandilas for the sum of £49 million. The work entailed 15 million m^3 of earthworks, Newton Chambers of Britain under sub-contract supplying the water control equipment. The same Consortium also became responsible for the power station building at £4.8 million. There were two major and two minor pumping stations in the project and the contract for the civil works went to Alhaji Ali Kotoko in consortium with Alhaji Ali Mohammed for £7 million. MAN of West Germany secured the two minor and the first stage pumping plants at £0.75 million.

In May 1977, Hawker Siddeley secured the contract for the second stage power supply at Marte at £5.9 million for the provision of four diesel generating sets making up the missing 17 MW and in July they won a third contract worth £3.6 million to supply the distribution networks from the station to the irrigation pumps, housing estates, and the towns within the irrigation perimeter.

In May 1977, twenty towns were to be connected up in Plateau State under rural electrification schemes. NEPA had completed a 132 kV transmission line Kaduna-Jos-Bauchi-Gombe to be later turned into 330 kV, and there were plans to commission the following:

Enugu — Yandev
Enugu — Oturkpo
Ukpilla — Benin
Abakaliki — Nkalagu
Gombe — Numan
Gombe — Biu — Maiduguri
Gombe — Ashaka — Potiskum

The first 120 MW unit of the gas fired steam turbine plant at Sapele, strictly Ogorodo, was scheduled for completion in April 1978. The station development had now been revalued at ₦265 million and the capacity upped from 480 to 720 MW on final completion in 1980, six units, of four and two, and erection was proceeding simultaneously in view of the demand by consumers.

In December 1977, complaints about the efficiency of NEPA became more and more vocal. Kainji, it was said, despite its not being built to capacity, was short of water. A year later, the trouble was too much water. The

Nigerian citizen had much patience but the press had none and spared no one. The new Chairman, Alhaji Yahaya Gusau, said rationing was inevitable. *"West Africa"* said "This particular disaster... is not of NEPA's making. But this has not been an unusually bad year for rain and it is extraordinary that so little seems to have been known about the behaviour of the great Niger that the Kainji station, where extra capacity is being installed, now proves not to be capable of producing the power which it was intended to. And if the possibility of a disaster of this kind was known all the time why was the programme of building and expanding thermal stations throughout the country not speeded up? After all Nigeria has abundant natural gas and fuel oil of her own and need not depend on hydro-electricity to what now seems a dangerous extent." *New Citizen* said the cause lay in the building of a dam on the Niger in the Republic of Mali, reducing the level at Kainji by 2.7 m.

Earlier in this history, a remark was made on the need to build up hydrological data over thirty-five years; was the data in this instance taken over too short a period? On the other hand, the behaviour of the river was well known and the cusecs well recorded. *West Africa* then made the most pithy comment of the times — "yet is there any evidence that the Five Year Development Plan drawn up to cover 1975-80, has really been revised to put first things first rather than to put everything together?" It is trusted that the fourth Five-Year Plan will, for the first time, do just that, and prove that Nigerians are no longer afraid to slow down.

NEPA's response was the promise by its General Manager, Alhaji Yahaya Dikko, that three more thermal stations would be commissioned from August 1978, Sapele (Ogorodo) first two sets with four to follow, Afam and Delta (6 × 20 MW), and that three × 20 MW gas turbines would be purchased for Lagos/Ijora as a short-term measure. A 90 MVA transformer had complemented two 60 MVAs covering Kano, Sokoto, Bauchi, Plateau, Benue, Borno, Gongola and Kaduna States. It did not help however that NEPA was short of two hundred qualified engineers and this was a direction in which Nigerian universities were expected to assist. As for Kainji where the reservoir contents had dropped from 11.8 bn gallons to 8bn gallons, they must await the July rains. But the Mali reported cause, the GM added, was a misconception. The dam was merely a proposal. The Commissioner for Mines and Power, Alhaji Kachalla Barko, announced that the Government had opted for water power because of its cheapness but that it would consider exploiting the country's gas and coal to an increased extent.

In April 1978, the second 330kV line, Kainji-Lagos, had been completed and three hydro-electric plants had reached the planning stage — Shiroro, Jebba and Lokoja, with capacities now put at 600, 545 and 1950 MW. A new Federal Commissioner of Mines and Power, Alhaji Shehu Kangiwa, commissioned the new Brown-Boveri 25MW gas turbine at Afam, first of four sets in the third phase extension, in August, bringing station capacity to 175 MW of its planned 250 MW output scheduled for December 1978. The contract for the four units had actually gone to Brown-Boveri for ₦17.5 million in June 1977.

In February 1979, it was announced that the Shiroro Gorge station would cost ₦250 million and would be in service in 1981. two years ahead of the ₦371 million Jebba hydro-station. Jebba would operate as the base load station to Kainji and Shiroro.

The Lokoja hydro-station would not cost less than ₦2000 million and the latest Minister for Mines and Power, Alhaji Mohammed Hassan, realised that thousands of people on the banks of the Niger and Benue would be displaced. Construction of the (now) 1870 MW station could not be put in hand before resettlement and the issue of lives dependent on fishing and agriculture had been resolved. The impounding would be felt along the Benue as far as Makurdi and along the Niger as far as Rabba, affecting eight Local Governments in Niger, Kwara, Benue and Plateau States. In consequence, despite the power potential, there was considerable debate as sharp voices of dissent as to the desirability of the project were raised. If it was to be built, it should obviously be put in hand before more projects were set up that might require resettlement. And two billion naira was a large sum of money to tie up in one place that might be vulnerable to an enemy, within or without. Resettlement at Lokoja was estimated to cost ₦450 million, a figure contained in the two billion naira total.

In 1979, projections to 1990 put the hydro-electric stations (excluding NESCO on the Plateau and the Cameroun stations now no longer a Nigerian responsibility) at:

Lokoja	1950 MW
Kainji	800 "
Shiroro	600 "
Makurdi	600 "
Jebba	545 "
Ikom	400 "

Blackouts continued through 1979, demand growing at 300%, Kainji being reduced to 300MW from its 420MW installed capacity, and industry being much affected by the load shedding. Standby generators became essential. Criticism was heard to the effect that older sets had been written off prematurely instead of being maintained in standby condition. The demand was such as was obviously never to have been contemplated but NEPA optimistically suggested a surplus in the late 80s. Meanwhile General Manager Alhaji Dikko reminded Nigerians that they could not expect supplies such as were to be found in USA, UK and USSR. NEPA imported 20,000 miniature circuit breakers to make it impossible for some of their 700,000 customers to increase their loads in an unlawful manner. Vigilance was required in cases of unauthorised connections. Debt collecting received a high priority; at 31/3/1978, sums outstanding were ₦70 million of which government agencies owed ₦19 million.

The Shiroro Gorge Dam was to be sited 168 km on the Kaduna river upstream from its confluence with the Niger and the contract for construction went to Torno of Italy for ₦200 million. In August it was decided to build an 800MW thermal plant at Imone, later described as Igbin, near Ikorodu, Lagos State, close to the Lagoon, to be called the Lagos Power Station. The plant's four 200MW units would draw on natural gas and residual fuel oil and drive steam turbines. A turnkey contract was to be let in November 1978 and would cover a 330kV line to Ikeja substation. First commissioning was put at December 1983, final by June 1985. Natural gas supply by pipeline from the oil-producing areas would be the responsibility of the Nigerian National Petroleum Corporation which hoped, by this means, to introduce LNG to industrial consumers in Lagos by 1999.

Then came 1980. Transmission lines were to go up Shiroro-Minna and Bida-Abuja. NEPA was intended to operate as a quasi-commercial enterprise. Production cost was 6.82 kobo/kWh but the current tariff yielded only 3.78 Kobo in return and accordingly the new tariff of 1/7/1979 was intended to reduce the 48% government subsidy. A consumer with a load in excess of 12kW was connected to the 3-phase supply. Single phase was charged at 6 kobo/kWh, three phase at 6.5 kobo/kWh, three phase above 75 kVA at rate of 6.5 kobo/kWh for first 50,000 kWh down in three further stages to four kobo/kWh for over one million kWh.

A sum of ₦35.7 million went to Water Resources & Engineering Construction Agency (WRECA) for the construction of the Challowa Gorge Dam of the Hadejia Jama are River Basin Development Authority, 60km south west of Kano City between Kiru and Karaye. The dam would impound 97 million litres, would be 7760m in length 39m high and have a total width of 10m. It would supplement the Tiga Dam and would irrigate 60,000 hectares, provide 200 tons of fish per annum and generate 8MW for rural areas.

A ₦36 million contract went to Stirling Astaldi of Italy for the Dadin Kowa Dam of the Upper Benue River Basin Development Authority in Bauchi. This dam which was on the Gongola river would irrigate 35,000 hectares and impound sufficient water for the generation of 146 million kWh per annum. A second contract for the design of the works went to the Canadian firm, Shawmont Nigeria Ltd.

By February, Afam extensions to serve Port Harcourt areas and Sapele were partly in use, the latter generating 480MW, Sapele having been commissioned in the previous September and now put at ₦230 million but further capacity of plus 300 MW to 1020 MW was planned for March 1981. The Ogorodo site, the responsibility of the Consultants, Shawmont Nigeria Ltd, was chosen because of the proximity of natural gas at Ugbekuku then being flared off together with, in that part of the country, soil conditions suitable for sound foundations, and availability of cooling water.

A survey completed in February 1980 put the 1985 demand at double the existing figure! Maximum demand was assessed at:

1979/80	1400 MW
1980/81	1800
1981/82	2200
1982/83	2600
1985/86	3600

The reasons for growth were associated with increasing industrialisation, spread to rural communities and desire for sophisticated consumer appliances. It was however a source of annoyance to many a Nigerian that for reasons of prestige hidden by the cloak of revenue, 95% of Niger Republic's electricity was generated by Nigeria.

The country's largest transformer substation at Ipaja by Ikeja was brought into use in March. It was a 330/132 kV of capacity 600 MVA, built at a cost of ₦10 million. All power from Kainji, Sapele, Afam and Ughelli was fed in before distribution to other parts of Lagos State. A 50km 132kV double circuit line would then be constructed to carry a 270 MW load to Ikoyi over a route of some complexity supported by 150 steel towers, twenty-five of which would be in swamp and fifteen in the waters of the lagoon.

Sapele was under strength at 237 employees, made up of:

Nigerian Engineers	9
Nigerian Pupil Engineers	6
British Electricity International	21
Technologists	12
Technicians	19
Operators	67
Operators-in-training	33
Administration & Supplies	70

but there seemed to be adequate provision for training on the spot.

Work was scheduled to begin on the ₦300 million Igbin Ikorodu station in October. Tenders inviting pre-qualification applications had been issued in February 1980 by Shawmont Nigeria Ltd. Offshore costs would, it was hoped, be aided by funds from IBRD.

In April 1980, NEPA announced its completion plans for the next five years:

Sapele steam	240 MW	1980
Sapele gas turbine	300 MW	1982
Afam additional gas	450 MW	1983
Jebba hydro-electric	540 MW	1983
Zungeru Falls hydro-electric	500 MW	1983
Katsina Ala hydro-electric	260 MW	1983
Shiroro hydro-electric	600 MW	1984
Ikorodu Igbin thermal	800 MW	1985
Makurdi thermal	800 MW	1986
Lokoja hydro-electric	1800 MW	1987

They also put a generation figure of 3000 MW to flared gas at wells. The 330 kV transmission would be extended by 1000 km:

Sapele-Benin	1981
Sapele-Aladja	1981
Benin-Ajaokuta	1981
Benin-Onitsha-Aba	1982
Afam-Alaoji	1982
Enugu-Makurdi	1983
Gombe-Maiduguri	1983
Birnin Kebbi-Sokoto	1984
Onitsha-Enugu	1987

132 kV lines would be extended 2000 km. It would seem obvious from a study of previous projections that the stations and network transmissions will not be completed

in the time scale envisaged.

Planned maintenance and anticipation of likely areas of storm damage, the collection of debts and prosecution for unlawful tapping, the spread of electricity to rural communities, the appearance of local manufacturing industry — these are the factors that must demand the attention of NEPA's management. An increasing depend- ence on water and natural gas has been shown over the years but the Government had, in June 1980, shelved the Lokoja Dam project.

Vast areas of the north, particularly west and east, remain a trail to be emblazoned along with the Middle Belt and land contiguous to Cameroun. The economics of Nigeria may be read from a study of the transmission line map. Finally, of the two bestowed gifts, one trusts that natural gas will find its own feet ahead of the potential energy provided by the difference in river datums.

Public Water Supplies

Two thirds of the earth's surface is covered by water and two thirds of one per cent only is fit for human consumption, untreated. Eighty six per cent of the rural population in developing countries do not have reasonable access to safe water. Water-borne diseases figure among the three major causes of sickness and death in tropical areas. Ancient civilisations knew of the value of wholesome water but the lessons were not handed down and had to be learnt again in the Industrial Revolution that brought pollution, cholera and typhoid in its trail. London domestics use 150 litres a day; the developing countries are lucky with 12.

Global Problems

Africa possesses some 40% of the earth's running water and millions of square kilometres of fertile land but only produces 2% of world food. Before examining Nigeria, remembering that the Futa Jallon Massif is the hydrographic centre of West Africa, it is as well to look at modern troubles elsewhere — issues that seem to compound the problems of unchecked industrial pollution and insufficiently treated sewage.

Canada is one of the few remaining countries with vast quantities of untapped fresh water. Her part of the Great Lakes alone accounts for ten per cent of the world's supply of fresh surface water. Her problems though are different, the presence of common salt used during the long winter on the icy roads and chemical and wood products from pulp mills. This has caused eutrophication.

Population density of the United States is only 10% of that of Britain. By 1970, total withdrawals had reached 370,000 mgd of which power/industry took 58% and irrigation 35%. Wells supplied 18.5% and of the remainder, surface water, 17.5% of which was saline. Nitrates from fertilisers were not thought of as health hazard to man and more concern was shown for thermal pollution causing lack of oxygen, with failure to support animal and plant. One cow, it was said, could produce a pollution equivalent to that from seventeen humans. The organisation for the department of the interior could well be copied by Nigeria as it embraced outdoor recreation, environmental review, and wildlife and parks. The United States has nine main drainage areas with pollution worsening in five, but improving in four. The battle appears to have been losing ground in terms of dissolved oxygen, the ammonias, and nitrates/nitrites.

Federal Germany faces an increase of 100% demand over thirty years, surface water presently meeting 35% of requirement. There was thermal station effluence in the Rhine whilst there was an increasing call for light water reactor nuclear stations. Sewage levies were to be raised to pay for the cost of treatment. Norway, Sweden and Finland are said to have no problems but Swedish law requires precautions to be taken by whosoever engages in activities detrimental to the environment. Chloride/alkali industries were responsible for 1mg mercury per kilogram of fish landed and the discharge of garbage and sewage from vessels was said to be equal to the untreated sewage of a population of

12,000 people. Great strides have however been made in Sweden with biological and chemical treatment of sewage. Finland makes a levy on each 1000 tonnes of oil imported and puts this sum to a kitty to pay for damage. Her seas and lakes are remarkably free. Not surprisingly, wood processing accounts for 88% of water pollution. The Nature Protection Association believes in making the polluter pay for his damage to the environment.

France, well endowed with rivers and under-utilized, controls six hydrographic basins with delegation of powers directed at national, basin, regional, county and municipal levels. She supplies 85% of her population by piped means, believing in the main, in a service provided by private companies. Plant is to a generous scale, and polluters must pay for oxidization or material in suspension increase, particularly in areas of shell fish cultivation and for this purpose data banks and early warning systems are employed.

The USSR had pollution troubles with the Caspian Sea, where the levels had fallen to 3m in thirty years, and the Volga and Ural rivers. Vessels for the collection of oil and surface rubbish, and microbes that thrive on petroleum have been introduced. An industrialisation of Lake Baikal resulted in the salmon catch reducing by half. Under Soviet principles, water was supplied free of charge and there was unfortunately little incentive to consider the consequence of pollution.

Japan has the problem of 31% of her peoples living on 1% of her land area. Her great enemy was the mining industry, exemplified by cooper, methyl mercury and cadmium poisoning of the paddy fields. Her present enemy is petrochemicals. She first laid down three standards, pH, chemical oxygen demand and suspended solids, followed in 1971 by a Pollution Bill, differentiating between human health and living environment.

The Indus carries more than twice the annual flow of the Nile the latter of which can be held back by the Aswan Dam. Israel's only resource is underground. Kuwait Oil Co. in 1950 financed the first desalinisation plant.

The Australian Snowy Mountain project with 130km of aqueduct and 30km of pressure tunnel contains 3000 million m^3 of water.

Consumption in the United Kingdom

In Malvern in 1975, it was found that unmetered consumption registered 115 litres/head and metered, 24 litres/head. The greatest consumption was found in detached owner-occupied quarters of the professional classes.

Meteorology of Nigeria

In Europe it is assumed that 80% of the average annual rainfall will fall in the three driest consecutive years. In Ghana at Takoradi, the figure was found to be 66%, occasioning the remark that West African weather was less reliable than UK in prediction. On the other hand, Takoradi saw a storm in June 1943 that gave a rise in the reservoir of 7ft. in 7 hours and a spillway discharge of 138 cusecs per thousand acres of catchment area. During the Guinea Coast wet season with the low pressure belt around Timbuktu, the South East Trades bring rain. In twenty years at Ibadan, there was no rain at all in ten Decembers, seven Januarys and six Februarys with the longest dry spell to 1945 marking 111 days. The average rainfall there was 49.2in. The Ogun with a catchment of 6000 sq. miles was often reduced to negligible flow in the dry season and the Oshun, to the west of it, was dry throughout in 1946. The cycle of wet years on the coastal belt coincided with the cycle of dry years in Sokoto and Katsina.

Some rain gauge records have been maintained for fifty years and it is known that average rainfall varies between enormous fluctuations, from 40in. in the north to 110in. on parts of the coast. Opobo had 109in. in 1923 and 220in. in 1934; Maiduguri was regarded as the most reliable table. In the north, impounding schemes have to take note of 9-10 months "dry" fed by 2-3 months wet. Rainfall is subject to evaporation and plant transpiration, fly off; lost to water table, cut off; induced to surface flows, run off. The proportion are dictated by local topography, geology and vegetation cover. More than half of Western Nigeria has but a thin soil covering over the basement complex and larger supplies can only be obtained by impounding the run off. On balance, the case for afforestation to impede the washing away of top soil is strong and this is a subject of which the people are ignorant of the consequences of shifting cultivation and the destruction of forest cover. It was at one time intended to develop the Ogun river for Ibadan water supplies but the intention was shelved because only a small part of the catchment was afforested. Evaporation from open grassland is higher than from forest but with transpiration, it is the other way round.

Geology of Western Nigeria

Western Nigeria was the most advanced in water schemes and 50% of the undertakings relied on impounded supplies. The northern half of the region is composed of the pre-Cambrian series of metamorphic and igneous rocks comprising the basement complex, outcropping in many places and where found in the valleys often of boulder form. South is a band of Eocene of the Tertiary age, the run-off from the formation being fairly prolonged with water percolating to some depth. The post-Eocene Coastal Plain Benin Sands which is interspersed with the Lignite series, are many hundreds of feet thick and extremely porous, the Lignite series appearing in shallow lenticular beds of shales and clays. Then there are the Delta deposits of the Pleistocene series which extend round the coast of the Bight of Benin, generally waterlogged and covered with swamp vegetation.

Practically all rainfall in the pre-Cambrian series emerges during the latter part of the wet season and the early part of the dry season. Run-off in the Eocene area is more prolonged and supplies must be taken from river intakes and boreholes. The rainfall is absorbed by the Benin Sands at an extremely rapid rate and emerges in springs whose level is only sufficient to provide natural drainage to the major rivers, generally as a pellucid water. Where the sand bends are intersected by the Lignite series, these form impermeable strata which may cause perched aquifers. The Benin Sands present the greatest problem as attempts to develop supplies by borings have resulted in piercing a perched aquifer so that the small supply has been lost in the great depth of these sands. Benin City and Agbor have excellent sub-artesian borehole supplies from these beds. The Delta silty deposits cause considerable trouble with ingress of sand to pumps. Warri is the only large town which derives its water supplies therefrom. Lagos is supplied from a perennial stream at Iju in the Eocene beds.

Early Designs Problems

Lest there be anyone who does not know what water is about, let such person be present at any Nigerian Railway station in the days of steam when a stopping train was expected. Immediately on coming to a rest, hordes of women and children with their buckets hastened to the locomotive in the hope that the firemen will operate the injectors. In anticipation, pails are put under the footsteps to receive the overflow whilst the injectors are put in trim. Even by 1948, Native Authorities could not bear the cost of pipe-borne water. However there were wells with calabash utensils to draw the contents. Whilst 1951 consumption per head per day ranged from fifty gallons in Bombay to 200 gallons in Chicago, Nigerian design was based on ten gallons; this was thought generous because it was not reached. Iwo, capacity 30 mg/month in fact fed 9 mg/month and only came up to scratch on Fridays, the Moslem Sabbath, when ablutions really became the order of the day.

It was no help to the waterworks engineer that the populace eschewed the holding of a census, assessing it as the latest taxation dodge. Survey maps of the period were not such as to make easy the calculation of catchment areas. Flow was measured by "V" notch in streams, rectangular notch in smaller rivers and current meters in larger rivers but readings lacked skilled attention and observation under the necessary number of years. The powers of the Water Authority vested in the Director of Public Works were adequate outside of rating but funds at his disposal were limited.

Purification Practices

In the course of its journey, water generally becomes polluted by bacteria, living organisms and mineral salts. Bacteria of the Coli-Aerogenes group, derived from excrement, are present in almost all surface supplies. Animal parasites such as the Bilharzia Vector and hookworm are present in some waters, and illnesses and diseases of bacterial origin, such as typhoid, dysentry, and gastro enteritis spread. The purification processes used in Western Nigeria for impounded waters comprises:

1. Coagulation with sulphate of alumina containing 15% Al_2O_3;
2. Floculation and settlement;
3. Rapid gravity filtration, pressure filtration, or slow sand filtration;
4. pH correction and sterilisation.

Aeration was used before coagulation employing towers packed with wooden slates and having forced draught blowers, removing H_2S from anaerobic water when using a low draw-off point and increasing pH from around 6.9 to 7.3. Iron compounds settled out and oxidation assisted in the removal of manganese compounds.

All urban waterworks built towards 1961 employed upward flow sludge-blanket settling tanks. Performance was superior provided correct alum dosage was affected. Tanks with over and under baffles were most satisfactory for sludge removal and circular clarifiers made for efficiency where trained operators were lacking. Alum dosage ranged from 30 to 120 ppm. Mr. T.A. Maclachlan, Chief Water Engineer, found no single plant in Western Nigeria giving a good tank effluent and he adopted the Ghana shake test. Rapid gravity filters were the standards designs using air scour and backwashing from elevated tanks.

In the pH sector, wider differences in practice were found between Ghana and Western Nigeria. In new works in Ghana, provision was made to add lime and/or copper sulphate to the raw water at the same place as the alum was added. If the pH become low, a good floc could not form and this was the reason for lime dosing. In Ghana, the filtered water was dosed with bleach powder solution and ammonium, therefore affording good contact time for the chloramine to sterilize the water. In Western Nigeria gas chlorine was added to the filtered water to give 1 ppm free chlorine and the pH was corrected to 7.6. Maclachlan had no doubt that the Nigerian practice was correct. In Ghana, many urban supplies covered large areas but to take a Nigerian example the chlorine dose at Ibadan had nearly vanished by the time it left the main reservoir. It was argued that once water was sterilised there was no need for residual chlorine but the danger persisted if pollution entered the system.

Not surprisingly, there were special difficulties in treating African waters. Kumasi supply was affected by algae (Euglena), water cabbage, bilharzia vectors and corethrid larvae. The impounded water had extensive shallow areas in which algae proliferated and there had to be recourse to spraying of copper sulphate solution. Water cabbage required removal when the rains brought it down to the reservoir. The life cycle of the bilharzia vector requires it to pass part of its life in a species of snail found in the reservoirs. The predominant inorganic compound causing difficulty in impounded supplies was manganese soluble in the manganous state but precipitated in the manganic. As its concentration at Ibadan in the west season was 1.5 ppm, experiments were conducted to find the best method of removal. This was accomplished by raising the pH to 8.2 when precipitation was obtained on the filters. The Government Chemist learnt of the use of copper as an immediate catalyst in the oxidation of manganous compounds but the addition of copper sulphate to coal water had no effect.

The most difficult problem at Ibadan

which had to do with organic pollution was the appearance of jellyfish during the rains of 1958 in the settling tanks. A change to a lower draw-off point however meant that the nuisance ceased to arrive at the works. Then with late final rains, the reservoir level rose and the current carried the jellyfish over the weir. The occurrence is common enough in East African reservoirs but 1958 marked the first visit to a West African impounding. Guinea-worms were to be found in many West African streams. Wells open to salmonellae pollution were said to be a big improvement because the effect of pure water supplies on an immigrant returning to his native village meant too often that he had lost his immunity to typhoid.

Early Lagos and Abeokuta

A dam on the Dago stream gave Zungeru a supply from 1904. Lagos was to have water from Ikoyi but test wells sunk on the race course in 1899 caused them to look inland. The study concentrated on the rivers Iju and Ilo. The Consulting Engineer, Mr. O. Chadwick, was not happy with the Ilo and Professor W.J.R. Simpson working on bubonic plague recommended the Iju as the Lagos source. This suggestion was fortunately followed before the devastating flu pandemic in 1918. W. Peat was the Water Engineer and the first step in 1909 was to be this laying of the railway siding from Agege, ultimately brought nearer, at Iju Jc, because of the diversion of the main line along the Ogun Valley. The siding, commenced in October 1910, approached the pumping station in a steep descent and terminated in coal, lime & alum, and run round sidings.

Iju was 17 miles from the centre of Lagos and the supply was pumped to the Shaga reservoir and then fell to Lagos. Three hundred Kennedy of Kilmarnock stand pipes were erected as distribution points for a flow that commenced in 1913 and they lasted well over half a century. The works were completed in December 1914 at a cost of £296,700 and provided 6½mgd. Formal opening was on 1st July 1915. Refinements were added in 1916 bringing the cost to £310,400, and shipping in the harbour was then supplied. Two driving and 3 steam forcing engines were employed to the 10mg settling tanks, the 8 slow and filter beds, the 2mg concrete floor and roof clear water tank, and the 6mg service reservoir. The pumping plant consisted of two sets of Hawthorn-Davey triple expansion engines running at 47rpm. Each set of pumps consisted of three barrels off a 36in. main pumping at 300,000gph against a head of 100ft. to the sedimentation tank. The four boilers were Lancashire coal fired. Mains were 28in. diameter to Lagos and Ebute Metta and thence 28 miles of 3in. to 15in. diameter distribution lines.

Abeokuta was constructed in 1911 at a cost of £56,000, drawing on the Ogun river, and with sedimentation treatment delivered 800,000 gpd although average consumption was around 0.5 mgd. It had a twin pumping set of capacity 1.3 mgd and the plant specifications were drawn up by A.M. Buchanan of London.

Other Pre-1920 Developments

Borings undertaken by 1919 disclosed the presence of artesian water between Udi and the Niger; artesian supplies for Sokoto were thought a possibility. World War I put programmes for Kano's proposed Challowa River Dam in abeyance. Plans for Port Harcourt and Kaduna were minor copies of the Lagos installation.

Storage capacity in the south west was based on a demand up to 270 days, equal to a maximum holding of 1500 million gallons, with provision for escape by spillway or sluice. Earth dams were the holding medium, 30-50ft. high, 1500ft. maximum length, stone pitching on the 3 : 1 upstream face, slope on the downstream side being 2 : 1. Core walls were built down to 45ft. to find a secure base and if deeper, aided by grouting of pipes sunk in drill holes.

Water was drawn off through screened intakes at different levels. A deterioration of quality as the distance from the surface increases sets in as the following figures show in parts per million:

	Surface	10' Depth	20' Depth	30' Depth
Albuminoid ammonia	.440	.517	.527	.933
Oxygen absorbed 3 hours 37°C	3.490	3.600	6.140	8.470
Total alkalinity as $CaCO_3$	72.500	72.500	120.000	122.500
Total hardness as $CaCO_3$	52.500	50.000	85.000	82.500
Total iron as Fe	1.140	1.880	18.000	26.000
Total solids 180°C 1 hr.	166.000	163.000	243.000	331.000
pH value	7.100	7.100	6.600	6.500
Acidity cc 0.5% Na_2CO_3/100cc	0.300	0.300	1.900	2.500

Shaki Dam in progress 1965

The upper intake was therefore fixed six feet below TWL of the reservoir with other intakes at eight feet intervals to be used successively as the water level dropped.

Post World War I Development

Waterworks were constructed as follows:

	Source	Capacity or use 000 gpd	Treatment	Plant	Built
Enugu	spring	700	aeration & chlorination	gravity	1925
Lokoja	spring	17	slow sand filter	gravity	1925
Ijebu-Ode	spring	300	partial	diesel	1927
Oyo	impounded	100	chlorination	diesel	1928
Aba	well	173	nil	steam	1928
Makurdi	river	16	nil	railway	1928
Onitsha	river	210	aeration pressure filter & chlorination	steam	1928
Kano	well	686	aeration pressure filter & chlorination	electric	1929
Kaduna	river	387	sedimentation rapid gravity filter & chlorination	electric	1930
Akure	well	7	nil	diesel	1931
Ife	impounded	120	chlorination	steam	1934
Benin	borehole	400	chlorination	steam	1934
Iseyin	spring	120	partial	diesel	1936
Calabar	spring	309	aeration chlorination	gas	1936
Okene	impounded	64	nil	gas	1937
Ilorin	well	22	pressure filter & chlorination	diesel	1937
Port Harcourt	borehole	319	nil	electric	1937
Yola	tube well	30	chlorination	steam	1937
Jos	impounded	147	pressure filter & chlorination	gravity	1939
Ogbomosho	impounded	250	aeration chlorination	diesel	1939
Zaria	well	357	aeration pressure filter & chlorination	electric	1939
Ilaro	spring	50	nil	diesel	1940

Yola had three 2in. diameter suction pipes from five 2in. diameter tube wells emerging from the steam pump chamber 220ft. distant off the Benue as a 4in. diameter rising main. Maximum water level above river bed occurred in 1915 and measured 18.7ft. Tube well tops were 4ft. below river bed.

By 1928, the Enugu supply had taken care of the coal mines. In 1929 Royal Engineers surveyed the 112 sq. miles catchment area of Ibadan, the largest city in Nigeria. Boreholes were sunk in the Eocene strata of Ilaro but were unsuccessful. Sub-artesian supplies had been detected at Warri and Asaba and found acidic with a pH value of 5.6 to 6.1, bacteria free, but required time for development.

Shaki Rising Main 1965

Pride of mention falls on Kano. Mr Gourley and Mr Johnson of Sir Alexander Binnie Son & Deacon arrived Lagos on 2nd February 1928 and accompanied Major R.L. Nunn, Senior Waterworks Engineer, to Kano, meeting there Mr. R.A. Brown, Executive Engineer. The question facing them was the Gangara gravitation scheme/Kano reservoir or Challowa pumping station/Goram Dutsi reservoir rising main. Present supply then was from 6400 wells dug in laterite within and without the city, 5200 of them of doubtful potability. Estimate was 700,000 gpd for the next forty years and the lessons of the extension of the Nigerian Railway to N'guru, not the original destination, were not lost sight of. The Challowa source was the most economical. Below the railway bridge the sand bed was naturally divided by rock basins into compartments each some 6500ft. in length requiring three to four intakes.

Challowa water was potable from the sand and the only treatment needed was aeration. Electric low lift pumps to deliver to the low level tank at main pumping station would be required, adjacent to the middle compartment intake. High level pumps would be driven by two diesel engines at 900,000 gpd to high level service reservoir on Goram Dutsi. At railway siding two miles in length for delivery of fuel would be required at Mundadu south of Kano. Goram Dutsi (dutsi means a stone in Hausa) was 1740ft. above Kano datum, a capacity of 1.5 mg would be required as the highest ground to be supplied was 1590ft. and there was ample head for distribution. Estimate was £217,000 with interest and sinking charges £12,345, fuel and lube £4600, staff £4500, per annum, so that cost would work out at 20.1d per 1000 gallons. Supply demand would be 100 kW and construction should commence by the August of 1928 to complete within the dry season.

The Gangara scheme would be cheaper but the dam would take three years and the Consultants were not satisfied with the local materials to hand. Silting up of the reservoir was another feared problem as they did not want South Africa's task of clearance every fifteen years. The water was acid, and would require alkaline reagents and filtration. Mains would be forty-seven miles in length with two miles in excavation at a depth of 53ft. and there were a number of streams to cross. The service reservoir would have to carry 2.5 mg, the cost of the scheme would be £535,000 and cost per thousand gallons would work out at 32.6d. The Challowa scheme was therefore the one recommended.

The 1940s

New works constructed were:

	Source	Capacity 000gpd	Treatment	Built	Plant
Ibadan	impounded	4000	sedimentation rapid gravity filter chlorination	1943	electric
Otta	stream	60	nil	1947	steam
Opobo	well	6.9	nil	1948	diesel

By 1949, average capital value was placed at £46,401, Akure being the cheapest installation at £1208, Lagos the dearest at the then figure of £400,458. Consumption per head per day varied from 0.6 gallons at Oyo to 32 at Ilorin with the average at 9.17 gallons. Schemes proposed in 1949 covered:

	Northern Provinces	Eastern Provinces	Western Provinces
Locations	16	8	27
Population covered	332,000	197,000	962,000
Estimate	£52,300	£154,600	£1,518,000
Most expensive installation	Ilorin	Umuahia	Iwo

In 1943, there came a scheme, the impounding at Minna of a supply to serve a population of 18,000, 180,000 gpd, pressure filter, under enlargement consideration in 1962 to 0.5 mgd. The reservoir drew on 3.5% of the catchment area and had a 60ft. weir. In 1943, the rainfall was 59.57in., precipitation 560.5mg and weir drainage 222.7mg or 39.8%. The dam straddled contours of 1075ft. and 1065ft. containing the water top at 1055ft. and having reservoir floor at 1000ft. The main to Minna was 7in. diameter and the dam was 520ft. long and 14ft. wide at the top.

The Ten-Year Plan, 1946-1956, voted £7.74 million for water, a different story to the half million loan of 1929 but it was said that Nigeria was the only country where urban supplies had to be self-supporting. In line with this parsimony was the fact that after the depression of the 30s, the eight waterworks engineers were reduced to one and never, before 1950, were there to be more than six in the country. The first reservoir to be constructed by a Nigerian engineer was Okene in 1937. The asset handover at Independence in 1960 was grossly inadequate. In 1955, there were only four government chemists to serve the country and a bacteriological laboratory had only just been started up.

Artesian supplies were given the Oji Leprosy Settlement. In 1948, cement lined wells sunk for Kaiama district villages cut out at a stroke a four-mile trek for water. In this decade, no large dams were constructed after Minna. Where necessary earth banks with impervious core and straight concrete overflow weirs had to make do. This, of course, was cheaper but thoughts turned to the American practice of omitting clay puddle cores in dams. To augment Kano supply, two 12in. boreholes were sunk in the Challowa downstream of the five caissons sunk in 1925 and equipped with Beresford electric submersible pumps throttled to give 8000 gallons/hour each.

New Undertakings and their Treatment in the Fifties

Among the new supplies were:

	Source	Capacity 000gpd	Treatment	Capital Value £000	Year
Ubiaja	spring	25	Nil	5	1951
Warri	borehole	200	complete	23	1952
Osogbo/Ede	impounded	2000	complete	438	1954
Ilesha	gravity	500	complete	129	1954
Ibadan extension	impounded	4000	complete	366	1956
Iwo	impounded	2000	complete	312	1956

The Osogbo/Ede scheme made use of four 30ft. wide by 15ft. high sluice gates impounding the water of the Erin-Ile river.

Plans were in hand for seventeen further stations from 1956, the most expensive of which was Akure/Ondo at £767,000 and the largest of which was Abeokuta New Scheme with 2 mgd. Eight schemes were for impounding, one for borehole and the rest river or spring. All were to have complete treatment. Two of the schemes depended on the erection of barrages of considerable length across the Ogun and Oshun rivers with lifting type sluice gates.

The first well-digging activity on a large scale was the product of H.A. Cochran who succeeded Dr. Raeburn as Director of Geological Survey and who gave his name as pronounced "Korkora" to the Hausa language; meaning "stone and cement lined well".

Treatment practised by 1960 in the north with average daily supply indicated, was:

	Source	Treatment	Consumption	
Bauchi	borehole	nil	0.10mgd	being doubled in capacity
Gombe	borehole	nil	0.15	being increased threefold
Gusau	river	filtration	0.12	
Ilorin	impounded	rapid gravity filter	0.22	new source with 400% potential
Jos	impounded	pressure filter	10.50	
Kaduna	river	pressure filter and horizontal flow sedimentation	1.80	being increased threefold
Kano	river	vertical flow sedimentation & pressure filter	2.50	being increased 340%
Makurdi	river	vertical flow sedimentation & rapid gravity filter	0.20	potential 30%
Maiduguri	borehole	chlorination	0.50	
N'guru	borehole	chlorination	0.20	
Sokoto	river	pressure filter	0.24	
Zaria	river	rapid gravity filter with polanite	1.70	

By 1960, twenty-two modern plants were at work in the west and thirty towns in the whole country had pipe-borne water. In rural areas, 5,000ft. of borehole were drilled in 1950 and water points were being added at the rate of 1,500 per annum. In Eastern Nigeria by October of 1960, there were forty such supplies including the deepest artesian borehole in Nigeria, producing 5000 g/hr, Nsukka Division. Boreholes in Borno had to be drilled 4000ft. to reach artesian supplies. Water in Sokoto was carried by donkey train in clay vessels.

In Eastern Nigeria by 1960, seven undertakings were rated as urban, being located at Port Harcourt, Aba, Umuahia, Enugu, Onitsha, Abakaliki and Calabar, with a total supply of 5 mgd under increase to 6 mgd. Aba, Abakaliki and Calabar contributed 1, 0.08, and 0.6 mgd respectively. An extension to Enugu yielded 1.5 mgd and work on nearby Nyaba river was likely to give a potential of 10 mgd. Onitsha and Umuahia extensions were to add 4 and 0.15 mgd respectively. Port Harcourt would be the largest plant in the east with 2.5-3.5 mgd.

Extensions to Lagos Water Supply

In Lagos, a new pumping station on the Ogun river was put in hand in 1946 to meet increasing demand and electrically driven pumps were used for the filters. A 24in. main was laid, Shaga to the township, to augment the existing 28in. main. These works were completed by 1954 and gave 11 mgd. A year later, it was realised that the improvement did not go far enough to meet the requirements of half a million people close to stand pipes and a quarter of a million people living too far away from a stand pipe. The aim was to supply 30 g/d per head for all, thought not over-generous in the tropics when the corresponding figures for Nairobi and Freetown were 45 and 38, and plan for a population of one million by 1970 in the metropolis.

Available funds and the need to cater for Victoria Island construction from Independence in 1960 dictated an initial improvement to 18 mgd with provision for the planned 30. Lagos drew on two rivers, Iju and Ogun. The former was clear and for ten months of the year yielded 14 mgd. In April and May however, the supply was apt to drop down to 7 mgd. The latter, on the other hand, was more than adequate but unfortunately very dirty and more costly to treat. Typical analyses of these rivers were given by A.G. Skinner, and they are reproduced below where samples differed.

	Iju	Ogun
pH	6.0	7.2
Acidity cc's 5% Na_2CO_3 per 100 ml	0.5	0.3
Chlorides as Cl, ppm	11	8
Chlorides as NaCl, ppm	18	13
Total hardness as $CaCO_3$, ppm	10.5	27.5
Total alkalinity as $CaCO_3$, ppm	17.5	47.5
Nitrates as N, ppm	0.5	1.0
Nitrates as N, ppm	0.001	0.004
Oxygen absorbed from Potassium Permanganate at 37°C for 3 hours, ppm	1.688	3.156
Total solids dried at 180°C for 1 hour, ppm	25	110

In 1952, a small pumping station on the Ogun was brought into use with a capacity of 300,000 g/hour feeding against a head of 150ft. into a 24in. main 3½ miles long to the headworks treatment plant. A new pumping station was then due to be built with provision for five 250,000 g/hour vertical spindle pumps and a new 36in. pumping main to the treatment plant, two of the pumps to be installed in the first instance connected to the existing 24in. main. Unfortunately it was not practicable to extend the existing pumphouse as it was too close to the river bank. An additional pumphouse was also built on the Iju using the same intake as that of the old steam pumps. These pumps had impellers and intakes permanently submerged.

Alum and lime were added, the latter having the advantage of making the sludge more readily removable. The rate of dosage varied according to the degree of Ogun water being treated but typical figures were:

Alum   2.52 parts per 100,000
Lime   1.10   "   "   "

Construction began on twelve vertical 30ft. square flow sedimentation tanks with water depth at 28ft., able to treat 450,000 g/hour of Ogun water, the Iju alone being channelled through the old sedimentation tank. In the full 30mg scheme twenty-two further such tanks would be installed. The original filtration plant consisted of eight slow sand filters with a total superficial area of 60,000 sq. ft. and the high theoretical capacity of 250,000 g/hour, lime being then added to bring the pH value up to 7.0 plus.

Six 45,000 g/hour Candy rapid gravity filters were completed in 1954; six further were built with provision for twelve more. The clean water tank held two million gallons. Water flowed by gravity to the filtered water pumps to be chlorinated to about 2 ppm residual chlorine. The pumps mentioned were three Hawthorn-Davey vertical steam pumps each of 100,000 g/hour capacity, operating at 24 rpm, fed from the same boilers as the raw water steam pumps, with a useful life of another twenty-five years.

The original 28in. cast iron main was laid at such a flat gradient in the vicinity of Agege that in some places it was slightly above the hydraulic gradient and it was necessary to keep the water level in Shaga reservoir within two feet of its maximum. The 24in. main land before 1951 to augment the 28in. main was laid to a better gradient. Combined mains capacity was 11mgd and as the demand had exceeded 8mgd by 1957 and was still rising, an additional trunk was clearly necessary. It was decided to lay a 42in. 12-mile mild steel main from Shaga to Yaba. This main would then lift capacity to 30 mgd. From Yaba, the existing mains had so many tappings that they had ceased to function as trunk supplies.

The existing six million gallon reservoir at Shaga with base at ground level had top water level raised by 1ft. 6in. by altering the overflow so as to make best use of available facilities. Three additional 6mg reservoirs would be built in the full 30mgd scheme. In the distribution system principal items of storage were two 1mg cylindrical hemispherical bottom balancing tanks with a top water level at 100ft. and bottom at 40ft. above ground. The tanks secured a beneficial stabilising of the pressure in the distribution system. Private storage in the domestic sector was thought to amount in the aggregate to two million gallons.

The Lagos 18mgd scheme cost £1.936 million and the proposed 30mgd scheme was put at £3.161 million, a further £1.225 million. Trunk mains and storage was the most costly item. Skinner supplied the following figures for recurrent costs:

	Actual 8mgd 1958	Estimated 18mgd 1962	Estimated 30mgd 1970
Cost/1000g	10.8d	9.1d	8.9d

World Bank Mission

The IBRD 1953 Mission examined the Nigerian strategy. It stressed the importance of rural supplies to farming communities and said that any barrage schemes would have to be under federal control. A Department of Hydrology should be set up to collect data without delay as most schemes depending on river flow required the background of at least fifteen years observations; no delay should be lost in the case of the Niger and the Benue. In the opinion of the Joint Group of Engineers, failure to propose further expenditure on urban and rural supply schemes was regrettable and unrealistic. Emphasis was placed on the fact that undertakings were a non self-accounting branch of Government and suggestions for the raising of a statutory corporation were made. The Bank drew attention to the relationship between a pure water supply and the maintenance of a high standard of public health where parasitic infestation and enteric group diseases were endemic.

Pre-Independence Practice

With the exception of one gravity and one pneumatic system, all Western Nigerian schemes pumped to the reservoir from which feed was by gravity. Boosters were fitted at times to produce further pressure zones and the pumps were either diesel or electric running at 500-600 rpm vertical engines or half that speed for horizontal engines. Vee belt drive was employed. Where necessary for auxiliaries, generating sets of 175-215 kW were used. Each site had a standby plant. Cooling systems used heat exchange or thermo syphon. Motors were 1450 rpm slip ring induction. Pumping heads of 300ft. were common with Ishan at 1100ft. as the maximum. "Horizontal split casing single and two stage pumps for the lower lifts, and multi-stage turbine pumps for high heads, were used".

The pneumatic system was installed at Warri where three electric pumpsets delivered directly into the main and maintained a pressure between limits against an air vessel. On reduction in main pressure, the pumpsets cut in on an individual basis if necessary. Boreholes were pumped from depth by deep well pumps of the piston type, submersible electric, or by air lift. The first was the most common but where there was any danger of drawing in sand, an alternative was used. Submersible electric motor turbine pumps came into use as maintenance problems lessened. As many well waters were acidic, corrosion problems occurred and cathodic protection considerations became necessary. Air lift was used for testing where the relative submergence of the education pipe was sufficient.

Service reservoirs were designed for one day's supply of filtered water, often, with increasing demand, insufficient with attendant risk if the pump failed. Concrete reservoirs were used where suitable rock was available to aggregate and the tendency was to use walls of gravity section, plain slab floors, and reinforced column, beam, and slab roofs. Reinforced concrete structures gave good results as more trained artisans became available. Reservoirs under 100,000 g were built to circular section. Pressed steel tanks on towers or at ground level were used where aggregate was unobtainable, as in the Benin and Delta areas.

For mains, asbestos cement pipes were used up to 10in., cast iron or steel above. Transportation to site undamaged was the great hazard — a hazard to last half a century, bit pipes to B.S.S. travelled the best. Steel was used in rock or to meet high heads. At the street fountain the head was a minimum of 20ft. and a maximum, to reduce leakage, of 60ft. Stand pipes were 600ft. apart and each was designed to supply 600 persons.

Rural supply installation stopped in the east for the seven years until 1955. In the west, it was the policy for beneficiaries to contribute 50% of the required labour free of charge towards the cost of the installation. This of course required trained staff to take care of the work and they were not there in the numbers required. The resources needed at the time were beyond the pocket of all concerned and a hazard to health remained in an area which touched 80% of the population. Where wells were dug, it was most important that the works protruded 3ft. above ground level to prevent foot infection with the drain supplies. In ten years, two thousand wells were sunk to an average depth of 19ft. A hand pump which would stand up to the treatment it received at the hands of the villagers was impossible to find and the most promising type was the oil bath lubricated crankshaft type requiring the full circle of a handwheel to obtain one stroke of the piston. Tube wells fitted with strainers were tried but with moderate success.

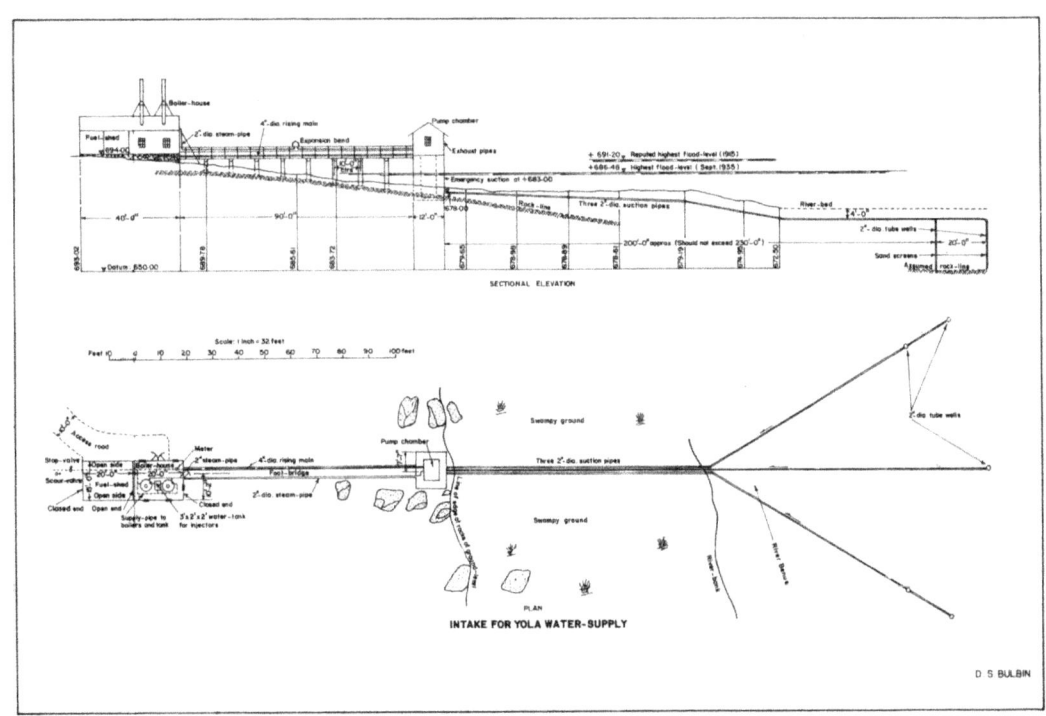

Intake for Yola Water Supply

With regard to financing, it was government policy that in the West, 50% of the capital value of an urban supply be borne by public revenue. The remaining 50% was loaned to the council operating the scheme and made repayable over thirty years at 3½% interest per annum. The council therefore became the outright owner in thirty years. All recurrent charges had to be budgeted for in the council estimates with provision for 1% of the total capital cost invested annually in a renewals fund. Owing to the shortage of civil engineers, much work was supervised by Consulting Engineers employing contractors whose overheads and profits inevitably increased the capital cost. For unmetered supplies, rating was based on a uniform tax levied on all male tax payers on a percentage of the assessed annual value of the tenement for private supplies. Government quarters were assessed on the floor area of the building. Metered consumers were charged at fixed rates per thousand gallons with discounts for missions and the like.

Post-Independence

In the East, several rural supply schemes were completed by September 1965, raising rural capacity from 1.3mgd to 6.7mgd on the way to a planned 16.5mgd. Oron, among the urban supplies, had a water tower and borehole pumps and Onitsha had been tested for larger diameter boreholes. In the same period, urban capacity in the East was planned to increase from 8.2mgd to 27.3mgd. Current financial policy there was for Government to pay for the cost of the capital plant up to reservoir and for the consumer to pay for the cost of the distribution system. An 18mgd water treatment plant was constructed by Taylor Woodrow and Dillingham Overseas Corporation in the West for Ibadan with low level pumphouse over the impounded waters. Also in the West came Ijebu-Igbo, a new supply for Western Nigeria Water Corporation, undertaken by a Crown Agents management team. This was a 4mgd scheme to replace a 0.5mgd undertaking that was quite inadequate for a population of 60,000.

The Ogun river received a hydrological survey. In 1971, the 2.6mgd sediment and chlorination Liberty Dam, three miles from Jos, to supply Jos and Bukuru, was scheduled to be completed by 1973.

The Third Five-Year Plan set aside, for State water supplies, larger sums than those voted for housing, co-operative community development, sewage and drainage, or town and country planning, namely:

	Area sq mile	Population 1972 millions	Provision ₦000
Benue Plateau	40,590	4.009	52,620
East Central	11,310	7.228	50,491
Kano	16,630	5.775	40,000
Lagos	1,381	1.444	44,400
Kwara	28,672	2.399	45,500
Mid Western	14,922	2.536	73,475
North-Central	27,108	4.098	41,550
North-Eastern	103,639	7.793	42,201
North-Western	65,143	5.733	34,250
Rivers	7,008	1,544	7,600
South-Eastern	11,166	3.623	31,200
Western	29,100	9.488	127,500

to which the Federal Government was to add ₦295,693,000. This was a contribution of ₦16 per head over the five years. Inevitably, Lagos took the lion's share at ₦31/head, once again every Tom, Dick and Harry being attracted to an overloaded capital when more funds should have been spent outside. Mid-West (capital Benin) came closest at ₦29/head, then a drop to Kwara (capital Ilorin) at ₦19/head, and then down to the figures of ₦13 and ₦7/head. Everything mattered and it took far too long for Abuja to be spelt out.

In part, the Government of the day said of the Five-Year Plan: "Despite tremendous efforts in this sector sizeable communities with no pipe-borne water exist all over the country. Even in towns with potable water supply, only an estimated 30% of the population are served with house connections, while the rest have to obtain their water from public taps. Daily consumption of water per head in most Nigerian towns is often less than 81 litres compared with a minimum of the 112.5 litres a day considered more appropriate. In rural areas while the bulk of the people live, only 10% have access to pipe-borne water. It is therefore government policy to make potable water available to a minimum target of 112.5 litres per person per day in all urban centres while at the same time ensuring that all communities with a population of 20,000 or more are supplied with pipe-borne water within the Plan period."

The Crown Agents sent, as their adviser to Kano State, a man who had been Deputy Water Engineer for Northern Nigeria. He stayed ten years and Kano extended from 5 to 25mgd, the plant necessary coming overland over the Sahara. In January 1976 Ward, Ashcroft and Parkman were involved in a scheme for increasing Kaduna supply from 14 to 60mgd to be ready by 1985, twelve storage reservoirs having to be erected. They were also asked to make an appraisal of the Yedseram Valley in North Eastern State, 60,000 hectares, for the purpose of irrigation.

In 1976, work began on enlarging Makurdi by no less than tenfold. Some fifteen neighbouring towns were to have a supply. A 4mgd scheme for Gboko-Yandev which would also serve the new cement works was put in hand. The Crown Agents showed their hand in supplying plant and equipment for improvements to Bauchi. The borehole supply was to be replaced by an impounded scheme and a 2⅔ mile dam had been designed by the Water Resources and Engineering Construction Agency, Kano. Target was 1½ mgd September 1978 and 10 mgd June 1980.

In the Third-Year Plan, the Crown Agents were asked to supervise the £8 million improvement to Zaria, one of the most attractive stations in the north, and ended up by employment of direct labour on site. A 1.25 mg ellipsoidal tank went up together with a handsome spillway on the impoundment.

Later, the Federal Government spelt out some of the 1975-80 intended schemes in detail; in ₦ millions:

Bakolori Sokoto-Rima development	150
South Chad irrigation	60
Baga Kirenowa polder	20
Kano extension	71
Hadejia irrigation	10
Jama'are River feasibility	4
Gongola dam	30
Mada River project	30
Kainji Dam irrigation	35
Shemanker Basin project	3
Dep River Basin	4
Ogun and Oshun projects	8
Cross and Imo project	19
Anambra River project	1
Kaduna Basin project	3
Qua-Iboe Basin project	4
Shasha and Owena Rivers project	1
Taraba and Donga Rivers project	6
Nun, Osse, and Ossiomo projects	8
Urban and rural State supplies	500

These schemes had to do with agriculture and power generation. A sum of ₦4 million was voted for the mapping of the various basins and ₦3.4 million for a study of underground resources. The Bakolori dam would irrigate 70,000 acres eight miles north west of the dam, fed thereto by a gravity canal, and was the largest irrigation experiment in West Africa. Supervising execution was Macdonald & Partners (MRT) of London. *West Africa* newspaper said that the dam stood out of a featureless landscape like a medieval cathedral.

Lagos in February 1980 still had too much rain water by far on their hands from inefficient and insufficient drainage of the roads but there was no drinking water for the outskirts because bills from the electricity authority had not been met and pumping had ceased. That matters could reach such a stage is one of the perennial problems long facing Nigeria. Supposedly to take care of everything, the Federal Ministry of Water Resources had been created way back in the 70s. Its responsibilities were set out in the Federal Gazette of 16th July 1975.

Ten River Basin Development Authorities had been created by Decrees of 1976:

Sokoto-Rima
Hadejia Jama'are
Chad
Upper Benue
Lower Benue
Cross River
Anambra-Imo
Ogun-Oshun
Benin River
Niger Delta

Sokoto city drew from Kware Lake thirteen miles to the north and supplied 8 mgd. Gusau, second city in the State, had a ₦12½ million barrage across the Sokoto River. Years ago, there was nothing but the railway's steam pumps down on the river pumping up to the station. To help solve the problems of Lagos, supply not meeting demand, Dr. K.J. Fisher of the University of Lagos drew attention to the number of industries or estates that had sunk their own boreholes to a depth below sea level and had in time been confronted with a lowering of the water table or a seepage of saline waters into the lower aquafers. Too often, bores were rejected instead of applying treatment to the supply. Comparative figures in the Ikeja area were:

	Untreated	Treated
pH	5.0	6.5-7.5
Total dissolved solids	80	100
Total hardness as $CaCO_3$ ppm	20	20
Chlorides	20	20
Sulphates	trace	trace
Dissolved iron ppm	2-5	0.5-0.1

There has been no mention of fluorides in Nigerian treatment. It was in Africa that the first plant was set up to use large scale municipal waste water reuse for drinking purposes. This was in Windhoek, capital of Southwest Africa in 1968; so arid was the region that the people were driven to considering every possible means of supply.

Nigeria is vast in size and population; much remains to be done to make life more comfortable and healthy.

Chapter 11

Opening up a Hinterland

The Stephensons left their mark all over a world that excluded West Africa and by 1906 route mileage had reached 268,588 in the Old World and 311,688 in the New, built by private enterprise in Europe and USA and departmentally in Australia and the Crown Colonies. Narrow gauge preponderated in S.America, Asia, Africa, and Australasia. Great height were reached and this statistics of the times is of present day historical interest:

profiles	above	10,000 ft.	25
"	"	11,000 "	14
"	"	12,000 "	11
"	"	13,000 "	8
"	"	14,000 "	5
"	"	15,000 "	2

The railways opened up beautiful parts of the world — the Mont Blanc summit, the Holy City of Mecca, the Yosemite Valley of California — and completion elsewhere brought in train the luxuries of civilisation.

Sir Winston Churchill said it was no good trying to lay hold of Tropical Africa with the naked fingers. "Civilisation must be armed with machinery if she is going to subdue these wild regions to her authority. Iron roads, not jogging porters; tireless engines, not weary men; cheap power, not cheap labour; steam and skill, not sweat and bumbling;" The *Railway Gazette* wrote that these factors obtruded upon the cost of construction — real estate, labour, and standards of build. In 1913 questions of exploitation of the indigenes were raised in the House. Were railways good for the European alone?

Many were the reasons for which railways were built: extraction of soil and ground wealth, pacification, slave trade suppression, treaty obligations, securing of a base on an international waterway, in furtherance of religion, eradication of disease, connection of more fruitful areas to places of famine, national defence, and policing of frontiers.

Surveys are of many kinds: geographic, topograhic, hydrographic, cadastral, nautical, aeronautical, geological and photogrammetric. Early engineers suffered from the lack of maps that even today many countries remain in this impoverished state with regard to common presentations, contours and soils. Often the best railway locations were based on the assumption that through the centuries the inhabitants had tramped out the best trade route. Later-day railway locations followed these steps:

1. Recce (the first engineering operation in an unexplored territory);
2. General line of route selected across area of recce;
3. Traverse to produce strip map with 5ft. contour intervals;
4. Paper location on contoured strip;
5. Reproduction of "4" on the ground with theodolite, compass, and level as a trial line;
6. Staking out 10ft. wide the best of "5".

The first two are given the most attention if subsequent abandonment is not to be encouraged so there must be a clear line of sight in dense territory with stumps cleared by bulldozer.

A thorough recce consists of taking:

1. vertical air photos of a 4-mile wide belt over the general line of route;

2. stereoscopic examination of "1" (enabling fault lines to be discovered) in conjunction with maps to produce on the former a series of recce lines;
3. traverse of the lines with compass, chain (or tellurometric measure of distance by radio waves), aneroid, with recourse to secondary lines where improvement appears possible;
4. plottings to scale 1:4800 to produce a plan embodying observations of the Recce Party as to adjacent topography;
5. traverse line determination to be followed by the Preliminary Survey Party.

Air photos in photogrammetric work are taken in 60% overlapping strips to a suitable scale, say, 4in. to one mile. If necessary, forest recce is helped by traces cut to magnetic bearings using a prismatic compass and lines determined from the map afterwards modified where required by the air photos. Aneroid levels must not be relied upon to give an accuracy closer than 15ft. intervals. It is easy in later years to condemn a survey of former years but the gradual opening up of the country that has led to the modern criticism must not be allowed to detract from the difficulties experienced when the environment was in virgin state and modern survey tools not to hand — when listening for a shout to obtain a direction. Chains in West Africa were 5/8in. wide steel band with the links marked by brass studs. The engineer had the miner's dial and the headman stood with the pole as far ahead as possible. A second engineer carried the dumpy level.

When Shelford was involved with West Africa, he attached great importance to caravan, timber, water, and the occupations of the people, and was well aware of the "dangers" of deceiving straight lines. A projected location was a Paper Location because it was projected in the office on the Preliminary Survey, a topographical survey of a belt of the country. A railway is not "located" until its centre line has been bench-marked and measurements established on the ground. Earth volume comparisons were:

Standard gauge	100
3ft. 6in. gauge	75
metre gauge	70

A question often asked at the turn of the century was whether one and the same engineer should be entrusted with the initial recce and the final location.

The ascending device of spiral upon bridge or spiral upon tunnel was not used in Nigeria. Nor was there recourse to vertical reversal switchbacks. On the other hand there was much adoption of mountain routes, deliberate increase in length and development to secure the manageable grade. A location following a water course, most easily determined, was much evident. Locations along grade contours spell economical construction with regard to cut and fill, and on a hillside excess of former over latter makes for stability. The statements concluding the chapter refer to survey and conditions met in Nigeria section by section.

Expansion and Development

The pioneer lines of Western Europe owed their all to British thinking with Belgium growing to a tract density of 28 km. per 100 sq. km. countryside by 1913. Such trackage facilitated Germany's occupation of the territory in the 1914-1918 war whilst the absence of such a doorway influenced the fortunes of the Eastern Campaign. The proliferation of gauges gave birth to the large mixed gauge junction at Hamm. It was in 1871 that railways had proved to be the material tool in Bismarck's hands for the creation of his empire. Italy became a modern state by much the same means. Before the 1914 war, the Royal Prussian State Railways used Carl Zeiss field glasses for its surveys. Railways came late to Persia in 1927 and no engineer wanted the problems of Palestine with thirty-six nationalities, five religions and eight languages.

It was not in Texas but Colorado that the USA was able to boast in 1907 of the highest station in the world at 11,629 ft; in Florida in the presence of warships the Key West line built seventy miles over the sea was opened. A land of scattered communities over a vastness where transportation failed to meet demand, the US build policy had been seaboard to interior away from the great waterways, later egged on by a Pacific coast navy base requirement for coal met from the Natanuska field of Alaska. Much labour was provided by the Italians who likened the climate in parts to their own; "the strong Neopolitan, the weaker Sicilian", but the Chinese beat the native and the immigrant Irish in their industry. In the American Civil War the system aided the Yankee. Routes could have been laid out straighter but government grants being on a mileage basis, the railway barons in their greed introduced curves to prolong distances.

After travelling miles between horizons of empty sky and empty earth to arrive at a stop, Robert Louis Stevenson wrote: "Seems incredible that the great child man finds entertainment in so bare a playroom." The golden spike that married the UP and CP systems in Utah bore the prayer, "May God continue the Unity of our Country as this Railroad unites the two great oceans of the world." Nevertheless, such penetration robbed the Indian and the buffalo of their way of life.

In Canada, broad to standard gauge conversion was carried out so as to be in conformity with the USA but the build policy was east-west so that the country "would not be carried away to the USA", its near neighbour. In Mexico, railways replaced man and mule from 1858 to carry the rich products of their earth and to connect their mountain fortress capital the 300 miles to Veracruz on the Gulf of Campeche, a step that threw light on the weakness of their defence frontiers with the USA.

In South America, British Guinea, present day Guyana, had taken a lead by construction in 1847 and by 1906 it had been dubbed "The land of tomorrow", the Trans-Andine, designed to eliminate passage round the Horn, a boon to Chile and Peru, Central Peru having to employ zigzag in its ascent over the Andes. Lines were built to eight gauges in the continent. "Distance" was the obstacle to Argentine progress but traverse over the Pampas in due course promoted meat export to the thousands and the gold and silver mule trains of the Conquistadores became a thing of the past as the world's highest railway took shape. Ecuador's 3ft. 6in. was laid on eucalyptus sleepers to carry the products of her petroleum fields. Nitrates of soda evacuation required lines. Sao Paulo doubled Brazilian coffee output. The harbour of the later famous Rio de la Plata attracted, like a magnet, the converging lines of the Central Argentine. Uruguay built lines to its strategic frontier with Brazil and Patagonia had to bridge Atlantic ports and the centres of population at the foot of the Andes.

In Central America, they said the Guatemala system introduced "inter oceanic communication gauge" in its Atlantic/Pacific route, Puerto Barrios to the capital, 195 miles away; abandonment for years at a time was to be its subsequent history.

Siam laid 4ft. 8½in. but considerations of through running to Burma, Indo-China and Malaya brought about conversion. It was only after the sweeping away of the Hamidian regime that Turkish construction became anything of importance, at a later date, a regional trunk route. The Hejaz commenced in 1901 was a "pilgrim" railway built for religious purposes dashingly disrupted in the Middle East Campaigns by T.E. Lawrence. The Trans-Persian was the child of a political marriage of three parents — Britain, France and Russia. In 1912 on the doubling of the Trans-Siberian, Paris to Peking in 9½ days became the aim whilst in the same year, a passenger from the Mersey to China could travel without being out of the hands of the Canadian Pacific Railway.

Australia's Nullarbor Plain supports the longest stretch of dead straight track in the world, 297 miles of it, whilst on the other side of the continent surveys in NSW cost between £8 and £80 per mile. North of NSW there are no perennial rivers into the interior and geography therefore saw to it that Queensland had her railways. Australia is a case where politics followed the railway instead of preceding it; Western Australia joined the Commonwealth on the promise of a transcontinental line to join her with the other states. In 1907 the New Zealand Premier announced that government aid would only be forthcoming where a profit could be anticipated. The remark was popular with the taxpayer but found no favour with the business and municipal community.

The gauge question in India was determined from two years observations of forty-three rated goods classes passing over the BBCIR in 1870. Two hundred and twenty-four to 5 cu. ft./ton with a good average at 80 cu.ft./ton was recorded and the analysis decided the basis for wagon size for the various gauges. On 31/3/1896, mileage open and sanctioned totalled 23,466 3/4 miles and by 1904 the gauge preponderance was:

5ft. 5in.	54.6%
metre	42.2%
narrow	3.2%

A through route of 1349 miles was possible on the Bombay-Jabalpur-Calcutta run in 1929 but one year later this had grown to the 2476 mile Mangalore-NW Frontier. The Indian systems were so far advanced, and their labour so much borrowed, that its metre gauge was adopted on railway systems thousands of miles away. The Indian networks commenced both from Bengal and Bombay, with opposition from the East Indian Company. On the Bolan Pass one train in sixteen hours accomplished the work of 2500 camels spread over a fortnight. Darjeeling-Himalaya — scene of splendour, welcome peace from the heat of the Plains — employed half loops and reverses in its climbs. Khyber Pass stations were virtually forts, ticket office windows combined with machine gun apertures, and the system with thirty-two tunnels in twenty-seven miles had no civil engineering superior in the world. The East Indian Railway lifted pilgrims to the Ganges. Thirty per cent of the North Western Railway was built for strategic purposes. The Government adopted 2ft. 6in. as standard for light rail and to this gauge the Barsi Light showed its paces, carrying 1500 passengers per train.

The famous Doctor Arnold of Rugby School welcomed any railway that destroyed feudalism. The vast distances in Africa meant that the gauge must be such for locomotives to carry adequate fuel and for vehicles to carry economical loads. By 1898 through connections, Cape of Good Hope to the Mediterranean had been visualised; Beira, over 2000 miles from Capetown, had been reached by 1902; the Victoria Falls Bridge, 1631 miles from Capetown, by 12th September 1905, twenty days from London. In 1906, Paris-Timbuktu could be accomplished in nineteen days and such is the fame attached to this oasis of the desert that the journey merits recording:

Paris-Bordeaux	1 day	rail
Bordeaux-Dakar	8 days	mailboat
Dakar-St Louis	1 day	rail
St Louis-Kayes	3 days	Senegal river
Kayes-Koulikoro	2 days	rail
Koulikoro-Timbuktu	4 days	River Niger

In 1912, construction in West Africa was thought to be lagging. At the end of World War 1, Cape to Cairo, as Horn to Mediterranean had then been called, was put at a possible:

Capetown-Bukama	8 days
Bukama-Albertville	8 days
Albertville-Victoria Nyaza	14 days
Victoria Nyanza-Butiaba	12 days
Butiaba-Khartoum	24 days
Khartoum-Cairo	3 days

This amounted to 69 days to cross the continent. Bukama was in the Congo, Albertville on Lake Tanganyika, Butiaba on Lake Albert. By 1933 the journey was down to thirty-nine days. By 1981 Rhodes' dream had narrowed to the railless gap Pakwach in Uganda to Wau in Sudan.

African systems compared with railways in other developing continents in 1929:

	Mileage/100 sq m	*Mileage/10,000 population*
Africa	0.33	2.66
S. America	0.79	8.14
Australia	0.90	45.00
India	2.97	1.28

So many factors are concerned with mineral discoveries and funds for investment that much should not be read into the foregoing analysis. The African systems were made up of 11% standard gauge, 55% 3ft. 6in., 34% metre and below. At Johannesburg in 1936, Southern Africa adopted the 3ft. 6in. as standard. On the 1st July 1931, the first train crossed the continent east to west, Lobito Bay to Beira, 2949 miles, using the tracks of the Benguela, Bas Congo, Rhodesia and Beira & Mashonaland, saving a sea voyage of 2644 miles. By July 1974, there were forty-nine systems operating on the African continent including the Sierra Leone then being phased out and the route distance touched 77,099 km. Niger, Chad, Rwanda, Burundi and Somalia had no railways and, except for the last, were landlocked. Most extensions planned by 1981 were to be found in the North African littoral.

The first railway opened in Africa was Alexandria-Cairo (1856), later in competition with the Suez Canal, the developing Egyptian system hugging the Nile The second railway was the Point/Durban in Natal, (1860), followed by the Cape of Good Hope Railway, Capetown-Wellington, in 1863, both standard guard but converted to 3ft. 6in. in 1878. The conversion was ordered on the recommendations of a select committee of the House of Assembly. Construction in South Africa was regarded as slow but it was galvanised by the discovery of diamond and gold. The Transvaal Republic declared Witwatersrand a public goldfield for which a railway was urgently needed.

The idea of the Uganda Railway was conceived at the Brussels Conference, Article I of the General Act, 2nd July 1890, the object being the suppression of the slave trade by providing easy access into the interior. The Act was called the "Slave Trade Treaty". The first rail was laid at Mombasa on 8th August 1896 and the first locomotive reached the shores of Lake Victoria on 20th December 1901, the line climbing 9010 ft. in 525 miles to Timboroa, peaking 9150 ft. on the Mau Escarpment. Although the line was called the Uganda Railway for years, there was not a yard of it in Ugandan territory, destination being reached only after a steamer voyage. Construction certainly required the use of astronomical and barometric readings together with an understanding of the map. H.M. Stanley of Livingstone fame told the recce party, "take a thousand men or make your will." It is to be doubted whether those who fell foul of the lions of Tsavo had made their will — twenty-eight of them, men, not lions.

Jiggers required amputation of the toe. The tsetse killed off 774 donkeys. The recce party had to bear in mind locomotive water supplies and find grades suitable for the traffic. Eighty-five per cent of the construction labour was recruited from India and arrangements were hampered by Indian plague regulations. Uganda controlled the headwaters of the Nile and therefore activities bore on the economics of Sudan and Egypt. Kenya, on the way, benefited from bi-carbonate of soda, coffee and sisal evacuation. The East African Railways was formed in 1948 by amalgamation of the Tanganyika Railway with the Kenya and Uganda Railway.

The vision of Cecil Rhodes and the financial genius of Alfred Beit saw to Rhodesia. The Sudan was to witness the largest reclamation over so vast an area ever attempted by mankind in its conquest for Egypt, railway construction reaching an unprecedented rate of progress; five water tanks per train supported the army in the field. Encouragement for cotton cultivation came later. No country bettered France in her appreciation of the need to place strategy and economics before profit. They laid down their plans for Africa twenty years in advance, being far ahead of the British in this respect. Kayes-Niger started it off in 1881 and by 1908 there were 2066 miles laid for seven systems. The mooted Trans-Sahara however never came about. In 1981 no projection came south of 27°North and no existing line ran north of 16°North.

The Congo systems with a cheap rate for ivory had to be built with labour recruited from as far away as China and suffered as a through line by using navigable sections of the Congo waterway. The Benguela was a sensible route for the evacuation of the Katanga mines but became the pawn of later-day political parties. German progress in Africa was so slow as to be deplored. Tanganyika, decimated by sleeping sickness, had little to offer but the distant great lakes. The excellent anchorage of Walvis Bay however settled the line to Swakopmund and to an area rich in mineral wealth. The original contract for the Ethiopian Railway signed with Emperor Menelik was cancelled by him on learning that political and not commercial issues were to be determining factors. Camel caravans made but ten miles a day to Harrar 280 miles inland.

The Tarkwa goldfields required a railway to bring in heavy machinery across the Anyrobra river and the inhospitable shores towards Cape Coast and Accra dictated the use of Sekondi although it was said that construction should have awaited a proper harbour — the future Takoradi. The thick forest, so thick that game could not be found after it had been dropped, was cut by matchet and survey accomplished by shouting and compass. The first rail was laid on 18th December 1898 on Baltic pine sleepers resistant to the white ant, local timbers being full of sap or the mahogany too hard. The line was badly built, "£3 million thrown away"; labour was supplied by Nigeria until the last Ashanti War put a stop to construction. Until the coming of the line, the crossing of the River Prah was a daily hazard. The 220 miles of Sierra Leone completed in 1905, a victim of later road competition, abounded in viaducts over the many streams. The Cameroun Railway halted for years at Yaounde until the Trans-Cameroun brought a horde of visitors to see the arrival of the first express at N'gaoundere km 935 from Douala on February 4th 1974. Tunnels were involved in the climb to 1087m. Plans to extend further to the Central African Republic had not, surprisingly, been shelved as the last decade of the century approached.

Tanzania was connected to Kenya. The Tan Zam railway was built by the Chinese and the railway opened up Zambia with Dar Es Salam Harbour to bypass Rhodesia, Mozambique and South Africa to import petroleum products and other commodities, and export copper. South Africa had taken over a 860km iron ore railway. Trans Gabon had seen new mileage along with Zaire. Zimbabwe was to put electrification in hand. Upper Volta was to extend eastwards. But no map of the world can pose more difficult questions to international railway construction into bordering territories than Africa where tradition and the need for foreign exchange has seen to an export/import pattern to Europe and the Americas. Politics will not sustain a railway.

Nigerian Railway Surveys

1907	Recce Ikiru-Eggan suggested Offa-Pategi-Eggan, passing through thick shea belt, avoiding Ilorin-Jebba territory which attracted only 10% of Province's taxation
1912	Proposed Sokoto-Katsina-Damberta-Kano; Sokoto-Bussa (either via Yelwa or Zuru) -Kaiama-Oyo-Ibadan; Ibadan-Ondo-Benin-Onitsha- Udi; Calabar-Udi-Ibi-Katagum-Bauchi-Rahama
1913	Proposed Warri-Benin-Niger River Ports; Cross River at Itu-Ikot Ekpene; Maiduguri/Yola-coast; Abeokuta-Ilesha; Jebba- Jega/Sokoto
1919	Proposed Zaria-Sokoto; Kano-Berbera on Niger frontier; Sapele-Pategi-junction with Minna/Baro line; Kano-Maiduguri; Jemaa-Bukuru-Bauchi-Maiduguri; Afikpo Road-Ogoja-Yola-Maiduguri; Aba-Itu
1923	Policy now to seek branches and not trunk routes. Recce in hand for Zaria-NW; Jebba-Yelwa-Sokoto through Jega and Birnin Kebbi; Jebba-Gunmi with branch Yelwa-Jega-Talata Mafara; Minna-Kaduna realignment location survey
1924	Tacheometric survey completed Zungeru-Minna realignment; paper location deferred as surveyors moved to proposed branch Zaria-Funtua
1926	Recce Zaria-Gusau and location Zaria-Funtua completed; traffic and engineering surveys Gusau-Talata Mafara and Umukoroshe-Owerri

	completed. Last named ground to be particularly easy country, no bridge and ruling grade 1 in 500. Preliminary survey Ifaw-Idogo.
1927	Location survey Ifaw-Idogo; Gusau-Kaura Namoda. Recce Odo Oba-Ife-Ipetu-Ondo-Akure; unexpected engineering difficulties met Ife-Ipetu. Preliminary survey Umukoroshe-Owerri continued towards Awka; heavy earthworks necessary; Recce Lafia-Maiduguri; bridging of 450ft. needed Kogin Namu. Recce via Wase. Nigerian Railway aimed at 150 miles survey per annum.
1928	Recce Odo Oba-Akure; revealed difficulty in obtaining standard grades and curves east of Ife. Traffic survey Umukoroshe-Owerri encouraging. Recce Lafia-Maiduguri extended to Lake Chad, bridging of Gongola to be at Kombo
1929	600ft. tunnel found necessary on proposed Odo Oba-Akure route; Lafia-Lake Chad length to Bama would be 465 miles
1947	Recce and location surveys recommended by West African Oil Seeds Mission for Rahama-Maiduguri
1949	Aerial and recce surveys N'guru-Maiduguri carried out by Colonial Development Corporation
1963	Elelenwa-Alesa Eleme oil plant line surveyed
1974	Long term plans for standard gauge calling for traffic and engineering surveys undertaken over following seven years

Nigerian Railway LIne Characteristics

Lagos-Abeokuta (97km)
Up through Agbado and Wasimi are minor summits of under 61m, from Ifo Jc. in the valleys of the Ewekoro and Igbin, surrounding hills below 87m, to Abeokuta at 31m in the valley of the Ogun; the transition is swamp to rain forest and the actual is suburbia for 26km and remainder through a mosaic of farmland and wooded shrub grassland. Typically of undulating soft sandstone plains and ridges, a belt of migmatite gneiss, and porphrytic biotite granite abound in Abeokuta. Alluvial soils soon left behind for ferralsols. For most of the way, the direction is NNW.

Abeokuta-Ibadan (96km)
The line climbs to 210m, most of the ascent accomplished on the Ilugun bank, crossing the Ogun in the Olokemeji Gorge where the peak of 264m (867ft.) is immediately adjacent, the highest and most beautiful landmark on the way. The route accommodates itself to the Ogun Valley from Abeokuta as far as Olokemeji whence use is made of the Afonrin. The approach and exit to the large sprawling town of Ibadan, a dissected plateau region, is tortuous, keeping to a minor watershed after crossing the Ona from the Ibadan Reservoir. The soil changes to ferruginous tropical and Ibadan is approached on Basement Complex rocks with scattered inselbergs not visible from the train. The direction is NE and then E, through rain forest, mosaics of farmland and wooded shrubland or immature forest with teak plantations en route.

Ibadan-Offa (153km)
Surmounting 299m at Oshogbo, 435.6m (1429ft.) at mile 213½ summit, an altitude not again to be reached this side of 811km from Lagos, rolling country introduces Offa at 421m (1315ft.). The climb is mainly managed in five ascending lengths and the Oba Hills of 300m are to be seen north of Iwo and countries higher than this as Ede is approached by a new alignment of 1930 mainly along the 260m contour, the line lying 50km to the west of the Effon Ridge peaks reaching 761m (2495ft.). The route crosses the Oba, then follows the valley of the Oshun, finally following the valley of the Otin from south of Inisa. Vegetation changes from rain forest to derived savanna, a mosaic of immature forest and at times in 60% crop cultivation. Soil remains ferruginous and there are quartz hills and ridges giving way to granite. The direction is NE.

Rock cutting towards Ibadan, 1900

Gradient profiles of Nigerian Railways showing location of stations

Offa-Jebba (142km)

The line falls 324m to cross the Niger at 97m (318ft.) with two intervening ascents at Jodomo and Beri Beri enroute: Beri Beri in rock cutting was lowered in the 1953 relay. Ikotun Hill at 514m away to the west of Offa is just below 8° 15′ latitude. The final descent to the Niger through man-made gorge with hills on either side of 214m and 273m was for years, until remodelling and dieselisation, the scene in the reverse direction of a banking engine. The route from Offa is in the valley of the Oyun, met again at Oyun River station, and Ilorin is met on the left bank of the Asa, the Oshin valley being used at Oke Dare through to Bode Sadu. Derived savanna gives way to guinea savanna, 60% farming/wooded shrub grassland/wooded transition, the palm belt having been left well behind at south of Offa. Soils remains ferruginous until the alluvial of the Niger. Basement Complex rocks with scattered inselbergs lead on to quartzite hills and ridges. The direction is NNW followed by NNE.

Jebba-Minna (255km)

This is a total climb of 159m to altitude 256m in up grades to Charati, down grades to Akerri, and final ascent to Maikonkele before Minna. Isolated hills reach 366m between the valleys of the diverging Niger and Kaduna. The latter is crossed at Zungeru at a height of 122m. Minna is a hilly countryside, the surrounding peaks reaching 468m. The direction is ENE and the line is mostly away from water courses after the bridging of the Niger until the crossing of the Eba at Kutiwengi, the Pimmi before Gierkun, the Mariga at Akerri, before falling partly into the Kaduna Valley at Wushishi and crossing the river itself at Zungeru. The line then follows the Kurako to Beji. Vegetation is Southern Guinea Savanna and the soil alluvial in the Niger proximity and ferruginous onwards. Away from Jebba, the line skirts aquatic grassland, passes through the Mokwa Research Plantations, crosses belts of riparian forest, on through wooded shrub grassland, arriving at Minna through cultivated farmland. West of the Kaduna, it is rolling sandstone plains with low hills but the approach to the Kaduna brings active floodplains of recent alluvium into context.

Minna-Zaria (243km)

This is one of the nicest stretches. The Kaduna is crossed at the high altitude of 598m and Zaria is reached on the Plains of Hausaland at 553m. This entails an immediate climb out of Minna to Shakwata, ascents to Gwada and Kuchi, and the arduous grade from the Serikan Pawa on a shelf to Bakin Kasua, climbs resuming after the Kaduna bridge through to Birnin Yaro, with long straight stretches north of Farin Rua. The line avoids spot heights of 709m and 665m after Bakin Kasua. Between Kaduna and Zaria, the highest elevation of the country is 696m to the west outside Labar Forest Reserve. The line crosses the Esse and follows a tributary to Gwada. The Muye and Dinga are crossed together with the long Serikan Pawa and the valley of the Godari is followed up Gwagwada bank before bridging the Kaduna. Direction is NE to Kaduna and then NNE to Zaria. Soils change to lithosols (immature soils) and Southern Guinea Zone gives way to Northern Guinea Zone — Gwari mixed farmland, patches of woodland, woodland transition, skirting broad-leaved woodland, to enter intense farming country towards Zaria. Dissected Basement Complex plains and pediments, after the river Dinya undifferentiated igneous and metamorphic to the west, granite to the east, to meet active floodplains of recent alluvium at the Kaduna and to arrive at Zaria with the first named alongside amethyst pits.

Zaria-Kano (140km)

The direction is NE over lithosolic soils. Kano is met at 493m but the Atlantic Divide marking the watershed between the ocean and Lake Chad, 1023.3 km from Lagos and after Gimi Dabosa station, has first to be surmounted at 689 m (2260ft.). Contours on each side of the line at Gimi Dabosa are 671m and spot heights range from 680m to 712m in the vicinity. Except for a climb after bridging the Challowa, the line falls all the way from the Atlantic Divide to Kano. Vegetation changes to Sudan Savanna. There is intense mixed farming, tobacco, cotton, ginger, groundnut and rice, to name but a few. There are shrub grassland and thorny thicket outskirts. The Challowa is the only river of note, crossed some 15km south of Kano, active floodplains denoting its passage. The Tiga reservoir is well to the east. The terrain marks sandy drift plains with scattered ironstone hills and outcrops overlying Basement Complex rocks.

Kano-N'guru (230km)

With a direction of ENE, the line falls to 357m at N'guru, a fall most pronounced from Jogana to Dabi. Mallam Maduri is on a slight rise but the ruling grade throughout does not exceed 0.5%. This is a branch line and in the main a surface track with one perfectly straight stretch extending over the last 129.5 km into N'guru station, covering no less than eight stations in its target approach. Soil is semi-arid brown and reddish brown undifferentiated leading onto regosols, an immature soil. Across Sudan Savanna to the borders of Sahel Savanna, the area traversed is farmland, intensively cultivated near Kano, leading onto shrub, wooded grassland transmission, and grassland (seven species of grass) at N'guru amidst thorn bush. Water is scarce and recourse is made to artesian supplies and impounding of the flood waters of the river Hadejia running parallel to the south. Only four bridges were required. Shelter belts have been built near the Department of Zinder, Republic of Niger, and large numbers of forest reserves parallel the track. Outside Kano, flood plains impinge before reaching longitudinal dune fields with clay depressions and diatomite at N'guru.

Port Harcourt-Enugu (243km)

Port Harcourt was settled by its port and Enugu by the location of the Udi coal fields so that we had two fixed points. Port Harcourt just avoids the Delta with its active floodplains and alluvial soils. From the dock a high level approach leads to the passenger station and separate goods yards at 20m elevation and the line then skirts the creeks of Diobu and Amadi to take up general direction NNE to Enugu over mostly ferrasolic soils. Straight stretches lead the way to Old Umuahia but with 270° of reverse curves to bridge the Aba at its lowest possible elevation in lowland rain forest. Much rich palm oil is evident over undulating sandy coastal plains with a steady easy climb to Umuahia at 189m. Here the terrain marks the toe of the Awgu Escarpment and by development the line skirts the sandstone ridges of Ameki, falling to 122m. Amber is found here. Just after km119 in this descent, the line passes through two of the three deepest cuttings of the Corporation at 55ft. (16.7m) and shortly afterwards is carried on one of the Corporation's two highest embankments, beyond km134, Uzuakoli-Nkpa section, also at 55ft.

The most difficult length for the locomotive is found at km146 in Ovim station approach where 180° of reverse curves are severely felt. (In the reverse direction Otampa and Ameki banks are the straining lengths). The line again maintains direction north of Otampa. North of Agbani, the Nyaba is crossed but the whole route is in no sense a valley route. A steady climb in open country, N'deaboh to Enugu, 227m, is relieved in the valley of the Ayo, lying well away from eastern 1200ft. (366m) contours, to enter Enugu east of the Udi cuesta over the length level Asata bridge. So the line traversed farmland, raffia and oil palms, and immature forest to enter further farmland, a dissected rolling sandstone plateau, undulating plains of shale and finally dissected sandstone pediment.

Enugu-Makurdi (220km)

The Benue crossing at the Munshi Narrows determined the northern fixed point, direction NE from Enugu. The soil, except for hard shale out of Enugu, was poor ferralsols, from Eha-Amufu for 31km, soft shale, close grained laterite and Oturkpo summit. Around Eha-Amufu, dissected sandstone pediments lie to the west, sandstone shale and clay to the east, after Oturkpo, undulating sandstone and shale plains with low hills. Enugu-Emene saw the heaviest earthworks for the necessary descent in cutting for 11km and Makurdi bridge approach was largely blasted out of sandstone ridge. Vegetation is derived savanna becoming southern guinea after Oturkpo bank. There is farmland on leaving Enugu and riparian forest is met at each river crossing. Wooded shrub grassland transition commences after Igumale, after Otobi mosaics of farmland, shrubs and patches of woodland. Line falls to elevation 131m by Eha-Amufu and maintains this approximate elevation throughout, meeting approach to Benue High Level at 128m by Agana. The exception is the climb Otobi-Oturkpo summit at 229m (750ft.) and immediate descent the other side to Taraku. The line crosses the Ekwulu at Emene, Okpauku at Igumale, Ogege at Utonkon and follows the valley of the Npude from Taraku and bridges, the Kwanwere at Moi-Igbo. From Agana, the line lies in a valley which has given rise to seven washouts in fifty-five years.

Rock cutting on the Kogun Kloof, 1926

Makurdi-Kafanchan (274km)

The northern fixed point was determined by the pass up the Plateau escarpment without recourse to tunnel but with the employment of 10° curves in the mountainous terrain. In fact, selected Kafanchan lay almost due north of Makurdi; alluvial soils out of the Benue, and ferruginous tropical soils mainly, but lithosols on the borders of Kafanchan. southern guinea Savanna has a touch of derived savanna by Kafanchan with farmland, riparian, wooded shrub, woodland patches, intensive crop cultivation by Lafia, teak plantations near Kaderko, shrub and a mosaic of farmland/grassland. A number of forest reservations are passed. North of the Benue is gently undulating sandstone and shale plains. Granite hills appear to the east of Mada, farther north and to the west lies undifferentiated igneous and metamorphic rocks until Kafanchan is approached amidst hills of younger granites.

In plan, the location avoids rock outcrops twice before Lafia and again after Barakin Abdullahi, crossing the Mada River after the station of that name, making a 225° change of direction at Anzo and approaching Gudi tortuously. There is a shift to the east before the Kogum River Forest Reserve, crossing the Kogum River, then going in straight stretches to Jagindi making use of the blind valley parallel to the Kogum Gorge. The path up the escarpment to Gerti is found by clinging to the Kogun Valley, a feat calling for no less than four changes in directional points of the compass, an employment called development. The ascent here is called the Kloof. A consequence is that with a long train, the locomotive and the guards van for a long time are proceeding in opposite directions. Kafanchan with environs is very open country with the Kagori Hills visible to the NE topping 4093ft. (1248 m).

In elevation, the line climbs without distress from the Benue to Agyaragu summit at 254m before descending through Lafia (207m) to Barakin Abdullahi at 144m. The line then climbs in two bites the ascent to the Kafanchan Tableland which marks a breathing space before further ascending grades up the Bauchi Plateau. The first climb is through the Mada Hills to Gudi, 75% on bank, and thence to Moroa River, respectively 231, 458 and 509 m. Pleasant coasting to Kogum River station is then followed by the second ascent through Jagindi (tied construction point) and Gerti, 511m and 665m respectively, the summit being 11km beyond Gerti. The foot of the Kogum Kloof was taken by the construction team to be at Delli at 704 km. In all, in the Kloof the line rises 272m (891ft.) in 26 km (16 miles) using many cuttings of 27ft. depth but just beyond km709 between Jagindi-Gerti, the cutting reaches 55ft. (16.7m) whilst an embankment to the same figure lies farther north at km 711 + 15 telegraph poles. (The original construction was built to 60ft. and 65ft. respectively.)

Northern and southern construction teams were linked in between Kafanchan and Gerti at km 719 + 14 telegraph poles and the monument testifies:

> "N E R
> Linked in 12th July 1926
> By H.E. Governor
> Sir Graeme Thompson KCB
> Chief Engineer A. Graham "

Kafanchan-Bauchi (238km)

The line used the original Kafanchan-Jos line as far as Kuru which became the junction. The direction is E to Tafawa Balewa and NNE thence to Bauchi. The soil characteristic is lithosols. Vegetation is plateau to northern guinea, some farmland, then wooded shrubland, then more cultivated land south of the Ganawuri Hills, Eucalyptus plantations and grasses follow until a pass through the bakin Kogi is reached. Rapids are found before Maijugu Zongo is reached after passes through wooded shrub scarps. By Bununu and through the Maijuju valley, and the scarps of the Oir and Kir Hills is Bauchi entered and left south of the township of that name. Its geomorphology comprises rolling plateau of undifferentiated igneous and metamorphic rocks with younger granites and basalt, dissected basement complex plains and pediments and finally basic intrusive rocks.

Kafanchan was selected by the surveyor for its acreage of good open flat land.

Kafanchan-Kagoro-Manchok steers just north of the 2800ft. (854m) contour of the Kagoro Hills. The peak height is 4093ft. (1248m) and falls into the valley of the Werram at 3600ft. (1098m). The required ascent over the Plateau was obtained by the use of 2% ruling grade and 12° curvature, a restriction dictated by the Jos-Bukuru 2ft. 6in. gauge formation of the Bauchi Light Railway whose terminal section from Zaria became Nigerian Eastern Railway 3ft. 6in. gauge territory, no point in the opposite ends of the line being other than to a common standard, it was thought. As it was, 41.2 miles (66km) had to accommodate a rise of 1626ft. (496m) —

Kafanchan	2607ft.	795m
Kagoro	2848ft.	869m
Manchok	3201ft.	976m
Quakwi	3623ft.	1105m
Hoss	4029ft.	1229m
Kuru at the Jc	4233ft.	1291m

The most difficult piece was the saddle at Hoss Nek. The line had to clear Kuru Hills peaks of 4659ft. and 4655ft.; it approached Kuru over 4150ft., 4200ft., 4250ft. and 4300ft. contours. From Heipan to Tafawa Balewa at km901 from Port Harcourt, a valley approach was adopted as the line fell off the Plateau, with an eventual rise preceding Bauchi located at 1988ft. (606m).

Bauchi-Maiduguri (468km)

The direction is E to Gombe, NNE to second crossing of the Gongola, NE to Maiduguri, entering N of the township and River Ngadda. The only perennial waters are the Hadejia, Yobe, and Lake Chad, all away from the location. From Bauchi, the line falls to the first crossing of the Gongola and beyond, rises to Gombe, falls to the second crossing of the Gongola, is 1015ft. (310m) at Gabai, summits at Biu Road, passes Ambiya at 1456ft. (444m) and falls to Maiduguri at 1042ft. (318m), in all, a grade unremarkable.

The flood plains of the Gongola were an obstacle. Then came in succession undulating sandstone plains, sandstone hills and pediments, basalt plateau and scarp and aeolian sand plains overlying Chad sediment. Further geological features followed in the nature of longitudinal dune fields with clay depressions, lacustrine sand plains and beach ridges until Maiduguri was reached. Soils are ferruginous tropical — ferrosols — lithosols — vertisols — semi arid brown and reddish brown to alluvial on borders of Maiduguri. Vegetation ranges from North Guinea Zone to Sudan Savanna. There are wooden shrubs in the valley, avoiding Gengila Hill at first Gongola bridging, with much intensive farming throughout and riparian at the crossing of the Guji and tributaries. At Gombe there is a detour round the slopes of Lijf Hill on the grassland approach to the second Gongola crossing. There is woodland transition at the crossing of the Anumma over broadleaved woodland to farming and shrubs through Jaori Forest Reserve to Maiduguri.

Kafanchan-Kaduna (179km)

The direction is NW over lithosol soils with an island of ferruginous. The summit of the Kloof escarpment is "projected" forward and is reached at 3023ft. (922m) at km 765½ from Port Harcourt after Jemaa station. Then follows a descent to 2085ft. at Kutura, a rise to Kajuru, the fall to the Kaduna valley; (elevations were NER datums). Iri Hill is 2909ft. (887m), sheersided Ludo Hill (Miniature Sugar Loaf) is 2893ft., off Kajuru station. The Serikan Pawa river is at 2000ft. south of Katura station and at 1300ft. where the Western main line crosses it at Serikan Pawa station, ensuring a rapid flow through the Kuder Hills. No forest reserves grace the scene and the line enters Kaduna east of the Industrial Estate and bridges the river after the junction with line from Lagos.

The most interesting feature of the line is the geomorphology. There are younger granites, Dissected Basement Complex plains and pediments to the east, then undifferentiated igneous and metamorphic rocks. The pediment "saucer" and the domed inselbergs, looking from a distance like craters on the moon, dominate the landscape. The last inselberg is off the road at Kaduna at 2778ft. (847m). Kafanchan waterfall, 200m west of the line and north of the station, attracts fishing in the plunge pool. The line passes through farm and woods shrub, Northern

Guinea Zone, enters transition and crosses innumerable tributaries of the Kaduna river before reaching Duchin Bako and Kurmin Biri after which it falls into numerous valleys including that of the Serikan Pawa as far as Kutura. The line has 'touched' plateau vegetation. From Kajuru it lies in the valley of the Romi, emphasising its presence after Kankomi. The surveyor made good use of mother nature.

Canadian class locomotive No 769 breasting the 4324ft. Summit on the Kafanchan-Jos branch in 1959

Terrain between Zaria & Gusau 1929

Kuru-Jos (35 m) (Mainline)

The picture was of plateau vegetation, major soil, lithosols, direction NNE and 4324ft. (1319m), the highest point on the Corporation's network, with little to choose in difficulty of travel in either direction. Jos was built on a spur between the Delimi River Valley and Canteen Creek, at an elevation of 4013ft. (1224m), much the same as the elevation of Hoss, so there was a climb either way to the 4324ft. summit. The section Bukuru-Jos crosses the valley of the N'gell and from Kuru to Jos there is evidence everywhere of the tin mining activity, the country being very open, with much cultivation, sometimes terraced. There are a number of eucalyptus plantations and non-thorny thicket east of Jos. Otherwise low grasses and absence of high foliage but presence of Bornhardts amongst the porphyritic biotite granites predominate. The scenery is fascinating and the environment is conducive to the health of the expatriate.

Zaria-Kaura Namoda (221km) (Branch Line)

The direction is NW to Gusau, NNW thence to Kaura Namoda, the line almost following a straight path, using the Gulbin Sokoto Basin and crossing the Gagere before Kaura Namoda. The branch, built to superior standards so that one class of locomotive could work over it to either of the two distant ports on the coast, had eleven switchbacks in its length, climbing out of Zaria and reaching maximum altitude at km 65 (mile 40½) at 737m (2416ft.), a little short of Funtua; Gusau is at 466m (1529ft.) and Kaura Namoda at 409m (1340ft.). Soil is lithosols and vegetation changes from northern guinea to sudan savanna before reaching Karazau. Crop cultivation, shrubland and thicket, the line to the west of grassland then crosses a belt of transition. It may be said that crops line the route. Dissected Basement Complex plains and pediments, sandy drift plains with scattered ironstone hills and outcrops; hills of schist, granite, and gneiss ensured no lack of ballast. Flood plains are met in the valley of the Sokoto at Gusau.

Minna-Baro (179km) (Original Main Line now a Branch Line)

The direction of this line is NW to Badeggi and NE to Minna, a climb of 614ft. (187m) from the Niger to the foothills of Minna, obtained by development on 20ft. banks and in 15ft. cuttings in 218 ascents and 128 descents. The Gbako Valley was entered via southern guinea vegetation followed by active flood plains, rolling sandstone plains and low hills. The scene became riparian skirting aquatic grasses and mosaics of Nupe cultivation with mixtures of grassland and woodland. Again into the valley of the Gbako to short of Ebba station, then the Jatau river also called the Ebba river, skirting woodland transition in an abrupt change of direction at Kataeregi to accommodate Yanpako Hill and again the Chanchaga flowing from the east. The line follows the Chanchaga through Lafiagi and crosses it at Sofon Dagga, keeping west of the right bank as far as Lapai whence the Bako is picked up. Many minor rivers are bridged but the area subject to flooding is always to the west. It was a location dictated by water courses in which orography paid little part. The soils were alluvials, ferralsols and ferruginous tropical.

Ifaw Jc-Idogo (44km) (Branch Line)

The direction of this line is W, a featureless cocoa branch devoid of structures, uninteresting except to the ornithologist. Features are lowland rain forest, top soil, ferralsols, farmland and immature forest to riparian bordering the river Yewa at Idogo, 19½ km east of the international border between Nigeria and Benin. There is coarse grained poorly sorted micaceous sandstone dissected by river valleys. In elevation, there is nothing much: Ifaw 75m, Ilaro 53m, Idogo 24m with the single summit at 141m, 10.5km from the junction, east of Ishawfin Halt. In addition to the Yewa, the Ore is crossed at Olorunda Halt, 40ft. banks necessary after the Halt; a 40ft. cutting is found east of Ilaro.

Index

Aburi Meeting in Ghana, 18
Action Group, 16
Adekunle, Brigadier Benjamin, 113
Adelanwa, Vice-Admiral, 121
Aero Contractors Company of Nig. Ltd., 145
Aerodrome Fire Fighting Service, 138
Aeronautical Services West Africa, 145
    (formerly Airstock West Africa)
    — Commercial Association, 47
    — Ferry Services, 59
    — Road Transport Symposium, 87
    — Steamship Company, 47, 52
    — Timber & Plywood Factory (AT & P), 158, 161
Aguiyi-Ironsi, Major-General Johnson, 17
Air Traffic Control, 135, 138
Akintoye, King, 9
Akintola, Chief S.L., 16-17
American Civil War, 46, 48, 195
American West African Line (AWAL), 55
Anglo-French Boundary Commission, 13
Annesley, Consul, 12
Armorial Bearings, 16
Atlantic Divide, 25
Atomic Energy Commission, 170
Australian Snowy Mountain project, 177
Aviation Planning Services, 149
Awolowo, Chief Obafemi, 16
Azikiwe, Dr. Nnamdi, 16-17

Baikie, 3, 6, 8
Balewa, Alhaji Abubakar Tafawa 15-16, 41, 89
Bank of British West Africa (BBWA), 49, 52
Banks, Sir Joseph, 3
Bath, 3
Beecroft, John, 8-9
Bello, Sir Alhaji Ahmadu, 16-17
Berlin Conference, 9
Bisalla, Major-General I.D., 19
Black Star Line of Ghana (BSL), 57
Borgu Game Reserve, 28, 93
Bourdillon, Sir Bernard, 133
British
    — Air Registration Board, 139
    — Aircraft Corporation (BAC), 144
    — Airports International, 150
    — American Air Services, 143
    — and African Steamship Navigation Company, 47
    — Cotton Growers Association, 49
    — Overseas Airways Corporation (BOAC), 134
    — Protectorate, 10
    — Railway Development Society, 80
Broad Gauge, 83
Bromfort Steamship Company, 54
Bubonic plague, 80
Bunning, Mr. 80

Caillie, Rene, 6
California Bearing Ratio (CBR), 84
Cameroun Development Corporation, 157
Carter Bridge 62, 89, 92, 106, 133, 160
Carter, Sir G.T., 9
Casement, Roger, 9
Cephalic Index, 32
Chargeurs Reunis Aeromaritime Coastal Service, 138
Church Missionary Society, 8
Churchill, Sir Winston, 51, 193
Commercial Pilots Licence, 144
Colonial Development Corporation [CDC], 87
Constitution
    — Macpherson, 15
    — 1979, 19
    — Pre-Independence, 15
    — Richards, 15
Crown Agents, 49, 58, 70, 87-88, 90, 99-102, 108, 112, 123, 160, 170, 190-191
Crowther, Bishop Samuel Ajayi, 6, 8, 14
Customs Quay (CQ), 105, 109, 112, 130

Delft Hydraulic Laboratory, 123
Dempster, John, 47
Denham, Clapperton & Oudney, 3
Denton, Capt. G.C., 9
Dikko, Alhaji Yahaya, 172-173
Dimka, Lt. Col., 19
Dosumu, King, 9
Dosumu Treaty, 16

ECOWAS (Economic Community of West African States), 80
Effiong, Major-General Phillip, 18
Egerton, Sir Walter, 10
Eko Bridge, 89

Elder, Alexander, 47
Elder Dempster & Co./Liries 9, 46, 52, 55, 56-58, 76, 78, 98, 127
Elder Colonial Airways, 133-134, 140
Electrical Wiring Regulation, 161
Electricity Corporation of Nigeria (ECN), 153, 158-161
Elizabeth II, Her Majesty the Queen, 15, 109
Exclusive Legislative List (International and Inter Regional Waterways) Order, 1955, 63

Fajuyi Lt. Col. Adekunle, 17
Federal Capital Territory, Abuja, 19, 22, 25, 40, 95, 150
Fodio, Sheikh Uthman dan, 3, 12, 45
Freeman, H.S., 9
French crisis of 1897, 10
Frontier Force, 15

General Act of Berlin, 62
Gifford, Sir George, 14
Girouard, Sir Percy, 10
Glover, Lt. John, 9
Glover's Hausas, 12
Goldie, Sir George Dashwood Taubman, 8, 47-48, 101
Government Coastal Agency, 108
Gowon, General (Lt. Col.) Yakubu, 17-18, 41, 89

Hanno, Carthaginian, 2
Hassan, Alhaji Mohammed, 172
Holland Afrika Line, 56
Holt, John, 47-49, 51-52, 55, 119
Holy War, 13
Hydrological Survey Department, 161

ILS (instrument landing system), 149
Imperial Airways, 132-134
Independence Bridge, 89
Indirect Rule, 10
Industrial Revolution, 176
Inland Waterways Department Hydrological Map, 25
International Highways, 93-94
International Legal States of Niger, 62
International Wildlife Protection, 28
Irish Electricity Supply Board, 170

Johnson, Governor Mobolaji, 94
Jones, Alfred Lewis, 47-48
Jones, Taffy, 83

Kainji Biological Pilot Research at Shagamu, 168
Kangiwa, Alhaji Shehu, 172
Kendall, Brigadier G.V., 12
Kogum River Forest Reserve, 205
Kosoko, King, 9

Labour Forest Reserve, 202

Lagos, Colony, 9
— Executive Development Board, 80
— Police, 12
— Protectorate, 61
Laird, Macgregor, 7-8, 46-47
Lake Chad Basin Commission, 62
Lancelot de Freitas, 2
Lander, Richard, 3-4, 7, 46
Lees, C.C., 9
Lever Brothers, 54-55
London Brighton & South Coast Railway, 52
Lower Benue River Basin Development Authority, 67
Lugard, Frederick Dealtry, 8-10, 12-13, 32, 62, 70, 82, 101, 103, 105, 114, 153

Macaulay, Herbert, 14
Macdonald, Major C.M., 9
MacDonald, Sir Claude, 10
MacGregor, Sir William, 10, 79, 101
Maloney, C.A., 9, 13
Middle East Reinforcement Route, 134
Mineral exploitation, 98
Mohammed, Brigadier Murtala, 19
Moor, Sir Ralph Denham Rayment, 9-11, 101
Murtala Mohammed Airport, 149-150

Napoleonic wars, 3
National Company of Africa, 8
National Council of Nigeria and the Cameroons, 16
National Electric Power Authority (NEPA), 169-175
National Maritime Museum Greenwich, 46
Nature Protection Association, 177
NEDECO and Bos Kalis Westminster Dredging, 65
Netherlands Airport Consultants (NACOBVO), 150
Niger Coast Constabulary, 12
Niger Coast Protectorate, 9
Niger Company Limited (see also Royal Niger Company), 10
Niger Dams Authority, 167-169
Niger Delta Development Board, 70
Niger/Nigeria Joint Commission, 62
Niger River Accord Decree, 64
Nigerian
— Air Services, 135
— Airports Authority, 146
— Civil Aviation Training Centre, 144
— Eastern Railway (NER) Enugu, 155
— Electricity Supply Company (NESCO), 155
— Field Society, 80
— Flying School, 144
— Government Electricity Undertaking (NGEU), 158
— National Line Limited, 57
— National Petroleum Corporation, 173
— Police Force, 14

Index

— Ports Authority, 98, 107-108, 119, 138
— Produce Marketing Company, 109
Night Water Police, 12
Nkalagu Cement Works, 159
Nok people, 2
Northern Peoples Congress, 16
Nuclear Non-proliferation Treaty, 170
Nzeogwu, Major Kaduna, 17

Obasanjo, Lt. Gen., 19, 150
Oil Rivers, 6
— Irregulars, 12
— Protectorate (ORP), 9, 12
Oji Leprosy Settlement, 185
Ojukwu, Lt. Col. Chukwuemeka Odumegwu, 17-18
Okotie-Eboh, Chief Festus, 17
Okpara, Dr. M.I., 16
Ollivant, G.B., 55, 58
Organic pollution, 180
Oron Museum, 46

Palm Line Agencies, 120
Palmer, I.T., 8
Pan American Airways, 134
Park, Mungo, 3-4, 20, 46
Phillips, F.A.O., 41, 52
Pollution Bill, 177
'Port of Koko', 122
Private Pilots Licence, 144
Protectorate
— of Northern Nigeria, 12, 79
— of Southern Nigeria, 6, 12, 79
Public Works Department (PWD), 81, 83

Queens Own Nigeria Regiment, 15-16

Regional Development Boards, 81
Republic of Biafra, 18
River Niger Commission, 62
Road Research Laboratory, England, 89
Road transportation system, 90
Robertson, Sir James, 16
Rohlfs, Gerhard, 3, 6
Royal Air Force, 13, 132-133, 135, 145
Royal Mail Group, 55
Royal Navy, 98
Royal Niger Company (RNC), 8-9, 49, 121 123, 125
Royal Irish Constabulary, 12
Royal Prussian State Railways, 194

Sacrifice Rocks, 63
Schon, J.F., 8
Shagari, Alhaji Shehu, 19
Shaw, Professor Thurstan, 1
Shipping Ring Commission, 52
Ships Entry Notice, 112
Shodeke, King, 12
Slave Market, 9
Slave Trade Treaty, 197
Society of Merchants, 8
Stanley, H.M., 9
Swedish Trade Mission, 170

Trade disputes, 8
Trans-Saharan highway, 80
Trans-Saharan railway, 15
Tropical Testing Establishment at Port Harcourt, 161
Trunk Development Plan, 92

Union de Transports Aeriens, 138
United African Company, 10, 54-55, 70-71, 125
United Arab Airways, 138
Unity and Faith, 16
Unegbu, Lt. Col. Arthur, 17

Venice of West Africa, 63
Vesting Day, 108
Volta Dam hydrostation, 159

Water borne diseases, 176
Water pollution, 177
Water Resources and Engineering Construction Agency (WRECA) Kano, 173, 191
West African
— Air Transport Authority, 135
— Airways Corporation (WAAC), 135
— Currency Board, 18
— Frontier Force (WAFF), 10, 12-14, 156
— Joint Overseas Group, 87
— Lighterage and Transport Company Ltd., 52
— Lines Conference, 55
West India Mail Service, 51
Windham, Captain, 2
Womens Riots of Aba and N'bawsi, 14

Yankari Game Reserve, 28-29, 95
Yar' Adua, Major-General Shehu Musa, 114, 120, 146
Yorubaland Protectorate, 9-10

Zochonis, Patterson, 49, 103